In the Eyes of the Dragon

Asia in World Politics
Samuel S. Kim, Series Editor

Cooperation or Conflict in the Taiwan Strait?
by Ralph N. Clough

In the Eyes of the Dragon: China Views the World
edited by Yong Deng and Fei-Ling Wang

In the Eyes of the Dragon

China Views the World

edited by

YONG DENG

and

FEI-LING WANG

ROWMAN & LITTLEFIELD PUBLISHERS, INC.
Lanham • Boulder • New York • Oxford

ROWMAN & LITTLEFIELD PUBLISHERS, INC.

Published in the United States of America
by Rowman & Littlefield Publishers, Inc.
4720 Boston Way, Lanham, Maryland 20706

12 Hid's Copse Road
Cumnor Hill, Oxford OX2 9JJ, England

British Library Cataloguing in Publication Information Available

Library of Congress Cataloging-in-Publication Data
In the eyes of the dragon : China views the world / edited by Yong
    Deng and Fei-Ling Wang.
        p.   cm.
    Includes bibliogaphical references and index.
    ISBN 0-8476-9336-8 (alk. paper). — ISBN 0-8476-9337-6 (pbk. :
alk. paper)
    1. China—Foreign relations—1976– 2. World politics—1989–
3. Nationalism—China. I. Deng, Yong, 1966– . II. Wang, Fei-
Ling. III. Title: China views the world.
DS779.27.I53   1999
327.51—dc21   98-46956
                                                                          CIP

Internal design and typesetting by Letra Libre

Printed in the United States of America

∞™   The paper used in this publication meets the minimum requirements of American National Standard for Information Sciences—Permanence of Paper for Printed Library Materials, ANSI Z39.48-1984.

Contents

Foreword

John W. Garver

One of the boons to Western study of China over the past decade has been the emergence of a cohort of younger scholars from the People's Republic of China (PRC). Born and raised in China, the members of this cohort experienced firsthand the political and economic tides that swept over that country in the 1960s, 1970s, and 1980s. They later found opportunities to undertake rigorous training in social sciences at American universities. The resulting synthesis of cultural sensitivity and rigorous theoretical insight led to academic contributions that greatly enriched the Western study of China. The essays presented in this volume are examples of this unique synthesis.

Virtually cut off from direct contact with mainland China after 1949, the Western sinological community relied on indirect sources to understand China. China-watching centers in Hong Kong provided libraries of mainland newspapers and journals, as well as opportunities to interview recent refugees from the mainland. Centers in Taiwan provided a different take on China—plus contact with a very different type of Chinese society. An older generation of Chinese scholars, educated in universities in the decades before 1949, deeply enriched Western understanding of China, but their personal familiarity with current events in China gradually faded. Even though extremely valuable, all these sources lacked the key ingredient of prolonged but up-to-date firsthand experience in the China of Mao Zedong and Deng Xiaoping.

With the opening of China in the 1980s, Western scholars returned to China to live, study, and work, often for long periods of time. Many of these scholars were fluent in Mandarin Chinese and were quickly able to establish contact with Chinese scholars working in areas of academic interest similar to their own. One common and central experience of this renewed contact, however, was an awareness of the great gulf in between academic approaches.

Western scholars, Americans especially, were products of an educational system and tradition that stressed theoretical and analytical approaches. American scholars were trained to seek the underlying dynamics and explanations of a phenomenon. They came armed with a "toolbox" of theoretical approaches, from which they pulled concepts to test against the empirical evidence they collected. Their purpose was to test hypotheses against evidence. They eschewed reliance on ideologically favored paradigms to the exclusion of other, possibly more powerful explanations. Chinese scholars of what passed for "social sciences" in China during the 1980s, in contrast, were typically products of a different tradition stressing historical description. Their concern was to trace the course of development of a phenomenon, showing little if any interest in explicit attempts at explanation. If there were attempts at explanation, as often as not they were left implicit and not linked to a framework of pure theory standing independently of the specific issue under investigation. Attempts at theoretical explanation were often cast in terms of Marxist class analysis—a tendency that was part of a larger problem, a pronounced tendency toward normative judgment. The purpose of Chinese scholarship was often to render final judgments of good and bad, whether those terms were defined in the categories of Marxism or in more traditional notions of Chineseness qua "good" and foreignness qua "bad." The strict separation between normative and empirical propositions that stood at the center of the Western academic project was alien to the traditional normative approach that nurtured Chinese scholars during the 1980s.

It thus remained to a new cohort of scholars—the authors of this volume being a part of that cohort—to bridge the chasm between rigorous analysis of Western social science and Chinese scholarship. During the 1980s a number of young, hardworking, and extremely bright Chinese traveled to the United States and other Western countries for graduate study. These people had cleared several highly selective tests designed to winnow out a select few from a very large base: They had made it into a Chinese university system that educates only about 2 percent of China's total population, had been admitted to graduate study either in China or abroad, and had then finished an extremely demanding graduate academic program at a U.S. university. This rigorous selection ensured that the survivors would be extremely bright and driven. Some of those people entered the social sciences, there imbibed with both the spirit and the theoretical "toolbox" of Western academia. This mastery of "Western" methods of rigorous, theoretically rooted empirical analysis, and the deep understanding of Chinese culture derived from having grown up in that culture, represented a great treasure for Western sinology.

I do not believe that one must be Chinese to fathom Chinese politics, history, and society. If I did, I would be in the wrong line of work. The record of extremely impressive foreign scholarship on China does not even bear out such a proposition. Yet it does seem likely that socialization as a child in a culture combined with decades of living and working as an ordinary person in the institutions of a society give one a nuanced understanding of the currents of that society that may be less visible to foreign analysts. This is an extremely subtle acuity. It may also be offset by certain blindnesses that derive precisely from sharing the assumptions and beliefs of a society. As the Chinese saying goes, *pang guangzhe qing* (by-standers may be clearer). Yet native acuity to subtle variations and influences is certainly a valuable asset that should be brought to the academic table. In a project such as this—seeking to understand how China's elites view the world—such a native acuity is an especially valued asset.

Native proficiency in Chinese language is another advantage brought to the scholarly table by the cohort of young, "Westernized" Chinese scholars. Aside from Western sinologists who learned Chinese in China as the children of missionary parents who had answered the call to serve in China, most Western sinologists began their efforts to master the Chinese language while in their twenties. A few individuals with a natural affinity for foreign languages achieved perhaps native-level proficiency through such adult study. Most, however, developed more limited capabilities. Although able to converse and read easily, reading speed especially was often relatively slow—at least in comparison with native and highly educated Chinese. This handicap was especially relevant to archival or documentary-based research. I am not aware of any systematic study of this topic, but my guess is that if it took an American sinologist who mastered Chinese in his twenties forty hours to read a book, a native, educated Chinese person could do it in perhaps ten. This meant that the cohort of young Chinese who entered Western academia during the 1980s and 1990s enjoyed the advantage of being able to scan large quantities of possibly useful material, then fully assimilate a wider array of genuinely useful documentary materials. Western scholars employed a number of stratagems to compensate for their relatively low reading speed. They employed Chinese research assistants to scan documents and identify the most useful ones. Such techniques helped, but at the end of the day the difference remained: Native Chinese scholars can simply read and assimilate Chinese language materials more quickly than nonnative Chinese speaking scholars. Assuming that a scholar's time is limited, this gives native speakers a substantial comparative advantage.

In this book, these impressive skills are turned toward the analysis of how China's elites view various aspects of post–Cold War international politics. This is an extremely important topic. It has been difficult for Americans to understand China and for Chinese to understand America. The history of Sino-American relations is replete with misperceptions and misunderstandings. A recent work by Richard Madsen, *China and the American Dream: A Moral Inquiry,* for example, chronicles the ways in which Americans have seen in China what they want to see since the early 1970s. The American discourse about China has had as much to do with American hopes for America as about the nature of Chinese society. From the Chinese perspective, another recent work by David Shambaugh, *Beautiful Imperialist: China Perceives America, 1972–1990,* documents the ideologically and culturally distorted perceptions of the United States held by many sectors of China's America-watchers. Members of the ruling elites of both countries are sometimes deeply misinformed about the other: Some of China's leaders believe that U.S. policy toward China is predicated on a strategy of containment, whereas some American leaders believe that China can and should become a free and democratic country. At the popular level, the U.S. media demonizes China because this caters to the negative views about China held by many ordinary Americans, whereas in China marginal intellectuals achieve instant celebrity by authoring anti-American diatribes such as *Zhongguo keyi shou bu* (China Can Say No).

It is difficult to say that U.S.-PRC conflict derives fundamentally from mutual misperception rather than from conflicting interests. Ignorance was deeper and misperceptions were stronger on both sides during the 1970s, when bilateral relations were good, than during the 1990s, when relations plummeted. The degree of convergence of geostrategic interests is the most important factor determining the quality of bilateral relations. But misunderstanding certainly contributes to strained relations between the two countries.

If the turbulent history of Sino-American relations makes important deeper mutual understanding, the growing position of both the United States and China in the post–Cold War era makes such understanding imperative. The collapse of the former Soviet Union and its empire, combined with the continuing vitality of the American polity and the American-led Western alliance that prevailed in the Cold War, have given the United States the position of the only superpower at this juncture in history. As the leader of a coalition of democratic nations that emerged victorious from the three epic global conflicts of the twentieth century, the United States enjoys a nearly unparalleled position of global preeminence at century's end. China, in contrast, stands outside the dominant global coalition of democratic powers, is resentful of that exclusion—indeed, many Chinese believe that the very existence of the coalition of democratic countries is a "remnant of Cold War mentality"—and apparently aspires to disintegration via "multipolarity" of U.S. preeminence. This resentment is significant, for China has emerged in the post-Soviet era as the only power willing and able to challenge and confront the United States directly—and even militarily.

China's impressive record of economic growth since 1978 has already given it the third largest economy as measured by parity purchasing power. Its relatively successful transition from command economy–style communism to a quasi–market economy has given it impressive dynamism, manifested inter alia in the massive amount of foreign investment flowing into China. In the late 1990s, China was the world's second largest recipient of foreign direct investment—second only to the United States. Parallel with China's record-setting, post-1978 economic growth has been systematic and relatively effective policies designed to foster technological development. China shows every intention of translating its growing economic power into political-military power as swiftly as is feasible. These attributes have substantially boosted China's international power ranking, making it the only genuine rival to the United States.

History is replete with confrontations between incumbent paramount powers and rising aspirant powers: Holland versus Portugal, Britain versus Holland, Germany versus Britain, Japan versus the United States, and so on. Sadly, this pattern of conflict seems to be more common than successful accommodation between incumbent and emerging powers. One overarching question we face as the twenty-first century unfolds before us is whether Sino-American relations will replay this bloody, costly drama of confrontation. The future course of Sino-American relations will be one of the most important variables determining the quality of international relations during the first quarter of the twenty-first century. If the two countries are able to cooperate, prospects for peace, prosperity, and the resolution of a myriad of pressing international problems will be far better. If the countries collide, the twenty-first century may well see more of the sort of tragic conflicts that defined the international history of the twentieth century.

1

Introduction: Toward an Understanding of China's Worldview

Yong Deng and Fei-Ling Wang

The consequences of power redistribution prompted by a rising new power have been a key subject that concerns practitioners and scholars of international relations. The twentieth century has witnessed several such rises, each with its own outcome for the international system. America's rise to the world's center stage was relatively peaceful, but the ascent of the Soviet empire triggered the Cold War with the West, which eventually led to its demise. Germany's and Japan's reemergence as great powers succeeded only after their failures in the two most destructive world wars. The variegated consequences and prices associated with rising powers suggest that the nature and intention of the rising power itself are perhaps more consequential than the systemic reconfiguration of capabilities in determining war or peace.

By the dawn of the new millennium, the People's Republic of China (PRC) has been widely perceived to possess the potential to evolve into a full-fledged superpower. Although few would dispute the view that "no other foreign policy issues deserve a higher priority" for the United States than to develop a sound China policy,[1] consensus is lacking as to how exactly this growing power should be assessed and dealt with. By elucidating how China views the post–Cold War world and its place therein, this volume helps to elevate the debate over China to a higher, more sophisticated and productive level. Understanding Chinese views and intentions is essen-

1

tial to determining whether, what, and how to deter, constrain, induce, and cooperate in dealing with China. For that purpose, the contributors rely primarily on original Chinese sources and extensive field research to examine respectively China's self-image and Chinese views on sovereignty, national interest, security multilateralism, international human rights, nuclear nonproliferation, Taiwan, the United States, and aspects of its relations with the reigning hegemon, the United States. By probing China's worldview, we hope to enhance understanding of the nationalist sentiments driving China's foreign policy.

THE DEBATE: HOW TO DEAL WITH CHINA?

In the United States, unwarranted expectations, heightened sentiments, and wishful thinking about building a "special relationship" with China have historically impeded a realistic understanding of the country. Since 1989, U.S. China policy lost its bipartisan consensus, existent since Pres. Richard Nixon's visit to China in 1972, and consequently has been beset by divisions in the American public image of China, among organized social interest groups, and between the White House and Congress.[2] Profound disagreements exist concerning how to make sense of China's domestic changes and foreign behavior and how best to deal with this rising power.

In the immediate aftermath of the June 4, 1989, Tiananmen Incident, many predicted the imminent collapse of the Chinese communist regime.[3] Yet prediction about domestic implosion soon gave way to the "China threat" theory. In the 1990s, China's growing strength and seemingly assertive irredentism over "lost territories" have fueled a new debate centering around a concern about how to deal with an ascending hegemon. Washington's proclaimed China policy currently goes under the name of engagement. Unsatisfied, however, many call for a containment strategy against Beijing.[4]

Arguments for Containment

Since *containment* is such a loaded word with Cold War connotations, supporters of this strategy tend to refrain from being explicit in their advocacy. Generally speaking, however, those who argue for this strategy focus on the growing Chinese power as a menace and impute aggressive intentions to China: that it would destabilize the East Asian region and undermine the U.S. national interest. Primarily seeing China as a threat, containment advocates believe a coalition along Chinese borders should be created to deter Beijing's aggressive behavior and put Chinese influence in check. In addition, the United States should withhold its support for China's economic development and for its participation in international institutions, such as the World Trade Organization (WTO), and instead insist on Beijing's complete conformity with regional and global multilateral regimes.

China's actual capacities are notoriously hard to ascertain due to its own secrecy and questionable statistics. Estimating Chinese power can be anybody's guess. Partial convertibility of Chinese currency to the U.S. dollar, in combination with extrabudget sources, including profits from the People's Liberation Army (PLA)–run businesses and arms sales, make Chinese defense expenditures a frequent subject of sensational speculation. A 1998 decree banning PLA-run businesses, issued by Chinese Communist Party (CCP) Central Military Commission chair Jiang Zemin, will certainly help increase transparency in China's defense spending. Those who advocate containment are often on the high side, with a tendency to overstate Chinese capacities. They also point to China's efforts to upgrade its capabilities for naval and airpower projection, weapon acquisitions (especially from Russia and Israel), and recent development of quick-response troops. The common premise of containment is that China is "the hegemon on the horizon."[5]

The tendency to overstate Chinese capabilities often goes along with a penchant for ascribing malign intentions to China and the destabilizing implications to the Chinese rise. China threat theorists subscribe to the realist logic that posits dangerous implications inherent in the rapid rise of a new power.[6] The realist view pervasive in American scholarship on international relations has provided broad assumptions in support of a containment strategy against China. From this perspective, China's threat to its neighbors and the reigning hegemon, the United States, is on the rise with growing Chinese power. Underscoring the Chinese danger, Lucian Pye writes, "In the past the emergence of all the great powers was accompanied by wars, as with Germany and Japan, or intense conflict, as in the case of the Soviet Union and the cold war."[7] Richard Betts asserts that "the principal U.S. strategic aim should be to prevent the emergence of a hierarchical regional system under any dominant power other than the United States. . . . A China, Japan, or Russia that grows strong enough to overturn a regional balance of power would necessarily also be a global power that could reestablish bipolarity on the highest level."[8] The conclusion is that the rising Chinese power would by necessity be fundamentally destabilizing and "is bound to be no strategic friend of the United States, but a long-term adversary."[9]

The Chinese threat is also seen from an assumption that fast economic and population growth generates lateral pressure for aggressive competition that is likely to end in war: When the nation experiences fast economic growth and upswings in the business cycle, the resultant ultranationalism in combination with raging demands for natural resources tempt the nation to embark on foreign aggression.[10] Accordingly, China's population pressure and insatiable demands for energies and natural resources could tempt it to violently expand its "living space" (*shengcun kongjian*) and push aggressively through the South China Sea.[11] Most pressingly, the South China Sea contains the critical sea-lanes by which most of Japan's and other Asian countries' energies are transported. China's unruly behavior toward the South China Sea could be especially destabilizing because it is where issues of sea-lane safety, sovereignty, economic interest, and regional security converge.

The challenge of managing an ascending China is reinforced by the view that China is "not your typical superpower."[12] Some sinologists have argued that China is more a civilization than a modern nation-state and historically had had little experience in interacting with other, legalistically equal sovereign states. And since it was forcefully drawn into the European-centered international system during the mid-nineteenth century, China endured a century of humiliations and sufferings at the hands of Western and Japanese powers. A China with profound historical grievances and unaccustomed to the prevailing norms and practices of international relations is, to say the least, hard to get along with, so the argument goes.

Moreover, China is not a democracy. A widely accepted democratic peace theory has provided an additional framework to highlight the China threat. The thrust of the theory holds as follows: Even though democracies may not necessarily be more peaceful than nondemocracies, they almost never resort to force against other democracies, whereas nondemocracies are the major threat to democracies.[13] The democratic peace tenet has made significant inroads in the official thinking guiding the U.S. foreign policy in the post–Cold War era. Pres. Bill Clinton, in his State of the Union address on January 25, 1993, stated, "Ultimately the best strategy to insure our security and to build a durable peace is to support the advance of democracy elsewhere. Democracies don't attack each other."[14]

In this logic, China threat theorists point to Chinese domestic repression. As the argument goes, one cannot trust a communist regime that has killed peaceful students in Tiananmen Square—and continues unabated human rights abuses—to respect the sovereign rights and concerns of other countries. Moreover, one cannot expect a regime that rejects the global standards on human rights and nuclear nonproliferation not to be eager to rewrite the rules of international society. Only a political democracy in Beijing, which some estimate could be twenty years away,[15] may obviate the China threat. Some observers argue that a China in transition may be even more dangerous, to the extent that the coexistence of the legacies of the old regime and the fragility of new institutions may unleash destructive nationalism and chauvinism beyond any control.[16]

Those who primarily see threat in China's rise invoke images, symbols, and analogies to suggest that China is not a legitimate great power that deserves respect but rather a hegemonic power that is on a course toward a coming conflict with the United States. China has been compared to an eighteen-year-old teenager—strong enough to knock people down but immature—and therefore it should be disciplined by the "adults" of the family of nations. China has also been referred to as an "800-pound gorilla" on the loose that does not accept the rules and regulations of the international system; and as a "mercantilist juggernaut" that leverages its market for high-tech acquisitions and favorable treatments.[17]

The most frequent historical analogy that has been used to highlight the Chinese danger is Germany, a Wilhelmine, even Nazi Germany. Edward Friedman writes, "As with Germany and Britain in the first part of the twentieth century, analysts worried that the downturn in Beijing-Washington relations could plummet toward all the horrors that exploded after the Great War, the First World War—fascism, depression, and another war."[18] Fareed Zakaria argues,

> Like Germany in the late 19th century, China is also growing rapidly but uncertainly into a global system in which it feels it deserves more attention and honor. Chinese military is a powerful political player, as was the Prussian officer corps. Like Wilhelmine Germany, the Chinese regime is trying to hold onto political power even as it unleashes forces in society that make its control increasingly shaky.[19]

In a similar vein, Arthur Waldron draws a parallel between China and Wilhelmine Germany: Like China today, Wilhelmine Germany was a new powerful state with an authoritarian regime, and Bismarck's departure unleashed social forces that led to the two world wars. The ominous question is: With the death of Chinese strong man Deng Xiaoping in 1997, will China become another Germany by the turn of another century? For Waldron, the U.S. policy on Taiwan thus becomes a choice with self-evident answers: "Would we support a democratic Taiwan against any or all threats—or would we perform a sort of Munich, and attempt to browbeat Taipei into backing down?" [20] The most explicit and crude advocates for containing China make frequent references to Hitler's Germany and militaristic Japan.[21]

Arguments for Engagement

Arguments for engaging China generally derive from the assumption that China's national interests and intentions can change and that it *can* become a responsible power due to domestic liberalization, external pressure, and internationally induced assimilation.[22] Engagement advocates point to how China's economic reform and integration into the capitalist world economy have engineered a break in Beijing's foreign policy outlook, from Maoist revolutionary diplomacy against the international system to a prevailing pragmatist paradigm seeking to take advantage of the opportunities provided by the capitalist economic system. They argue that China's enmeshment into the regional and global economies has translated into pacific effects on Chinese foreign policy. China is now preoccupied with its economic modernization, the success of which depends on investments, capital, markets, and technologies from Asian neighbors and the West. China's prosperity depends on regional stability. China's penchant for the status quo in terms of East Asian security is evidenced by China's withdrawal of support for communist resurgents throughout Southeast Asia, as well as China's acquiescence to the U.S. security presence in the western Pacific.

From this perspective, alarmist views about China's capacities and intentions are largely unwarranted. Proponents of engagement argue that China, compared to the United States, is still an underdeveloped country with enormous domestic challenges that will keep its hands full for quite a while. Most of China's gross national product (GNP) increase will be consumed by its growing population, with a current annual net increase of some 13 million. Contrary to the inflated threat that alarmists see in China, those who favor engagement point to China's myriad security vulnerabilities, painting a China barely able to fend for itself.[23] Beijing's recent military modernization program does not indicate aggressive ambitions but rather is driven by an attempt to update its outdated weaponry and to make up for the neglect of defense during much of the 1980s. China's efforts to increase its blue-water navy and airpower capabilities are basically a reactive move in light of the growing military capabilities of its neighbors.[24] Moreover, one should expect some increase of military spending from a growing power like China. Hence, there are no grounds to associate China's recent military modernization with perilous Chinese intentions for foreign aggression. Instead, China is a "conservative power," too weak and too preoccupied domestically to challenge the status quo and balance of power in East Asia.[25]

Most China scholars support engagement because they detect evidence of China's gradual evolution toward a more open, liberal, and possibly democratic society. For example, Yasheng Huang shows that since the late 1980s regular, competitive, and direct elections for officials at the village level across China's vast countryside have given Chinese peasants, more than 72 percent of the population, the first taste of grassroots democracy.[26] Susan Shirk points to how internationalization has generated domestic social groups, sectors, and regional interests in support of continued reform in China: "Once the wall between China and the world economy was partially dismantled, international economic forces evoked positive domestic responses to China's reform drive."[27] These changes, though gradual in pace, are fundamentally transforming Chinese society.

Even though different in dimension, perspective, and assessment of the extent of change in China, most China scholars share a guarded optimism that a more open and democratic China can be brought into being through further domestic reform and international interdependence. International enmeshment facilitates China's social learning in terms of the values, norms, principles, and rules of the international system and adds China's stakes in the existing institutions and order. China's worldview and definition of national interests can be transformed toward greater compatibility with the rest of the world through transnational activities and networks, including tourism, academic and cultural exchanges, and commercial ties.[28]

To facilitate China's evolution along that line, as Robert Sutter argues, the United States has a key role to play in shaping China's future largely through constructive engagement.[29] Despite Chinese realpolitik, Tom Christensen argues, "by engaging China and encouraging its participation in multilateral forums and confidence-building regimes, over the long term the United States may help soften China's skepticism about these institutions, which could help stabilize East Asia."[30] Similarly, Chalmers Johnson cautions against a U.S.-Japanese alignment to contain China. The United States and Japan are the two richest countries that possess power to shape Chinese foreign behavior through inducements (a strategy that Japan has been executing all along).[31]

Engagement: Rhetoric and Reality

Vast disparities exist in the understanding of Chinese capabilities and intentions, and theories suggest divergent strategies for dealing with China. Containment views stem from various forms of deterministic thinking. Realist logic underlying much of the containment argument negates the authorship of the agent (the state) in determining its behavior. Rather, it posits that state behavior is driven by the international structural force, that is, its position in the distribution of power across the international system. It follows that a rising power such as China will inevitably find the existing system nonconducive to its interests, which in turn necessarily conflict with those of the reigning hegemon, the United States. In the China debate, containment arguments based on the democratic peace theory simply label a country as either democratic or authoritarian and hold that the rise of a nondemocratic power such as China is inevitably threatening.

Deterministic logic similarly underlies the historical analogies used frequently in the containment argument. But as Robert Jervis maintains, decisionmakers often "too quickly" *and* mistakenly rely on their perceived historical lessons in making policies to avoid repeating past failures, with the assumption that "the contemporary situation resembled the past one so closely that the same sequence would occur."[32] The danger is that historical analogies are often used for advocacy, not for informing diagnosis but in lieu of serious analysis.[33] A Cold War precedent was that in the 1980s U.S. politicians used the Hitler analogy in reference to the Soviet Union to justify larger defense spending and a "peace through strength" strategy. Despite frequent references to Hitler, according to Alexander Dallin, "there was not a single effort, on the record, to ask whether the assumptions regarding Nazi Germany were equally applicable to the Soviet Union: by implication, they must be."[34] In an amazingly similar fashion in the current strategic debate over China, those raising the historical analogy of Hitler's Germany simply use history as an anecdote without bothering to systematically examine the truthfulness of what is implied: that China is or will become like Nazi Germany.

Fortunately, in the current China debate no policymaking official has used the Hitler reference to drum up a China threat. As many have pointed out, containment as a policy is a nonstarter. For one thing, a military and political alliance to encircle the enemy nation, a key requirement of containment, is almost impossible to form.[35] Containment advocates' call for the United States to establish a coalition with Russia, Japan, India, and Vietnam to counterbalance Chinese power appears to be a pipe-dream.[36] As a matter of fact, the Association of Southeast Asian Nations (ASEAN) and Japan are adopting their own style of quiet, nonconfrontational engagement with China, and there is no sign they prefer a U.S.-led containment strategy.[37]

Arguments for containment highlight the challenges and difficulties in coping with the Chinese rise; nevertheless, containment is not only un-desirable but also infeasible. On balance, arguments for engagement tend to be based on a more factual, nuanced understanding of the realities in China and the international environment. The pronounced official U.S. policy has been one emphasizing engagement, whereas containment has never been an explicit option. The Secretary of State under the George Bush administration, James Baker, argued in 1991 that China's strategic importance as shown in issues of weapons proliferation control, the U.S.-led international coalition in the Persian Gulf, and conflicts management in Asia "underscores the need for sustained engagement with China on issues of common concern."[38] President Clinton's policy was initially held hostage to his own campaign attack of Bush's policy of "coddling" the dictatorship in Beijing. But in the course of strategic debate, a consensus on the outlines of engagement emerged around 1994–1995; the underlying reasoning was articulated by Assistant Secretary of Defense Joseph Nye Jr.:

> It is wrong to portray China as an enemy. Nor is there reason to believe China must be an enemy in the future. . . . In the face of uncertainty among the experts, suppose that we simply posited a 50 percent chance of an aggressive China and a 50 percent chance of China becoming a re-

sponsible great power in the region. On this hypothesis, to treat China as
an enemy now would in effect discounting 50 percent of the future. Moreover, a containment strategy would be difficult to reverse. Enmity would
become self-fulfilling prophecy.[39]

Despite Bush's and Clinton's avowed commitment to engagement,
ever since the Tiananmen crisis in 1989 U.S.-China relations have been
beset by an array of irritants and crises. Disagreements over human rights,
China's most-favored-nation trading status, weapons proliferation, Taiwan,
Hong Kong, and the Dalai Lama brewed raging frustrations, resentments,
and recriminations in both capitals. Anti-American feeling in China was fueled by the Yinhe tangle, the U.S. opposition of China's bid to host the
2000 Olympic Games, and human rights–related incidents, culminating in
1996–1997 in the publication of a group of wildly popular and virulently
anti-American books (such as *China Can Say No*) that promote nationalistic
and even xenophobic rhetoric.[40]

A survey published in *China Youth Daily* in September 1995 indicates that
87.1 percent of the young respondents regarded the United States as the
most unfriendly country to China.[41] The U.S.-China relations have bumped
into crisis after crisis, leading closer than ever since 1972 toward a military
clash over Taiwan in March 1996, when the United States sent two carrier
battle groups into the Taiwan Strait. From the Chinese perspective, U.S. policies on Taiwan, diplomatic normalization with Vietnam, and reaffirmation of
the U.S.-Japan security treaty belied the proclaimed engagement strategy. All
these incidents and crises appeared, instead, to have stemmed from a containment agenda against China. Anti-American sentiments peaked in
1995–1996. However, the majority of students and intellectuals we talked
with in Beijing during summer 1997 still believed that the United States had
a strategy toward China, and that the strategy was containment.

TOWARD A SOUND CHINA POLICY:
TAKING THE CHINESE VIEWS SERIOUSLY

Containment advocates are too deterministic and suffer from a lack of serious analysis. Engagement arguments are often equated with appeasement
in the U.S. domestic debate. Engagement policy ignoring Chinese concerns
is often viewed by Beijing with suspicion and even hostility. We propose that
the debate over China can be elevated to a higher, more sophisticated and
productive level if the Chinese side of the story is taken into account. A
sound China policy, based on an effective engagement strategy, entails a
thorough and accurate understanding of Chinese views and intentions.

Engagement is not appeasement or antithetical to disagreements. Indeed, some of the bilateral issues between China and the United States are

rooted in the inherent tension between a rising power trying to find its rightful place and an established hegemon seeking to defend and define the rules of the game in the international system. Although engagement presupposes a critical attitude against many of the present Chinese views and behaviors,[42] it nonetheless signifies a positive attitude that "the U.S. has rejected the argument that conflict with China is inevitable."[43] Insofar as the goal of engagement is to ensure that China becomes a responsible and conformist power, engagement "contains elements of constraints."[44] Differences, disagreements, and even conflicts on many issues will persist in Sino-American relations. But the overall relationship should not be held hostage to one single issue, be it human rights or trade; instead, particular policy issues should be subordinated to the larger engagement strategy rather than the other way around.[45] The mood of the relationship tends to be easily poisoned when the overall relationship is dictated by one issue.

To bring China into the international system peacefully requires China's proper response; hence, it is imperative to treat China as a partner whose legitimate concerns should be addressed.[46] The current engagement discourse tends to fixate on how the United States should deal with China without giving adequate attention to how China would respond. This one-sidedness contains a major flaw: Unilateral fixation tempts one to set preconditions for China to meet and ignores China's concerns and demands, thereby fueling Chinese fear of containment and suspicion about U.S. intentions. A purpose of engagement is to forge a nonhostile environment in which issues of disagreement can be managed and dealt with. Setting preconditions for China on issues of ongoing dispute between the two countries, such as human rights, the use of force over Taiwan, and trade, will only elicit hostility from Beijing.[47]

China, like any other major power, has legitimate national interests. In the strategic debate, whether or not China rightfully has concerns and demands is often unclear. The realist logic, which posits inevitable Sino-American conflicts and destabilizing implications accompanying a stronger China, negates China's legitimate national interest, thereby justifying an ignorance of Chinese intentions. An effective engagement policy entails a recognition and accommodation of China's preeminent security interest in maintaining regime survival and integrity, prohibiting Taiwan independence and other vital regional security concerns.[48] In particular, "increasing confidence concerning America's Taiwan policy is most fundamental because this dimension of U.S. policy colors Beijing's attitudes in the other areas."[49] Engagement without considering legitimate Chinese concerns and interests could be, and has been, interpreted by the Chinese as a comprehensive containment strategy aiming to belittle, destabilize, and hold back China. By addressing Chinese demands properly in time, the established powers can help make China a benign instead of a predatory power before a nationalistic flame turns the rising dragon into a fire-breathing monster.

How China relates to the international system has been a perennial issue besetting both the Chinese nation and the world since China was violently and forcibly drawn into the European-centered international system in the mid-nineteenth century. Although China's past search for its rightful place in the world has been especially traumatic, never before has the Chinese leadership posed the questions for its people so explicitly than now: What kind of China will be brought to the twenty-first century? What kind of attitudes should China have to welcome the twenty-first century? This book is intended to enhance the understanding of the Chinese debates, views, and policies in coming to terms with these questions. It is our conviction that the outside world, with a better understanding of China's worldview, can help the Chinese to answer these critical questions in a way that makes the Chinese rise more as an opportunity than as a threat.

ABOUT THE BOOK

With that in mind, this book sets to explore the Chinese views of the post–Cold War world and to interpret the concerns and intentions as well as the likely international demands of the PRC. The following chapters deal with China's self-perception and views on national interests, human rights, multilateralism, weapons proliferation, the United States, Taiwan, the World Trade Organization, trading relations with the United States, and other vital issues. We hope these discussions, taken as a whole, can illuminate key aspects of China's worldview. We try as meticulously and objectively as we can to report our findings in our attempt to interpret Chinese views.

To that end, we rely heavily on firsthand Chinese-language materials published inside and outside China. Secondary English-language literature is used to various extents when appropriate. All of the authors have conducted extensive field research in the PRC and have accumulated substantial data and observations through formal and informal interviews. Efforts are made to utilize the available quantitative data, yet this volume is largely a qualitative analysis of the massive information gathered. Although we are fully aware that any good understanding of China's worldview must relate to its historical roots, this project nevertheless concentrates on contemporary developments since the end of the Cold War.

No matter how thorough, objective, and accurate we have conscientiously tried to be in our endeavor to probe China's worldview, our findings are not free from uncertainties and incompleteness. The inconclusiveness is partially inevitable due to the inherent methodological limitations of qualitative studies in the social sciences.[50] Our chosen subject matter adds greater methodological challenges. China, as suggested by its totem of the dragon,[51] presents multidimensional, complex, and sometimes even mysterious images. The Maoist legacy of policy secrecy and the authoritarian nature of the PRC's political system have presented extra difficulties. After some twenty years of reform and opening-up, China has now become a greatly diversified society, featuring a much less centralized government, a commercialized press, and an increasingly pluralistic intellectual community. Modern investigative tools of social science inquiry, such as independent and systematic surveys and polling, have just barely started in the PRC.

We hope that the scrupulous reading of Chinese materials and frequent field research help surmount some of the methodological difficulties to minimize mistakes in our findings. Most of our contributors are Western-trained China experts with American doctorates in political science and are native speakers of the Chinese language. All of us have lived in China for extended periods of time and have been studying China for many years. Currently, most of us are university-based scholars actively publishing in the field of Chinese foreign policy studies.

Our backgrounds and expertise should hopefully equip us with enough closeness and appropriate distance to our subject matter so as to present an in-depth and accurate analysis. This does not mean that we share the same views and arrive at the same conclusions regarding China's worldview and its international future; in fact, the authors in this book do not always agree among ourselves. Taken together, however, what all of us reject is the doomsday view of the China threat. Instead, we argue that even though China's international view is uncertain, continuous domestic reforms and deepening enmeshment in the international system in combination with an engagement strategy from the reigning hegemon, the United States, and other major powers can induce China to pursue a foreign course that is compatible with the international and regional order.

Chapter 2, by Fei-Ling Wang, explores China's self-image and strategic intentions. China's is a self-image rife with contradictions. The juxtaposition of increased self-confidence within the Chinese nation and a peculiar but persistent sense of political insecurity among PRC leadership has deeply colored China's strategic considerations. With limited and rather transparent external demands centering around the political survival of the PRC regime and the national unification cause, Wang concludes, China's self-image and strategic intentions are likely to sustain a conservative and pragmatic foreign policy in the near future.

Chapter 3, by Yong Deng, probes the Chinese theorizing on national interests in international relations in the 1990s. His findings support the argument that China's national-interests conception is still dominated by realpolitik thinking. But they also show that liberal values do exist and are gaining some legitimacy in China's discourse on international relations. Doubtless, encouraging a liberal-oriented redefinition of national interests would bring about a more cooperative China less apt to redraft the rules of the game in foreign relations. However, Deng notes immense difficulties dampening the prospects of liberalization in China's worldview, not the least of which is the "liberal dilemma" rooted in the inability of Chinese "liberals" to reconcile internationalist thinking with their nationalism and sovereignty concerns.

Chapter 4, by Jianwei Wang, examines China's perceptual evolution and consequent policy changes regarding multilateral diplomacy and multilateralism in collective security. Wang discusses, at the global level, China's attitudes toward UN peacekeeping operations in recent years and finds that China, although it supports most of the UN Charter Chapter VI operations, is reluctant to endorse Chapter VII operations. At the regional level, Wang explores China's calculation and policy response toward a regional security regime as reflected in its "new thinking of security cooperation." The evidence suggests that overall China has become more receptive to security multilateralism and that this reflects behavioral adaptation as well as some conceptual changes.

Chapter 5, by Ming Wan, discusses Chinese views on human rights and democracy, not only those of the government but also those of the society. On the one hand, Chinese society is not ready at this stage to push for democracy and human rights. Despite serious social and economic problems, the Chinese society is largely content with the country's economic performance. The government and society share a broad consensus, emphasizing stability as a precondition for economic development. The current regime enjoys significant popular support, whereas the dissident movement attracts little sympathy in China. On the other hand, since the late 1970s ordinary Chinese have become more conscious of their rights, especially property rights. More importantly, the society supports the regime because of a cynical calculation of its best interest; the party-state is seen as a necessary evil for achieving the development goals that the society supports. The party-state will find it difficult to maintain its power when the society's calculations change due to economic crises, enhanced political awareness, or available alternatives.

Chapter 6, by Weixing Hu, explores China's views and policy on the issue of nuclear proliferation. China has moved up on the learning curve on nuclear nonproliferation since it ratified the Nonproliferation Treaty (NPT) in 1992. Beijing's consciousness of nuclear proliferation risks has increased steadily in recent years, and its long-standing mistrust and suspicion toward the NPT regime was replaced by a more cooperative posture. This change is not a short-term maneuver. Rather, it represents a major shift in Beijing's perception of this international regime in particular and in its approaches to arms control and international security in general. Using the concept of learning, Hu explains how the interaction of domestic dynamics and external factors has effected changes in Beijing's nuclear export controls, thereby bringing China's behavior closer to the international standard.

Chapter 7, by Ming Zhang, reports on the Chinese public images of the United States, which have become a volatile factor in Sino-American relations. Noting the complexity and contradictions in the Chinese perception, Zhang finds that the Chinese public images of the United States have most noticeably undergone a shift from a romantically positive one in the 1980s to a negative one in the 1990s. The suspicion, anger, frustration, and assertiveness the public has expressed toward the United States stem from a negative view on American society, politics, media, and foreign policy, but how these sentiments will evolve remain uncertain.

Chapter 8, by Yasheng Huang, examines a number of problem areas in the economic relationships between China and the United States. Since 1980, China has moved from an autarkic economy to an important player in the world economy. Along with this development in foreign trade and investment, China has also entered into increasing economic policy conflicts, mainly with the United States. Issues such as trade deficits, intellectual property rights violations, domestic market protection, technology transfer, accession terms to the World Trade Organization, dumping, unfair competition, and the like have increasingly dominated the agenda between China and the United States. Huang argues that a number of unique features of China, the nature of its political regime, its size, its development strategies, the functions of Hong Kong, and the role of foreign-invested enterprises in the bilateral trade have all contributed to the complexity of the economic relations between China and the United States.

Chapter 9, by Bin Yu, examines the development of China's regional policy during the reform decades. This conscientiously conceived and carefully executed regionalization effort is in sharp contrast to the PRC's "lack" of a regional policy under Mao. As a result, China's overall foreign policy has scaled down from global to regional, from political-security–oriented to trade-development–centered, from high-profile to low-profile, from ideological to pragmatic. This "regionalization" of China's foreign policy has been the result of both a long-term effort to create a periphery conducive to China's modernization and a short-term need to offset the post-Tiananmen Western sanctions. Ironically, such a reorientation of China's foreign policy has not necessarily led to a more desired outcome. A more stable and peaceful regional environment cannot be constructed without a more stable working relationship with the United States, the sole superpower that has been deeply involved in Asian affairs and forwardly deployed around China's periphery.

Chapter 10, by Suisheng Zhao, analyzes China's views and policy on Taiwan. Although Beijing's peaceful offense after 1979 had brought about some desirable changes in cross-strait relations, its military exercises, including missile tests aimed at Taiwan prior to Taiwan's first direct presidential election in March 1996, created an international crisis. By focusing on the shift in Beijing's perceptions, Zhao's account helps us understand the major causes and objectives of China's military exercises. He argues that the Taiwan Strait crisis of 1995–1996 was not the result of differences in ideology or social and political systems between the two sides or because Beijing planned to press Taipei for immediate reunification. Rather, it resulted, to a great extent, from Beijing's perceptual shift concerning Taiwan's internal political development and external status. The military exercises served as a crisis bargaining strategy supplementary to peaceful offense.

Chapter 11, by Thomas Christensen, concludes this volume by analyzing the deep roots of the Chinese worldview being explored. Tying together all the chapters, Christensen describes the external and internal causes of the rise of a possible Chinese "hypernationalism" in the post–Cold War era. He echoes most contributors' findings that the major powers need to engage China with caution, thoughtfulness, and good information about internal factors in China. He warns that two traps need to be avoided: counterproductive external pressures that may fuel Chinese nationalism, and passive concession that may reward belligerent foreign policies of a rising China.

As editors, we wish to thank all the contributors for not only completing their individual chapters in a timely fashion but also working closely with us through the project. Their professionalism and friendship are greatly appreciated. The book benefits immensely from a two-day workshop held in Atlanta in early February 1998, where contributors gathered to thoroughly discuss an earlier draft of all chapters. We would like to acknowledge the generous financial support from the International Studies Association (ISA) made available through its 1997/98 Workshop Grants. We are grateful to Vicki L. Golich and other members of the 1997/98 ISA Grants Committee for their confidence in this project, and to Dana Larsen at ISA headquarters for logistical support. The Sam Nunn School of International Affairs at the Georgia Institute of Technology kindly provided the venue and support for our workshop. We thank William J. Long, Wanda G. Moore, and Joy W. Daniell for their help.

We presented our earlier findings and benefited from comments and discussion at two panels at the 1998 ISA annual meeting held in March 1998 in Minneapolis, Minnesota. Susan McEachern, our editor at Rowman & Littlefield, had enough confidence in this project at the proposal stage to extend us a book contract and some seed money for the subsequent symposium. She has since offered wise counsel. We also thank the publisher's anonymous reviewer for a strong vote of confidence and for suggested revisions. Professors Chih-Yu Shih, Song Xinning, and Zhang Xiaojin and many other individuals, whose names are not listed here, have provided encouragement and advice to us in this project, for which we are deeply thankful.

Yong Deng and Fei-Ling Wang

NOTES

1. Doak Barnett et al., *Developing a Peaceful, Stable, and Cooperative Relationship With China* (New York: National Committee on American Foreign Policy, July 1996), 1.

2. Michael Hunt, *The Making of a Special Relationship: The United States and China to 1914* (New York: Columbia University Press, 1983); Harry Harding, *A Fragile Relationship: The United States and China Since 1972* (Washington, D.C.: The Brookings Institution, 1992).

3. For a discussion of this view, see Avery Goldstein, "Trends in the Study of Political Elites and Institutions in the PRC," *China Quarterly*, no. 139 (1994): 714–730.

4 A representative argument is Richard Bernstein and Ross H. Munro, *The Coming Conflict with China* (New York: Knopf, 1997). Their views are summarized in *Foreign Affairs* 76, no. 2 (March/April 1997), 18–32, and *The Weekly Standard*, 24 February 1997, 18–20.

5. Denny Roy, "Hegemon on the Horizon? China's Threat to East Asian Security," *International Security* 19, no. 1 (Summer 1994): 149–168.

6. See, for example, Robert Gilpin, *War and Change in World Politics* (New York: Cambridge University Press, 1981); Paul Kennedy, *The Rise and Fall of the Great Powers: Economic Change and Military Conflict from 1500–2000* (New York: Random House, 1987); and A. F. K. Organski and Jacek Kugler, *The War Ledger* (Chicago: University of Chicago Press, 1980).

7. Lucian Pye, "China: Not Your Typical Superpower," *Problems of Post-Communism* 43, no. 4 (July/August 1996): 11.

8. Richard K. Betts, "Wealth, Power, and Instability: East Asia and the United States after the Cold War," in *East Asian Security*, Michael Brown, Sean M. Lynn-Jones, and Steven E. Miller, eds. (Cambridge: M.I.T. Press, 1996), 72.

9. Bernstein and Munro, "The Coming Conflict with China," 22.

10. Nazli Choucri and Robert C. North, *Nations in Conflict: National Growth and International Violence* (San Francisco: W. H. Freeman, 1975); Greg Cashman, *What Causes War? An Introduction to Theories of International Conflict* (New York: Lexington Books, 1993).

11. Concern has been raised about how China is going to feed its 1.2 billion population with the annual growth of 13 million additional mouths. In 1993, China became a net oil importer, reversing its erstwhile status as an oil exporter for at least two decades. China's present-day deficit in oil trade reaches about 600,000 barrels a day and is expected to surge to more than 1 million by 2000 and nearly 3 million by 2010. Kent E. Calder, "Asia's Empty Tank," *Foreign Affairs* 75, no. 2

(March/April 1996): 55–69. According to one Chinese estimate, the oil deposits under the seabed in the South China Sea amount to 105 billion barrels. Another Chinese account estimates the oil deposits to be 20 percent larger than Kuwait's oil. Western estimates are more conservative, ranging from 3 billion barrels to 15.6 billion barrels. For the two Chinese estimates, see John Garver, "China Pushes Through the South China Sea," *China Quarterly*, no. 132 (December 1992): 1015; and Calder, "Asia's Empty Tank," 61.

12. Pye, "China: Not Your Typical Superpower."

13. See, for example, Michael W. Doyle, "Liberalism and World Politics," *American Political Science Review* 80, no. 4 (December 1986): 1151–1169; Bruce Russet, *Grasping the Democratic Peace* (Princeton: Princeton University Press, 1993); and Henry S. Farber and Joanne Gowa, "Polities and Peace," *International Security* 20, no. 2 (Fall 1995): 123–146.

14. Transcript of the speech in *The New York Times*, 27 January 1994, A-11.

15. Henry S. Rown, "The Short March: China's Road to Democracy," *National Interest* (Fall 1996): 61–70.

16. For the argument that the process of democratization may enhance war-proneness in a transitional society, see Edward D. Mansfield and Jack Snyder, "Democratization and the Danger of War," *International Security* 20, no. 1 (Summer 1995): 5–38.

17. See the special issue of *Business Week* on "Rethinking China," 4 March 1996, 57–65.

18. Edward Friedman, "The Challenge of a Rising China: Another Germany?" in *Eagle Adrift: American Foreign Policy at the End of the Century*, Robert J. Lieber, ed. (New York: Longman, 1997), 219.

19. Fareed Zakaria, "Speak Softly, Carry a Veiled Threat," *New York Times Magazine*, 18 February 1996, 36–37.

20. Arthur Waldron, "Deterring China," *Commentary* 100, no. 4 (October 1995): 21.

21. Charles Krauthammer, "Why We Must Contain China," *Time*, 31 July 1995, 72; Gideon Rachman, "Containing China," *Washington Quarterly* 19, no. 1 (Winter 1996): 129–139.

22. For an insightful discussion of the engagement logic, see Joseph S. Nye Jr., "China's Re-emergence and the Future of the Asia-Pacific," *Survival* 39, no. 4 (Winter 1997–98): 65–79.

23. Andrew Nathan and Robert Ross, *The Great Wall and the Empty Fortress* (New York: Norton, 1997).

24. For a discussion of these points in the context of South China Sea disputes, see Michael Gallagher, "China's Illusionary Threat to the South China Sea," *International Security* 19, no. 1 (Summer 1994): 169–194.

25. Robert Ross, "Beijing as a Conservative Power," *Foreign Affairs* 76, no. 2 (March/April 1997): 33–44.

26. Yasheng Huang, "Why China Will Not Collapse," *Foreign Policy* no. 99 (Summer 1995), 54–68.

27. Susan Shirk, "Internationalization and China's Economic Reforms," in *Internationalization and Domestic Politics*, Robert Keohane and Helen Milner, eds. (New York: Cambridge University Press, 1996), 196.

28. Andrey K. Cronin and Patrick M. Cronin, "The Realistic Engagement of China," *Washington Quarterly* 19, no. 1 (Winter 1996): 141–169.

29. Robert G. Sutter, *Shaping China's Future in World Affairs: The Role of the United States* (Boulder, Colo.: Westview Press, 1996).

30. Thomas Christensen, "Chinese Realpolitik," *Foreign Affairs* 75, no. 5 (September/October 1996): 52.

31. Chalmers Johnson, "Containing China: U.S. and Japan Drift Toward Disaster," *Japan Quarterly*, October-December 1996, 10–18.

32. Robert Jervis, *Perception and Misperception in International Politics* (Princeton: Princeton University Press, 1976), 274–278.

33. For a discussion of historical analogies being used for policy advocacy, see Yuen Fong Khong, "Korea and the Vietnam Decision of 1965," in *Learning in U.S. and Soviet Foreign Policy*, George W. Breslauer and Philip E. Tetlock, eds. (Boulder, Colo.: Westview Press, 1991), esp. 307–310.

34. Alexander Dallin, "Learning in the U.S. Policy Toward the Soviet Union in the 1980s," in Breslauer and Tetlock, *Learning in U.S. and Soviet Foreign Policy*, 407.

35. George Kennan, "Containment: Then and Now," *Foreign Affairs* 65, no. 4 (1987): 885–890.

36. The call for regional alliance to contain China is in Krauthammer, "Why We Must Contain China," 72.

37. For discussions of Chinese relations with Japan and Southeast Asian countries, see Yong Deng, "Chinese Relations with Japan: Implications for Asia-Pacific Regionalism," *Pacific Affairs* 70, no. 3 (Fall 1997): 65–80; and his "Managing China's Hegemonic Ascension: Engagement from Southeast Asia," *Journal of Strategic Studies* 21, no. 1 (March 1998): 21–43.

38. James Baker, "America in Asia: Emerging Architecture for a Pacific Community," *Foreign Affairs* 70, no. 5 (Winter 1991/92): 16.

39. Joseph Nye Jr., "The Case for Deep Engagement," *Foreign Affairs* 74, no. 4 (July/August 1995): 94.

40. Song Qiang et al., *Zhongguo keyi shuo bu: Lengzhanhou shidai de zhengzhi yu qinggan jueze* (*China Can Say No: The Political and Emotional Choice in the Post–Cold War Era*) (Beijing: Zhonghua gonshang lianhe chubanshe, 1996); and their *Zhongguo haishi neng shuo bu—Zhongguo keyi shuo bu xupin: Guoji guanxi bianshu yu women de xianshi yingfu* (*China Still Can Say No—The Sequel to China Can Say No: The Variables in International Relations and Our Realistic Responses*) (Beijing: Zhongguo wenlian chubanshe, 1996).

41. *Beijing Review*, 21–27 October 1996, 13.

42. Many commentators are uncomfortable with the dichotomous recommendations of engagement versus containment and have proposed strategies such as "polite containment," "enmeshment," and "constrainment" that combine elements of both. See, for example, Gerald Segal, "East Asia and the 'Constrainment' of China," *International Security* 20, no. 4 (Spring 1996): 107–135; Denny Roy, "The 'China Threat' Issue: Major Arguments," *Asian Survey* 36, no. 8 (August 1996): 758–771.

43. Nye, "China's Re-emergence," 76.

44. Ibid., 75.

45. Steven Mufson, "Standing Disputes Await Albright in Post-Deng China," *Washington Post,* 24 February 1997, A-13.

46. Many commentators (including Chinese officials) have suggested that China should be treated as an equal in the U.S. engagement policy. To the extent that engagement implies change on the part of China, it is doubtful that genuine "equality" is possible.

47. For a typical view of "conditional engagement," see James Shinn, ed., *Weaving the Net: Conditional Engagement with China* (New York: Council on Foreign Relations Press, 1996). For a thoughtful critique of this approach, see Peter Van Ness, "The Impasse in U.S. Policy Toward China," *China Journal* no. 38 (July 1997): 139–150.

48. For an alternative U.S. China policy, see Fei-Ling Wang, "To Incorporate China: A New Policy for a New Era," *Washington Quarterly* 21, no. 1 (January 1998): 67–81.

49. James Schlesinger et al., *Toward Strategic Understanding Between America and China* (New York: National Committee on U.S.-China Relations, December 1996), 3.

50. Gary King, Robert O. Keohane, and Sidney Verba, *Designing Social Inquiry: Scientific Inference in Qualitative Research* (Princeton: Princeton University Press, 1994), 31–32.

51. The dragon became the totem of the Chinese nation two thousand years ago at the latest. The dragon, as the Chinese interpret it, is an almighty, unpredictable, and eternal creature. It is not necessarily bad-tempered and is not an evil monster, as Europeans might believe. In appearance, the dragon is a mixture of boar, deer, lion, snake, horse, lizard, and fish.

2

Self-Image and Strategic Intentions: National Confidence and Political Insecurity

Fei-Ling Wang

How does China view itself after two decades of phenomenal growth and changes? What are the security concerns and likely demands of the increasingly powerful People's Republic of China (PRC)? To address these questions, this chapter aims at an analysis of China's strategic intentions by examining China's self-image.[1] Perhaps as a reflection of the speed and depth of the great changes and the immense potential and uncertainties the nation has been experiencing, China has a self-image that is filled with contradictions. An increased self-confidence of the Chinese nation and a peculiar but persisting sense of insecurity of the Chinese Communist Party (CCP) leadership have deeply colored China's strategic considerations. Likely to be more assertive and even nationalistically demanding, the PRC, under the current political regime, appears to prefer a conservative foreign policy for the sake of its political stability. Ironically, perhaps, the more capabilities the PRC develops and the bigger role Beijing plays internationally, the more acute the sense of CCP's political insecurity is likely to become, and thus the restraining effect of such a mentality on China's foreign policy will become even stronger.

Increasingly confident and self-assured, China is now rightfully feeling safe as a nation. Many of its people believe that a rejuvenation of Chinese civilization is approaching. Despite the noticeable nationalist sentiment, aspirations, and even ambitions common to a rising power, China appears to have accepted two basic facts of today's international relations: First, the world is organized in a nation-state political system and an international market economy rather than anything like the "Chinese world order" of the Middle Kingdom; second, China is still clearly a backward or developing nation that lacks the economic clout, capital, and technology necessary to realize its potential as a great power. Thus, the self-evaluation of Chinese capabilities as well as the intended purpose assigned to those capabilities have been limited. More important, the PRC government in Beijing has demonstrated a profound concern bordering on a strong sense of insecurity—a siege mentality, if you will—primarily caused by the political trepidation of the CCP leadership. The debilitating impact of such a mentality may have effectively constrained the foreign policy of a rising Chinese power. With a general sense of national security, a peculiar leadership mentality under siege, and the limited and rather transparent external demands centered around the political survival of the CCP regime and the unification course, China's self-image and strategic intentions are likely to sustain a conservative and pragmatic foreign policy for the PRC in the near future.

CAPABILITIES AND NEW CONFIDENCE

The rising capacity of the PRC has been widely analyzed. International financial organizations such as the World Bank and the International Monetary Fund as well as the Chinese government have similarly concluded that China's gross domestic product (GDP) grew at an average annual rate of 9.8 percent from 1979 to 1997 (11.8 percent in 1994, whereas the average world annual rate of economic growth was only 3.3 percent, 2.5 percent for developed nations, 5 percent for developing nations). Eliminating the inflation factor, China's GDP increased fourfold in fifteen years and is now the seventh largest in the world.[2] Internationally, China rose from the twenty-seventh–ranked trader in 1978 to tenth in 1998 (not including the ninth ranking of Hong Kong, which was returned to the PRC in 1997). China has accumulated the largest reserve of foreign currency, after only Japan ($139 billion by 1998 compared to only $167 billion in 1978). Since 1992, the PRC has been the second largest recipient of foreign investment after the United States. China has become the fifth largest foreign holder of U.S. Treasury bonds ($43 billion by 1997) and the largest foreign buyer of T-bonds in 1996.[3]

Under Zhu Rongji's able leadership, the economy's worrisome overheating appears to have eased considerably as the official inflation rate reduced from 16.7 percent in 1995 to less than 7 percent in 1996.[4] This has bolstered Beijing's confidence in managing the economy. Consequently, the CCP leadership declared at the Fifteenth CCP National Congress in fall 1997 that an accelerated market-oriented reform of the money-losing state-owned enterprises (SOEs) is now on the agenda.[5] The financial crises of 1997–1998 in Southeast Asia and Korea have exacerbated the difficulty in reforming the core of China's Stalinist-socialist economy. The lesson that the Chinese leadership seems to have drawn from the Asian crises is that even though reform should be approached with caution it must continue in order to build a modern market economy capable of competing globally.

Given the massive population and huge domestic market, a still very cheap labor force of nearly 800 million, one of the largest natural endowments in the world, and the rapidly advancing market institutions, the high economic growth of the PRC is expected to continue into the twenty-first century to produce a world-class continental power. External forces could make a major difference, especially if applied as a cohesive and effective effort (like the containment effort led by the United States during the Cold War). Yet containment aimed at curbing the Chinese growth or limiting Chinese power appears to be unfeasible. Chinese analysts have generally dismissed the possibility of a new Cold War–type of containment against China.[6] One senior analyst concluded internally in 1997:

> The bi-partisan mainstream of the United States has realized that the rise of China is hard to stop and cannot be ignored; it is unfeasible to contain China, it must use engagement as the means and "incorporation" as the end; only that way, it can serve the U.S.'s own political, security, and economic interests. The United States needs engagement policies as the channels of keeping "Westernizing" and "dividing" (*xihua* and *fenghua*) China. From a long-term perspective, the strategic objectives of the U.S. China policy is, through a trinity-policy of "economic participation, political pressures, and ideological infiltration," to lure and force the Chinese to gradually change its domestic and foreign policies and eventually to incorporate China into an international system dominated by the West. For that, the U.S. government must keep engaging China and avoid confrontation.[7]

The widely held optimistic forecast of rising Chinese power based on high economic growth has often been presented in China as an echo to such estimates made by foreign observers. One analyst in Beijing reported that "more and more Westerners have viewed it to be final that China has become a world-class power."[8] Such an "universal" feeling has substantially enhanced China's self-image by the late 1990s. Accordingly, talks about a larger Chinese role in international affairs emerge. Clearly, one sees a rise of confidence among Chinese elites, who generally have a deep sense of history and often a strong feeling of mission. One economist, noted for his independent analysis of Chinese capabilities, concluded that the current era has been China's "greatest era of reform and most prosperous era of construction" in history. Furthermore, after the United States and Japan, China has now been granted "the third rare historical opportunity in 100 years" to have an economic takeoff into the status of a world economic power.[9]

A book by a group of scholars and analysts, prefaced by a longtime close associate of Jiang Zemin, asserts that China has had a "Chinese miracle" of economic development, a "structural transformation" of its society, and a "polyarchical configuration" of its culture and ideology.[10] "Rapidly growing Chinese economy will inevitably become the locomotive of the world's economy in the 21st century." Thus,

> A rising China will never be a nation that is satisfied with only food and shelter. Her development and progress will definitely make increasing contributions to peace and prosperity of the world. China was such a [nation] in the past for several thousands of years, it will definitely become such a nation again in the next millennium. . . . Our nation used to be a crucial player on the playground of international politics. [Its] enhancing economic capabilities, and its status of being a major nuclear power and a permanent member of the UN Security Council, will give our nation a larger and larger role in world affairs. [O]ur nation enjoys a position as an irreplaceable major world power.[11]

Other analysts who are more ideologically oriented believe that China is carrying out the mission of rejuvenating the Chinese civilization and restoring its past glory as well as undertaking the grand task of safeguarding and promoting socialism, which requires patience and hard work. One faculty member of the CCP's Central Party School summarized Deng Xiaoping's "strategic thoughts" as "so long as China's socialism does not collapse, socialism will forever stay in the world. If by the middle of the next century, China develops to be a midlevel developed country and realizes its development strategy, socialism will become invincible."[12]

In short, many in Beijing believe that "it is impossible that China will lie there motionless forever (as Napoleon allegedly suggested almost two hundred years ago). The 1.2 billion Chinese people, who are their own masters, want to develop and move on. This is a historical trend that nobody can hold back."[13]

CAUTIONS AND DOUBTS

Due caution, however, must be exercised when assessing China's capabilities. Despite the seemingly high trade surplus the PRC currently enjoys, its economy is still basically a low-tech one. "China's leading exports are products that have not been produced in large quantity by American factories for more than a decade."[14] In many important aspects, China still remains a developing country with a large number of poor people and mounting economic, social, and political problems. Between the goals of a strong state and a rich nation, the Chinese still are far from being able to achieve both. Militarily, China remains a very modest power, and it simply cannot purchase modern military might from abroad given its limited military budget.[15] Furthermore, "analysts need to provide more evidence that demonstrates whether China's [People's Liberation Army or PLA] . . . is catching up, merely keeping pace with, or perhaps falling behind" the existing major powers.[16] Chinese elites are clearly aware of China's lack of power-projection capabilities, especially beyond its immediate neighborhood.

Checks on the growth of Chinese power are visible, although none has appeared to be fundamentally undermining. Rising individualism and consumerism, the inevitable products of a market economy, are likely to reduce the resources available to the state's foreign ventures. The ongoing political and economic decentralization may cut deeply into Beijing's ability to utilize domestic resources. Obstacles and potential hazards to the economic development are abundant. Compared to the world average, for example, China's per capita arable land, water, mineral, and energy deposits are poor. Feeding the Chinese has even become a serious challenge, something viewed by analysts as being currently under "very great pressure."[17] Cautious estimates about the Chinese economy abound in the Chinese press and academic writings. The current reform of state-owned enterprises and the chronic issue of massive rural underemployment, compounded by the now increased competition from the Southeast Asian economies on the international market, have prompted many to develop conservative forecasts about the future of the Chinese economy.

The concerns and reservations are well reflected in China's self-assessment. The CCP leadership has been insisting that it needs at least another fifty years (from the mid-1990s) to turn China into a "middle-level developed" country. Scholarly discussion of the "national conditions" of China is often filled with deep and often well-grounded concerns over some of the monumental problems China is facing: a huge population that grows by more than 10 million every year; hundreds of millions of low-skilled or unskilled laborers needing jobs; the chronic problem of state enterprises; and the decline of both political legitimacy and governing authority of Beijing in a nation that is rich in regionalist traditions and developing very unevenly. It is remarkable to notice that Chinese analysts often tend to be less optimistic than their Western counterparts in assessing the rise of Chinese power. The Western "inaccuracies" in estimating Chinese power and its impact, explain some Chinese analysts, were caused by Western analysts' "epistemological limits" or their "evil intentions" of manipulating world opinion and hurting China.[18]

One Chinese economist believes that there are at least four serious challenges to China's ascendance as a world economic power: conflicts between the central government and local governments; the increasing gap between the developed areas and the less developed areas; the worsened relationship between the CCP/PRC government and the people; and the problems of economic instability. There are also unspecified "political risks that cannot be ignored."[19] Others acknowledged in 1997 that there was a "hard-to-ignore belief crisis and other social problems" and a danger of possible "Yugoslavia-nization" of the PRC.[20] Yet another group of scholars close to the CCP leadership listed as many as twenty-seven "key" issues, centered around the decline of central political and fiscal authority, that need to be addressed in China today.[21] In the view of many Chinese elites, the very promising future of the PRC, therefore, is not guaranteed. It has been concluded that the next fifteen to twenty years will be "the most critical historical moment for the rise/success or fall/failure of this ancient civilization in the East."[22]

The rising Chinese national power is believed to have three features: massive aggregation of the power elements and great potential; low per capita resource and thus small power-projection capability; and "poor quality and low efficiency." Overall, China's "comprehensive national power" is ranked roughly the same as Japan's (behind the United States and Russia), and as only a "regional power" in East Asia.[23] There is a recognition of the significant gap between China's perceived or potential role and its acquired capabilities. China has thus basically viewed itself as "a regional, or transregional, major power with glistening global color" or "a quasi global power" with regional capabilities and room to maneuver.[24] As China is now more closely scrutinized by the existing major powers and aspires to be more active in international affairs, the self-recognition of the gap between a "major power" role and China's deficiency of capabilities is likely to be even more apparent.

VALUES AND NORMS: HOW DIFFERENT ARE THE CHINESE?

Many analysts, especially realists, believe that the power position of nations fundamentally conditions and even determines options and actions in international relations. A nation experiencing significant power increase will necessarily make new demands, search for new policies, and initiate new activities. Driven by its national objectives and feeling constrained by external conditions and especially by existing major powers, a rising power has a great propensity to demonstrate a challenging attitude, an aggressive involvement, even an imperialist agenda. History has plenty of such examples. From the rise of Great Britain, the United States, to that of Germany, Japan, and the former Soviet Union,[25] a rising power always prompted a change in international relations that was often war-prone, costly, and bloody. Yet looking at the different consequences of the rises of Germany and Japan versus that of the United States may reveal that the inevitable accommodation of a rising power does not have to be costly and destructive. The cause of the differences, it seems, is the different intentions of the rising power in question and the different international responses. The key variables here seem to be the different norms and values a rising power may have vis-à-vis the existing major powers. If there are a reasonably similar norms and values between the rising power and the existing powers, a peaceful incorporation and a rapid, smooth integration into the existing international framework is more likely. If, however, a rising power is dominated by a strong and aggressive agenda that demands major change and even an overhaul of the existing international order, it may force the existing powers into either a prolonged and costly cold war of containment, a bloody and often uncertain real war to settle the disputes, or surrender, which is normally out of the question.

Under international political anarchy or the nation-state system, nations by definition have different objectives and agendas. Intentions of a rising power like the PRC are generally the result of its domestic institutional arrangement, primarily the historically defined political structure, economic system, cultural and religious factors, and leadership mentality. The analysis of the intentions of the rising power, therefore, should be valued at least as importantly as the analysis of its capabilities. Intentions of the rising power may in fact be the factor that determines whether the rising power is a challenging, aggressive, even imperialistic power or merely a more powerful nation with accommodatable demands. The differences in values and utility functions, more than the growing capabilities, perhaps deserve more scrutiny. The Chinese seem to be aware of this. The official *Renmin ribao* reported: "Whether a country constitutes a threat to world peace (or other countries) depends not on its size, strength, or growth rate but on what type of foreign policy it adopts."[26] Therefore, officially Beijing has been very cautious about using words that may be interpreted as challenging the West. The reform and opening have transformed the Chinese value system toward assimilation with the West. Yet deep differences exist between China and the West, primarily in the areas of ideology and human rights, especially political rights. That understanding, however, needs to be further analyzed here in the West to avoid misjudging China's power and intentions (thus prompting improper responses) due to an exaggeration of its peculiarities.

Unlike the former Soviet Union, Beijing now has a diminishing ideological identity and no religious affiliations. Indeed, Chinese communism
and the CCP have been very different from their Soviet counterparts since
the very beginning. The Chinese, including most of the CCP cadres, have
now apparently become involved in a grand marketization of their economic, social, and even political lives. Western values and the Western way
of life have not only become the models for the Chinese youth; they have
been authentically practiced in the PRC. One now perhaps needs to travel
to southern China, for example, to see, ironically, what "genuine" capitalism is.[27] Field trips in China easily reveal that the American way of life and
American entertainment and media have deeply captured the hearts and
minds of educated youth. A variety of beliefs, ranging from voodoolike su-
perstition, various denominations of the world's major religions, to ances-
tor worship, has been competing with official communist ideology. Christianity, especially Protestantism, has been growing the fastest, even in
Chinese villages.[28]

The Chinese economy has been rapidly moving toward an essentially
capitalist or market economy, albeit one that is incomplete and heavily distorted. The authoritarian, "communist" CCP regime now controls roughly
the same proportion of the Chinese economy as Paris does of the French
economy. Official statistics showed that the PRC's direct state control of industrial production declined from 70 percent in 1979 to 5 percent in 1995,
and control of retail pricing fell from 95 percent in 1979 to less than 6 percent in 1994.[29] Beijing's authoritarian control of labor allocation declined
similarly fast during the past fifteen years.[30] Extensive economic and culture bonds have already developed between China and the outside world,
primarily the West. Some even estimate that as much as 20–40 percent of
China's gross national product (GNP) now comes from foreign trade.[31]
Trade, business, and profit rather than ideology have become the national
objectives for erstwhile revolutionary Chinese. Pursuing profits in the international market has colored Chinese foreign policy, now with a rather
typical neomercantilist bent.[32]

As the heir to the ancient Chinese civilization, the PRC enjoys a stable
and fairly homogenous culture relatively free of religious zeal. Despite lin-
gering problems with Tibetans, Muslims, and Mongols, China appears to
be under firm control of the Han Chinese, who constitute the majority in
every part of China except Tibet.[33] A common written language and the re-
lentlessly promoted Mandarin pronunciation have made China one of the
few densely populated countries to have just one language. There has been
little, if any, question about such homogeneity and unity. Politically, such a
homogeneous nation provides the Leninist authoritarian regime with
strong support during an era of rapid economic development and social
change. Produced by the powerful Confucian culture and then nourished

by the existing culture, the family structure has always been the cell of the Chinese nation and the basis upon which the Chinese state was maintained. The Chinese culture that originated from this historical legacy has thus generated a peculiar view on the government-subject relationship. "The ruler or government, as the grand family/clan head (*dajiazhang*), has an obligation to work for the well-being of its subordinate members. . . . [Thus the] legitimacy of the government does not come from votes but from promoting the welfare of the people."[34]

To many inside and outside the government, the CCP earned its *dajiazhang*, or patriarchal, power through long, violent struggles. To perhaps even more, the rapid economic development of the PRC and the economic meltdown of the former Soviet Union have been sufficient reasons to justify the monopoly of political power by the CCP. Still preaching its Chinese version of communism, the "revolutionary" CCP has nonetheless lost almost all of its revolutionary drive and courage. This one-party rule, currently under Jiang Zemin, is seen as having no serious alternative or organized competitor,[35] even though it may logically conflict with the market-oriented economic development that requires and produces diversity, mobility, and political participation. As long as the CCP can continue to generate or allow for a satisfying economic development, political stability in the PRC is expected.

Despite the marketization of its economy and the discoloring of its official ideology, the CCP regime itself is likely to be the source of differences between China and the West. The most apparent and well-known difference has been Beijing's treatment of individual rights, especially political rights. The most vivid illustration of that was the lively verbal exchanges between the U.S. president and the Chinese president during their joint press conference at the Sino-American Summit in Washington in fall 1997.[36] Fully aware of those differences, Beijing defends itself by arguing for a nationally defined concept and criteria as to human rights.[37] The Chinese concept of human rights is said to include four components: the right to survival; the right to development; political rights of citizens; and social rights. The Western concept of political and civil rights is considered to be just one part of human rights. Emphasizing the right to survival and development, the Chinese government and scholars argue, is currently more important than providing Western-style civil and political rights to the 1.2 billion Chinese.[38]

Westerners, especially American politicians, have taken the differences regarding human rights very seriously (too much so, arguably). The Chinese, however, do not seem to share nearly as much concern. Conveniently standing behind the shield of national sovereignty and internal affairs, Chinese elites seem to believe that differences in human rights, as long as Western human rights advocates do not succeed in hijacking foreign policy toward China, are of minor importance and will wither away as Chinese economic development proceeds and China becomes stronger (and thus a lesser target for criticism).

Perhaps in a sign of self-awareness of the shortcomings of China's political system, Chinese intellectuals generally adopt a defensive position rather than promoting its political system. Other than a few popular readings, there are hardly any Chinese writings, openly published or internal, suggesting that the Chinese ought to impose their understanding of human rights onto the West as the country strengthens. On the contrary, many imply that the Western notion of human rights may eventually take root in China, suggesting that the Western criticism of Chinese human rights simply reflects "impatience" rather than evil intent. More specifically, many seem to believe that Beijing should at least acknowledge partial responsibility for the tragedy in June 1989, yet they commonly prefer what Deng Xiaoping allegedly instructed: Avoid the controversy for the sake of political stability and let history make the final judgment in the future. A common response has been that the Westerners' criticism of China for its human rights problems has been prompted by a fear of a different and strong China, ignorance of the Chinese culture and history, or evil intent to make China an enemy.[39] And though Western criticism might cause some movement in Beijing to improve its human rights record for practical considerations and diplomatic interests, it may also produce considerable resentment and misgiving among Chinese youth, who tend to view Western criticism of the Chinese political system as an attack on the nationhood and statehood of China.

The PRC's different treatment of human rights, especially political rights, is likely to continue for some time. An official reversal on June 4, 1989, exonerating political dissidents, still appears to be politically very costly to the CCP leadership. The proponents of China's political democracy and individual freedom are expected to keep up the pressure. A certain improvement in the human rights record of the PRC, and some form of "delinking," or deemphasis, of this difference in the West, however, are very likely, perhaps very desirable to the Chinese as well as the existing major powers. Early signs of willingness to make changes to head off Western criticism can thus be detected, even in the writings of some pro-CCP analysts.[40] The quiet release of Wei Jingsheng, the most symbolic Chinese political prisoner since 1979, in November 1997 may further demonstrate that Beijing is willing to make some gestures to improve its image in the West.

In short, unlike other rising powers in modern history, the PRC has no known international ambitions based on ideological, religious, or racial claims. (Even the United States had a clearly imperialistic impulse, the "manifest destiny" that impelled the young American republic toward imperialism nearly two centuries ago.) The differences between China and the existing major powers, mainly centered around Beijing's political system, are easy to see and may rightfully cause concern in the West. They are likely to be a major point of contention in the near future. Yet China seems to have accepted the basic ideological orientation of the West and thus has little ambition to impose its views onto other nations. The peculiar Chinese value system and norms, already blended into the official national interests of the PRC, should be interpreted, perhaps more accurately, as a cover and a defense of the CCP's political interests, which do not fit the Western value system. Unlike an "ordinary" rising power, therefore, Beijing lacks the moral calling to undertake adventurous foreign policies, let alone an expansionist or colonial program. Furthermore, behind the value differences there lies a very strong political reason for conservatism in China's foreign policymaking: a peculiar siege mentality and a persisting sense of insecurity among the CCP leadership.

THE BEST NATIONAL SECURITY ENVIRONMENT VERSUS CCP'S SENSE OF INSECURITY

There seems to be an intriguing and profound contradiction in China's self-image, especially as to strategic concerns. On the one hand, Chinese leaders and analysts have openly concluded in the 1990s that China now clearly feels secure and enjoys its best security posture "since World War II" or "even since the Opium War" of 1840–1842.[41] On the other hand, there has lingered a strong insecure feeling within the CCP leadership. Often, this feeling manifests in the siege mentality. Beijing's sometimes "irrational" responses to criticism of its political actions have been largely motivated by this mentality.

Thanks largely to the foresight of American statesmen, mainly Franklin D. Roosevelt, China already has a nominally satisfied "world power" status. Now the PRC is one of the five permanent members of the UN Security Council and one of the five "legal" nuclear powers. The nominal world power status and the apparent national security, however, have not stopped Chinese elites, especially the CCP leadership, from longing for an "equal" treatment and a lesser threat from the existing powers. One only needs to browse the speeches and writings of Chinese political leaders and academicians to see a deep fear of foreign-induced political instability, conceivably justifiable concerns over "hegemonic" interventions in Chinese "domestic affairs," a near-paranoid sense of insecurity for a possible international siege or containment against China, and a strong longing to be treated "equally" by the leading nations. Such a feeling of insecurity and unfulfillment is perhaps natural to a rising power. The intensity of the PRC's clear sense of insecurity, however, perhaps should be better explained as the continuity of the CCP's besieged mentality, which contrasts strikingly with the well-grounded sense of national security in China.

The ruling CCP regime demonstrates a peculiar mentality that mixes an ambitious sense of mission with a strong fear of being under siege. Despite its ambitious plan and confidence of leading China into the promised land of "lost" greatness, respect, prosperity, and power, the CCP regime has been contested in its legitimacy; its authority and official ideology are under constant challenges from within and without, especially after 1989. These internal and external pressures have forced Beijing to search for sanctuary in economic prosperity and nationalistic feeling, or "patriotism." Not surprisingly, given the authoritarian nature of the PRC political system, the CCP's insecurity has essentially been translated, through its organizations and propaganda machines, to be in the "national interests" of a rising Chinese power. The result, as Yong Deng shows in the next chapter, is a fixation on and worship for "national interests" in China's discourse on international relations during the 1990s. Thus a false sense of national insecurity and siege has heavily influenced Chinese strategic considerations, despite the fact that the Chinese nation has never been so secure in nearly two centuries. The leading arguments offered by the CCP to combine its political interests with the national interests of China have been that "only the CCP can save China," "China can only develop well under the CCP leadership," and "no CCP, no New China." Such arguments have been persuasive to many Chinese, since they describe the nature and course of state-led modernization. Moreover, valuing one's political system as a vital part of national interest is not exclusively a Chinese logic.

The CCP seems to be content with its domestic political monopoly. External respect or disrespect and criticism, however, have now become the leading sources of CCP's political legitimacy or destabilization. Beijing was preparing for an "inevitable" world war at any time until 1983, when Deng Xiaoping assessed that a new world war was unlikely within ten years. The new leadership under Jiang Zemin in 1995 reestimated that "it is possible to earn an international peace for the next fifteen years" until 2010, when China and, in the leadership's calculation, the CCP regime would expect to be strong enough to rid itself of the danger. A military invasion by foreign powers may be remote now, yet the CCP's sense of siege and insecurity persists.

Despite China's obviously secure environment, the CCP regime may indeed have good reasons to feel insecure in the post–Cold War world, where the dominant powers, led by the United States, have appeared to be at odds with this last "communist" government. The growing Chinese capabilities have actually heightened the West's scrutiny and criticism of the CCP political system. It is not difficult to imagine, looking out from Zhongnanhai (CCP headquarters), the serious threat to China (actually, to the

CCP political regime) of the democracy-promoting and human rights–advocating United States. The State Council of the PRC thus concluded:

> As long as China remains a socialist country with the Communist Party in power and as long as China does not adopt the American style political system, no matter how much Chinese economy develops, how much democracy is introduced in politics, and how much human rights is improved [the United States] will just look but not see and listen but not hear. As what people often said: "prejudice is far worse than ignorance. . . . [The United States is just] using human rights [issue] to interfere in Chinese domestic politics and promote hegemonism and power-politics.[42]

Consequently, as Jianwei Wang shows in this volume, PRC analysts talk about a "comprehensive security" goal, look out with highly alerted eyes, and view international organizations or collective security arrangements very suspiciously.[43] A foreign ministry–backed journal published an article asserting that a "grand strategy" of China must consider a "comprehensive security" of "domestic and external security" and "not only military security but also political, economic, and cultural security."[44] Beijing vigilantly watches for dangers. Other than the United States, which is clearly the direct and likely most serious threat, nearly all of China's neighboring countries are viewed internally as potentially "troublemaking": Japan "is transforming from a potential threat to a real threat," Russia is "our long-term potential rival," India "is the potential source of insecurity and instability in our southwestern regions," the Association of Southeast Asian Nations (ASEAN) is the "direct party of struggle over our sovereignty of Nansha (Spratly) islands," and the development of "a larger ASEAN" would be a serious and unfavorable challenge to China.[45] (With the additions of Vietnam in 1995 and Laos and Myanmar in 1997, ASEAN now has nine members.)

A sense of being under siege is clearly, if not prevalently, identifiable in Beijing today. Even though it is correct that differences between the PRC and the United States are not exactly ideological or political,[46] the Western/American threat to the CCP regime, not necessarily the Chinese nation, apparently weighs heavily in Beijing's strategic calculation of the post–Cold War world. Practically, however, between the national sense of security and the insecurity of the ruling regime, Beijing has become profoundly sensitive and susceptible to external pressures and incentives.

STRATEGIC CONCERNS AND THE RISE OF NATIONALISM

Given its siege mentality, the CCP regime has concluded that fundamental Chinese national interests should include three components:[47] first, to safeguard the PRC political system, that is, the stability of the CCP regime; second, to maintain a peaceful international environment for the economic development of China; third, to unify the motherland, that is, to take back Hong Kong (which happened in 1997), Macao (to be realized in 1999), and Taiwan (no timetable yet, but at least the status quo must be preserved).

The political stability of the CCP regime seems to be the top concern to Beijing. And even though economic development is seen as the foundation for that goal, unification of the motherland may be delayed for the sake of political stability. Beijing has demonstrated remarkable patience and flexibility in its attempt to lure Taipei to the negotiation table to address the unification issue without upsetting the political stability of the CCP. Officially, Beijing has said that everything but its political system is on the table.[48] Essentially, besides Taiwan, the Chinese leadership currently appears to have asked for very little beyond its own survival. Recalling what Germany, Japan, the former Soviet Union, and even the United States wanted during their rises through the global ranks, the world may indeed feel lucky this time around.

There are other concerns. There is friction between the PRC and the major powers, mainly the United States, on issues of market access, membership in the World Trade Organization (WTO), intellectual property rights protection, and Tibet. There is also the Sino-Indian border dispute, a Sino-Japanese dispute over Diaoyu (Senkaku) Islands, and disputes over the South China Sea islets. These, however, are not the main strategic concerns of the PRC. In general, Beijing inclines to either make compromises after hard bargaining or postpone a settlement on issues. Deng Xiaoping's low-profile and conservative guidelines for Chinese foreign policy after 1989 appears to be still in effect even after his death, despite surging criticism from some radical nationalist youth.[49] Based on that, Jiang Zemin proposed a sixteen-word U.S. policy in 1993: *Zeng jia xin ren, jian shao ma fan, fa zhan he zuo, bu gao dui kang* (to enhance trust, reduce trouble, develop cooperation, and refrain from confrontation).[50] It clearly reflects a cautious, low-profile, cooperative, and patient approach.

Accompanying the rising status of national power is a rising, broad-based nationalist sentiment for a "Greater China" or "Greater PRC." Several popular readings have cashed in successfully on those sentiments, and serious scholars have at times argued for a more assertive and demanding Chinese foreign policy.[51] By the late 1990s, strong interest among Chinese readers has sustained the publication of dozens of books filled with nationalistic rhetoric and even xenophobic writings. Some, like the cleverly titled *China's Grand Strategy*, even outline a future of China's destined "reintegration of Asia" and "new leadership" of the world in the next fifteen to thirty years.[52] As Ming Zhang shows in his chapter, a leading target of China's rising nationalism, not surprisingly, has been the United States. With an over-whelming desire to avoid direct confrontation with the lone superpower, some Chinese have nonetheless predicted a collision course and succession process between the United States and China in the not very distant future. At the very least, they say, the rising Chinese power will despise American criticism and act accordingly, especially in neighboring regions. One expert of American studies concluded in 1995,

> Data show that in recent years, in the eyes and minds of the Chinese public including most of the intellectuals and young students, the United States has changed from a friendly country to a bully and anti-China country. As time goes by, the [United States] will eventually realize what kind of consequences its bad image in China will have to its interests in the Asian-Pacific region.[53]

Another internal article published by the military in late 1996 concluded that "the United States has been against us everywhere on the important issues and wants to contain us at every moment. For a considerably long period of time in the future, the United States will be the most direct and most serious threat to us."[54]

Still under the conscious control by the CCP regime, the rising nationalism nonetheless deserves close attention from major powers. Ironically perhaps, the same CCP regime that is criticized by the West may actually do a better job of controlling potentially dangerous nationalism that is bound to be more common and even radical in a more powerful and confident China. Any political regime in Beijing must address the potentially explosive issue of Taiwan and China's other interests that conflict with other nations. A noncommunist Chinese government is by no means more likely to compromise on the issues of Tibet or the South China Sea islets. On the contrary, a "democratic" regime in Beijing, free from the debilitating concerns for its own survival but likely driven by popular emotions, could make the rising Chinese power a much more assertive, impatient, belligerent, even aggressive force, at least during the unstable period of fast ascendance to the ranks of a world-class power. A democratizing China with apparent and perhaps justifiable strategic concerns and demands may actually be much more likely to become a systemic challenger.[55] The authoritarian CCP regime has been able to shield itself from the newly rising nationalist sentiment.[56] Beijing, for example, has recently tried to stop the spread of radical nationalist sentiment in the PRC.[57] But a "democratic" regime would have a very difficult time preventing such thoughts and ideas, which are natural for any nation experiencing drastic changes and growth, from affecting and even controlling the rising Chinese power.

CHINESE DEMANDS

Besides the "let me live" political request of the CCP, the rising Chinese power is not completely lacking real, even ambitious demands. As one analyst wrote in 1996, "The growth of the Chinese national power is the logical consequence of its economic reform. And the adjustment or development of Chinese foreign policy is the logical consequence of the growth of its power."[58] The most pressing desire, however, still appears to be on the issue of Taiwan.[59] As recounted by Suisheng Zhao in this volume, the developments in 1995–1996 highlighted the explosive nature of this issue and led many in Beijing to believe that a military solution has appeared to be harder to avoid. If many on the island are attempting to change the status quo by seeking the full title of independence, increasingly many in Beijing may have also decided to solve the problem at an earlier date. The recent surge of nationalist sentiment has largely focused on a "decisive" and rapid solution to the division of the motherland. As a historical curse cast upon the CCP regime, unifying the motherland and finally eliminating domestic political rivalries on Taiwan are intertwined with the political legitimacy of the CCP regime itself and thus have become an issue of vital national and political interest. Multiple sources in Beijing have indicated that the CCP leadership is determined to use force to prevent Taiwanese independence, even at the risk of openly opposing American military might.[60] For Chinese leaders, there is indeed very little room for maneuver on the issue of Taiwan. Premier Li Peng told the visiting vice president of the United States, Al Gore, in 1997 that "the issue of Taiwan has always been the most important and most sensitive core issue of the Sino-American relationship."[61]

The Taiwan card will continue to be the ace in the hole in the game being played by those on either side of the Taiwan Strait, as it will be for the United States and others. Yet it is a very sensitive issue that constantly reminds many Chinese how bluntly the existing major powers, primarily the Americans, have been trespassing on Chinese "domestic" affairs with their deliberately "ambiguous" policies. On this issue, we detect very little difference among the Chinese elites, officials, youth, and even political exiles. One senior official close to Jiang Zemin openly stated at Harvard University on the unification issue that Beijing has no room for negotiation and that maintaining the status quo is in both Chinese and American interests.[62] The Chinese seem to have realized that the United States is not necessarily interested in having an independent Taiwan. One internal journal asserts, "The issue of Taiwan is a card in the hands of the United States with relevance to its strategic interests in Northeast Asia. The U.S. will inevitably use this card to bargain with [China]. To maintain the status quo of division between the two sides of the Taiwan Strait fits best [American] interests."[63]

Another likely Chinese demand will be China's rights over the islets in the South China Sea and the related and much talked about expansion of the Chinese naval force. Despite insisting it has indisputable sovereignty over all of the islets and surrounding waters, Beijing has agreed to shelve the disputes and allow some "joint explorations" to proceed.[64] Aware of its own limited naval capabilities and the still uncertain value of the region, Beijing seems to have decided to postpone a showdown on this issue to avoid prematurely "internationalizing" the issue, that is, bringing in the United States.[65] The growth of the Chinese navy has caught more attentive eyes. Indeed, Chinese analysts have clearly longed that "had we had a strong enough fleet to appear in the Taiwan Straits first, who would have dared to try to interfere with Chinese domestic politics with force?"[66] A senior officer in the PLA navy recently advocated that Beijing should put more emphasis on the development of naval power and use it more routinely to protect growing Chinese maritime interests. He also hinted that China may indeed demand more maritime rights and interests in the future—the so-called maritime space—which, according to his calculation, is disproportionately small for the Chinese (only 30 percent of the size of Chinese territory versus the world average of 94 percent). Yet he apparently also believes that the UN's Law of the Sea is in China's interests and that the PLA navy wants to "protect our legitimate interests" as stipulated by the Law of the Sea.[67]

The rising Chinese power may proactively seek, beyond Taiwan and the South China Sea and on a more grand scale, according to some analysts in Beijing, a "countercontainment" strategy against the existing major powers to secure its political regime and create room for making new demands, especially in East Asia. Sounding like a realist strategist, Deng Xiaoping prescribed the following for the PRC in the 1980s:

> How much role we can play in international affairs depends on how much achievement of our economic construction. If our country developed and became more prosperous, we would play a larger role in international affairs. Our current role in international affairs is not small; but if our material basis and material capabilities are enhanced, [our] role will be even larger.[68]

More active Chinese participation in the management of international affairs and a more evenly constructed multipolar world sound more satisfactory to Beijing. Therefore, the PRC prefers to first be given a great power (*daguo*) responsibility in the Asia-Pacific region to ensure a "just and rational" new security order in the region. A quadrangular arrangement of the United States, Japan, China, and Russia should replace the unfavorable bilateral U.S.-Japan alliance. China can then "rightfully" play

its role of "balancer" and thus "share" the major powers' responsibility for
the region's security.[69] Beyond that, China could take advantage of the differences between the United States and its allies in Europe—the strategy
of utilizing the West-West conflicts by forging more ties between the rising
Asia and the European Union. On the last day of 1996, the official *Renmin
ribao* illustratively ranked "the successful Asian-European Summit" (held
in Malaysia in March 1996) as the number-one item on its annual list of
"Top Ten International News in 1996." An American-European-Asian
tripolarity may thus replace the American-European-Japanese dominance,
and a five-power (the United States, Russia, China, Japan, and European
Union) structure may replace the current one superpower–plus–multiple
major powers situation.[70] An internally published analysis argued more
bluntly that

> we must seize the opportunity, develop ourselves, and to further strengthen
> our position and function in our neighboring areas. . . . [We] must be
> strategic and grasp the initiatives in the management of the affairs in our
> neighboring regions . . . to skillfully handle the several triangular relation-
> ships for the strategic interests of China: the big China-U.S.-Japan triangle
> and the [five] small triangles of China-Japan-ASEAN, China-Japan-Russia,
> China-India-Pakistan, China-Japan-South Korea, and China-North Korea-
> South Korea.[71]

In very general terms, some Chinese analysts have suggested that in
the twenty-first century China's strategic goal of international politics and
diplomacy "should be for a peaceful, democratic, harmonious and cooperative new international political-economic order." Such a new order will
depart from a five-century history of hegemonic struggle. China should
work to reach "such a goal: Through the rise of a multipolar world, [we]
will make the lone superpower of the United States to have a smooth and
dignified 'soft landing' type of transformation to become a normal major
power, a normal pole."[72] Yet such an aspiration has not been a consensus in
the PRC. To deal with the United States with extra care, however, has appeared to be the common view in Beijing. Internally, analysts suggest that
China may oppose the "hegemonic policies" of the United States yet needs
"to recognize its superpower status and its influence on the global major issues."[73] A more scholarly work concluded that "the United States is the
world's only superpower after the Cold War and its position will continue
for at least another 20–30 years to come. . . . Thus, avoiding military confrontation with the United States is in China's long-term strategic and security interest."[74]

A rising Chinese power is likely to develop new and more concrete demands, and Beijing may argue for an effective, if not entire, accommoda-

tion. The nature of those demands will depend on the circumstances in the future and mainly the responses of the major powers to the stated demands of the PRC. So far, few of Beijing's known demands have appeared to threaten the vital interests of the established powers or constitute a fundamental challenge to the existing international political and economic orders. They appear to be largely related to neighboring areas and seeking out a true major power status, not just a nominal one, for the PRC. Furthermore, the realpolitik logic and realist rationale, as well as geopolitical perspectives of the Chinese strategists,[75] have appeared to be very Western-like and have few ideological or racial overtones. Of course, realpolitik logic may lead Beijing to demand more when it becomes much stronger. A natural inference is that Chinese demands, especially on the issue of Taiwan, if ignored by the major powers for too long, could well ignite and fuel a dangerously aggressive nationalism in a stronger and perhaps a more democratic China.

CONCLUSION

China currently enjoys its best security posture since the nineteenth century and the highest economic growth ever in its long history. The rapidly growing Chinese economy is making the PRC a rising power that may rival even the most powerful nations in the foreseeable future. But the much-anticipated ascendance to world-power status is by no means guaranteed. What China wants and how it will act are not settled, even among the Chinese themselves. China's self-image has reflected and been affected by that fact. A more powerful China is likely to further increase self-confidence among Chinese leaders. Primarily on the issue of human rights, China will be, or arguably must be, different from the West for some time to come. Under the overall self-labels of "socialist market economy with Chinese characteristics" or "the primary stage of socialism with Chinese characteristics," China has shown a mixed self-image, one that is filled with increasing self-assurance, assertiveness, and some ambitious aspirations but also with deep concerns, uncertainties, and fears. Moreover, Beijing has a peculiar but persistent mentality of being politically under siege and thus experiences a strong sense of insecurity. The growth of China's capabilities has ironically enhanced Beijing's political insecurity, as the West is now compelled to increase its scrutiny and criticism of the CCP's political system in the rising Chinese power. The political insecurity of the CCP regime has already been translated into the definition of the Chinese national interest. The rising power of China has thus far shown a clear, though perhaps false sense of insecurity. Consequently, China has only a short list of fairly transparent and limited demands, centered around the CCP's political survival and a reunification with Taiwan.

The peculiar self-image and the limited strategic intentions are likely to sustain a rather conservative, conformist, and defensive Chinese foreign policy. The "approval" and support from the existing major powers have been viewed as a source of legitimacy to the CCP regime, which is eagerly searching for exactly that for its own political self-preservation. In fact, the CCP has pinned its legitimacy and ruling ability on that effort with a wholesale slogan: "to connect to the tracks of the world" (*yu shijie jiegui*).

The rapid socioeconomic and inevitably political development, such as national democratization in the PRC, however, may soon solve the political insecurity issue for China, thus leading to a more confident and active rising power. Two external factors could also profoundly affect China's self-image, its strategic intentions, and moves abroad: drastic events concerning Taiwan or enhanced encroaching actions by the existing major powers. Such external developments could force China to act out its persisting sense of insecurity. In either case, China's self-image would predictably be highlighted and enhanced by foreign stimuli and thus become more assertive, singular, even twisted. China's strategic intentions, therefore, could become much more nationalistic and even dangerously militant and aggressive. But the window of opportunity does exist for both China and the established powers to avoid such a costly and violent scenario.

NOTES

An article addressing U.S. China policy, based on the analysis of this chapter, has been published as "To Incorporate China: A New Policy for a New Era," in *Washington Quarterly* 21, no. 1 (Winter 1998). A grant from the Georgia Tech Foundation helped the research for this paper. The author thanks Yong Deng and the other contributors of this book for their very helpful comments.

1. Scholars have long argued for the existence of different types of "powers" separated primarily by their strategic intentions rather than their capabilities. Robert Gilpin, for example, described the "status quo power" versus "challenging power" in *War and Change in World Politics* (New York: Cambridge University Press, 1981). China's strategic intentions have been discussed, to various extent, in recent works, such as Lowell Dittmer and Samuel Kim, eds., *China's Quest for National Identity* (Ithaca: Cornell University Press, 1993); Samuel Kim, ed., *China and the World: Chinese Foreign Relations in the Post–Cold War Era* (Boulder, Colo.: Westview Press, 1994); Thomas Robinson and David Shambaugh, eds., *Chinese Foreign Policy: Theory and Practice* (New York: Oxford University Press, 1995); and Michael Swaine and Donald Henry, *China: Domestic Change and Foreign Policy* (Santa Monica, Calif.: Rand Corporation, 1995).

2. *China in Brief: Factors Fueling China's Rapid Economic Development* (Beijing: New Star Publishers, 1995),1–3; *Renmin ribao (People's Daily)*, 25 September 1998, 1.

3. *Renmin ribao (People's Daily)*, 25 September 1998, 1; *Time*, 3 March 1997, 45.

4. *Renmin ribao (People's Daily)*, 3 January 1997, 1.

5. Jian Zemin's report to the Fifteenth CCP National Congress, 12 September 1997.

6. Author's interviews in Beijing and Shanghai, 1996–1997.

7. Liu Jiang (deputy chief of Xinhua News Agency's International Department): "Shixi Zhongmei jianshixin zhanlue huoban guanxi" ("Preliminary Analysis of the Sino-American Strategic Partnership"), *Shijie xinshi yanjou* (*Studies of the World Situations*) no. 47 (1997), 2. See also his "Zhongmei guanxi de xianzhuan he fazhan qushi" ("The State and Prospects of Sino-American Relations"), *Shijia xinshi yanjou* (*Studies of the World Situations*), no. 26 (1997), 3.

8. Yan Xuetong: "Xifangren kan zhongguo de jueqi" ("Westerners View China's Rise"), *Xiandai guoji guanxi* (*Contemporary International Relations*), no. 9 (1996), 37.

9. Hu Angang, *Zhongguo xiayibu* (*The Next Step of China*) (Chengdu: Sichuan Renmin Press, 1996), 1, 20–22, and 221.

10. Wen Jieming et al., eds., *Yu zhongshuji tanxin* (*Chatting with the General Secretary*) (Beijing: Zhongguo shehui kexue Press, 1997), 13.

11. Ibid., 70 and 232–233.

12. Zhang Tuosheng, ed., *Huanqiu tongci liangre: Yidai lingxiumen de guoji zhanlue shixiang* (*Same to the Whole Globe: The International Strategic Thoughts of a Generation of Leaders*) (Beijing: Zhongyang wenxian Press, 1993), 312.

13. Lu Shi, "Zhuding puomie de bairimeng" ("A Daydream Doomed to Be Shattered—Refuting the 'Theory of Containing China'"), *Guangmin Ribao*, 25 August 1995, 3.

14. Seth Faison: "The Giant Follows Asia's Growth Path," *The New York Times*, 4 March 1997.

15. Robert S. Ross: "Beijing as a Conservative Power," *Foreign Affairs* 76, no. 2 (March/April 1997), 36–38. For an analysis of the modest military spending by the PLA, see Shaoguang Wang, "Estimating China's Defense Expenditure," *China Quarterly*, no. 147 (September 1996): 889–911.

16. Avery Goldstein, "Great Expectations: Interpreting China's Arrival," Working Papers Series of the Christopher H. Browne Center for International Politics, University of Pennsylvania, March 1997, 52.

17. Wen Jieming et al., *Chatting with the General Secretary*, 66 and 82.

18. Yan Xuetong, "Westerners View the Rise of China," 45.

19. Hu Angang, *The Next Step of China*, 28–34, 65, and 66–218.

20. Wen Jieming et al., *Chatting with the General Secretary*, 172–174 and 252.

21. Xu Ming, ed., *Guanjian shike: dangdai zhongguo jidai jiejue de 27 ge wenti* (*Crucial Moment: The 27 Issues that Need to Be Urgently Solved*) (Beijing: Jingri zhongguo chubanshe, 1997).

22. Wen Jieming et al., *Chatting with the General Secretary*, 2.

23. Yan Xuetong, *Zhongguo guojia liyi fengxi* (*An Analysis of China's National Interests*) (Tianjin: Tianjin renmin chubanshe, 1996), 88–95.

24. Song Xinning, *Guoji zhengzhi jingji yu zhongguo duiwai guanxi* (*International Political Economy and Chinese Foreign Relations*) (Hong Kong: Hong Kong Social Science Press, 1997), 204, 208, and 281.

25. Whether the former Soviet Union was a genuinely rising power is debatable. With an economic system destined to fail, the surge of Soviet power was

clearly unbalanced, unsustainable, and perhaps exaggerated as well. A different age of globalized economy and communications as well as the existence of nuclear weapons thus facilitated the inevitable implosion of such a premodern power.

26. *Guanchajia* (*Observer*), "Zhongguo fazhan youliyu shijie heping yu jinbu" ("The Development of China Benefits the World Peace and Progress"), and "Jin-fang lengzhan siwei taitou" ("Watch for the Rise of Cold War Thinking"), *Renmin ribao*, 22 December 1995 and 26 January 1996, respectively.

27. For a recent report on the position of Chinese workers in China's "sweat-shop socialism" that reminds one of Charles Dickens's or Charlie Chaplin's times, see Anita Chan and Robert Senser, "China's Troubled Workers," *Foreign Affairs* 76, no. 2 (March/April 1997), 104–117.

28. For a case study of religious diversification in the Chinese rural areas, see Yang Hongshan, "Wandong nongcun 'jidujiao re' diaoca yu sikao" ("An Investigation of and Reflection on the 'Christianity Craze' in Rural East Anhui"), *Jianghuai luntan* (*Jianghuai Forum*), no. 4 (1994).

29. *Xinhua Daily Telegraph,* 25 September 1995, 1.

30. Fei-Ling Wang, *From Family to Market: Labor Allocation in Contemporary China* (Lanham, Md.: Rowman & Littlefield, 1998).

31. For an analysis, see Nicholas R. Lardy, *Foreign Trade and Economic Reform in China, 1978–1990* (New York: Cambridge University Press, 1992), app.

32. Robert Kleinberg, *China's "Opening" to the Outside World: The Experiment with Capitalism* (Boulder, Colo.: Westview Press, 1990).

33. Only in Ningxia and Guangxi are the Chinese Muslims and the Zhuang people the majorities. Yet the distinctions between these two groups of "minorities" and the Han are increasingly hard to see now.

34. Ren Xiao, "Zhenzhi wenhua de fanxing" ("A Reflection on Political Culture), *Zhongguo shuping* (*China Book Reviews*) (Hong Kong), no. 1 (1994), 117.

35. Jianwei Wang, "Coping with China as a Rising Power," in *Weaving the Net: Conditional Engagement with China,* James Shinn, ed. (New York: Council on Foreign Relations, 1996), 133–174. See also Yasheng Huang, "Why China Will Not Collapse?" *Foreign Policy,* no. 99 (Summer 1995), 54–68.

36. The complete text of the press conference is in *The New York Times,* 30 October 1997, A-14.

37. For an examination of China's view on human rights, see Ming Wan's chapter in this book (Chapter 5, "Human Rights and Democracy").

38. For an elaboration on these views, see Yan Xuetong, *An Analysis of China's National Interests,* 201–207, 217–252.

39. Almost all of the PRC official responses and many of the Chinese writings (such as the edited volumes by Wen Jianming and Xu Ming cited earlier) have unmistakably expressed such views. Radical publications are even more confrontational to Western criticisms.

40. For an interesting discussion on the "need" to develop and reform Marxism as the official ideology, to refine Chinese culture through market competition, and to reappreciate the value of individualism, see Wen Jieming et al., *Chatting with the General Secretary,* 76–85.

41. The CCP's Fourteenth National Congress concluded in this way in 1992. For scholarly elaboration on this general assessment, see Shen Qurong (vice presi-

dent of the China Institute of Contemporary International Relations—a major think tank in the Chinese foreign policy community), "Security Environment in Northeast Asia: Its Characteristics and Sensitivities," *Contemporary International Relations* (Beijing) 2, no. 12 (December 1992), 13. Yang Chenxu (president of the China Institute of International Studies—the think tank of the Chinese foreign ministry), "Jianxi dongya anquan wenti" ("An Analysis of East Asian Security Issues"), *Guoji wenti yanjiu* (*International Studies*), no. 3 (1994), 21 and 19. For an overview of Beijing's general assessment of its security environment, see Tae-Hwan Kwak and Edward A. Olsen, eds., *The Major Powers of Northeast Asia* (Boulder, Colo.: Lynn Rienner Publishers, 1996), 41–68.

42. Press Office of the State Council: "Weihu renquan haishi ganshe neizheng?" ("Protecting Human Rights or Interfering with International Affairs?"), *Renmin ribao*, 29 March 1996.

43. For an examination of China's views and policies regarding collective security, see Jianwei Wang's chapter in this book (Chapter 4, "Managing Conflict: Chinese Perspectives on Multilateral Diplomacy and Collective Security").

44. Tang Yongsheng, "Zhonghe anquan yu zhongti zhanlue" ("Comprehensive Security and Grand Strategy"), *Shijie zhishi* (*World Affairs*), no. 20 (16 October 1996), 16–17.

45. Yang Jianyong, "Guanyu woguo zhoubian anquan huanjing de fenxi yu sikao" ("An Analysis and Relection on the Neighboring Security Environment of Our Nation"), *Yatai cankao* (*Asia-Pacific Reference*) (an internal publication, Beijing), no. 34 (August 19 1996); Ren Rongrong: "Dadongmeng de jueqi he zhongguo de duice" ("The Rise of a Greater ASEAN and China's Policy"), *Yatai cankao* (*Asia-Pacific Reference*), no. 38 (16 September 1996).

46. Jianwei Wang, "Coping with China as a Rising Power," 134.

47. For an examination of China's conception of national interest, see Yong Deng's chapter in this book (Chapter 3, "Conception of National Interests: Realpolitik, Liberal Dilemma, and the Possibility of Change").

48. The author was told by senior CCP officials repeatedly during 1995–1996 that even the national flag, name, and anthem of the PRC can all be changed through negotiations between Beijing and Taipei for the new united China. By 1998, there was a growing view in Beijing arguing for the political "disadvantages" of a rapid reunification with Taiwan.

49. Song Qiang, et al., *Zhongguo haishi neng shuo bu—Zhongguo keyi shuo bu xupin: Guoji guanxi bianshu yu women de xianshi yingfu* (*China Still Can Say No—The Sequel to China Can Say No: The Variables in International Relations and Our Realistic Handling*) (Beijing: Zhongguo wenlian chubanshe, 1996). This is the sequel to the controversial but immensely popular book, *Zhongguo keyi shuo bu—Lengzhanhou shidai de zhengzhi yu qinggan jueze* (*China Can Say No—The Political and Emotional Choice in the Post–Cold War Era*) by the same authors. For a critical review of the two books, see Fei-Ling Wang: "Ignorance, Arrogance, and Radical Nationalism," *Journal of Contemporary China* 6, no. 14 (Spring 1997), 161–165.

50. Zhongguo Tongxun News Agency, "PRC: Review of Developments in Sino-U.S. Relations," 18 November 1996, in Foreign Broadcast Information Service-China (FBIS-CHI-96–224). Also in Xinhua News Agency, "China: Qian Qichen Discusses World and Foreign Affairs," 30 December 1996, in FBIS-CHI-96–251; Wang

Jisi: "Ezhi haishi jiaowang?" ("Containment or Engagement?"), *Guoji wenti yanjiu* (*International Affairs*), no. 1 (1996), 6. A slightly different version of this article appeared in *Beijing Review*, no. 43 (21–27 October 1996), 6–9.

51. For example, Luo Weilong, "Zhongguoren yao shuo bu" ("The Chinese Want to Say No"), *Taipingyang xuebao* (*Pacific Journal*), no. 2 (1995).

52. Cai Xianwei, *Zhongguo da zhanlue: Lingdao shijie de lantu* (*China's Grand Strategy: A Blueprint for Leading the World*) (Haikou: Hainan Press, 1996). For a critical review of this book, see John W. Garver, "China as Number One," *China Journal* (forthcoming, 1998).

53. Niu Jun: "Duoshi zhichiu: Zhongmei guanxi de xianzhuang ji qianjing" ("The Troubling Time: Current Situation and Prospects of Sino-American relations"), *Meiguo yanjiu* (*American Studies*), no. 4 (1995), 134. For the opinion surveys showing the United States was the "most disliked country" among Chinese youth, see Xu Ming et al., *Crucial Moment*, 547–548.

54. Yang Jianyong, "An Analysis and Thinking on the Neighboring Security Environment," 6.

55. For an analysis of the relationship between war-proneness and political democratization, see Edward D. Mansfield and Jack Snyder, "Democratization and the Danger of War," *International Security* 20, no. 1 (Summer 1995).

56. Ming Zhang, "The Shifting Chinese Public Image of the United States," *Strategic Forum* (National Defense University, Washington D.C.), no. 89 (November 1996).

57. Hong Kong newspapers reported that Beijing ordered in fall 1996 a ban on media coverage of the two very popular readings advocating radical nationalism and crude anti-Japanese and anti-American sentiments. Ma Shih-t'u, "Why Have the CCP Authorities Banned 'China Can Say No'?—'China Can Still Say No' Is Accused of Heterodoxy," *Hong Kong Hsin Pao* (*Hong Kong Economic Journal*), 29 October 1996, 18, in FBIS-CHI-96-218.

58. Zhao Gancheng: "Yatai diqu xinzhixu yu zhongguo de zeren" ("The New Order in Asia-Pacific and the Responsibility of China"), *Guoji wenti luntan* (*Forum on International Issues*), no. 2 (1996), 53.

59. For China's views and recent policies on Taiwan, see Suisheng Zhao's chapter in this volume (Chapter 10, "Taiwan: From Peaceful Offense to Coercive Strategy").

60. Author's interviews with PRC officials and PLA officers in 1995–1996. The vice chairman of the PRC Central Military Commission, Gen. Zhang Zhen, reiterated publicly the situations in which the PRC will definitely use force to solve the Taiwan issue. Chang Hsiao-Ming: "Zhang Zhen Stresses That Taiwan Issue Must be Solved by Force in Three Situations, and Under Eight Circumstances," *Hong Kong Ping Kuo Jih Pao*, 19 December 1996, A18, in FBIS-CHI-96-245.

61. *Renmin ribao*, 26 March 1997, 1. Foreign Minister Qian Qichen said publicly that "the key to the stabilization and development of Sino-American relationship is a proper handling of the issue of Taiwan." *Renmin ribao*, 4 March 1997, 4.

62. Liu Ji, "21 shiji zhongmei guanxi de xuanze" ("Choices for Sino-American Relations in the Twenty-First Century"), speech at Harvard University's Fairbank Center for East Asian Studies, 27 May 1997. English text is in *Journal of Contemporary China*, no. 17 (March 1998).

63. Tang Yongxing: "Zhongmei guanxi jinru yige xinde lishi jieduan" ("Sino-American Relations Have Entered a New Historical Stage"), *Shijia xinshi yanjou* (*Studies of the World Situations*), no. 26 (1997), 5.

64. Foreign minister Qian Qichen said that Jiang Zemin reached an agreement with the Philippines in 1996 on that position. Xinhua News Agency, "China: Qian Qichen Discusses World and Foreign Affairs," 30 December 1996, in FBIS-CHI-96-251.

65. Wang Yizhou, "Lianheguo haiyangfa gongyue yu zhongguo" ("The UN Law of Sea and China"), *Taipingyang xuebao* (*Pacific Journal*), no. 2 (Summer 1996), 9–17.

66. Wen Jieming et al., *Chatting with the General Secretary*, 232–238.

67. Liu Zhenhuan (director of the PLA navy's Military Research Institute), "Ping lianheguo haiyang fa" ("Comment on the UN Law of the Sea"), *Guofang (National Defense)*, no. 15 (15 November 1996), 14–16.

68. Deng Xiaoping, *Deng Xiaoping Wenxuan (1975–1982) (Selected Works of Deng Xiaoping)* (Beijing: Renmin Press, 1986), 204.

69. Zhao Gancheng, "The New Order in Asia-Pacific," 49–51. Also see Shi Yongming, "Yatai anquan huanjing yu diqu duobian zhuyi" ("Security Environment in Asia-Pacific and Regional Multilateralism"), *Guoji wenti yanjiu* (*International Affairs*), no. 1 (1996), 41–47.

70. For a discussion of those ideas by Chinese scholars and analysts, see Xiao Ding, "Ya ou hezuo yu fazhan wenti yantaohui jiyao" ("Summary of the Symposium on Asian-European Cooperation and Development"), *Xiandai guoji guanxi* (*Contemporary International Relations*), no. 7 (1996), 42–53.

71. Yang Jianyong, "An Analysis and Thinking on the Neighboring Security Environment of Our Nation," 10–12.

72. Xu Ming, *Crucial Moment*, 8–9 and 17–18.

73. Tang Yongxing, "Sino-American Relations Have Entered a New Historical Stage," 4.

74. Yan Xuetong, *An Analysis of China's National Interests*, 158.

75. Thomas Christensen, "Chinese Realpolitik," *Foreign Affairs* 75, no. 5 (September/October 1996), 37–52.

3

Conception of National Interests: Realpolitik, Liberal Dilemma, and the Possibility of Change

Yong Deng

M any scholarly analyses in North America have pointed to a hard-core, well-entrenched Chinese realpolitik worldview with little in-grained liberal thinking.[1] In a similar vein, during the 1990s Western and U.S. politicians have criticized the Chinese government for its alleged narrow-minded, backward view, especially on issues concerning human rights and irredentist claims. China is said to hold an outmoded Westphalian notion of sovereignty and an obsolete definition of national interest in a world of growing interdependence and globalization. The critique of the Chinese worldview raises questions: What precisely is the nature of Chinese realpolitik thinking? Are there contending views? What are the prospects for change?

The concept of national interest lies at the core of the predominant paradigm governing any state's foreign policy. For example, Mikhail Gorbachev's "new thinking," which caused a cataclysmic revolution in the former Soviet Union's foreign policy, was predicated upon a redefinition of Soviet national interests, one key tenet being a recognition of and emphasis on common interests of humanity. Thus, studying the Chinese view on national interests would allow us to look into China's broad assessment of the nature of international relations (IR), namely, the paradigmatic thinking governing its foreign policy.

This chapter probes the Chinese theorizing on national interests in the 1990s, focusing on aspects of the conceptual framework from which interpretations on specific policy issues are derived. The explication of Chinese views is mainly based upon a reading of the most influential textbooks and representative, major scholarly works published in China during the 1990s. Apart from the publications consulted here, the analysis below also relies on my interviews with scholars in Beijing for the past several years. There is no doubt that Chinese scholars enjoy some freedom in expressing their views; however, one should not exaggerate the difference between scholarly and official analyses in the Chinese context. Writings on IR are still heavily censored, and publication often requires official clearance.[2] China's nascent IR scholarly community also suffers from self-censorship and inaccessibility to information necessary to form independent thinking. Moreover, lack of critical tradition and inadequate personnel with rigorous scholarly training further compromise the ability of China's IR scholars to offer views differing from or critical of the official pronouncements.[3] Here I subscribe to the widely noted observation that analyses in China's international studies community are intertwined with official thinkings, and that a line between the two is hard to draw.[4]

This chapter seeks to open up the "black box" of the Chinese conception of national interests in international relations. With the premise that the Chinese conception of national interests is not fixed or immutable, I hope to equip the analysis with some leverage to account for the possibility of change. To that end, I do not consider the Chinese conception in terms of two mutually exclusive categories: realpolitik thinking and liberal values. Instead, I consider it in terms of a realpolitik-idealpolitik spectrum so that the approximate weight of one type of thinking relative to other contending views can be appraised. I delineate a dominant realpolitik paradigm but also discern contending liberal views. Finally, I attempt a tentative examination of the possibility of liberal ascendancy in the Chinese conception of national interests in international relations.

REALISM WITH CHINESE CHARACTERISTICS

Realism, as a school of thought in Western IR theory, consists of three main assumptions: (1) the nation-state is the primary actor in international relations, hence realism is said to be state-centric; (2) there is a lack of central authority equivalent to domestic government, hence international politics is characterized as anarchy; (3) international politics is essentially power politics. The core tenet of realism is the emphasis on the dichotomy between domestic and international politics. For Martin Wight, the goal of domestic politics is the pursuit of "good life," whereas the highest value of international politics is "survival." "International politics differ from domestic politics in being less susceptible of a pregressivist interpretation. . . . International politics is the realm of recurrence and repetition; it is the field in where political action is most regularly necessitous."[5] Without a system of government, "it is roughly the case that, while in domestic politics the struggle for power is governed by the framework of law and institutions, in international politics law and order are governed and circumscribed by the struggle for power."[6]

Neorealism seeks to refine classical realism into a parsimonious, scientific theory by treating the international system as a structure shaping the unit/state behavior. Since self-help is the ordering principle of the decentralized, anarchic international system, states are subject to the same imperative for survival, hence they are compelled to pursue uniform tasks. States only differ in their respective capabilities as determined by the distribution of power in the international system.[7] Although neorealism overlooks the "second image" discounting this level of analysis as reductionist, it nonetheless accepts the basic assumptions of classical realism. With these assumptions, realism puts forth a theory of national interests, whose lawlike postulate is articulated by Hans Morgenthau: "The main signpost that helps political realism to find its way through the landscape of international politics is the concept of interest defined in terms of power. . . . We assume that statesmen think and act in terms of interest defined as power."[8] For realism, then, the state is a unitary actor insulated from the domestic society, and "statesmen" are supposed to represent the objectively existent "national" interests.

The Chinese realist conception of national interest demonstrates several important Chinese characteristics.

Worship for National Interest

As a leading Chinese scholar points out, the Chinese conception of national interests is guided by a materialist theory. "Compared with the Westerners, the Chinese are more accustomed to analyze international relations from the perspective of practical interests." Thus, "they are less likely to believe that some spiritual beliefs [values, religions, and ideologies] themselves can also be a driving force behind diplomacy. . . . The Chinese see international exchanges more in terms of the motives of interest and the gains-losses thereof."[9] Because Chinese analysts tend to interpret the foreign policy of the Western countries from an exclusively interest-oriented approach, there is always a huge perceptual gap besetting China's relations with the West.[10] They view Western human rights diplomacy as driven by power politics and reject Samuel Huntington's "clashes of civilizations" thesis as a misrepresentation of the post–Cold War world.

Many Chinese authors note that national interests are "objectively existent" and that they should be studied with "scientific methods." The author of the first monograph exclusively devoted to analyzing China's national interests makes these claims of scienticism most explicitly.[11] The Chinese belief in scientism is reminiscent of the embrace of logical positivism and scientific behavioralism as the epistemological and methodological foundation for neorealism in the North American IR theory.[12]

For many Chinese officials and scholars alike, national interests are the embodiment of the nation as a whole, and their pursuit is the natural and "inalienable right" of the nation-state.[13] In international politics, "relations in interests are the fundamental factor influencing foreign behavior, and national interests are the most long-lasting, the most influential factor and the most basic motive of the state's foreign behavior."[14] Put differently, "national interests are the primary, direct motive. The rest of the dynamics are secondary and permeate national interests."[15] For a high-ranking scholar-official, upholding national interests should be the highest principle in China's dealings in international affairs.[16] In the words of the late Chinese leader Deng Xiaoping, "National sovereignty and national security should be the top priority." "National rights [guo quan] are more important than human rights," and the latter should by no means be allowed to undermine the former.[17]

Chinese realist analyses even assume that once countries start to deal with each other based on their national interests conflicts will be settled and the world will be peaceful.[18] One prominent scholar even claims that "international sovereign national interests are mutually compatible."[19] Given the prevalent worship for national interests, it is no wonder that Chinese officials and scholars alike all claim that one of Deng Xiaoping's major intellectual contributions was his emphasis on national interests as the "highest principle" governing international relations. Deng was hailed as responsible for having single-handedly shifted China's erstwhile approach in drawing its foreign policy lines according to the social system and ideology to the rightful emphasis on dealing with international relations based on national interests.[20]

The Domestic/International Dichotomy

As Raymond Aron points out, for the postwar realists such as Hans Morgenthau, "To invoke national interest is a way of defining not a policy but an attitude, of problemacizing against ideologies of perpetual peace, international law, Christian or Kantian morality, against the representatives of special interest groups who confuse their own interests with those of the collectivity as a whole and in time."[21] Interestingly, the Chinese discussions of national interests also have an antiideological sociological background.[22] During the Maoist era, Chinese theory on national interests was based on the Marxist class analysis, which posits, since the state is the tool of the ruling class, national interests are naturally the interests of the ruling class. In the post-Mao era, the invoking of *national* (instead of class) interest is a reaction against the revolutionary diplomacy, that is, what the Chinese authors call the "ideologization" besetting Chinese foreign policy, especially during the 1960s.

In order to abandon the Marxist analysis while still maintaining the ideological facade, Chinese IR scholars now differentiate between two attributes of national interests: one representing the ruling class in domestic politics, the other the nation as a whole in international politics. Even though authors during the late 1980s and early 1990s still considered national interests as predominantly a property of the ruling class,[23] an account in 1994 emphatically placed "the *national* attribute" as the primary attribute of national interests.[24] China's realists often simply assert the compatibility of the two attributes without engaging in explaining how the attributes can be theoretically reconciled into a "unity."[25] The most recent, first scholarly book on Chinese national interests goes even further by starting with an uncompromising attack on the class analysis. For its author, the confusion of national interests with state interests may have arisen from the fact that in the Chinese language both the nation and state are often understood to refer to the same thing, *guojia* (state). He goes on to make a clear distinction between the *guojia* interests in domestic politics and international politics. Whereas the former refers to the interests of the state that belong to the ruling class, the latter refers to national interests, which belong to the nation as a collectivity and are enjoyed by both the rulers and the ruled.[26]

The emerging consensus among Chinese authors is that national interests in international relations can be understood sui generis and are to be separated from domestic politics. An editorial in a leading official weekly on the return of Hong Kong attacks those Chinese who seek private, sectoral interests at the expense of national interests and those who believe pursuing national interests is obsolete and may hurt economic cooperation in this age of global interdependence. The editorial proclaims that the unit of the intense competition for comprehensive power is still the nation-state, and "national interests take precedence over everything else."[27]

The Five Principles of Peaceful Coexistence

Chinese realists subscribe to the state-centric notion, albeit often less explicitly than do their Western counterparts. China's reification of sovereignty by extension implies a world of atomized nation-states entangled in power politics. Even the recent debate over civilizational clashes and human rights is viewed in terms of the struggle between the Western cultural expansion versus the third world countries' attempts to defend their "cultural sovereignty." The Western pressure on "political ideologies, lifestyles, and values" is but the Western attempt to reinforce its hegemony over the rest of the world, in particular to "discipline" a rising China.[28] The spread of "global culture" has reduced the differences in national attributes, leading to a "homogenization of civilizations." The rhetoric of "intercivilizational conflicts" is but a facade of long-standing struggle for power among sovereign nation-states.[29] Real or imagined, civilizational clashes are but a continuation of power politics waged by the West against non-Western nations, including China.

In the 1990s, there has been a renewed emphasis in China on the so-called Five Principles of Peaceful Coexistence first enunciated in the 1950s. These principles are: mutual respect for territorial integrity and sovereignty; mutual nonaggression; mutual noninterference in internal affairs; equality and mutual benefit; and peaceful coexistence.[30] Since 1988, Deng Xiaoping and other Chinese officials and scholars have even preached frequently that these principles should be the guidelines for the "new international political order."[31]

Insofar as the principles boil down to a "respect" for sovereignty, whose "core is a notion of political authority as lying exclusively in the hands of spatially differentiated states," they constitute the basis for "an anarchy of mutual recognition," and, therefore, tend to "promote egoistic over collective conceptions of interest."[32] Henceforth, it is ironic that although the principles are ostensibly intended to counter "hegemony and power politics" (*baquan zhuyi he qiangquan zhengzhi*) and the Western human rights diplomacy they in fact defend the Westphalian anarchic nature of international relations, thereby reinforcing the structural source for power politics.

Power Politics

Like their counterparts in the West, Chinese realists see the world in terms of power politics. But to understand Chinese power politics thinking, one has to understand the fact that Chinese discourse on world politics is profoundly conditioned by the historical memory of the "one hundred years of sufferings and humiliations" at the hands of Western powers and Japan, which is held as the collective experience of the Chinese nation.

Chinese realists view the world as almost exclusively an arena of interactions between sovereign states engaged in merciless competitions. Despite their cognizance of interdependence and multilateralism, they are not concerned about how these new forces are reshaping the structure and process of the international system. Rather, they view the growing transnational and multilateral networks through a state-centric prism, focusing only on how China could take advantage of these new "external environments" to protect and maximize its national interests.

In the most systematic Chinese account of national interests, the criteria for judging national interests are said to include the international environment, national capabilities, technological development, and the subjective assessment of these three factors. Although the first three factors essentially refer to the world power configuration and China's position therein, the last factor refers to the "objective" assessment of China's position in that power distribution.[33] To be sure, Chinese realists differ slightly from the classical realists in the West with respect to the hierarchy of issue areas. Although the traditional Anglo-American realists considered military security as "high politics" and social and economic issues as the domain of "low politics," Chinese contemporary realists tend to place greater emphasis on economic and technological development. This difference is attributable to China's recent conviction that international politics is now characterized by "the competition for comprehensive power" (*zhonghe guoli de jiaoliang*) on a wide range of battlegrounds in, inter alia, military, political, economic, and technological areas. Most Chinese analysts believe that, with the end of the Cold War, "bloc politics" and ideological differences are less important; instead, national interests, especially economic interests, rise to preeminence.[34]

The controversial but well-connected scholar He Xin compares international politics to a world of sheep and wolves. "If the flock of sheep builds some walls and fences specifically designed to protect themselves, it is not because they are not open-minded enough; but rather, it is for the sake of not being swallowed by the wolves. But from the wolves' point of view, these fences are probably not necessary, or are even provocative."[35] He frequently cites Hans Morgenthau and Friedrich List's arguments to advocate his realpolitik worldview and neomercantilist policies.[36] For He Xin, Morgenthau paints the world as a struggle for power, and List provides much-needed prescriptions for an economic nationalism, centered around state intervention and protectionism in the world of limited resources and the hierarchical division of labor.[37]

Viewing international politics as essentially a struggle for power, "the post-Mao China seems to have turned dependency theory on its head," taking advantage of interdependence while rejecting any modification of its essentially ultraegoistic view on national interests.[38] And Chinese decision-makers continue to view the world as essentially conflict-prone, interstate relations as zero-sum power struggles, with violence by no means being rendered less common a solution.[39] In the Chinese realpolitik worldview, the international system essentially consists of atomistic nation-states locked in a perpetual struggle for power.

EMERGING LIBERAL VIEWS

My research also finds that in the 1990s other counterviews largely corresponding to liberal values do exist and are expanding their space in

China's discourse on international relations. In contrast to realism, *liberalism* in international relations emphasizes the roles of the state *and* nonstate actors and sees international politics largely in terms of a positive-sum game as opposed to a zero-sum game. Liberalism gives great attention to the mitigating effect of interdependence, multilateral institutions, and international regimes on international anarchy. Specifically, international liberalism consists of beliefs in: (1) "the pacific effects of trade" (*commercial liberalism*); (2) "the pacific effects of republican government" (*democratic liberalism*); (3) "the importance of rules and institutions in affecting relations between countries" (*regulatory liberalism*); and (4) "the transformative effect of transnational contacts and coalitions on national attitudes and definitions of interests" (*sociological liberalism*).[40]

In the Chinese IR writings, there is an identifiably growing recognition of the interdependent reality in the world. The late 1980s and 1990s have seen highly frequent references to interdependence in international relations, in contrast to the complete absence of the concept of "interdependence" in earlier Chinese writings. For example, a *People's Daily* editorial on the Asia-Pacific Economic Cooperation (APEC) quasisummit read: "Exchanges in economics, trade, investment, science and technology, and information have increased steadily in recent years, spawning the growing interdependence" of the world economies.[41] Chinese president Jiang Zemin spoke like a Western liberal at the November 1994 APEC summit:

> Modern technology has narrowed the distance between regions. Many challenges facing mankind often transcend national borders. Many issues, such as economic relations, trade exchanges, scientific and technological development, environmental protection, population control, disaster mitigation and relief, drug ban, crime prevention, prevention of nuclear proliferation, and AIDS prevention and treatment are of a global and interdependent nature, and all of them require cooperation and commonly observed standards. Since the 1980s, trade contacts, market development, capital flows, industrial reallocations, scientific and technological exchanges, and information outflows have increased noticeably among members of the Asia-Pacific region, leading to closer contacts.[42]

China once disparaged the postwar, *embedded liberalism*–based international political economic order and its keynote institutions, the International Monetary Fund (IMF), the World Bank, and the General Agreement on Tariffs and Trade (GATT), as "citadels of international capitalism."[43] Yet since the late 1970s China reversed its erstwhile hostility and joined both the World Bank and IMF in 1980, and since 1986 it has formally bid for GATT (the World Trade Organization [WTO] after 1995) membership. China's enmeshment in these institutions has facilitated information exchange and social learning as evidenced in changes in China's domestic institutions, policies, and organizations, legal frameworks, and attitudes toward the world economy.[44] To be sure, the liberal rhetoric, particularly if from official statements, should always be taken with a grain of salt. Efforts have to be made to probe beneath the liberal proclamations to determine genuine beliefs from pure rhetoric. But the prevalence of the rhetoric itself demonstrates that liberal views are gaining some legitimacy in the Chinese conception of the world, facilitating at least "tactical" if not "cognitive" learning.[45]

In the 1990s, Chinese officials and IR scholars have paid more attention then ever before to "globalization" in the post–Cold War era. "Transnational, supranational, and global forces are at work, and global problems are proliferating," observes former vice president of the Chinese Academy of Social Sciences (CASS) Li Shenzhi. Because of globalization, he argues, the actors and rules in future international relations will be vastly different from today, and the changes will not be like past ones, involving only redistributions of power and interests among existent nations and states. Rather, concepts of nations, sovereignty, and national boundaries will change, with nonstate actors (such as international organizations and multinational corporations) and domestic factors (including individual choices and values) playing greater roles. It behooves all nations to seek new common solutions through multilateral cooperation. Li asserts, "If China chooses chauvinism, it will be China's and the world's disaster; if China chooses globalism, it will be China's and the world's fortune." In this age of globalization, according to Li, the solution to the perennial Chinese *ti-yong* debate should be "treating the universal laws of globalization as 'essence' (*ti*), and Chinese characteristics as 'function' (*yong*)."[46] Reversing completely the official doctrine of "Chinese learning for essence, Western learning for practical use" on its head, Li's view is truly revolutionary and as such is the most liberal written statement I encountered during my research.

One major scholarly work published in 1995 is devoted to examining the impact of interdependence and globalization on international relations. The monograph lists ten factors that are challenging the traditional notion of state sovereignty: (1) incongruence between the nation and the state; (2) the weakening of the state capacities and responsibilities; (3) inequality in resources and diplomatic quality; (4) weak cultural identification and regime legitimacy; (5) the strengthening of international interventions and international laws; (6) a greater role of international organizations; (7) the growing power of nongovernmental forces; (8) "borderless" economies and global interdependence; (9) the deepening of global crises; and (10) air space and outer space activities and the rising consciousness of sea territories. The book posits that the concept of sovereignty is a dynamic, historical notion subject to change.[47] In this age of globalization, the globalized problems call for global solutions. The state may be endowed with more opportunities, interests, and rights even as its autonomy may be limited and its sovereign rights lost. "The more it gets, the more it loses; the more rights it enjoys, the more obligations it assumes."[48] For the author, globalist thinking should be an integral part of globalization, "not just because of the new threat for security and survival, but also for transforming ourselves and molding ourselves as human beings according to the new characteristics of the era."[49]

Another scholar even touches upon how changes in information technologies and production patterns have brought about changes in the views on human rights. She calls for greater attention to the ideational change, because "a change in ideas often paves the way for changes in behavior. And the norms and customs could well arise based on this kind of idea change."[50] Wang Jisi may be the first Chinese scholar to have introduced to his Chinese colleagues the debate over relative versus absolute gains in American IR theory.[51] Having laid bare the logic of relative gains underlying Samuel Huntington's theory of civilizational clashes, Wang admonished his Chinese readers that in order to prevent international conflicts from becoming a self-fulfilling prophecy they must not fall into Huntington's misleading intellectual trap of realpolitik.[52]

On the issue of Chinese nationalism, there has been a debate in China between nationalists, who see the world in terms of cutthroat power politics, and internationalists, who see interdependence in a more positive light.[53] Similarly, in juxtaposition with ideological and geopolitical views on the United States and U.S.-China relations, there is also a "global interdependence perspective" that largely corresponds to "idealism."[54] On the security issue, somewhat liberal views are evident too. Noticeably, a growing number of Chinese analysts are starting to advocate multilateral collective security, as it is believed to serve China's national interests. Even on the issue of nuclear arms control, there is a nascent "security interdependence" perspective as opposed to the prevailing self-help views.[55]

Yan Xuetong, director of the Center for Foreign Policy Studies at the China Institute of Contemporary International Relations, argues that under an "individual security system" the individual country's security depends on the strength of the individual country itself and its allies. However, under a collective security system, the security of the individual country is protected not only by the country's own defense but also by the collective security arrangement. A collective security system differs from a military alliance in that the former does not target a predetermined third-party enemy but is directed against threats wherever they arise. For him, collective security is analogous to collective health insurance, obviously far better than fending for oneself. The large amount of expenses that the individual can count on from the collective health insurance *when one is sick* makes the regular payments all the more worthwhile.[56]

As Jianwei Wang discusses in his chapter, Chinese analysts all express support for the confidence-building, multilateral security endeavors sponsored by the official Association of Southeast Asian Nations Regional Forum (ARF) and for some other track II (i.e., nongovernmental) programs of security dialogue in the Asia-Pacific region. One Chinese commentator writes that we live in a "global society with high interdependence where one country's security and other states' interests are vitally interrelated. Safeguarding the common interest of global security is increasingly becoming a universal consensus."[57] ARF represents a new approach to security because the dialogue and cooperation it promotes are not to target a common enemy country but to promote regional stability. This is a kind of security attained not through armament or military alliance but through building mutual confidence and common interests. The *White Paper on National Defense,* released by the Information Office of the People's Republic of China State Council in July 1998, reaffirms China's support for this "new mode of security thinking" that seeks to enhance "mutual security" without targeting against any third country.[58] To be sure, China's support is motivated by several considerations, not the least of which is that an embrace of the "new thinking" helps to counter NATO expansion and the lately revised U.S. security treaty with Japan. Nonetheless, China's "change of mind," however reflecting "tactical" rather than "cognitive" learning, is quite remarkable, given Beijing's long-standing opposition to the idea of security multilateralism.

REALPOLITIK DOMINANCE AND LIBERAL DILEMMA

Despite a wide range of views existing along the realpolitik-idealpolitik spectrum in the Chinese conception of national interests, the dominant thinking is still realist. Even though Chinese scholars well versed in Western IR theory have introduced some liberal schools of thought to their readers, it is clear that their primary interest lies in realist and neorealist variants of theory.[59] Since the mid-1980s, approximately eighteen English-language IR books have been translated and published in Chinese. Except for some textbooks, most of the theoretical works that interest Chinese IR scholars belong to the realist camp, including notably those by Hans Morgenthau, Kenneth Waltz, and Robert Gilpin. The most popular and widely cited book is Hans Morgenthau's classic realist statement, *Politics Among Nations: The Struggle for Power and Peace.*

Many of the Chinese scholars who give attention to interdependence are primarily concerned with how China can best seek interests while avoiding harm—without recognizing important costs of interdependence

that could incur on China.[60] A prominent Chinese scholar rejects outright
views on the erosion of sovereignty as "incompatible with our emphasis on
the sovereign interests."[61] Moreover, the Chinese discourse on interdependence and globalization is often more meaningful in terms of domestic politics than in terms of international relations, insofar as it is intended
for domestic politics to justify China's economic restructuring and opening up to the outside world. *Globalization* for China means it will "act in accordance to international customs, to connect track to global customs"
(*zhao guoji guanli ban shi, yu guoji guanli jiegui*).[62] In his political report to
the Fifteenth Communist Party Congress in September 1997, Pres. Jiang
Zemin cited globalization as a reality in the contemporary world in support of his call for deepening economic reform and privatization of state-
owned enterprises.[63]

Among Chinese "liberals" we see self-doubt and bewilderment in their
thinking. The most typical is perhaps Wang Yizhou, who has most consistently wrestled with the implications of globalization and interdependence. He openly admits his perplexity over the coexistence of power politics and globalization, centering around the question of whether
globalization is Western-dominated hegemony or a "positive, triumphantly
proceeding" process of "open and progressive" evolution. As a scholar
from a "weak, developing country," he confesses his agony over the realiza-
tion of the cruel reality of power politics and hegemony imposed upon the
weak in the everyday life of world politics.[64] On the one hand, awareness of
the common problems facing humankind, such as "ecological protection,
population growth, arms race, racial discrimination, and cultural differences," compels you to at least try to be more "internationalist," abandoning the narrow-minded parochialism and self-centered nationalism. On
the other hand, when you witness the most advanced and most "internationalist" country engage in hegemonic behavior in the pursuit of narrow,
myopic self-interest under high-sounding excuses, you cannot help but
raise doubts about your belief in the "common interest." Unconsciously or
consciously, the sense of you as "a member of the nation" is consequently
reinforced. "I do not know how to explain my orientations, but must admit
that I haven't straightened out some of the puzzles and I don't have clear
answers to some of these questions."[65] Despite his emotional agony, Wang
Yizhou concludes: "Rationally speaking, the international society is still in
the state of anarchy governed by power politics."[66]

Similarly, others who are sympathetic to liberal views are concerned
about the reality wherein interdependence and globalization enhance the
leverages of and give excuses to Western powers to exercise power politics
in interfering in other countries' domestic affairs. Those who are engaged
in the discourse on globalization seem unable to reconcile nationalism and
state sovereignty with globalization. Consequently, most conclude with an

emphasis on state sovereignty or "national rights" and on global management as a process that should not be dominated by any big power. In the face of the seemingly endless crises in Sino-American relations during the 1990s, Chinese liberals have in fact started to question the sincerity of the United States in encouraging a rise of a liberal and *strong* China.

CONTENDING VIEWS AND THE POSSIBILITY OF CHANGE

Conceptual change regarding the Chinese definition of national interests in international relations is contingent upon the outcome of interactions between the extant dominant views and countervalues. Specifically, the ability of the counter, liberal views to assert ascendancy depends on three factors: (1) the internal coherence and academic rigor of the contending liberal view vis-à-vis those of the dominant realist view; (2) the loss of credibility of the dominant realpolitik paradigm proven by its ineffectiveness in upholding national interests; and (3) the liberal views' "fit" with the broad, prevailing values and institutions in the society.[67]

Internal Coherence

Like its Western counterpart, Chinese realist thinking is flawed in terms of conceptual coherence and internal logic and is vulnerable to critique from various perspectives. The criticism of the erstwhile dominant class analysis has gone so far in China's realist intellectual scheme that international politics is in effect compartmentalized from domestic politics. Consequently, national interests become a predetermined abstract concept existing independent of the social forces.

Since national interests can be explained sui generis in insulation from domestic politics, "the realist hypothesis that 'the statesman thinks and acts in terms of interest defined as power' becomes unfalsible," and consequently "is capable of legitimating an unlimited range of practical suggestions as to present policy."[68] For example, E. H. Carr, the most important spokesman of realism prior to World War II, praised Chamberlain's appeasement policy toward Hitler as "a reaction of realism against utopianism."[69] Yet postwar realists attributed the disastrous failure in preventing World War II to some "utopianism." And it was exactly the realist crusade against utopian ideologies that led to the postwar ascendancy of political realism.

Without attention to domestic politics and hence without a theory about how national interests are formed in the first place, Chinese realists cannot provide a critical analysis of their nation's foreign policy. For instance, even if there was a set of interests belonging to the nation as a collectivity, the degree of identification with the interests may vary across the individual, sector, and region. Given that China's economic opening-up

policy is in its national interests, those who benefit most, such as consumers, light industry, agriculture, and coastal regions, identify more
strongly with the policy than do those who bear the brunt of the deleteri-
ous effects of interdependence, such as the producers, heavy industries, in-
terior provinces, and government bureaucrats.[70] Deng Xiaoping's "southern tour" in early 1992 was in fact intended to elicit support for his
economic reform and opening-up policy from those who had benefited
most from this policy.

If national interests are "objectively existent" "interests of the national
collectivity," "represented by the government,"[71] is there any policy that
does not uphold and maximize national interests? Or how do we know
which policy fails to best serve national interests? Chinese realists seem unable to adequately address these questions. As a result, for them, the only
"slip" in Chinese foreign policy since 1949 was the incident that involved
the burning of the British consulate in August 1967, because the craze of
the Cultural Revolution led to the masses' ignorance of "genuine" national
interests.[72] Similarly, the communiqué passed by the Third Plenum of the
Eleventh Party Central Committee in December 1978 provided an unprecedented critical look at some of Mao's domestic policies such as the
Great Leap Forward, the Antirightist Movement, and the Cultural Revolution; it nonetheless refrained from mentioning any of the specific excesses
or mishandlings in China's foreign policy.

Despite their claim to the contrary, realists basically do not have a theory of national interests. They also do not have a theory of change in the
national interests conception.[73] For Chinese analysts, one would expect
the issue of change to command their theoretical attention, given the fact
that the very notion of the modern nation-state is a recent import from the
Eurocentric international system. Chinese authors more or less accept
John King Fairbank's and Joseph Levenson's well-known view that premodern China was more a cultural entity, *tian xia* (all under Heaven) defined
by Confucianism, than a political unit in the modern sense. And the Chi-
nese-dominated East Asian order is distinctive from the Westphalia system
in that pax sinica is not based on the principles of sovereignty or legalistic
equality among sovereign states. But regrettably even those Chinese authors who are beginning to show interest in the historical evolution simply
list a host of well-known ancient Chinese mottoes about "harmony,"
"peace," "benevolence," and "kingly way." Their discussions are often dis-
jointed and invariably fail to incorporate a truly historical perspective into
the conceptualization of national interests. Indeed, the distinctive Chinese
historical experiences, culture, and philosophy have not been vigorously
explicated and drawn on to inform their contemporary search for an international theory with "Chinese characteristics." Instead, those who advocate
an IR theory with Chinese characteristics often rehearse the Five Principles

of Peaceful Coexistence, together with some slogans about "peace and development" without much substantive content.[74]

The alternative views, broadly categorized as idealism, are able to provide a better theory of national interests by their attention to domestic factors and the interaction between domestic and international forces. The constructivist and ideational literature, which has gained some prevalence in Western IR theory during the 1990s, presumably has the most to say about the constitution and change in national interests. Yet as of this writing, this literature has not made any inroad into China's IR studies. Regrettably, in face of the glaring lack of internal coherence of the dominant conception, Chinese "internationalists" have failed to articulate a more coherent alternative theory of their own to challenge the ascendancy of realist views.

Realpolitik's Ineffectiveness

The conception of national interests serves as a mental map through which decisions regarding foreign policy events are reached. To the extent that any conceptual framework involves an element of expectations about what should happen, there is a possibility that what is expected may not be fulfilled by what actually happens. If what things turn out to be match the expectations of the counterconception instead of the dominant notion, then political elites may consider the current views to be flawed and choose to adopt the available and politically salient "new ideas," thereby generating impetus for change.[75]

Paradigmatic effectiveness depends upon the national goals of the time. By the 1990s, China has reversed its erstwhile penchant and rhetoric for overthrowing the capitalist-dominated international system and, instead, is now seeking to take advantage of the opportunities offered by the world system.[76] To be sure, the most important "event" responsible for this change is post-Mao China's embarkation on the "Second Revolution," the primary goal of which is economic modernization. All Chinese authors now agree that diplomacy constrained by ideology or the facade of communist internationalism had not upheld Chinese national interests, and they argue for distinguishing between ideological fantasy and China's real economic and political interests. Publicly, Chinese scholars and officials alike often call unabashedly and unapologetically for China's global strategic thinking to be oriented by China's own most predominant and long-term national interests.[77]

Thanks in part to this realist instrumentalism, China has attained in the 1990s the greatest security seen since the mid-nineteenth century; it faces no imminent threat from any major power. Moreover, this interest-oriented policy has won China aid, capital, technology, and markets that have propelled its spectacular economic growth. Yet forces of internationalism have impinged upon China's insistence on sovereignty and noninterference, reigniting the perennial nationalism-versus-internationalism debate within the Chinese society, and even causing a crisis in Chinese national identity.[78] As discussed above, many Chinese analysts are starting to recognize the transformative power of interdependence and globalization on traditional notions in international politics, leading to growing receptivity to liberal ideas.

In the 1990s China's conception of national interests, particularly relating to sovereignty, territorial integrity, trading behavior, human rights, and regional security multilateralism, has met with increasing queries and criticisms from some of its Asian neighbors and Western countries. The ultrarealist notion of national interests is confronting increasing difficulty to the extent it diverges from the expectations of "how an actor *should* behave," stemming from the emergent new norms prevailing in the international society.[79] Caught somewhat by surprise, China finds its diplomacy contains limited room for maneuver in the post–Cold War era, and it is compelled to adopt a low-key posture. Many Chinese scholars and officials are feeling frustrated by China's inability to make foreign policy initiatives. One prominent CASS scholar summarized the predicament well: Supposedly, China's current foreign policy guideline is "seeking interests while avoiding harm" (*quli bihai*); yet in reality "the primary goal is avoiding harm" (*yi bihai weizhu*) without being able to actively promote China's national interests.[80]

Societal Values and Institutions

The conception of national interests is embedded in the broad domestic values and institutions prevailing in society. The political salience of a set of ideas is determined by its fit with underlying social values and existing political structures. It is also determined by the status, power, and influence of the bearers of these ideas. An idea carries greater weight if born by well-placed elites.[81] In other words, the ascendant paradigm governing a state's foreign-policy making is also sustained by the predominant values in the political discourse and the prevailing patterns of state-society relations.

As discussed earlier, what is implied in post-Mao China's dominant conception is that national interests exist objectively "out there," waiting to be discovered through a process of rational, empirical inquiry. And this "objective" (interest-oriented) approach serves as a touchstone against which all other (ideology-oriented) approaches are to be tested. The epistemological foundation for this conception is a fundamentally empiricist guideline of "seeking truth from facts," which has effectively become an official dogma since Deng Xiaoping and his supporters dethroned Hua Guofeng and his cohorts in the late 1970s.[82] Although the positivism underlying neorealism in American IR theory has been under vehement attack since the 1980s,[83] no effort has so far been made to question the scienticist assumptions in the Chinese conception of national interests.

During the post-Mao era, liberal values have made significant inroads in the broad political discourse in China despite several major setbacks, including one after the Tiananmen crackdown. To be sure, liberal views are by far not well entrenched. But with time they will be carried by more and more key players among China's foreign policy elite. The plausibility of liberal views seems to be tied to the prevalence of reformist factions in China's domestic political struggle. The ascendancy of liberal-minded leaders will have a critical impact, boosting the rise of the liberal conception of national interests. Generational change also matters. What is noteworthy is that almost all of the aforementioned liberally inclined younger scholars have studied in the West and have had extensive exposure to Anglo-American IR literature. In contrast, most of the core members in China's current top leadership and many older scholars have had little experience with the West and tend to be suspicious of the outside world.[84] As time passes, the younger generation of leaders and scholars with a more liberal worldview will likely have growing influence in defining Chinese national interests.

There is no doubt that liberal values are gaining ground in Chinese society, albeit gradually. For example, those along China's southeastern coast have simultaneously embraced national, regional, and cosmopolitan identities and values in a mutually reinforcing way.[85] As Ming Wan suggests in Chapter 5, it is doubtful that Western values can be transposed to China. Nonetheless, further economic liberalization and gradual emergence and solidification of democratic institutions will add the plausibility of liberal values to contest more forcefully the Chinese definition of national interests.

CONCLUSION

The supremacy of national interests in the Chinese worldview does not necessarily suggest Beijing will become either more benign or predatory in its behavior. But it does allow Chinese scholars and leaders to break away from the confines of Maoist ideology and to define national interests based on pragmatism. What determines Chinese behavior lies in *how* China defines its national interests and goals, which are in turn determined by its national-identity conception.[86] As is well known, China's elusive quest for national identity has prompted wild swings in its international role since the Opium War.[87]

This analysis shows that the substantive content of the Chinese conception of national interests is not monolithic or static but rather is dynamic and contested. Even though supporting the argument that China's conception of national interests is still dominated by realpolitik thinking, the findings presented in this chapter also show that counter, liberal values do exist and are expanding their space in China's discourse on international relations. A China whose liberal conception of national interests gains ascendancy would mean a China that is more cooperative and less apt to redraft the rules of the game in its foreign relations. Thus, encouraging a liberal-oriented redefinition of national interests toward compatibility with the international system is essential for making the Chinese rise more an opportunity than a threat. There are indeed signs that the liberal considerations are having some impact in policy, as China is noticeably more susceptible to ideas and policies of interdependence, multilateralism, and collective security.

However, immense difficulties exist, dampening prospects for liberalization in the Chinese conception of national interests. China's "liberals" have failed to provide a logically compelling attack against the realist conception, and they have not systematically engaged in formulating their own alternative framework. Liberal "projects" cannot thrive before Chinese intellectuals and IR scholars come to reach some kind of reconciliation between nationalism and globalism. The Chinese liberal dilemma will remain hard to resolve as long as China is still committed to its own nation-building and territorial integrity remains its primary national goal. As argued by Fei-Ling Wang in his preceding analysis, the plausibility of liberal thinking will be significantly limited in a China with an insecure state struggling with legitimacy and suspicious of international influences. Realpolitik perspective will prevail as long as China's international identity is defined in terms of a nationalistic view of modern Chinese history, in which China was brutally victimized in a hostile and threatening world.

Meanwhile, the fact that China is still in search of its "Chineseness" suggests the possibility that China's national identity and its interests are open for contestation and redefinition.[88] Despite the difficulties confronting Chinese liberal IR thinking, many factors and forces are also pointing to the possibility of a conceptual shift in China's foreign policy outlook. The growing legitimacy of transnational issues in the age of globalization has generated a powerful "compliance pull," undermining the validity of Chinese realpolitik views and putting them on the defensive. Thanks in part to the "legitimacy problem" in its worldview, China's foreign policy is confronting increasing challenges despite the unprecedented security the nation now enjoys. Greater exposure of the Chinese IR community to Western liberal IR theories will help Chinese liberals in critiquing realism and in developing their own program. The international community should continue to socialize China into the prevailing norms, values, and rules through constructive engagement.

In the end, change is contingent upon the interactive patterns of varying views along the wide spectrum of liberalism and realism rooted in the contending social forces and embedded in broader social values and polit-

ical institutions. Displacing the realist dominance, therefore, depends criti-
cally on the developments of the value change and institutional evolution
in the Chinese society at large. Further political and economic liberalization provides the social values and political ground whereby the intellectual reformulation of Chinese national interests along liberal lines can
only flourish.

NOTES

This chapter is a revised version of my article, "The Chinese Conception of National Interests in International Relations," in *China Quarterly*, no. 154 (June 1998):
88–109.

1. Samuel Kim has argued this view in his numerous works. See "China In and
Out of the Changing World Order," Occasional Paper No. 21, World Order Studies
Program, Princeton University Press (1991); "China's International Organizational
Behavior," in *Chinese Foreign Policy: Theory and Practice*, Thomas Robinson and David
Shambaugh, eds. (New York: Oxford University Press, 1993). See also Thomas W.
Robinson, "Interdependence in China's Foreign Relations," in *China and the World:
Chinese Foreign Relations in the Post–Cold War Era*, Samuel Kim, ed. (Boulder, Colo.:
Westview Press, 1994); Thomas Christensen, "Chinese Realpolitik," *Foreign Affairs*
75, no. 5 (September/October 1996): 37–52.

2. For example, several books cited in this article had been delayed or denied
for publication due to official disapproval and had to be published by local publishers outside Beijing or even in Hong Kong.

3. It is said that Chinese Pres. Jiang Zemin has for the past few years encouraged scholars in major universities and think tanks to come up with more independent, in-depth analyses of foreign affairs in the spirit of "having multiple
voices internally, while speaking in one voice externally." But the result has been
frustrating. The Chinese leaders have realized that as a great power China must
have its own independent voice in the world. Right judgments on international situations also help domestic policymakings and implementations. See the briefing
of Chinese Vice Premier and Foreign Minister Qian Qichen's talk in commemorating the fortieth anniversary of the establishment of the leading think tank, the
China Institute of International Studies, *Guoji wenti yanjiu* (*International Studies*),
no. 1 (1997): 1.

4. See a recent article by Barry B. Hughes, Steven Chan, and Charles W. Kegley
Jr., "Observations on the Study of International Relations in China," *International
Studies Notes* 19, no. 3 (Fall 1994): 17–22. My assumption is further testified by a re-
cent review article on Chinese views on international relations, which finds the offi-
cial, scholarly, and populist perspectives do not differ much in terms of core views.
See Christopher Hughes, "Globalization and Nationalism: Squaring the Circle in
Chinese International Relations Theory," *Millennium: Journal of International Studies*
26, no. 1 (1997): 103–124.

5. Martin Wight, "Why Is There No International Theory?" in *Diplomatic Investigations*, Herbert Butterfield and Martin Wight, eds. (Cambridge: Harvard University Press, 1966), 26.

6. Martin Wight, "Western Values in International Relations," in *Diplomatic Investigations*, 101. E. H. Carr explicitly addressed the contrast between domestic and international politics in terms of the tension between realism and idealism in Western political theory; see *The Twenty Years' Crisis, 1919–1939* (London: Macmillan, 1939).

7. Because neorealism focuses on the international structure as its level of analysis, it is also known as "structural realism." For the most systematic articulation of structural realism, see Kenneth Waltz, *Theory of International Politics* (Reading, Mass.: Addison-Wesley, 1979). For a penetrating critique of Waltz's views, see John G. Ruggie, "Continuity and Transformation in the World Polity: Toward a Neorealist Synthesis," *World Politics* 35, no. 2 (1983): 261–285. There are many variants of neorealist theory, a good review of which can be found in James E. Dougherty and Robert L. Pfaltzgraff Jr., *Contending Theories of International Relations*, 4th ed. (New York: Longman, 1997), especially chaps. 2 and 10.

8. Hans Morgenthau and Kenneth Thompson, *Politics Among Nations: The Struggle for Power and Peace*, 6th ed. (New York: Knopf, 1985), 5 and 11.

9. Wang Jisi, "Wenming chongtu lun de lilun jichu yu xianshi yiyi" ("The Theoretical Foundations and Practical Implications of the Theory on Civilizational Clashes"), in *Wenming yu guoji zhengzhi—Zhongguo xuezhe ping hengtingdun de wenming chongtulun* (*Civilizations and International Politics—Chinese Scholars' Responses to Huntington's Theory of Civilizational Clashes*), Wang Jisi, ed. (Shanghai: Shanghai renmin chubanshe, 1995), 189–190.

10. Wang Jisi, "The Theoretical Foundations." See also his "'Wenming chongtu' lunzhan shuping" ("A Critical Review of the Debate over Civilizational Clashes"), in Wang Jisi, ed., *Civilizations and International Politics*.

11. Yan Xuetong, *Zhongguo guojia liyi fengxi* (*Analysis of China's National Interests*) (Tianjin: Tianjin renmin chubanshe, 1996). See also his "Guojia liyi de fengxi fangfa" ("The Analytical Methods of National Interests"), *Zhongguo shehui kexue jikan* (*Chinese Social Sciences Quarterly, Hong Kong*), no. 20 (Autumn 1997).

12. Yoseph Lapid, "The Third Debate," *International Studies Quarterly* 33, no. 3 (1989): 235–254; Stanley Hoffmann, "An American Social Science: International Relations," *Daedalus* 106, no. 3 (1979): 41–60.

13. This expression was coined by Liang Shoude, dean of the School of International Relations, Beijing University; see Liang Shoude and Hong Yinxian, *Guoji zhengzhi xue gailun* (*Introduction to International Politics*) (Beijing: Zhongyang bianyi chubanshe, 1994), and Liang Shoude, "Guoji zhengzhi xue zai zhongguo" ("The Study of International Politics in China"), *Guoji zhengzhi yanjiu* (*Studies of International Politics*) 1 (1997): 1–9.

14. Feng Tejun and Song Xinning, eds., *Guoji zhengzhi gailun* (*Introduction to International Politics*) (Beijing: Zhongguo renmin daxue chubanshe, 1992), 123.

15. Liang Shoude and Hong Yinxian, *Introduction to International Politics*, 58–60.

16. Wang Huning, "Deng Xiaoping tongzi dui guoji zhanlue de sikao" ("Comrade Deng Xiaoping's Thoughts on International Strategy"), *Wenhui bao*, 26 February 1994, 1.

17. Deng Xiaoping, *Deng Xiaoping wenxuan* (*The Selected Works of Deng Xiaoping*), vol. 3 (Beijing: Renmin chubanshe, 1993), 331; 347–348.

18. For example, Deng Xiaoping once told his visitor in Beijing, the former U.S. president, Richard Nixon, that "national self-interests should be the starting

point of international relations. . . . In this way, all problems can be resolved properly. . . . Thus, your trip to China in 1972 was not only wise but also bold. I know you are anti-communist, and I am a communist. Yet we both hold our national self-interests as the highest principle when talking about and dealing with problems." Deng Xiaoping, *The Selected Works*, 330.

19. Liang Shoude, ed., *Guoji zhengzhi xinglun* (*New Introduction to International Politics*) (Beijing: Beijing daxue chubanshe, 1996), 60.

20. Peng Guangqian and Yao Youzhi, *On Deng Xiaoping's Thoughts on Strategy*, chap. 6; Gao Jingdian, *A Study on Deng Xiaoping's Thoughts on International Strategy*; Wang Taiping, ed., *Deng Xiaoping waijiao shixiang yanjiu lunwenji* (*A Collection of Research Papers on Deng Xiaoping's Thoughts on Diplomacy*) (Beijing: Shijie zhishi chubanshe, 1996).

21. Raymond Aron, *Peace and War: A Theory of International Relations* (translated from the French by Richard Howard and Annette Baker Fox) (New York: Praeger, 1967), 599.

22. Some may argue that support for supremacy of national interest is in itself a form of ideology. But this "antiideological" background has to be considered in the Chinese context.

23. Jin Yinzhong and Ni Shixiong, *Guoji guanxi lilun bijiao yanjiu* (*A Comparative Study of International Relations Theory*) (Beijing: Zhongguo shehui kexue chubanshe, 1992), 116–122.

24. Liang Shoude and Hong Yinxian, *Introduction to International Politics*, esp. 75–76; 83–87.

25. For the most rigorous articulation of this view, see Song Xinning, "Guojia liyi de lilun renshi" ("A Theoretical Understanding of National Interests"), *Zhongguo shehui kexue jikan* (*Chinese Social Sciences Quarterly, Hong Kong*), no. 20 (Autumn 1997). See also, Zhang Jiliang, *Guoji guanxi gailun* (*An Introduction to International Relations*) (Beijing: Shijie zhishi chubanshe, 1990), 58; Feng Tejun and Song Xinning, eds., *Introduction to International Politics*, 123–125; Gao Jingdian, ed., *Guoji zhanlue xue gailun* (*Introduction to the Study of International Strategy*) (Beijing: Guofang daxue chubanshe, 1995), chap. 1.

26. Yan Xuetong, *Analysis of China's National Interests*, 4–11.

27. Wei Yang, "Guojia liyi gaoyu yiqie" ("National Interests Take Precedence over Everything"), *Liaowang* (*Outlook*), no. 19 (1997): 1.

28. Wang Huning, "Wenhua kuozhang yu wenhua zhuquan: duizhuquan guannian de tiaozhan" ("Cultural Expansion versus Cultural Sovereignty: A Challenge to the Concept of Sovereignty"), in Wang Jisi, ed., *Civilizations and International Politics*.

29. Hu Wei, "Lun lengzhanhou guoji chongtu: dui 'wenming fanshi' de piping" ("Conflicts in the Post–Cold War World: A Critique of the 'Civilization Paradigm'"), *Fudan xuebao: shehui kexue ban* (*Fudan Journal: Social Sciences Edition*), no. 3 (1995): 254–262.

30. See the special edition of *Xiandai guoji guanxi* (*Contemporary International Relations*), no. 6 (1994), which is devoted to commemorating the fortieth anniversary of the announcement of the five principles of peaceful coexistence.

31. Deng Xiaoping, *The Selected Works*. See also Gao Jingdian, ed., *Deng Xiaoping guoji zhanlue shixiang yanjiu* (*A Study on Deng Xiaoping's Thoughts on International*

Strategy) (Beijing: Guofang daxue chubanshe, 1992), chap. 3; Wang Taiping, *A Collection of Research Papers on Deng Xiaoping's Thoughts on Diplomacy;* Peng Guangqian and Yao Youzhi, eds., *On Deng Xiaoping's Thoughts on Strategy,* chap. 3.

32. Alexander Wendt, "Collective Identity Formation and the International State," *American Political Science Review* 88, no. 2 (June 1994): 388 and passim.

33. Yan Xuetong, *Analysis of China's National Interests,* chap. 2.

34. See, for example, Zhao Xiaochun, "Lun lengzhan hou guojia liyi de xinbianhua" ("On New Changes in National Interests in the Post–Cold War Era"), *Guoji guanxi xueyuan xuebao* (*Journal of the Intitute of International Relations*), no. 1, 1995: 1–7.

35. He Xin, *Zhonghua fuxing yu shijie weilai* (*China's Revival and the World's Future,* vols. 1–2) (Sichuan: Sichuan renmin chubanshe, 1996), 338.

36. Friedrich List (1789–1846), one of the earliest critics of Adam Smith and the liberal classical economics, is also considered one of the classical spokesmen for contemporary neomercantilism and economic nationalism. According to some, his views have helped inspire the state-driven East Asian model of political economy. See, e.g., James Fallows, "How the World Works," *Atlantic Monthly* (December 1993): 61–87. The Chinese version of List's most important book, *The National System of Political Economy,* first appeared in 1927. The translated version was republished in the 1960s and 1980s mainly because of its relevance to Marxism. For the Chinese Marxists, though List's critique of classical economics contributed to Marxism, his analysis of capitalism as a national system made his theory "unscientific" and "wrong," and his theory also contributed to capitalist vulgar economics. For the Chinese "Marxian" interpretation of List, see Hu Qiling's "Preface to the Chinese Version" (written in 1980) of *The National System of Political Economy* (Beijing: Shangwu yinshuguan, 1997), 1–9.

The book was reprinted again in 1997 and is increasingly being read as a book advocating economic nationalism.

37. For He Xin on Morgenthau and List, see his *China's Revival and the World's Future,* esp. 69; 130; 153; 628–631; 661–662.

38. Kim, "China and the World in Theory and Practice," in Kim, *China and the World,* 29.

39. Alastair Iain Johnston, "Learning Versus Adaptation: Explaining Change in Chinese Arms Control Policy in the 1980s and 1990s," *China Journal,* no. 35 (January 1996): 31.

40. Both Keohane and Nye's views are summarized in Joseph Nye Jr., "Neorealism and Neoliberalism," *World Politics* 40, no. 2 (January 1988): 246.

41. *Renmin ribao* (*People's Daily,* overseas ed.), 16 November 1994, 1.

42. Beijing XINHUA Domestic Service in Chinese, 15 November 1994, in Foreign Broadcast Information Service (FBIS)—China, 15 November 1994, 2.

43. Thomas W. Robinson, "Interdependence in China's Foreign Relations."

44. Harold K. Jacobson and Michel Oksenberg, *China's Participation in the IMF, the World Bank, and GATT: Toward a Global Economic Order* (Ann Arbor: University of Michigan Press, 1990). For a detailed discussion regarding how China has "learned" to cooperate in the context of Asia-Pacific regionalism, see Yong Deng,

Promoting Asia-Pacific Economic Cooperation: Perspectives from East Asia (London: Macmillan, 1997), chap. 3.

45. *Tactical learning* involves "change in means but not in ends," whereas, *cognitive learning* involves "a modification of goals as well as means." For further discussion, see Jack Levy, "Learning and Foreign Policy: Sweeping a Conceptual Minefield," *International Organization* 48, no. 2 (Spring 1994): 279–312.

46. Li Shenzhi, "Quanqiuhua: ershiyi shiji de daqushi" ("Globalization: Grand Trend in the Twenty-First Century"), *Keji daobao* (*Science and Technology Herald*), 3 June 1993, 5; "Quanqiuhua yu zhongguo wenhua" ("Globalization and Chinese Culture"), *Meiguo yanjiu* (*American Studies*) 1 (1995): 126–138. Since the mid-nineteenth century, the Chinese elite have wrestled with the *ti-yong* question as to how much they can borrow from the Western world to modernize China (*yong* or "function") while still keeping Chinese values and cultural identity (*ti* or "essence") intact.

47. Wang Yizhou, *Dangdai guoji zhengzhi xilun* (*Analysis of Contemporary International Politics*) (Shanghai: Shanghai renmin chubanshe, 1995). Another Chinese author also lists ten influences of globalization on world politics and economics: economic interdependence, technological and information development, the erosion of state sovereignty, the globalization of production, the formation of the global market, transnational activities of multinational corporations, greater global financial risks, mutual international coordination, new challenges and opportunities for developing countries, and increasing global problems. See Wang Hexing, "Quanqiuhua dui shijie zhengzhi, jingji de shida yingxiang" ("Ten Influences of Globalization on World Politics and Economics"), *International Studies*, no. 1 (1997): 10–15 and 33.

48. Wang Yizhou, *Analysis of Contemporary International Politics*, 40–41.

49. Ibid., 43.

50. Zhu Wenli, "Dui dangqian guoji guanxi bianhua de jidian renshi" ("A Few Thoughts on the Changes in Contemporary International Relations"), in Liang Shoude, ed., *New Introduction to International Politics*, 68–76.

51. Realists are generally concerned with relative gains (how benefits are to be distributed), namely, the question of "who will gain more," whereas liberals care more about how the state gains in absolute terms. For a summary of the neorealist-neoliberal debate over absolute versus relative gains, see Robert Powell, "Anarchy in International Relations Theory: The Neorealist-Neoliberal Debate," *International Organization* 48, no. 2 (Spring 1994), esp. 334–338.

52. Wang Jisi, "The Theoretical Grounds and Practical Implications of the Theory on Civilizational Clashes," 196–199; 205.

53. Yu Bin, "The China Syndrome: Rising Nationalism and Conflict with the West," *Asia Pacific Issues* (Analysis from the East-West Center), no. 27 (May 1996).

54. Jianwei Wang and Zhimin Lin, "Chinese Perceptions in the Post–Cold War Era: Three Images of the United States," *Asian Survey* 32, no. 10 (October, 1992): 902–917.

55. Banning N. Garrett and Bonnie S. Glaser, "Chinese Perspectives on Nuclear Arms Control," *International Security* 20, no. 3 (Winter 1995/1996): 43–78.

56. Yan Xuetong, *Analysis of China's National Interests*, 160–163.

57. Tang Tianri, "Anquan hezuo de xin moshi" ("New Model in Security Cooperation"), *Liaowang (Outlook)*, no. 31 (1997): 44. Like most of his Chinese colleagues, the author uses the occasion to criticize the revised U.S.-Japan military alliance. This invites questioning of his real motive behind promoting collective security.

58. The Information Office of the PRC State Council, "Zhongguo de guofang" ("China's National Defense"), *Renmin ribao,* 28 July 1998, 2.

59. The earliest book introducing Western (mostly realist) international relations theories is Chen Hanwen, *Zai guoji wutai shang: Xifang guoji guanxi xue jianjie (On the International Stage: A Brief Introduction to Western IR Theory)* (Chengdu: Sichuan renmin chubanshe, 1985). Other major introductory books include Ni Shixiong and Jin Yinzhong, eds., *Dangdai meiguo guoji guanxi lilun liupai wenxuan (Selected Readings in Contemporary American International Relations Theory)* (Shanghai: Xuelin chubanshe, 1987); Jin Yinzhong and N. Shixiong, *A Comparative Study of International Relations Theory;* and Song Xinning, *Guoji zhengzhi jingji yu zhongguo duiwai guanxi (International Political Economy and Chinese Foreign Relations)* (Beijing: Hong Kong shehui kexue chubanshe, 1997).

60. See, for example, Wang Yong, "Lun xianghu yicun dui woguo guojia anquan de yingxiang" ("On the Impact of Interdependence on Our National Security"), in Liang Shoude, ed., *New Introduction to International Politics.*

61. Liang Shoude, "Maixiang ershiyi shiji de shijie yu zhongguo de waijiao zhanlue" ("The World Forging Ahead Toward the Twenty-first Century and China's Diplomatic Strategy"), in Liang Shoude, *New Introduction,* 33.

62. Liang Shoude, "The World Forging Ahead"; see also articles in the special section on globalization in *Fudan Journal,* no. 6 (1996): 23–39.

63. *Renmin ribao (People's Daily,* overseas ed.), 22 September 1997, 2.

64. Wang Yizhou, *Analysis of Contemporary International Politics,* esp. p. 13.

65. Ibid., pref.

66. Ibid., 41.

67. My categorization draws on Jeffery W. Legro, "Conceptual Revolutions in Foreign Policy: America after the World Wars," paper presented at the Annual Meeting of the American Political Science Association, San Franscisco, 28 August–1 September 1996; Albert Yee, "The Causal Effects of Ideas on Policies," *International Organization* 50 (1996): 69–108; and Judith Golstein, *Ideas, Interests, and American Trade Policy* (Ithaca: Cornell University, 1993).

68. Justin Rosenberg, "What's the Matter with Realism?" *Review of International Studies* 16, no. 4 (October 1990): 290–291.

69. Rosenberg, "What's the Matter with Realism?" p. 292. For E. H. Carr's view, see *The Twenty Years' Crisis, 1919–1939,* 1st ed., 14.

70. Susan Shirk, "Internationalization and China's Economic Reforms," in *Internationalization and Domestic Politics,* Robert Keohane and Helen Milner, eds. (New York: Cambridge University Press, 1996).

71. Yan Xuetong, *Analysis of China's National Interests,* 6–8.

72. Ibid., 101. Li Xiangqian, "Dangdai zhongguo waijiao xingxiang lun" ("On the Diplomatic Images of Contemporary China"), in Wang Taiping, ed., *A Collection of Research Papers on Deng Xiaoping's Thoughts on Diplomacy,* 66.

73. Martha Finnermore, *National Interests in International Society* (Ithaca: Cornell University Press, 1996).

74. Professor Liang Shoude is the most ardent advocate of an IR theory with "Chinese characteristics." See his *Introduction to International Politics,* passim; "Lun guoji zhengzhi xue de zhongguo tese" ("On the Theory of International Politics with Chinese Characteristics"), *Guoji zhengzhi yanjiu* (*Studies on International Politics*), no. 1 (1994), 15–21; and "The Study of International Politics in China." Many younger Chinese scholars disagree with Liang and others. For a summary of the debate over the issue of "Chinese characteristics in IR theory," see Song Xinning, "The IR Theory-Building in China: Tradition, Function, and Characteristics" (manuscript, Department of International Politics, Chinese Renmin University, 1997), 3–5.

75. Legro, "Conceptual Revolutions in Foreign Policy," 12–13; Golstein, *Ideas, Interests, and American Trade Policy,* 12–15.

76. Samuel S. Kim, "Thinkining Globally in Post-Mao China," *Journal of Peace Research* 27, no. 2 (1990): 191–209; see also his "International Organizations in Chinese Foreign Policy," in Allen S. Whiting, ed., *The Annals of the American Academy of Political and Social Science,* vol. 519 (January 1992): 140–157.

77. He Xin, *China's Revival and the World's Future,* 22–27.

78. Lowell Dittmer and Samuel Kim, eds., *China's Quest for National Identity* (Ithaca: Cornell University Press, 1993).

79. Peter Katzenstein, ed., *The Culture of National Security: Norms and Identity in World Politics* (New York: Columbia University Press, 1996); Ann Florini, "The Evolution of International Norms," *International Studies Quarterly* 40, no. 3 (September 1996): 363–389.

80. Author's interviews in Beijing during May to June, 1997. The source of the quote must remain anonymous.

81. Golstein, *Ideas, Interests, and American Trade Policy.*

82. For two succinct analyses of how Deng Xiaoping's views on "seeking truth from facts" won the debate over truth and the power struggle with Hua Guofeng and other dogmatic Maoist followers, see Harry Harding, *China's Second Revolution* (Washington, D.C.: Brookings Institution, 1987), chap. 3; and Richard Baum, *Burying Mao: Chinese Politics in the Age of Deng Xiaoping* (Princeton: Princeton University Press, 1994), chap. 2.

83. There is a growing body of literature produced mostly from the British school of international relations that explicates and criticizes realism's positivist assumptions; see Barry Buzan, Richard Little, and Charles Jones, *The Logic of Anarchy: Neorealism and Structural Realism* (New York: Columbia University Press, 1993); Richard Ashley, "The Poverty of Neorealism," *International Organization* 38, no. 2 (1984): 225–286; and Roger Tooze, "The Unwritten Preface: International Political Economy and Epistemology," *Millennium: Journal of International Studies* 17, no. 2 (1988): 285–293.

84. David Shambaugh, "Containment or Engagement of China? Calculating Beijing's Responses," *International Security* 21, no. 2 (Fall 1996): 180–209.

85. Lynn White and Li Cheng, "China's Coast Identities: Regional, National, and Global," in Dittmer and Kim, *China's Quest for National Identity.*

86. Wendt, "Anarchy is What States Make of It: The Social Construction of Power Politics," *International Organization,* vol. 46 (1992): 395–421. See also his "Collective Identity Formation and the International State," 384–396.

87. For the best treatment of this subject, see Dittmer and Kim, eds., *China's Quest for National Identity.*

88. Both Western and Chinese scholars agree on China's lack of stable national identity. See Li Shenzhi, "Globalization and Chinese Culture;" Dittmer and Kim, eds., *China's Quest for National Identity;* Hughes, "Globalization and Nationalism."

4

Managing Conflict: Chinese Perspectives on Multilateral Diplomacy and Collective Security

Jianwei Wang

One salient characteristic of post–Cold War international relations is the upsurge of multilateral diplomacy at the global, crossregional, regional, and subregional levels. *Multilateral diplomacy* is defined here as interactions among nation-states in permanent and ad hoc global and regional international organizations, conferences, and talks in which more than two actors are involved simultaneously. The seed of multilateral diplomacy was sown when the United Nations was established in 1945. However, the globalization of the Cold War soon turned the UN into a battleground for East-West confrontation. Consequently, the function of multilateral diplomacy was severely constrained by a rigid bipolar framework. The collapse of the bipolar world structure opens a new era for multilateralism. First, the relaxation of relations among major powers revitalized the function of the UN Security Council in which the Big Five are more likely to reach consensus on important issues of international peace and security. Second, the end of the Cold War gave momentum to the development of regionalism in those areas that used to be stiffly demarcated by opposing political and military blocs, thus intensifying intraregional multilateral interactions. Third, multilateral solutions to interstate or even internal conflicts became feasible and more effective with the superpower competition abated in many geographic hot spots.

73

For a long time, China had been largely excluded from global and regional multilateral diplomacy. China did not restore its membership in the
UN until 1971. During most of the 1960s, China endured a partially self-
imposed diplomatic isolation with limited bilateral (not to mention multilateral) diplomacy. China's only experience in multilateral diplomacy was
its interaction with the Soviet bloc and, to a much less extent, with some
Asian countries during the 1950s. These experiences did not always leave
the Chinese with a sweet taste. China did advocate the formation of a
united front against the Soviet expansionism of the 1970s. But in practice,
this diplomatic strategy was seldom carried out in a multilateral fashion.
For China, therefore, multilateral diplomacy was uncharted terrain.
China's foreign relations since the 1980s, particularly since the end of the
Cold War, witnessed a slow but steady perceptual and behavioral change in
its multilateral diplomacy. This chapter attempts a preliminary exploration
of China's cognition and practice of multilateral diplomacy in one issue
area: collective security at the global and regional levels. In its classic definition, *collective security* means that all countries act in unison in taking military and nonmilitary enforcement measures to halt aggression and restore
peace. For the purpose of this chapter, it is understood in a broader sense
to include China's involvement in various forms of multilateral security
consultation and cooperation.

CHINA'S ATTITUDE TOWARD THE
UN COLLECTIVE SECURITY

In recent years, the United Nations ushered in a new era of multilateral
diplomacy on various issues. In the security domain, a noticeable development has been the flourishing of UN peacekeeping operations. More new
peacekeeping missions were initiated during 1988–1994 (twenty) than during the previous forty years.[1] At its peak in 1995, the total deployment of
UN military and civilian personnel reached almost 70,000 from seventy-
seven countries. In 1997, there were seventeen peacekeeping missions,
compared to only eight in 1987.[2] As a permanent member of the UN Security Council, China bears special responsibility for authorizing and financing these peacekeeping operations.

Subtle Change of Perception

China's memory of UN collective security is by no means positive, and it
can be said that China was among the first targets of collective security action. After the Korean War broke out in June 1950, the UN Security Council first legitimized the U.S. military intervention on the Korean Peninsula
under the UN flag. Then, after China entered the war, the U.S.-influenced
UN General Assembly adopted a resolution to brand the People's Republic

of China (PRC) as an aggressor and recommended that all states embargo strategic and military material to China. Not surprisingly, collective security measures taken by the UN, in Beijing's eyes, meant imperialist aggression and intervention.

Immediately after China reactivated its involvement in the UN in the early 1970s, it was rather passive toward UN multilateral diplomacy in general. It invented "nonparticipation" in the voting process in the Security Council. The rate of its nonparticipation was very high. Of the 101 resolutions adopted by the Security Council between November 24, 1971, and December 22, 1976, China posted a 39 percent rate of abstention and nonparticipation.[3] Beijing was particularly skeptical about the legitimacy of UN peacekeeping operations. Most such UN actions were seen as interference in countries' internal affairs and as the undesirable result of U.S.-Soviet hegemonic power competition. Therefore, China avoided dispatching troops in the name of the UN under any form. Although China did not want to appear to be obstructionist, it either did not participate in or was absent from the vote on almost every UN peacekeeping operation during the 1970s. For instance, China opposed UN Emergency Force II (UNEF II) in the Middle East in 1973 and dissociated itself from all related votes and discussions in both the Security Council and the General Assembly. China also refused to pay its share of the financial cost for UNEF II and the UN Disengagement Observer Force (UNDOF).[4] China also did not make any contribution to the UN peacekeeping forces in Lebanon in 1978.[5]

The change in the Chinese attitude toward UN multilateral diplomacy, including collective security, came with the adjustment of foreign policy in the early 1980s. At the Tenth Party Congress of 1982, Beijing declared that it would pursue a foreign policy of independence to replace the previous strategy of uniting with the United States against the Soviet Union. As part of this strategic shift, China intensified its activities in the United Nations. In Premier Zhao Ziyang's report on government work in 1986, for the first time he clearly defined multilateral diplomacy as the integral part of China's foreign policy of independence.[6] By the end of 1986, China was involved in virtually all the important elements of UN intergovernmental multilateral diplomacy.[7] China's evaluation of the UN role in international affairs, including maintaining international peace and security, has thereafter become more positive. In various speeches by Chinese leaders inside and outside the UN, China acknowledged that the UN, although it has various weaknesses and made mistakes in the past, overall has contributed to the peace and prosperity of mankind in an important way.[8] As the most universal and authoritative of any intergovernmental organization (IGO) of sovereign nation states, its position and influence in international affairs are irreplaceable. In the post–Cold War era, the function of the UN should be increased rather than reduced.[9]

Reflecting China's more upbeat evaluation of the UN and China's more proactive diplomacy in the system, its attitudes regarding UN peacekeeping operations also underwent noticeable change. In 1981, China for the first time voted for the extension of UN Peacekeeping Forces in Cyprus (UNFICYP).[10] In 1982, China paid dues toward the UN peacekeeping operation in Lebanon. It also sent out a fact-finding mission to the Middle East to study the UN peacekeeping operation there.[11] China started to perceive UN peacekeeping operations through a more functional and less ideological lens. In 1988, the year UN peacekeeping forces were awarded the Nobel Peace Prize, China officially became a member of the UN Special Committee on Peacekeeping Operations.[12] In 1990, China began to send military observers to peacekeeping operations. Since then it has sent 437 military observers in thirty-two groups to join six UN peace-keeping operations.[13]

China and UNTAC

China's endorsement of UN peacekeeping operations reached a milestone during the UN peacekeeping operation in Cambodia during the early 1990s.[14] The Cambodian conflict was a legacy of the Cold War and the longtime rivalry between the United States, the Soviet Union, China, and Vietnam in Southeast Asia. By the end of the 1980s, a consensus began to emerge among regional and global players involved that the conflict did not serve anybody's interest and should come to a halt. After the four factions in Cambodia failed to reach an agreement at the first Paris Conference in 1989, the peace process shifted to the UN Security Council itself. As a permanent member of the UN Security Council, the way in which China played its cards in this game was key to the success of resolving the conflict in Cambodia.

It was not a secret that China had long been a staunch supporter of the infamous Khmer Rouge, the most powerful faction among resistance forces operating against the Vietnamese occupying Cambodia. In the early 1990s, however, China's policies toward the Cambodian conflict in general and the Khmer Rouge in particular underwent significant change. First of all, with the improvement of Sino-Soviet and Sino-Vietnamese relations— exemplified by the Sino-Soviet summit and the withdrawal of Vietnamese troops from Cambodia in 1989—China's underlying rationale for supporting the Khmer Rouge lost its validity. Second, at that time, China still suffered from its post-Tiananmen diplomatic isolation, and its international image was very much in ruin. Thus, it was in China's national interest to keep its distance from the notorious Khmer Rouge and to prove that it was a responsible power.

These circumstances, coupled with China's new perception of the UN and its peacekeeping operations, brought about a new pattern of Chinese behavior in terms of UN collective security. China moved away from its traditional position that the UN should never interfere in a sovereign country's internal affairs. During the consultation of five permanent members of the Security Council, China worked hard to bring the Khmer Rouge into line. By the end of 1990, the Big Five worked out a draft peace agreement that was eventually accepted by all four factions in Cambodia with some modifications. At the second Paris Conference on Cambodia in October 1991, all four factions in Cambodia as well as nineteen other countries signed the Paris Agreement, thereby completing a comprehensive political settlement of the Cambodian conflict. In accordance with the agreement, the UN Security Council passed Resolution 745 to establish the UN Transitional Authority in Cambodia (UNTAC) to monitor the implementation of the Paris Agreement. UNTAC kicked off its mission in March 1992. At its peak, it involved almost 16,000 military personnel, 3,600 civilian police, and 2,000 civilian staff, making it approximately 22,000-strong—one of the largest peacekeeping operations in the UN history.[15]

China's support of UNTAC was unprecedented in Chinese multilateral diplomacy. In addition to its size, UNTAC was also the most "intrusive" peacekeeping operation in terms of the UN's involvement in a country's internal affairs. The Paris Agreement provided UNTAC with a broad mandate to exercise authority over functions normally reserved for a country's internal apparatuses, such as political elections, civil administrations, economic rehabilitation, and the guaranteeing of human rights. In other words, the mission was a "second generation" peacekeeping operation, a mixture of "peacekeeping, peace maintenance, and peace building," and went far beyond the narrowly defined traditional mandate of partitioning warring parties. For more than a year, UNTAC actually governed an independent sovereign country.

China not only underwrote the operation politically and financially; it also sent a military unit to participate in UNTAC. Acting on the request of Cambodia's Prince Norodom Sihanouk and then UN Secretary-General Boutros Boutros-Ghali and with the approval of China's Pres. Jiang Zemin, the Chinese government sent forty-seven military observers and an engineering battalion of four hundred men to Cambodia, comprising China's first blue-helmeted troops.[16] The performance of Chinese troops during the operation was highly praised by UNTAC authorities, and the UNTAC military commander honored their accomplishments by awarding each member a bronze UN medal.[17] China also suffered its first casualties in a UN peacekeeping operation when several Chinese peacekeepers were killed in Khmer Rouge attacks.

UNTAC's mission soon encountered serious problems when the Khmer Rouge declared it would not participate in the disarmament process and consequently refused to participate in new government elections. The critical question then became whether the peace process should continue and whether the election should be held as scheduled in May 1993. The UN Security Council decided to throw its weight behind UNTAC. China went along with the Security Council and voted in the affirmative for almost all the Security Council resolutions during the critical time leading up to the election. Beijing put pressure on the Khmer Rouge to comply with the Paris Accords and agreed that the election should move on even without its participation. Although the Khmer Rouge refused to participate, it did not systematically disrupt the election, as many people feared. China's pressure on the Khmer Rouge apparently made a difference. China publicly announced in April 1992 that it would not support any Cambodian party that would resume the civil war. China also warned Khieu Samphan, the Khmer Rouge leader, during his visit to Beijing in late May not to disrupt the election.[18]

Chapter VI and Chapter VII Operations

China's active participation in UNTAC was a significant departure from its past behavior in multilateral diplomacy for collective security purposes. However, it should not be seen as a norm that China would follow most of the time. As mentioned earlier, China's cooperative diplomacy in conflict resolution in Cambodia took place under some special conditions. The most important factor was that the conflict directly involved China's interest; China also had considerable influence on the warring parties in Cambodia. In addition, although UNTAC was very intrusive in its political and civil mandates, its military mandate was very limited. It was clearly planned to be a UN Charter Chapter VI operation in terms of military force, that is, the peacekeeping forces were to be employed to maintain a cease-fire already agreed upon by warring parties; no military force would be used except for self-defense. It was never intended as a Chapter VII operation, whereby military force could be used to enforce the peace (such as disarming uncooperative factions). This is important to understanding China's persistent support for the mission. China tends to be more reserved about collective security measures that use military force directly; it is also wary of enforcement actions, such as economic sanctions. Even during the UNTAC operation, after the Khmer Rouge had reneged on its commitment, some UN members and officials suggested that the UN should change UNTAC from a Chapter VI to Chapter VII operation, taking tougher measures such as economic sanctions and the use of military force against the Khmer Rouge. China was uneasy with these ideas. In the whole process, China cast its only abstention vote on a Security Council resolution in November 1992. The resolution raised the possibility of imposing an economic embargo against the Khmer Rouge. China pointed out that it fully supported the Paris Agreement's implementation yet could not support the resolution's provisions, which seemed to encourage an economic sanction.[19]

China's cooperative involvement in UNTAC has not been repeated in other UN peacekeeping operations. In most cases, China would likely support UN peacekeeping operations under Chapter VI but is more reluctant to endorse Chapter VII missions absent clear-cut foreign aggression or invasion.[20] For instance, China supported most UN Security Council resolutions against Iraq for its invasion of Kuwait, including economic sanctions. But when the Security Council came to vote on the resolution to authorize the United States and its allies to use military force to drive Iraq out of Kuwait, China abstained. China is even more conservative if the conflict in question is domestic in nature. For instance, China abstained on all UN resolutions imposing sanctions on the former Yugoslavia.[21] And China's diplomacy in the ongoing Iraq crisis since the 1990–1991 War further illustrates its reservation on using coercive means to impose the UN will on a sovereign country. Although China repeatedly asked Iraq to strictly, comprehensively, and completely implement UN Security Council resolutions on weapons inspection and went along with the consensus on this issue, Beijing made it clear that it opposed using force even if Iraq refused to comply. In the meantime, it also pointed out that the Security Council's Special Commission should have a more just appraisal of Iraq's implementation of the UN resolutions and the UN-imposed economic sanctions should not continue indefinitely.[22] China took a similar position on the issue of economic sanctions against Libya.[23]

China is often struggling with the cognitive dissonance between its strong views on, sometimes even obsession with, national sovereignty and the perceived necessity of collective security in international conflict resolution. Chinese diplomats held that UN peacekeeping operations, though a useful measure of collective security, should abide by the principle of respecting national sovereignty and noninterference in domestic affairs. In principle these peacekeeping operations should be agreed upon in advance by the concerned countries or parties. Although recent UN peacekeeping operations have been more heavily involved in internal conflicts, this should not be used as a pretext to interfere with internal matters.[24] The UN peacekeeping forces should under no circumstances take sides and become a party to an internal conflict. Its mandate should not go too much beyond maintaining peace and providing humanitarian assistance. For this reason, China is not enthusiastic about using UN peacekeeping forces to arrest those responsible for human rights violation and genocide during internal conflicts. In regard to Rwanda, for instance, China abstained on the Security Council recommendation to establish the International Criminal Tribunal and to arrest those who were responsible; China considered the matter to be outside the jurisdiction of the Security Council.[25]

In the final analysis, China's conditional endorsement of UN collective security is related to the strong Chinese belief that peacekeeping operations can accomplish only so much in terms of conflict resolution. It can be used only as a supplement to political solutions, and it should not and cannot substitute political solutions per se. China is thus concerned with the overgrowth of UN peacekeeping operations in recent years. Then–Foreign Minister Qian Qichen argued that the sources of international conflict are very complicated and multifaceted. It is unrealistic for the UN Security Council to take care of all conflicts in the world. Therefore, peacekeeping operations should take into consideration limited UN resources.[26] When conditions are not yet ripe, a peacekeeping operation should not be undertaken.[27] The UN's tendency to authorize a few major powers like the United States or military alliances like NATO to control peacekeeping operations was questioned by the Chinese.[28] Beijing held that peacekeeping operations should be genuinely multilateral and should not be hijacked by major powers or military blocs for their own foreign policy agenda. Peacekeeping also should not be expanded at the cost of other UN mandates, such as economic and social development.

Conflict Between National and Collective Interests

However, just like other major powers, China's treatment of UN peacekeeping operations is colored by its calculation of national interests, though China often declares that its position is impartial and even selfless. Despite its recent increase in economic and military power, China is not a major power with global interests. Such a power status leads to two tendencies in its diplomacy. First, China is generally not interested in remote conflicts where China's interest is not significantly affected. It has not been particularly eager to pour its financial and human resources into conflict resolution in those areas, compared to some medium-sized powers, such as Australia and Canada. As the late Chinese leader Deng Xiaoping repeatedly said, China cannot afford to care too much about what is going on in other countries; what China really cares about is how to cultivate a good international environment to develop itself.[29] Yet just because it does not have many vested interests in these conflicts, China is in no mood to jeopardize its image in the UN and its relations with major powers by acting as an obstructionist. In other words, China does not always strongly stand by the principles it declares. So even when China disagrees with UN collective security measures, it normally does not attempt to block Security Council action so that a consensus of the Security Council can be maintained. China would rather abstain from rather than veto most Security Council collective security resolutions, explaining any reservations after the fact.

Yet China would not hesitate to use its status as a Permanent Member of the Security Council to push its own foreign policy priorities. One issue that has colored China's behavior regarding UN collective security in recent years is Taiwan, as the island has intensified its effort to raise its international profile. In February 1996, then UN Secretary-General Boutros-Ghali recommended an extension of the UN peacekeeping mission in Haiti for another six months. China indicated that the recommendation was too extensive given the UN's financial situation. It threatened to veto the proposal. A compromise was worked out eventually, granting an extension for a period of four months with a contingent of 1,200 troops and 300 international civilian police—far less than the Security Council wanted. The real reason behind China's objection was related to Haiti's official ties to Taiwan and its invitation of Taiwan's vice president, Li Juan-zu, to attend Haiti's Pres. Lavalas Rene Preval's inauguration.[30] China took even more dramatic action in 1997 regarding the UN peacekeeping mission in Guatemala. It cast its first veto of a Security Council resolution in twenty-five years, blocking the proposed UN peacekeeping mission to Guatemala in retaliation for Guatemala's support of Taiwan. China was the only member of the fifteen-nation Security Council to vote against a U.S.-sponsored resolution calling for the dispatch of 155 military observers to oversee compliance with a peace accord signed between the Guatemalan government and leftist rebel leaders. China was especially offended by Guatemala's four years of support in the UN General Assembly for Taiwan's bid to win UN membership and by its inviting Taiwan's foreign minister, John Chang, to the signing of the peace agreement in Guatemala City. In statements in both the UN and Beijing, China declared that it favored the peace process in Guatemala and would like to vote for it. But it could not countenance a country doing things that harm China's sovereignty and territorial integrity while asking for China's cooperation in the Security Council.[31] In the meantime, China left the door open for further negotiation with Guatemala after conveying its strong message via veto. With ten more days of intensive consultation, China and Guatemala reached a secret deal.[32] Then the Security Council voted again and unanimously approved the resolution to authorize the deployment of UN peacekeeping mission in Guatemala.[33] These two cases indicate that China is willing to use multilateral diplomacy as an instrument to push its own foreign policy agenda at the expense of UN Security Council consensus.

SEARCHING FOR COLLECTIVE SECURITY IN THE ASIA-PACIFIC REGION

Multilateralism is underdeveloped in the Asia-Pacific compared to other regions in the world, such as Western Europe. The Cold War polarization between communist and anticommunist countries, the political, economic, and cultural diversity and heterogeneity in the region, a strong commitment to national sovereignty, and political independence resulting from colonial history all contributed to the historic paucity of multilateralism in the Asia-Pacific. During the Cold War, most security and economic issues in the region were dealt with on a bilateral basis, as exemplified by the U.S.-Japan and U.S.–South Korean security alliances as well as the Sino–North Korean and Sino-Soviet security alliances. The American attempt to establish a NATO-type multilateral security regime such as the Southeast Asian Treaty Organization (SEATO) never got very far. The Soviet maneuver of establishing an "Asian collective security system" during the 1970s was rejected outright by most countries in the region. The only exception was the formation of an indigenous multilateral organization—the Association of Southeast Asian Nations (ASEAN)—in 1967 as an attempt by Southeast Asian countries to survive the struggle of major powers in the region and to maintain a nonaligned identity outside any major power security alliance. Just like the situation at the global level, China often perceived itself as a target of rather than a participant in regional multilateral diplomacy.

Economic Versus Security Multilateralism

In the post–Cold War period, multilateral regionalism has gained momentum in East Asia. The decline of East-West confrontation in the region removed a major barrier of more dynamic interaction and contact among countries in the region. The economic transition from planned economy to market economy in most socialist countries, with the exception of North Korea, facilitated a higher level of economic interaction and integration in the region. As a result, functional economic interdependence in terms of trade, investment, as well as human resources has increased significantly, crying for more standardization and coordination of economic activities. In the security sphere, the strong desire of Asia-Pacific countries to maintain regional stability and prosperity in the post–Cold War period compelled concerned countries to take collective measures to deal with potential hot spots, such as Cambodia, the Korean Peninsula, and the South China Sea. Moreover, the rise of China and Japan, the collapse of the Soviet Union, and the uncertainties surrounding the U.S. presence in the western Pacific also demand a multilateral regional approach to security.

China was keenly aware of the transformation of the power structure in the Asia-Pacific. As early as in 1991, it realized that the triangular relationship among China, the United States, and the USSR was gradually evolving into a quadrilateral relationship among the United States, the USSR, China, and Japan. The interactions among the four major players and the critical role played by the diplomatically shrewd ASEAN nations formed a multilateral political, economic, and military structure in the region. The careful handling of this multilateral relationship is of crucial importance to the establishment of a new political and economic order in the Asia-Pacific.[34]

However, the extent to which China should adopt a multilateral approach in addressing issues directly involving China's interest as well as other regional issues is still an open question in China's foreign policy establishment. Generally speaking, China has been more active in economic multilateralism but more reserved about multilateralism in the security domain. With regard to security multilateralism, China has been more receptive to unofficial or so-called track II (i.e., unofficial or nongovernmental) security discussions but more cautious about establishing an official mechanism for multilateral security consultations.[35]

China's cautiousness about security multilateralism is related to its basic assessment of the security situation in the Asia-Pacific. According to Beijing's analysis, in the post–Cold War period, Europe and other parts of the world have been plunged into protracted turbulence, yet the Asia-Pacific has remained relatively peaceful and stable. Since the 1990s, no new interstate military conflict has broken out, and old hot spots like Cambodia have settled down or eased considerably. The possibility of any major new conflict is low today. It is the first time China has faced no direct military threat since 1949, possibly since the Opium War of 1840.[36] Under such circumstances, China sees no hurry to establish a multilateral security regime in East Asia. As a Chinese scholar remarked, from the Third Plenary Session of the Tenth Central Committee of the PRC, security interests gradually lost their priority to economic interests in China's national agenda.[37] That explains why China has been very interested and active in economic multilateralism but not so much in security multilateralism.

Of course, China does not see its security environment as all rosy and without challenges. In the short term, the security threat to China comes from two directions: national separatism and territorial disputes.[38] The former points to the separatist movement in Taiwan, Tibet, and Xinjiang; the latter points to the numerous territorial disputes China has with neighbors. Overall China does not see multilateralism as the most effective approach to address these security concerns; instead, multilateralism may indeed make the situation more complicated. Particularly on the issue of separatism, China sees multilateral diplomacy playing only a minor role, as the issue often strides the boundary between domestic and international affairs. With regard to the Taiwan and Tibet issues, China insists both are under the jurisdiction of the Chinese government, although one can argue these issues could have regional security repercussions and should not be covered by bilateral diplomacy, let alone multilateral diplomacy. China strongly opposes the so-called internationalization of these issues. Territorial disputes such as the South China Sea, in contrast, can be more fruitfully handled by bilateral consultations, as a multilateral approach will most likely put China on the spot and minimize its advantage as a major power vis-à-vis its smaller neighbors.

China also notes that the Asia-Pacific region is characterized by diversity rather than uniformity. Countries in the region are still divided over what kind of regional security framework should be established, and there is no consensus. Any possible framework must therefore take into account the diverse needs of different countries.[39] Under such conditions, a region-wide multilateral security arrangement such as the Conference on Security and Cooperation in Europe (CSCE) is premature and may well be counterproductive. Based on its own experience, China believes that in any institutionalized multilateral regime sooner or later there would be competition for leadership.[40] China, still considering itself relatively weak among the major powers in the region, does not want to be involved in such a struggle too early, as it could find itself in an unfavorable position. Related to this, a formal multilateral security mechanism requires a high degree of military transparency, and China is not ready to accept this for fear of exposing its military weaknesses.[41] Many Chinese analysts still believe that a formal security regime often needs an enemy. In this respect, China suspects that proposals for a collective security regime in the Asia-Pacific may have the implication of containing China as a rising power. Beijing has no intention to prematurely committing to any security regime that might reduce its own freedom of action in the future.

Nonetheless, China understands that under post–Cold War circumstances, multilateral security is a trend reflecting legitimate concerns of small and medium-sized countries seeking a stable and predictable regional security order. Indeed, the drive for multilateral security has been partially stimulated by the growing Chinese military and economic might in the region. As a Canadian scholar pointed out, "Repeated statement of benign intent by Chinese officials, invocation of the 'Five Principles of Peaceful Coexistence,' and even concrete steps by Beijing to improve bilateral relations with most of its Asian neighbors are increasingly ineffective in meeting international concerns."[42] China thus has to be more sensitive to growing apprehension among Asia-Pacific countries. A refusal to be involved in multilateral security will be regarded as an ominous sign that China wants to act on its own. Therefore, China's mere endorsement and participation in multilateral security could be a more effective means to dispel the perception of the "China threat" than reiterating the pledge that China will not seek hegemony in the region. In addition, if China is constrained by a multilateral security regime, other major powers would be likewise constrained. Finally, involvement is also a more assured way to prevent security multilateralism from exclusively targeting China.

The Relationship with ASEAN

These perceptions of regional multilateral security have been reflected in China's dealings with ASEAN. In recent years, China's ties to ASEAN, the only comprehensive regional organization with some limited security mandate, have been considerably strengthened. By the early 1990s, China normalized its relations with all ASEAN countries, and China began its dialogue with ASEAN in 1991 as a consultative partner. Since then, the Chinese foreign minister has attended ASEAN's foreign ministerial meeting every year. In March 1996, in a letter to Ali Alatas, chairman of ASEAN's Standing Committee and Indonesia's foreign minister, Chinese Foreign Minister Qian Qichen indicated in clear terms China's intent to become ASEAN's full dialogue partner. ASEAN responded positively on June 24, when Alatas notified Qian in a letter about a consensus of ASEAN foreign ministers to upgrade China as a full dialogue partner. In July 1996, China, together with India and Russia, attended the ASEAN ministerial meeting as a full dialogue partner for the first time.[43]

Over the years, China has established a network of multilevel dialogues with ASEAN. The framework has five parallel mechanisms: China-ASEAN political consultation of senior officials; a China-ASEAN joint economic and trade committee; a China-ASEAN joint committee of science and technology; a China-ASEAN joint committee; and an ASEAN Beijing committee.[44] In December 1997, a new mechanism of consultation between China and ASEAN was set into action. The first informal China-ASEAN Summit was held in Kuala Lumpur, thus raising the dialogue to the highest level. China's Pres. Jiang Zemin declared that the meeting "marks the beginning of a new stage of development in Chinese-ASEAN relations."[45] The range of issues covered by the China-ASEAN dialogue has also been gradually expanded from economic issues to security issues, including promotion of confidence-building measures, peacekeeping, maritime search and rescue, preventive diplomacy, nonproliferation,[46] and even sensitive topics such as the South China Sea.[47] It is likely that the summit meeting will be regularized and institutionalized.

Due to ASEAN's original mandate to create the Zone of Peace, Freedom, and Neutrality (ZOPFAN), for a long time security issues were not even on the formal agenda of ASEAN meetings. But with the great power competition receding in the region, ASEAN's function in regional conflict resolution has increased. ASEAN countries were instrumental in the peaceful settlement of the Cambodian conflict. China supported and appreciated ASEAN initiatives in this regard. In the post–Cold War environment, China continued to support the limited role of ASEAN in regional conflict resolution. In July 1997, Cambodia's Second Prime Minister Hun Sen violently ousted his rival, First Prime Minister Prince Norodom Ranariddh, thereby raising the possibility of another civil war in the country. China endorsed ASEAN's mediating role in the conflict and stood by ASEAN's call for all parties involved to accept the outcome of the parliamentary election in July 1998 so that a viable government could be formed in Cambodia.[48]

However, China's response to establish broader and more formal security regimes has been calculated. One important reason is the adverse impact that such an arrangement may have on security issues involving vital Chinese interests. In earlier years, China would insist on excluding sensitive issues (such as the South China Sea and Taiwan) from the security consultation in any official capacity. China made a clear distinction between "low" politics (economic and other functional issues) and "high" politics (security issues). Although China could allow Taiwan and Hong Kong to join the Asia-Pacific Economic Cooperation forum (APEC) as regional economies, it regards the discussion of security issues as a prerogative exclusively reserved for sovereign national government. In 1993, under the sponsorship of research institutions from ten countries, a nongovernmental organization (NGO), the Council for Security Cooperation in the Asia Pacific (CSCAP), was established. It comprises national delegations, each of which includes not only scholars and policy analysts but also government officials participating in a private capacity.[49] China and Taiwan were both invited. Beijing, however, regards CSCAP as semigovernmental and therefore declined to join the organization unless Taiwan was excluded.[50] A compromise was reached in June 1996 after more than two years of intense consultation. China became a formal member of CSCAP; representatives from Taiwan will participate in the capacity of individuals.[51]

China also resisted pressure to allow Taiwan to become a member of the ASEAN Regional Forum (ARF). ARF was established in 1994 to discuss security issues informally between ASEAN and other concerned countries in the region. It marked the beginning of security multilateralism in the region at the official level. China endorsed ARF and participated in its meetings but did not want ASEAN countries to dictate the agenda of ARF. China realized that ASEAN countries intended to use ARF to tie down Beijing on issues such as the South China Sea. Instead, China tried to shape the agenda of ARF by putting forward its own proposals, focusing on less controversial security issues.

At the third ARF meeting in Jakarta in 1996, Foreign Minister Qian suggested that ARF start a dialogue on defense conversion and begin discussions on comprehensive security cooperation. In terms of military cooperation, he offered a number of proposals of confidence-building on such matters as notifying and inviting other ARF members to observe joint military exercises and reducing and eventually eliminating military reconnaissances targeted at a certain member of the forum. At the same meeting, China agreed to cosponsor with the Philippines the 1997 meeting on confidence-building measures in Beijing. This marked the first time China hosted an official multilateral conference on security.[52] China also advocated discussions on topics such as the development of military medicine and the science of military law.[53] So far China has preferred that ARF remain an informal dialogue mechanism rather than a formal organization. It has no interest in seeing it become an arbitrator of regional conflict.[54] Qian Qichen pointed out that ARF could play an increasingly important role in maintaining regional peace and stability so long as it gives full consideration to the region's diversity and develops itself incrementally on the basis of the shared interests and needs of its members in the spirit of consensus and seeking common ground while reserving differences.[55]

As it is at the global level, China is very skillful at using regional multilateral diplomacy to promote its own security priorities and interests. This can be seen in its engagement with ASEAN. The stickiest issue in Beijing's relationship with ASEAN is the South China Sea dispute. On this issue, most ASEAN countries have a united front against China's claim. China's seizure of the Mischief Reef in 1995 raised a lot of eyebrows in the region. One objective for China's intensifying its engagement with ASEAN was to ease tension on this issue. Needless to say, China will do whatever feasible to strengthen its presence in the South China Sea, and China is not in a position to soften or give up its sovereignty claim over the Spratly Islands. Yet China does not intend to dramatically change the status quo in the region. Although Beijing still maintains that the disputes over the South China Sea be settled by concerned countries through bilateral consultation,[56] at least in public statements it is open to the possibility of multilateral economic cooperation, such as joint exploration of natural resources in the area.[57]

When compared to China's concern over Taiwan, the importance of the South China Sea is of the second order. In this regard, Beijing has pursued a strategy of using more reconciliatory gestures on the South China Sea to win stronger support from ASEAN on Taiwan. In recent years, whenever a move in the South China Sea raised some collective concerns from ASEAN countries, China would back off. In the annual dialogue between China and ASEAN, China normally would refuse to discuss security concerns over the South China Sea, as Beijing's territorial claims overlap with many ASEAN countries. This attitude changed in 1997. In the mid-April China-ASEAN dialogue held at the mountain resort of Huangshan in China's Anhui Province, Beijing agreed for the first time to talk about ASEAN members' claims in the South China Sea and offered to frame a code of conduct governing ties with ASEAN.[58] In the meantime, China pushed ASEAN to sign a political accord with China to confirm a closer relationship between Beijing and ASEAN, including an affirmation of Beijing's "one China" policy. Some ASEAN officials had reservations about the idea and instead argued that China should sign ASEAN's Treaty of Amity and Cooperation.[59] In the "Joint Statement of the Informal Summit Meeting Between the Leaders of China and ASEAN" in December 1997, both sides got what they wanted. Although ASEAN reconfirmed its one China policy in general, China also recognized that the Treaty of Amity and Cooperation, together with the UN Charter and the Five Principles of Peaceful Coexistence, provide principles to guide China–ASEAN relations.[60]

Establishing a Peace Mechanism on the Korean Peninsula

China's perceptual change toward regional security multilateralism can be further observed in its diplomacy on the Korean Peninsula. For a long time, China insisted that the Korean conflict had to be settled between the two Koreas (the Republic of Korea [ROK, or South Korea] and the Democratic People's Republic of Korea [DPRK, or North Korea]) as well as between the DPRK and the United States. China supported the DPRK's demand to have direct dialogue with the United States but declined direct involvement in negotiations for establishing a peace mechanism on the peninsula.

In April 1997, U.S. Pres. Bill Clinton and South Korean Pres. Kim Young Sam proposed four-party discussions (including North and South Korea, the United States, and China) to replace the armistice that ended the Korean War with a formal peace treaty. For a time China was cool to the idea and did not want to commit itself to this multilateral approach. Beijing was unhappy partially because it was not involved in the initial discussion between Washington and Seoul on the proposal. It was reported that China arranged a secret bilateral talk between South and North Korea in Beijing after the U.S.-ROK proposal was put on the table. The purpose was to indicate to Washington that China had considerable influence over developments on the peninsula and that it must be more fully involved in working out a solution to the Korean problem.[61] Another reason was that North Korea was still suspicious about the utility of such a talk and would like to see South Korea excluded.

By July 1997, however, China's attitude changed from noncommitment to strong support toward the four-party talks. The Chinese foreign ministry announced that as a signatory of the Korean armistice agreement and one of the neighboring countries of the peninsula China would agree to participate in the quadrilateral talks and promised to play a constructive role in the process of establishing a peace mechanism.[62] China was heavily involved in the consultations and was instrumental in getting North Korea aboard. China's support infused new momentum in the process, as it was the only country that had good relations with all parties. Following several preliminary talks in New York City, the first formal quadrilateral talk was held in Geneva in December 1997. The four parties met again in Geneva in March 1998, and the focus of the discussion shifted from procedure matters to substantive matters. Although no substantial progress has been made so far,[63] a multilateral framework of negotiation has been put in place. The multilateral diplomacy in turn promoted bilateral dialogue between the two Koreas. During the Geneva talks in March 1998, North

Korea indicated that it was willing to resume direct official talks, suspended since 1994. Talk at the vice foreign minister–level was held in Beijing in April 1998.[64]

New Modes of Security Cooperation

China's conception and practice of regional multilateral security in recent years have gradually evolved into the so-called new thinking or new model of security cooperation. In April 1996 China signed an agreement on military confidence-building in the region between China and Russia and other three Central Asian republics to create a stable and peaceful border of 7,000 kilometers. All sides committed to a series of military confidence-building measures in the border area. This is an interesting experiment of combining bilateral and multilateral diplomacy. The Chinese official newspaper praised the document as the first of its kind in the Asia-Pacific region in terms of multilateral peace and security.[65] Foreign Minister Qian cited the agreement, together with the quadrilateral talks on the Korean Peninsula and ARF, as examples of "new models of security cooperation."[66]

Although the definition and content of this new model of security cooperation need more conceptualization and elaboration, some main features have emerged from the Chinese articulation. First, this model features "equal participation and negotiated consensus."[67] As with economic multilateralism, China prefers APEC-style security multilateralism, characterized by weak institutionalization and informal dialogue, and based on a combination of the collective guidance and voluntary action of individual members.[68] China is interested only in informal and multilevel security consultations and dialogues, including bilateral, subregional, and regional mechanisms. At this stage, Beijing does not see a need to install a cross-regional and institutionalized security regime. For that reason, China opposed the idea of turning APEC into a highly institutionalized political structure for Asia-Pacific security.

Second, the new mechanism of security cooperation in the Asia-Pacific should not be based on any bilateral or multilateral military alliance. Beijing argued that military alliances or blocs were the residuals of the Cold War and that they should be abandoned given post–Cold War circumstances, as countries in the region no longer faced a common threat or enemy. As Foreign Minister Qian put it, the purpose of multilateral security arrangements such as ARF is "not to defuse a common threat, but rather to achieve a common goal; that is, regional peace and stability."[69] Therefore, China strongly opposed any effort to strengthen military alliances resulting from the Cold War confrontation. According to Beijing, "Security systems based on military alliances and arms competition have been unable to ensure peace. Expanding military blocs and enhancing military alliances under new circumstances can do little to bring about greater security."[70] For that reason, the U.S. policy of expanding NATO as well as consolidating the U.S.-Japanese security alliance were perceived as a reflection of "Cold War mentality." In the Asia-Pacific, then, multilateral diplomacy as embodied in China's cooperation with ASEAN is perceived as leverage to offset the influence of the bilateral security alliance between the United States and Japan.[71]

Third, economic security should be the priority of regional security cooperation because economic growth and common prosperity are the material bases for regional and global security. At the annual ARF meeting in July 1998, newly appointed Chinese Foreign Minister Tang Jiaxuan pointed out that the East Asian financial crisis had caused such tremendous damage that it was as destructive as a war. It fully indicated that economic security "has increasingly become an inseparable part of national or regional stability."[72] Multilateral security regimes such as ARF therefore should take measures to safeguard economic security, such as strengthening supervision over and taking strict precautions against excessive financial speculation.

The effort to conceptualize a "new model" for security cooperation indicates that Beijing has attached more strategic importance to regional multilateral security. Consistent with this perceptual change, China has become more and more receptive to the idea of multilateral consultation and cooperation on security issues. Besides ARF and CSCAP, China has participated in other major mechanisms of security consultation in the region, including the Conference on Interaction and Confidence-Building Measures in Asia (CICA) and the Northeast Asia Cooperation Dialogue (NEACD).[73] During Chinese Premier Li Peng's visit to Japan in November 1997, a former Japanese prime minister, Yasuhiro Nakasone, proposed "a new framework for political talks among leaders of four powers (Japan, China, the United States, and Russia) to promote stability and peace in the Asia-Pacific region. Although Li did not immediately commit himself to the plan, he nevertheless thought it was an extremely important issue that deserved serious consideration.[74] As mentioned earlier, Chinese Pres. Jiang Zemin attended the historic multilateral talks among ASEAN, China, Japan, and South Korea (the so-called 9+3) as well as those between ASEAN and China (9+1) in December 1997. This was the first time that the countries of Northeast Asia and Southeast Asia got together to discuss various issues, including security, indicating an enlargement of the security dialogue in the region. Such 9+3 and 9+1 summit meetings were held again in December 1998. China's Vice President Hu Jintao attended the meetings. One reason that China was enthusiastic about the summit is that outside powers such as the United States were not included, signaling a more indigenous framework of multilateral security consultation. In addition, recent developments in the region, including the East Asian finan-

cial crisis and the South Asian nuclear crisis, further enhanced China's influence and its sense of urgency for regional security consultations.[75]

CONCLUSION

China's perception and practice of multilateral diplomacy and collective
security have been evolving at both the global and regional levels. The evolution reflects some value and conceptual changes as well as behavioral
adaptation to the changing international environment. This process constitutes one way in which China has gradually integrated itself into the international community.

Compared to China's diplomacy during the 1970s and early 1980s,
there is no doubt that multilateralism and collective security have increased in legitimacy and weight in China's post–Cold War foreign policy
thinking and behavior. Behind the change are some new understandings
of international relations. First, since the late 1980s, Chinese leaders and
elites increasingly have accepted the fact that the world in which China
exists is characterized by a high degree of interdependence, not just in
economic terms but also in security terms. Consequently, "one country's
security is closely related with other countries' interests."[76] In such a world
of interdependence, traditional bilateral diplomacy is not sufficient to
handle issues that can be effectively addressed only multilaterally. Second,
from the very beginning, China was uncomfortable with the prospect of a
unipolar world in which the United States dominates the agenda of world
politics. China sees such a situation as transitional in nature and believes
that the world will inevitably move from the unipolar structure to a multipolar structure. Normatively China regards a multipolar world as more desirable, safer, and fairer. One important thrust of China's diplomacy in recent years has been to speed up the advent of a multipolar structure in
world politics. In such a world, China would contend that bilateral or exclusive multilateral political and military blocs or alliances are obsolete.
Correspondingly, more open and inclusive multilateral economic, political, and security frameworks should be established. China has realized
that it is only natural that a world with a high degree of functional interdependence and strategic multipolarity will be accompanied by a new
mode of multilateralism. In other words, multipolarization and multilateralism are closely linked and compatible.[77] For instance, China's support of
ASEAN is partially because the role of ASEAN and the "ASEAN way" reflect "the trend of global multipolarization."[78]

Although China is not yet a full-fledged global power, with its remarkable rising as a major economic and military force in the Asia-Pacific region China has been paying more attention to multilateral diplomacy for
two reasons. First, as China's power increases, it has become more confi-

dent that it cannot sit by and be acted upon but rather is able and should take advantage of multilateral diplomacy. In the past, China was passive in this regard largely because it was weak and often the target. Even in the midst of the Tiananmen crisis, when Deng Xiaoping warned that China should never take the lead in international affairs, he also declared that by any standard China is a pole and that China has to "do something" in international affairs.[79] China's proactive diplomacy in recent years, particularly in 1997, has indicated that Beijing wants to have its say in shaping the post–Cold War international order. Second, the phenomenon of China as a rising power also raised international concerns as to Beijing's intentions and behavior. To convince the world that it means to join rather than to disrupt the existing international system, China must explain and sell its foreign policy, not just in the bilateral setting but also in the multilateral setting. China's increasingly receptive attitude toward the idea of multilateral consultation on security issues indicates this conceptual change.

Yet China considers national sovereignty and noninterference in internal affairs as the highest principle of international relations. To the extent that China can embrace multilateralism, it has to be based upon respect rather than disregard for national sovereignty. China insists that collective security measures can only go as far as concerned nations or parties are willing to accept them. As a rule of thumb, collective security should not be militarized, functioning only as a supplement to political solutions to international conflicts. Some sensitive issues, such as national unification and territorial disputes, should basically be exempt from the multilateral scrutiny. Although nonsovereign entities or players could be involved in economic multilateralism, security is the taboo reserved only for sovereign nation-states. In addition, China believes that collective multilateralism should not be used as a disguise for undue influence of one or two major powers. Under no circumstances should multilateral security be applied as a panacea. Particularly as applied to internal conflicts, collective security, such as UN peacekeeping operations, can accomplish little. As one Chinese commentator remarked: "Cooperative security does not mean the collective interference in international disputes to seek a complete settlement to all security issues."[80]

In China's own practice, bilateral diplomacy still has a higher priority. Beijing believes that a meaningful multilateralism can be based only on good bilateral relations, particularly among major powers. In the Asia-Pacific region, for instance, China considers the bilateral relations between China and the United States, China and Japan, and the United States and Japan—the so-called New Triangle—the key to maintaining peace and stability in the region.[81] China's practice of multilateral diplomacy also shows a tendency for being selective and utility-oriented. Although Beijing puts more value on bilateral diplomacy, it could use the multilateral approach to offset other bilateral arrangements. Beijing often criticizes other countries that use multilateral diplomacy to realize unilateral foreign policy goals, but it spares no effort to take unilateral actions to safeguard its own national interest at the expense of collective security.

In the future, multilateral diplomacy obviously will become an increasingly important instrument of Chinese foreign policy. China no longer objects to collective security for its own sake. However, at this stage, the multilateralism China embraces most, particularly in the domain of security, is "nominal" rather than "qualitative" multilateralism.[82] The challenges for Beijing lie in two aspects. The first is how it will balance its responsibility and rights as a major power, its foreign policy priorities, and concerns within the international community as to UN multilateral diplomacy. The second is how to become more sensitive to the multilateral security implication of its vital national interests in issues such as Taiwan and the South China Sea. The economic meltdown in Asia since 1997 has doubtless enhanced China's wherewithals to have its way as well as multilateral diplomacy.

NOTES

1. A. Leroy Bennett, *International Organization: Principles and Issues* (Englewood Cliffs, N.J.: Prentice Hall, 1995), 176; Karen A. Mingst and Margaret P. Karns, *The United Nations in the Post–Cold War Era*, (Boulder, Colo.: Westview, 1995), 65.

2. "United Nations Peace-keeping" and "UN Peace-keeping: some questions and answers," The United Nations Department of Public Information (DPI), United Nations Headquarters internet homepage.

3. Samuel S. Kim, *China, the United Nations, and World Order* (Princeton: Princeton University Press, 1979), 209.

4. Ibid., 219, 232.

5. Bennett, *International Organizations*, 100.

6. Han Lianlong et al., eds., *Dangdai zhongguo waijiao (Contemporary China's Diplomacy)* (Beijing: Zhongguo shehui kexue chubanshe, 1987), 384.

7. Ibid., 384.

8. Wang Baoliu, "UN faces arduous task," *Beijing Review* (July 31–August 6, 1995): 16–17.

9. "Qian Qichen Delivered a Speech at the UN Conference," *People's Daily*, 28 September 1995.

10. Samuel S. Kim, "China's International Organizational Behaviour," in Thomas Robinson and David Shampaugh, eds. *Chinese Foreign Policy: Theory and Practice* (Oxford: Clarendon Press, 1994), 421.

11. Han Lianlong et al., *Contemporary China's Diplomacy*, 385.

12. Xiao Yu, "China and UN peacekeeping operations," *Beijing Review* (October 2–8, 1995): 16.

13. These operations include the United Nations Truce Supervision Organization (UNTSO) in the Middle East, United Nations Iraq-Kuwait Observation Mission (UNIKOM), United Nations Mission for the Referendum in Western Sahara (MINURSO), United Nations Transitional Authority in Cambodia (UNTAC),

United Nations Operation in Mozambique (ONUMOZ), and United Nations Observer Mission in Liberia (UNOMIL). *White Paper on China's National Defense, People's Daily,* 28 July 1998.

14. For a detailed analysis of peacekeeping operations in Cambodia, see Jianwei Wang, *Managing Arms in Peace Processes: Cambodia* (United Nations: United Nations Institution for Disarmament Research, 1996).

15. Yashshi Akashi, "The Challenges Faced by UNTAC," *Japan Review of International Affairs* (Summer 1993): 187.

16. Xiao Yu, "China and UN Peace-keeping Operations," 16–17.

17. Ibid., 19.

18. Trevor Findlay, *Cambodia: The Legacy and Lessons of UNTAC,* SIPRI Research Report No. 9 (Stockholm: Stockholm International Peace Research Institute, 1995), 87–88.

19. *UN Chronicle* (March 1993), 25.

20. In other words, in Chinese eyes, there is a clear boundary between "peace-keeping" and "peace-enforcing." Under most circumstances, UN peacekeeping operations should not involve peace-enforcing. Sun Wei, "'Peace-keeping' or 'Peace-enforcing,'" *Beijing Review* (July 24–30, 1995): 20.

21. John Tesitore and Susan Woolfson, eds., *A Global Agenda: Issues Before the 50th General Assembly of the United Nations, 1995–1996* (Lanham, Md.: Rowman & Littlefield, 1995), 32.

22. "Foreign Ministry News Briefings," *Beijing Review* (December 1–7, 1997): 9; (December 8–14, 1997): 8.

23. *The China Press,* 7 March 1998.

24. *People's Daily,* 11 November 1997.

25. Tesitore and Woolfson, *A Global Agenda,* 33.

26. *People's Daily,* 28 September 1995.

27. *White Paper on China's National Defense.*

28. *People's Daily,* 14 April 1997.

29. "China Will Never Allow Other Countries to Interfere in Its Internal Affairs," *Selected Works of Deng Xiaoping,* vol. 3 (Beijing: August 1st Press, 1993), 360.

30. Tesitore and Woolfson, *A Global Agenda,* 29–30.

31. John M Goshko, "China Vetoes Use of UN Personnel to Supervise Peace Agreement in Guatemala," *Washington Post,* 11 January 1997.

32. As a part of the deal, Guatemala refused to participate in or jointly sign the bill to put Taiwan's return to the United Nations on the agenda of the fifty-second UN General Assembly meeting. "Foreign Ministry News Briefings," *Beijing Review* (October 6–12, 1997): 9.

33. John Tessitore and Susan Woolfson, eds. *A Global Agenda: Issues Before the 52nd General Assembly of the United Nations, 1997–1998* (Lanham, Md.: Rowman & Littlefield, 1997), 27.

34. "Prospects for new Asian-Pacific political order," Foreign Broadcast Information Service, JPRS-CAR-91–030, 30 May 1991, 3.

35. China participated in most of the track-II discussions, but Chinese representatives did more listening than talking. Their attitude was neither hostile nor enthusiastic, merely passive. See Susan Shirk, "Chinese Views on Asia-Pacific Regional Security Cooperation," *Analysis* (National Bureau of Asian Research) 5, no. 5 (1994): 7.

36. Xuetong Yan, "China's Regional Policy," paper for the Association of Chinese Political Science (ACPS) annual meeting, Honolulu, 3–5 July 1994, 2; Guo Zhenyuan, "Asian-Pacific Region Remains Peaceful," *Beijing Review* (5–11 February 1996): 13.

37. Xuetong Yan, "China's Regional Policy," 3.

38. Ibid.

39. Guo Zhenyuan, "Asian-Pacific Region Remains Peaceful," 13.

40. "The Political and Economic Situation China Is Facing in the Asia-Pacific," in *Zhongkuo Waijiao (China's Foreign Affairs)*, Chinese Renmin University Social Sciences Information Center, 8–23, 1995.

41. Susan Shirk, "Chinese Views on Asia-Pacific Regional Security Cooperation," 11–12.

42. Paul Evans, "The New Multilateralism in the Asia-Pacific and the Conditional Engagement of China," in *Weaving the Net: Conditional Engagement with China,* James Shinn, ed. (New York: Council on Foreign Relations, 1996), 252.

43. Ren Xin, "Sino-ASEAN Relations Enter New Stage," *Beijing Review* (19–25 August 1996): 10.

44. *People's Daily,* 28 February 1997.

45. Jiang Zemin, "Towards a Good-Neighboring Partnership of Mutual Trust Oriented to the Twenty-First Century," *Beijing Review* (5–11 January 1998): 10.

46. *White Paper on China's National Defense.*

47. *People's Daily,* 12 June 1996.

48. Murray Hiebert, "All for One," *Far Eastern Economic Review,* 7 August 1997, 26.

49. Harry Harding, "International Order and Organization in the Asia-Pacific Region," in *East Asia in Transition: Toward a New Regional Order,* Rober Ross, ed. (Armonk, N.Y.: M. E. Sharpe, 1995), 343.

50. Paul Evans, "The New Multilateralism," 261.

51. *China Times,* 13 September 1996.

52. "Dialogue Key to Peace, Prosperity," *Beijing Review* (12–18 August 1996): 6.

53. *White Paper on China's National Defense.*

54. "The Political and Economic Situation China Is Facing in the Asia-Pacific," in *Zhongkuo Waijiao (China's Foreign Affairs)*, China Renmin University Social Sciences Information Center, 8–25, 1995.

55. "Dialogue Key to Peace, Prosperity," 6.

56. *People's Daily,* 25 October 1997.

57. *People's Daily,* 12 August 1997.

58. Michael Vatikiotis, "Friends and Fears," *Far Eastern Economic Review,* 8 May 1997, 15.

59. Michael Vatikiotis, "Big Squeeze," *Far Eastern Economic Review,* 13 June 1997, 12–13.

60. *People's Daily* (overseas ed.), 16 December 1997.

61. Nigel Holloway, "Appointment in Beijing," *Far Eastern Economic Review,* 13 June 1996, 15.

62. "Foreign Ministry News Briefings," *Beijing Review* (28 July–3 August 1997): 8.

63. The talk was deadlocked because North Korea demanded that the agenda include discussion of withdrawal of U.S. troops and the signing of a peace agreement between Pyongyang and Washington; the United States refused. "North Korea Blames U.S. for Problems," Associated Press, 24 March 1998.

64. Gu Zhenqiu, "To Seek Permanent Peace," *People's Daily,* 7 April 1998.

65. *People's Daily,* 27 April 1996.

66. "Qian Addresses 52nd Session of UN Assembly," *Beijing* Review (20–26 October 1997): 7.

67. Ibid.

68. *People's Daily,* 23 November 1996.

69. "Forum Urged to Focus on Peace, Security," *Beijing Review* (11–17 August 1997): 4.

70. "Qian Addresses 52nd Session of UN Assembly," 7.

71. Tang Tianri, "The New Model of Security Cooperation," *Outlook,* no. 31 (1997): 44.

72. "Full Text of Chinese FM's Address at ARF," Xinhua, 27 July 1998.

73. *White Paper on China's National Defense.*

74. *Hong Kong Standard,* 12 November 1997.

75. "Full Text of Chinese FM's Address at ARF," Xinhua, 27 July 1998.

76. A Ying, "New Security Mechanism Needed for Asian-Pacific Region," *Beijing Review* (18–24 August 1997): 6; Tang Tianri, "The New Model of Security Cooperation," 44.

77. The Chinese foreign ministry spokesman pointed out that the world is moving toward the direction of multipolarity. Accordingly, countries should beef up multilateral consultation and communication at various levels. *China Press,* 14 November 1997; *Beijing Review,* (22–28 December 1997): 14.

78. *People's Daily,* 8 August 1997.

79. "International Situation and Economic Issues" and "Seize the Opportunity to Develop the Economy," *Selected Works of Deng Xiaoping,* vol. 3, 353, 363.

80. A Ying, "New Security Mechanism Needed for Asian-Pacific Region," 6.

81. "China Once Again Asks Japan to Clarify the U.S.-Japan Defense Guidelines," *China Press,* 21 January 1998.

82. John Ruggie differentiates between *nominal* and *qualitative* multilateralism. The former is based on a definition employed by Robert Keohane, which points to "the practice of co-ordinating national policies in groups of three or more states." The latter is an institutional form that coordinates relations among three or more states on the basis of "generalized" principles of conduct. See John Gerard Ruggie, "Multilateralism: The Anatomy of an Institution," *International Organization* 46, no. 3 (Summer 1992): 561–598.

5

Human Rights and Democracy

Ming Wan

N o issue in Sino-American relations invokes as much condemnation and indignation as does human rights. At stake, however, are much more than moral concerns and hurt national feelings. As pointed out by Richard H. Solomon, assistant secretary of state for East Asian and Pacific Affairs during the Bush administration, human rights is a "deal breaker" between China and the United States.[1] To many Americans, the Chinese government is ultimately untrustworthy, as it is undemocratic. To the Chinese government, U.S. human rights pressure compromises its legitimacy, thus casting a different light on what might be called "normal" disputes in international relations, such as trade, arms sales, and intellectual property rights.

This chapter discusses Chinese views on human rights and democracy. When we discuss China's views, we need to answer a crucial question: Whose views in China are we talking about? Western attention has mainly focused on the Chinese government's declared policies and Chinese dissidents' opinions. Policy prescriptions and media commentaries are too often based on a simplistic view of China, where a repressive communist government is ruthlessly preventing a society of aspiring democrats, represented by courageous human rights fighters like Wei Jingsheng, from achieving well deserved civil and political rights. America's finger-pointing and diplomatic pressure, however, have led to little perceived progress in China. Human rights intervention rarely yields immediate results when target countries, especially major powers such as China, put up strong resistance. But a lack of understanding of political and social developments in

China contributes to misjudgments about the timing and degree of pressure on China. China specialists in the United States have illustrated the scope and complexity of the rapid economic, social, and political transformations in China, but their scholarship has yet to have a noticeable impact on the media and the public. The media have seized upon human rights as the focus of their coverage on China. The intense, negative coverage of China has shaped and fed off the negative public perceptions of the country. Such negative publicity and public sentiment constrain the willingness and ability of the U.S. government to promote a better relationship with China.

What has been missing in the public debate in the United States is the Chinese voice. The American public hears propaganda by the Chinese government and effective sound bites by Chinese dissidents. But not many people know or even care what "the silent Chinese majority" thinks. The silent Chinese majority is actually quite vocal in its own circles and is strongly opinionated about China and the U.S. policy toward China. To understand the feasibility and desirability of human rights pressure on China, one needs to know Chinese perspectives, not only those of the government and dissidents but also those of the society at large.

This chapter includes four sections. The first two sections discuss the views on human rights and democracy held by the Chinese state and Chinese society since the late 1980s, when China came under greater Western pressure. My main goal is to present Chinese views as objectively as possible. This is a difficult task, because Chinese views on human rights and democracy are increasingly diverse, not only among the government, society, and dissidents but also within each of these three broad categories. Chinese views are also evolving in view of changing domestic and external circumstances. To a lesser extent, I critique Chinese views where necessary. Although Chinese views are realities that prudent policymakers should recognize, like them or not, it is important to reflect on their efficacy.

The third section examines the complex relationships between the government and society. The 1989 Tiananmen Incident polarized the government and residents in major cities. But important developments have taken place since then. A broad developmentalist consensus between the government and society has emerged, emphasizing stability as a precondition for economic development. China's concerns for stability and growth condition its gradualist, cautious, even suspicious views on human rights and democracy.

The concluding section highlights the implications of this discussion for Sino-American relations. Given the views held by ordinary Chinese and the current relationship between the government and society, human rights has become largely a foreign policy issue for a majority of Chinese. Human rights in China will remain an issue in the United States due to

American political traditions and domestic politics, a fact of life acknowledged and increasingly understood by China. But if the U.S. government goes beyond a baseline of just speaking up about human rights issues and instead imposes severe pressure on China over human rights or makes explicit linkage with other issues, such policies now find an unresponsive Chinese audience and invite nationalist reactions. An interventionist policy works only when the society of the target nation seeks and appreciates such intervention. But there does not exist a broad support base in China at this historical moment for U.S. human rights intervention and pressure.

OFFICIAL CHINA ON HUMAN RIGHTS AND DEMOCRACY

Evolution of Government Views on Human Rights and Democracy

As Hungdah Chiu noted, not a single article devoted exclusively to human rights was published in China before Mao Zedong's death in 1976.[2] The Chinese government's engagement in human rights dialogue with the outside world started with the reforms of 1978. Ironically, Western scrutiny of China's human rights situations intensified just as China started making progress in this area.

The Information Office of the State Council has issued fifteen white papers (listed below) since November 1991, and nine of these deal with human rights. Three of the nine discuss human rights in general, and all three cover similar issues, thereby shedding light on change in government views in the 1990s.

> *Human Rights in China* (November 1991)
> *Criminal Reform in China* (August 1992)
> *Tibet—Its Ownership and Human Rights Situation* (September 1992)
> *The Taiwan Question and Reunification of China* (August 1993)
> *The Situation of Chinese Women* (June 1994)
> *Intellectual Property Protection in China* (June 1994)
> *Family Planning in China* (August 1995)
> *China: Arms Control and Disarmament* (November 1995)
> *The Progress of Human Rights in China* (December 1995)
> *The Situation of Children in China* (April 1996)
> *Environmental Protection in China* (June 1996)
> *The Grain Issue in China* (October 1996)
> *On Sino-U.S. Trade Balance* (March 1997)
> *Progress in China's Human Rights Cause in 1996* (March 1997)
> *Freedom of Religious Belief in China* (October 1997)

The general human rights white papers treat rights to subsistence and development as taking precedence over civil and political rights in China's current situation. Economic rights are therefore listed first in all these documents. The 1991 white paper maintains that "the right to subsistence is the most important of all human rights, without which the other rights are out of the question." It also begins with a six-paragraph discussion of imperialist aggressions against China, which are regarded as a gross violation of national rights and individual human rights of the Chinese. The 1995 white paper toned down the antiimperialist theme and summarized past Chinese humiliation in a single sentence. Instead, the paper highlights China's rapid economic growth, rising incomes for rural and urban residents, the declining mortality rate, and government efforts to assist the poor. The 1997 white paper follows the format of the 1995 document and focuses on China's economic performance in 1996.

The three documents discuss China's political and civil rights after economic rights. Similar to its discussion of economic rights, the 1991 document first comments that the Chinese "did not have any democratic rights to speak of in semi-feudal, semi-colonial China" and that they "gained real democratic rights after the founding of New China." It emphasizes the Chinese constitution, the people's congresses at all levels, and multiparty cooperation led by the Communist Party. The following two white papers omit the historical discussion. The 1995 paper discusses the Administrative Procedural Law of 1990 and the State Compensation Law of 1994, which have given citizens more rights against arbitrary state actions. The 1997 paper highlights laws passed during the previous year that give further protection to citizens. Both papers discuss grassroots democracy. In particular, the 1997 paper details how local elections have become more democratic. "All the overseas people who have no prejudice but have a good understanding of China's actual situation have fully acknowledged the building of democracy at grassroots levels in China," the paper concludes.

The arguments in the three documents are echoed in speeches, statements, and publications of party and government organs. In addition, the Chinese government has established some "nongovernmental" research centers on human rights, such as the China Society for Human Rights Studies, founded in 1993. Much writing on human rights has been produced by these agencies and groups. Based on one estimate, some five hundred articles appeared in newspapers and journals in Beijing and other regions during the early 1990s.[3] There are also dozens of books on human rights.

These publications offer diverse views on human rights and democracy, but there are some general themes. A sample of the human rights articles in *Beijing Review,* an official English-language news magazine aimed at the foreign audience, reveals a few such themes.[4] There is denial of human rights problems in China at the beginning, then a protest against Western human rights pressure as interference in China's domestic affairs. Some authors claim that China indeed protects human rights. A favorite argument is that different countries have different situations. There has been much defense of China's policies in Tibet. An increasingly important theme is the preference for economic and social rights over civil and political rights. Some articles criticize human rights violations in the United States, especially after the 1992 Los Angeles riots, and point out contradictions in U.S. human rights policy. There is also criticism that the United States has used human rights as an instrument of power politics.

The volume of Chinese writing on human rights decreased for a time after U.S. Pres. Bill Clinton delinked human rights and China's most-favored-nation (MFN) trading status in May 1994. However, since the issue remains important in Sino-American relations, there is renewed interest in the topic in official Chinese media, which now take a more offensive approach. For example, in retaliation to a January 1996 Human Rights Watch report, which alleged that children in some Chinese orphanages have died of neglect and starvation, the Chinese government sponsored a commentary in *People's Daily* in February that criticized the conditions of children in the United States.[5] In another case, the China Society for Human Rights Studies authored a paper in March 1996 entitled "A Comparison of Human Rights in China with Those in the United States." This paper responds to the U.S. State Department's annual report and concludes that China is doing better than the United States in twenty-four areas. In a most recent case, a commentary titled "Ruthless Freedom" in *People's Daily* on September 4, 1997, blamed the Western media for Princess Diana's tragic death: "Diana became . . . the prey of news media, and Western 'press freedom' is doubtlessly the death sentinel."[6]

The published views of the government show considerable progress. The government no longer denies the importance of human rights and has accepted human rights in China as a legitimate issue for bilateral and multilateral dialogues (but not for sanctions or condemnation). More importantly, the country has improved human rights in a broad sense, thus giving some substance to government propaganda. Despite this improvement, however, Beijing's propaganda remains an instrument for the government to cover up existing human rights violations in the country. Whatever their positions on China, sophisticated analysts seldom base their views on the ineffective propaganda of the Chinese government.

Who Is the Chinese Government?

How should we read these Chinese human rights commentaries? It should be noted that the views of Chinese propaganda agencies do not automatically translate into state policies. The Chinese government is not a uniform body with the same views on human rights and democracy. There are two crucial cleavages in this area, one factional and the other institutional.

First, the contest of factions shapes the policy parameters for the government. It goes without saying that whether a relatively liberal or conservative faction dominates the top leadership has a decisive impact on what the government says and does regarding human rights and democracy.[7] The liberal faction has gradually lost out in the intraparty contest for power, with Hu Yaobang's dismissal in 1987, Zhao Ziyang's fall in 1989, and Qiao Shi's forced retirement from the Central Committee of the Communist Party in 1997. A decisive factor in the defeat of the liberal faction was Deng Xiaoping's insistence on promoting economic reform without political reform. Labeled "Deng Xiaoping theory," this pragmatism remains the guiding line for the current president, Jiang Zemin. A centrist, cautious, and pragmatic leadership prevailed at the Fifteenth Party Congress held in September 1997, the first of the post-Deng era. The new leadership will further economic reform but appears in no hurry to adopt any political reform that it considers destabilizing and disruptive to China's modernization. This sets limits on what the government will say and do in the area of human rights and democracy.

Second, in the Chinese configuration of power, the agencies directly involved in human rights issues are the Propaganda and Education (*xuanjiao*) system (*xitong*) and the Foreign Affairs system (*waishi xitong*).[8] The propaganda *xitong* serves as the mouthpiece of the party. The Central Propaganda Department of the Communist Party is the leading agency. Overseas propaganda is orchestrated by the Bureau of Overseas Propaganda. The white papers discussed earlier were the products of the bureau.[9] In contrast, the foreign affairs *xitong* is responsible for implementing China's foreign policy, including human rights diplomacy. The leading foreign affairs group was led by Prime Minister Li Peng until March 1998, with the Chinese Ministry of Foreign Affairs (MFA) as the key implementing organization. The functionaries in the two *xitongs* often come from different backgrounds; those in the foreign policy apparatus often majored in foreign languages and international relations, whereas those in the propaganda agencies mainly studied Chinese language, Chinese history, party history, and political theories.[10]

The propaganda and foreign affairs *xitongs* as parallel institutions are not well coordinated. Foreign policy bureaucrats generally ignore propaganda functionaries.[11] The UN Human Rights Division of the foreign ministry conducts its own research on human rights laws and treaties and has little contact with human rights scholars in universities or research institutes.[12] With the foreign affairs *xitong* charged with defending China's national interests, career diplomats consider it humiliating if China is condemned at the UN Human Rights Commission, regardless of their personal convictions. More than their counterparts in democratic nations, Chinese diplomats are interested in self-preservation, which means avoiding "diplomatic accidents" or diplomatic failures. As a result, the country's human rights diplomacy is actually much more pragmatic and flexible than government rhetoric would suggest.[13]

However, the two *xitongs* are connected at the top. The party leadership sets guidelines for both *xitongs* to coordinate what the government says and does. Although the propaganda *xitong* is at times more zealous than the party leadership, the rhetoric reflects the political environment in China, which conditions the country's foreign policy as well. Commentaries of the Xinhua News Agency or *People's Daily* and statements of the foreign ministry now sound strikingly similar, an indication of converging views on human rights and democracy among government officials.

The Chinese government's views on human rights and democracy are best represented by China's current leader, Jiang Zemin. His state visit to the United States (October 26–November 3, 1997) provided a rare opportunity for the outside world to hear his personal views on these issues. In an interview with *The Washington Post* on October 17 in preparation for the visit, Jiang made some off-the-record remarks about human rights, which he later gave permission to be published. He applied Einstein's theory of relativity to politics in that "democracy and human rights are relative concepts and not absolute and general." "One country's human rights situation cannot be separated from the actual conditions of that country," he argued. "Undoubtedly, there can be [diplomatic] discussion on the human rights issue, but I hope that the West understands that our primary issue is to assure that all Chinese people have adequate access to food and clothing."[14]

Jiang presented himself as an open-minded leader during his visit, but he sharply differed with his American hosts on human rights issues. The spontaneous exchange between Jiang and Clinton at a joint press conference on October 29 illustrated this well. In response to a reporter's question about the 1989 Tiananmen Incident, Jiang claimed that "the Communist Party of China and the Chinese government have long drawn the correct conclusion on this political disturbance, and facts have also proved that if a country with an over 1.2 billion population does not enjoy social and political stability, it cannot possibly have the situation of reform and opening-up that we are having today." Clinton responded that the Chinese government "is on the wrong side of history" on this issue. Jiang also held spirited debates over human rights with congressional leaders. The two presidents took their debate to Beijing during Clinton's reciprocal visit to China in summer 1998. Their joint news conference and Clinton's lecture at Beijing University were both broadcast live on Chinese television, an unprecedented move indicating the Chinese leadership's confidence in making public its differences on human rights and democracy with the Americans.

Jiang's statements on human rights and democracy were severely
criticized by human rights groups, the media, and congressional leaders.
But his views reflect the dominant view in the Chinese government.
What has emerged as a convergence point for most government and
party agencies is "developmental authoritarianism," which calls special
attention to China's national conditions (*guoqing*). According to this
view, stability is critical for achieving economic development as the
country's primary objective. Jiang said specifically in his speech at the
Fifteenth Party Congress in September 1997 that "without stability, nothing could be achieved."[15]

The government agencies not centrally involved with human rights
have more pressing issues at hand: to promote economic reform, avoid political turmoil, raise living standards for their districts or working units, and
promote their own careers. My field research in China and discussions with
Chinese cadres visiting the United States have repeatedly confirmed that
developmentalist concerns prevail among Chinese officials. As a typical example, a deputy head of a major state enterprise from a northern city who
visited the United States for the first time explained that provincial cadres
have all heard about human rights as an issue between China and the
United States but that it is not important for common folks, as there are
more urgent problems. Curious about the human rights situation in the
United States, he concluded during his visit that the United States is
blessed with tremendous natural resources, giving it leeway to allow greater
personal freedom than poorly endowed China; the Chinese should focus
on improving their living standards; and stability is important for economic growth, given China's unique conditions.[16] Such views are common
in the Chinese government.

There is certainly dissent within the party and the government. A former government official, for example, recently authored and distributed a
platform labeled "the democratic faction's program proposals," which
called for separation of the party from the government, elections for all
levels of government, freedom of the press and religion, autonomy for
Tibet, a reversal of the verdict on the 1989 Tiananmen demonstrations, introduction of a free market, and pro-Western foreign policy.[17] More liberal
views and policy prescriptions have challenged the party orthodoxy in the
past and will continue to do so in the future. It is my hope that such
healthy dissent will grow and become the mainstream view within the party
and the government. However, it is important to note that the author of
the reform proposals no longer works in the government and that no one
else signed the platform. An effective and coherent opposition force for
political reform in China will take time to emerge. Until then, we should
base analysis on the actual stage of political development in the country
rather than on wishful thinking.

"THE SILENT CHINESE MAJORITY"
ON HUMAN RIGHTS AND DEMOCRACY

It is difficult to know the opinions of ordinary Chinese in the absence of systematic national polls to allow time-series and cross-section analysis of public opinion. Since the views of the majority of the society are not easily heard, both the government and dissidents claim to represent Chinese society. The Chinese government routinely refers to itself as "the Chinese government and Chinese people." Such claims are challenged by dissidents. For example, Xiao Qiang, executive director of Human Rights in China, based in New York, commented that "the world rarely hears Chinese (or Tibetan) voices for democracy and human rights, because they have been totally suppressed by Jiang's government."[18] However, the fact that the voice of Chinese society is not heard does not necessarily mean that society shares the views of dissidents.

Observers outside China normally speculate based on anecdotal evidence and reasoning. More importantly, their assessments are often shaped by explosive media events like the 1989 Tiananmen Incident. As James D. Seymour observed, during the Tiananmen Square demonstrations "it became obvious that international human-rights principles, however poorly understood, found a receptive audience in China's city dwellers, who reject both ultraconservative and moderate conservative lines on this subject."[19] But the opinions expressed at moments of passion do not necessarily represent the views and calculations of the society under normal circumstances.

In this section I have pieced together a picture of Chinese society based on occasional opinion polls conducted in China in recent years as well as interviews and participation in seminars, conferences, and internet groups. This rough picture displays four interesting features about Chinese society.

First, the majority of Chinese now prefer social order and stability to freedom. Based on a survey conducted in Beijing in December 1995, Yang Zhong, Jie Chen, and John M. Scheb II found that fully 61.8 percent of those polled strongly agreed that they "would rather live in an orderly society than in a freer society which is prone to disruption"; another 33.8 percent agreed with the statement. Only 3.6 percent and 1.6 percent disagreed or strongly disagreed.[20] The survey question is based on the premise that freedom leads to instability, which is not necessarily true. The government clearly emphasizes such a connection to its own advantage. The phrasing of the question, therefore, may well have led to a high degree of support for order over freedom than an alternative phrasing may have. However, the notion that freedom may lead to instability strikes a cord among many ordinary Chinese, given their collective experience with past political experiments and turmoil. The answers to this question thus do illustrate considerable worry among ordinary Chinese about political change that promises greater freedom yet may also undermine stability. This relates to my next observation of Chinese society.

Second, Chinese are generally cautious toward political and economic change. The extraordinary political energy exhibited during the 1989 Tiananmen Incident illustrated the potential of Chinese society for political change. Under normal circumstances, however, although the Chinese majority support greater freedom as a matter of principle, they are not active politically. In the survey mentioned previously, about 90 percent of the Beijing residents interviewed favor or strongly favor political tolerance, a free press, and contested local elections. But 71.4 percent agreed or strongly agreed that "the well-being of the country is mainly dependent upon state leaders, not the masses," and 63.5 percent strongly agreed or agreed that "in general, I don't think I should argue with the authorities even though I believe my idea is correct." Ordinary Chinese also feel strong hesitation and caution even in the economic realm despite almost two decades of rapid economic transformations. Many urban Chinese still want to maintain certain elements of the planned economy. The same survey shows that only 33.1 percent of urban residents wanted a predominantly market economy; a mere 1.9 percent wanted a pure market economy. In contrast, 17.5 percent wanted a predominantly planned economy, and 26 percent wanted a mixed economy—half planned and half market. As the government is now focused on reform of state enterprises, resistance will come from conservatives as well as ordinary people.

Third, Chinese political culture still exhibits some undemocratic attributes that may create problems if the country underwent democratization now. Based on a national survey conducted in China in 1990, Andrew J. Nathan and Tianjian Shi identified potential difficulties in Chinese political culture for immediate democratization; compared with citizens in advanced nations, Chinese show lower levels of awareness of the government's impact on daily life, lower expectation of fair treatment from the government, and lower tolerance of ideas with which they disagree. Although educated Chinese score higher in perceived government impact and political tolerance than less-educated countrymen, they are still "substantially less likely to hold democratic orientations than people of the same educational levels elsewhere."[21] Caught in a catch–22, Chinese will find it difficult to acquire the attributes necessary for democratization in the absence of democratic experience.

Fourth, Chinese are becoming more individualistic, the young especially so.[22] They are also increasingly aware of their rights, property rights in particular. A poll conducted in 1994 in Beijing indicated that when presented with "stories" of rights violations an absolute majority of people were aware of their rights, with urban residents more informed than rural residents. Urban residents are more aware of property rights than rural residents.[23] Chinese are increasingly driven by economic interests in their behavior. In fact, Chinese society is more concerned about economic rights than about social and political rights. This pattern is illustrated by a project, the Social Development and Protection of Civil Rights in China, conducted by a Chinese research team during 1992–1995.[24] According to the team's field research, people are more concerned about property rights than about political and civil rights, whether they live in cities or the countryside, in advanced or backward regions. In the countryside especially, unless there is serious injury or assets are lost, people tolerate abuse despite private resentment.[25] This is shown in a nationwide survey the research team conducted. The first two questions in Table 5.1 are indirect questions about property rights. People are highly resentful if the fruits of their labor are seized by cadres. In contrast, almost one-third of those polled exhibit no resentment when someone enters their house without permission, an act that violates privacy. The table shows that people are even less assertive about their political rights.

A greater awareness of property rights will in the end lead to a greater awareness of political and civil rights among Chinese, as is indicated by the

TABLE 5.1 Awareness of Rights

Questions	No Resentment	Little Resentment	Some Resentment	Considerable Resentment
Some cadres receive income even though they do not work	13.40	13.25	21.66	26.26
State and collective assets go into the pockets of a small minority	12.12	10.96	15.71	23.19
Someone enters your house without permission	31.98	20.82	17.32	15.25
No opportunity to voice opinions on making of policy and law	51.36	17.87	15.96	7.84
Not knowing the background of candidates in election of people's delegates	36.48	17.23	19.01	14.81

SOURCE: Gao, "Zhongguo gongmin quanli yishi de yanjin", p. 44. Translation by the author of this chapter.

experiences in Taiwan and South Korea. But based on the evidence we have, this connection has yet to be made in China. In fact, according to the 1992–1995 national survey mentioned previously, 35–50 percent of those polled answer that rights for personal safety, election and dismissal of cadres, and not being abused in confinement are given by the state and government. Only 1–3 percent think people are born with these rights. Since the start of the reform, almost all new rights have been granted by the state. There have been few initiatives from below seeking greater rights.[26]

A powerful combination of aversion to political instability and awareness of economic interests and rights provides a fertile ground for developmentalist and instrumentalist views of human rights. This means that the focus for most Chinese is not the inherent value of democracy and human rights but what these concepts can do for their living standards and for the country. People are not convinced that human rights and democracy will necessarily improve daily life, given China's unique conditions. Such views are reinforced by general satisfaction among Chinese with their rising living standards, the country's rising power, and their wish to see a powerful and prosperous China. In addition, by looking at the former Soviet Union, many Chinese have drawn a negative conclusion about the wisdom of promoting democracy at all costs.

Such prevailing views among ordinary Chinese explain why human rights and democracy continue to be perceived as foreign concepts removed from daily life. The *Washington Post* published an article on the Chinese reaction to Jiang's October 1997 visit to the United States; a Beijing barber was quoted as saying that he did not care about U.S. pressure on human rights in China. "I live better, I eat better. The rest doesn't matter."[27] This is a common view among ordinary Chinese at this stage of political development. There has been a significant decrease in Chinese acceptance of U.S. pressure over human rights. This in part explains the confidence behind the Chinese leadership's decision to broadcast live Clinton's speech and the joint news conference during the 1998 summit. Given such a social and political environment in China, it is not surprising that U.S. pressure has contributed to rising nationalist sentiments in Chinese society.[28] What is striking about China today is the strong political conservatism combined with nationalist emotions, even among intellectuals. There are clear misperceptions about U.S. intentions toward China and about China's situation itself; the United States is not conspiring against China, and, even given China's current *guoqing*, a greater degree of liberalization will stabilize rather than destabilize the country. Yet the Chinese views I have discussed so far nonetheless condition policy debates and decisions in China and should be taken seriously by foreign analysts.

RELATIONS AMONG THE STATE, SOCIETY, AND DISSIDENTS

Contrary to the West's perception that the Chinese government is an illegitimate regime that has survived solely by coercion, there is now considerable public support in China for the government. As shown in Table 5.2, Jie Chen, Yang Zhong, and Jan William Hillard found strong popular support for the political regime in a public survey conducted in Beijing in December 1995.[29] In addition, it appears that popular support has grown. In a nationwide survey conducted by a team of American-trained Chinese scholars during 1986–1987, there was only "moderate" support for the political regime, even though support for the country was strong.[30] It is difficult to draw definite conclusions based on the two surveys, which followed different procedures. But the findings confirm rather than contradict personal observations that there is stronger public support for the government now than during the mid-1980s.

TABLE 5.2   Popular Support for the Political Regime

	Strongly Disagree % (#)	*Disagree* % (#)	*Agree* % (#)
1. I am proud to live under the current political (socialist) system	.9 (6)	3.7 (25)	41.6 (281)
2. I feel an obligation to support our current political system	.0 (0)	2.5 (17)	35.3 (238)
3. I respect the political institutions in China today	1.3 (9)	5.5 (37)	48.3 (325)
4. I think the basic rights of citizens are (relatively well) protected by the Chinese political system	1.9 (13)	11.4 (77)	62.8 (425)
5. (In general) I think the courts in China guarantee a fair trial	3.6 (24)	14.2 (95)	66.0 (443)
6. I believe that my personal values are the same as those (advocated by the government) of our political system	1.8 (12)	18.2 (122)	61.0 (408)

SOURCE: Chen, Zhong, and Hillard, "The Level and Sources of Popular Support for China's Current Political Regime," p. 49.

Dissidents play at most a marginal role in shaping China's political, economic, and social developments. Opinion polls have not posed specific questions about Chinese society's views on Chinese human rights and democracy advocates or groups. But anecdotal evidence suggests little support from ordinary Chinese citizens. Chinese democracy advocates have had difficulty forming associations with social groups like peasants and workers. An important reason for this is that they often take elitist attitudes toward ordinary Chinese, seeing themselves as pioneers of freedom in China while judging peasants as unable to understand democracy or militant workers as a threat to a functioning democratic system.[31]

We should pause here for a moment to question the validity of the survey results cited. Two objections might be made to these surveys. First, one might speculate that the Chinese respondents may be too afraid to give their true opinions. This is a common problem that pollsters are aware of when they conduct surveys in China. To alleviate people's fear of government retaliation, all answers are confidential. There has been no known case where the government has tracked down survey respondents for retaliation. Chen, Zhong, and Hillard argue that Chinese are much freer in their responses than is assumed by the Western media. This is in part due to the absence of government regulations on public survey research until 1997.[32]

The second possible objection is more serious: Chinese society's calculations and views are in part a reflection of the harsh political reality that the government has created in the first place. There is certainly not a level playing field between the government and dissidents. The party-government has forcibly prevented dissidents from presenting their views and alternative programs to ordinary Chinese. They have sent almost all leading dissidents either abroad or to prison, thus separating them from the larger society. Wei Jingsheng, who was expelled from China in November 1997, had resisted going abroad precisely to prevent diminishing his influence in China. While hoping that Wei will become the leader who unites a fragmented Chinese dissident community overseas, many people worry that he will be destroyed in factional infighting or lose his "value" in exile.[33]

More importantly, the government has monopolized the use of violence and financial benefits. On the one hand, the 1989 Tiananmen Incident was a reminder to Chinese society that the government is willing and able to use brutal force against citizens. On the other hand, the government possesses financial resources to benefit society. These sticks and carrots have distortional effects on the calculations of Chinese people, keeping them away from political protests and cooperation with dissidents. One may thus speculate that opinion polls and interviews might produce drastically different results if society was exposed to the views of dissidents. This is conceivable. But we should not exaggerate this possibility. After all, most

Chinese scholars in the United States offer considerable support for the Chinese government and largely accept the premise of developmentalism despite their exposure to alternative views and their strong objection to certain government policies. And Chinese dissidents have had only a limited impact on the political attitudes and behavior of Chinese students and scholars living and working overseas.

Chinese society's broad developmentalist and instrumentalist views on human rights and democracy provide a partial explanation for the growing popular support for the party-government and lack of support for dissidents. The society supports the state because it supports the state's goals of developing the national economy and building a strong nation and because it agrees that political stability is necessary to realize these objectives. Popular support rises when the nation makes progress in achieving these goals.

I want to point out, however, that the real story between the state and the society is much more complicated than the simple lineal relationship between popular support and shared goals. If we examine the nature of popular support, we see that society is supporting the government not because of a closer identification with the government but, paradoxically, because of its "distancing" from it. The society has not been thrilled with the government's performances in specific issue areas. Chen, Zhong, and Hillard found that the Chinese who were polled gave rather poor scores to government performance in a number of issue areas: controlling inflation, providing job security, minimizing the income gap, improving housing conditions, maintaining social order, providing adequate medical care, providing welfare to the needy, and combating pollution. A majority of respondents scored government performance as poor or only fair.[34] There is also no evidence that the people support the government based on blind faith in the party-state. Quite the contrary: There has been widespread distrust of the party-state. In the 1986–1987 national survey mentioned earlier, there was moderate support for the political system and goals of the party (average 62 percent approval rating), yet slightly more than half of the respondents actually opposed the party and officials. In fact, more than 80 percent of those polled claimed that party members are not good models.[35]

Such distancing between the society and the government is the inevitable result of reform. Reform is about adjusting the relationship between the state and society; it is about giving society the rights to engage in economic and commercial activities as they please. As economic reform deepens and widens, ordinary Chinese enjoy greater freedom in areas such as employment, travel, residence, and schooling. The party-state has retreated from one area after another, even though it has been stubborn in cracking down on any open and organized attempt at challenging its political leadership.

This distancing applies to all major social groups, which defend their self-interests against the state and other groups. In particular, we need to examine Chinese intellectuals, who are widely seen as the most enlightened group in China and the best hope for improving human rights and democracy. *Chinese intellectuals* refers to a loose group of college-educated professionals who may also take up positions of importance in the party and the government. Despite much persecution and suspicion by the party during the early years, Chinese intellectuals on the whole once strongly identified with the party and the state. But as Merle Goldman, Perry Link, and Su Wei point out, Chinese intellectuals during the Deng era came to be more identified with the society and the nation than with the party-state. But those authors also recognized that "the traditional concept of a political center (or 'heavenly authority')—which is implicitly 'higher' than the people, on which the people are dependent, and to which it is the highest calling of the scholar to offer advice and service—remains deeply embedded in China's political culture."[36] Merle Goldman commented separately that Chinese intellectuals "are undergoing a radical transformation, intellectually and economically, in their relationship with the state" and "may choose to be an independent force or an organized alternative, in alliance with other social groups, to the established government."[37]

Even more than intellectuals, Chinese farmers, who account for the majority of the Chinese population, have distanced themselves from the party-state. As Kate Xiao Zhou points out, Chinese farmers "did not self-consciously seek democracy. They sought more immediate, perhaps more far-reaching goals, such as family control of land use. But their modest seeking restored an open class system and laid a greater emphasis on decisionmaking by individuals."[38] Although Chinese farmers do not have much voice in a society where urbanites dominate, they are changing China in a fundamental way through their actions.[39] It is also in villages where direct elections have been held since 1988, when the National People's Congress passed the Organization Law of Villagers' Committees. The implementation of the law has been driven by popular demands. It is villagers who prevent township officials from controlling elections.[40]

It is precisely this distance between the party-state and society that is helping the party to maintain its leadership in the country. Consistent with its developmentalist views of human rights and democracy, Chinese society has adopted increasingly developmentalist and instrumentalist views toward the party and government, meaning that most Chinese citizens and intellectuals now see the party as a necessary evil for the common good during the daunting challenge of modernization. Lack of alternatives and aversion to chaos and instability also influence this way of thinking. Ironically, such a cynical view of the party and the state can serve to strengthen the basis for party control. Emotional attachment to the party-state generates a sense of disappointment and betrayal. In contrast, cynical and instrumental views keep some distance between the society and the party-state. Since the party-state is no longer interested in revolutionizing the society, it does not need to mobilize the society. For the society, cool calculations rather than affection condition their support for the state. Such an instrumentalist view of the government also means that the government needs to respond to societal needs to maintain its power.

The party understands that its existence is largely contingent upon its willingness and ability to address issues that are of immediate concern to the society. The government has responded, if not in a timely and exact fashion, to public concerns about issues such as inflation, crime, and corruption. Then Vice Prime Minister Zhu Rongji, who is now China's premier, brought down the inflation rate from almost 25 percent in 1994 to 2.8 percent in May 1997 while managing more than 9 percent annual growth. More importantly, food prices have also stabilized with heavy food subsidies from the government.[41] In 1996 the government also launched the "strike hard" campaign against violent crimes, which was welcomed by Chinese society but criticized by human rights groups for not following legal procedures.

Corruption is now a serious concern for ordinary Chinese. The government's performance is mixed in this area. Chen Xiaotong, the son of a former Beijing party chief, Chen Xitong, was sentenced to twelve years in prison in August 1997. His father was expelled from the party in September after he allegedly took $25 million in kickbacks for construction projects and stealing public funds; he lost his membership of the Politburo in April 1995 and was sentenced to sixteen years in prison in 1998. Another Beijing party official was sentenced to twelve years in prison for corruption in November 1997.

The government's biggest challenge in the coming years will be high unemployment. As calculated by Chinese scholar Hu Angang, China had 15.5 million unemployed workers in cities (an unemployment rate of 7.5 percent) in 1997 and 175 million surplus laborers in the countryside (an unemployment rate of 34.8 percent) in 1995.[42] As the party decided to reform failing state enterprises at the Fifteenth Party Congress, millions of workers will lose jobs, thus creating potentially serious social problems for the government.

The party-government increasingly turns to economic performance for legitimacy as well as for resolving practical issues. It is often suggested by Chinese scholars that China needs to develop at least a 7 percent gross national product (GNP) growth rate per year to prevent social chaos. But this is a very fragile foundation. The financial crisis in Asia, starting in 1997, does not bode well for China. The country has thus far been shielded from the crisis due to its relative insulation from the global financial market, its enormous foreign trade surplus, and its massive reserves. The Beijing government has shown considerable confidence in weathering the storm, but the country is likely to experience serious economic problems down the road, given its weak banking system, failing state enterprises, and growing competition from other Asian nations that have drastically devalued their currencies. Even a slowdown in economic growth, let alone a meltdown, will test the government's ability to govern.

Given all these challenges, the party-state is living dangerously. How the party-state adapts to these challenges will in part shape its own destiny: whether it is dumped into the dustbin of history or continues to dominate China's political development. It should also be recognized that precisely because of the society's instrumentalist view of the party-state, the party will inevitably face major challenges when the calculations of the society change either due to their enhanced political awareness or due to available alternatives.

CONCLUSION

This discussion of Chinese perspectives on human rights and democracy has important implications for Sino-U.S. relations. Although the United States has to act upon its own moral concerns and political interests, it is important to recognize how concerned the majority of Chinese are about human rights and democracy at a given period of time. One basic assumption in much writing about China is that the United States really represents Chinese society against a repressive government. This assumption provides legitimacy for U.S. intervention in China. But American concerns and the concerns of Chinese society do not always correspond. Although those concerns overlapped during 1989–1990, there is a divorce at the present, which explains why U.S. human rights policy has not worked and has contributed to rising nationalism. If the silent Chinese majority does not respond to Western pressure, such interventionist diplomacy is unwise; any pressure without support from ordinary Chinese will fail. The Chinese have the right to evolve morally on their own terms and at their own pace. Unless it has broad support from Chinese society, the United States will face a situation in which it tries "to save China from the Chinese."

NOTES

1. Richard H. Solomon, "Is the Door Nixon Opened Going to Close?" *Washington Post*, 16 February 1997, 3(C). He mentioned two such issues; the other issue is Taiwan.

2. Hungdah Chiu, "Chinese Attitudes Toward International Law of Human Rights in the Post-Mao Era," in *Chinese Politics from Mao to Deng*, Victor C. Falkenheim, ed. (New York: Paragon House, 1989), 239.

3. Yu Quanyu, "Ba renquan lilun yinxiang shenru" ("Furthering Human Rights Research"), which appears as the preface for the books in the Human Rights Book series by Liaoning renmin chubanshe (Liaoning People's Press) in 1994. The period covers a few years before the end of 1994.

4. This summary is based on twenty-six essays published in the magazine between mid-1989 and mid-1994.

5. "China Hits Condition of Children in U.S.," *Washington Post,* 23 February 1996, 8.

6. "China Paper Blames Death on Media," Associated Press, 4 September 1997.

7. Note that the term *liberal* is used in the context of Chinese elite politics. Hu, Zhao, and Qiao are more liberal-minded than other leaders in the party. They are, of course, not liberals by U.S. standards.

8. For a discussion of how the Chinese *xitongs* work, see Kenneth Lieberthal, *Governing China: From Revolution Through Reform* (New York: W. W. Norton, 1995), 192–207. In addition to the foreign affairs and propaganda *xitongs,* the political and legal affairs (*zhengfa*) *xitong* controls China's courts, prisons, and "reeducation through labor" camps. Its practices toward political dissidents, Christian priests, and Tibetan monks create international issues that the propaganda *xitong* has to defend and the foreign policy *xitong* has to resolve. But this chapter does not discuss China's judiciary system.

9. The Information Office of the State Council, set up in June 1991, is under the dual leadership of the State Council and the Central Propaganda Department. The officials in the office are from the propaganda *xitong.*

10. In recent years, as overseas propaganda becomes an increasingly important assignment, the propaganda *xitong* has also tapped into the same talent pool as the foreign affairs *xitong.*

11. In fact, Chinese diplomats sometimes complain that the propaganda agencies have performed poorly in creating a positive image for China, especially regarding Tibet. Discussion with a senior official of the Chinese Foreign Ministry, December 1997.

12. Author's interview with a senior official of the UN Human Rights Division of the Chinese Foreign Ministry, Beijing, May 1996.

13. For China's diplomatic efforts at defeating Western attempts to pass a resolution condemning China at the UN Human Rights Commission, see Human Rights Watch/Asia, "China: Chinese Diplomacy, Western Hypocrisy, and the U.N. Human Rights Commission," vol. 9, no. 3(C), March 1997.

14. *Washington Post,* 19 October 1997, 22(A).

15. Steven Mufson, "Jiang Opens Communist Congress with Calls for Change, Stability," *Washington Post,* 13 September 1997, 19(A), 22(A).

16. Author's interview, Washington, D.C., 9 November 1996.

17. Steven Mufson, "Former Chinese Official Advocates Democracy," *Washington Post,* 12 January 1998, A-13.

18. Xiao Qiang, "Let Freedom Ring in Beijing," *Washington Post,* 29 October 1997, 23(A).

19. James D. Seymour, "Human Rights in Chinese Foreign Relations," in *China and the World: Chinese Foreign Relations in the Post–Cold War Era,* Samuel S. Kim, ed. (Boulder, Colo.: Westview Press, 1994), 206.

20. Zhong Yang, Chen Jie, and John Scheb II, "Political Views from Below: A Survey of Beijing Residents," *PS: Political Science and Politics* 30, no. 3 (September 1997): 476. The survey was conducted in cooperation with the Public Opinion Research Institute of People's University. A total of seven hundred Beijing permanent residents were selected through random sampling procedures (response rate at 97 percent). Answers were anonymous.

21. Andrew J. Nathan and Tianjian Shi, "Cultural Requisites for Democracy in China: Findings from a Survey," in *China in Transition,* Tu Wei-ming, ed. (Cambridge: Harvard University Press, 1994), pp. 95–123.

22. Yongnian Zheng, "Development and Democracy: Are They Compatible in China?" *Political Science Quarterly* 109, no. 2 (Summer 1994): 241–242. He cites a survey conducted in China that was originally published in Shang Xiaoyuan, *Zhongguoren de ziwo yizhixing renge* (*The Chinese Self-Controlling Personality*) (Kunming: Yunnan renmin chubanshe, 1989).

23. Shi Xiuyin, "Zhongguo shehui zhuanxing shiqi de quanli yu quanli" ("Public Power and Rights During the Transformational Period in China"), in *Zouxiang quanli de shidai zhongguo gongmin quanli fazhan yanjiu (Towards An Era of Rights: Research on Development of Civil Rights in China),* Xia Yong, ed. (Beijing: Zhongguo zhengfa daxue chubanshe, 1995), 108–114.

24. See Xia Yong, *Towards an Era of Rights.* The research team conducted a survey in six provinces, with a sample of 6,000 (5,461 valid returns). The team also conducted field research in ten Chinese provinces and cities, with over 230 interviews.

25. Gao Hongjun, "Zhongguo gongmin quanli yishi de yanjin" ("The Awakening of Consciousness of Rights among Chinese Citizens"), in Xia Yong, *Towards an Era of Rights,* 43.

26. Ibid., 46–47.

27. Steven Mufson, "This Just In: Gosh, Everything's Swell," *Washington Post,* 31 October 1997, 20(A).

28. For China's popular image of the United States, see Ming Zhang's chapter in this book (Chapter 7, "Public Images of the United States").

29. Jie Chen, Yang Zhong, and Jan William Hillard, "The Level and Sources of Popular Support for China's Current Political Regime," *Communist and Post-Communist Studies* 30, no. 1 (1997): 45–64. The survey used for this article is the same as discussed in the article "Political Views from Below" by Zhong, Chen, and Scheb.

30. Cited in Alfred L. Chan and Paul Nesbitt-Larking, "Critical Citizenship and Civil Society in Contemporary China," *Canadian Journal of Political Science* 28, no. 2 (June/July 1995): 293–309.

31. Lei Guang, "Elusive Democracy: Conceptual Change and the Chinese Democracy Movement, 1978–1979 to 1989," *Modern China* 22, no. 4 (October 1996): 437–438; Andrew G. Walder and Gong Xiaoxia, "Workers in the Tiananmen Protest: The Politics of the Beijing Workers' Autonomous Federation," *Australian Journal of Chinese Affairs,* 29 (January 1993): 1–29; and Daniel Kelliher, "Keeping Democracy Safe from the Masses: Intellectuals and Elitism in the Chinese Protest Movement," *Comparative Politics* 25, no. 4 (1993): 379–396.

32. The Chinese government imposed restrictions on survey research in 1997. Now researchers need advanced government approval for the content of their surveys.

33. Tang Jie, "Weijingsheng ruhe zaixian yingxiong bense" ("How Can Wei Jingsheng Be a Hero Again?") *Shijie zhoukan (World Journal Weekly)*, 21 December 1997, 12. Wei himself has indicated that he wants to avoid the mistakes other Chinese dissidents in exile have made. "China: Exiled Wei Plans to Press Homeland on Human Rights," *Financial Times*, 12 January 1998.

34. Chen, Zhong, and Hillard, "The Level and Sources of Popular Support for China's Current Political Regime," 51.

35. Chan and Nesbitt-Larking, "Critical Citizenship and Civil Society in Contemporary China," 306.

36. Merle Goldman, Perry Link, and Su Wei, "China's Intellectuals in the Deng Era," in *China's Quest for National Identity*, Lowell Dittmer and Samuel S. Kim, eds. (Ithaca: Cornell University Press, 1993), 153.

37. Merle Goldman, "Politically-Engaged Intellectuals in the Deng-Jiang Era: A Changing Relationship with the Party-State," *China Quarterly*, no. 145 (March 1996): 51–52.

38. Kate Xiao Zhou, *How the Farmers Changed China: Power of the People* (Boulder, Colo.: Westview Press, 1996), 12.

39. For studies of Chinese peasants, also see Edward Friedman, Paul Pickowicz, and Mark Selden, *Chinese Village, Socialist State* (New Haven: Yale University Press, 1991).

40. Liangjiang Li, "Popular Demands for Village Elections in Rural China," *Human Rights Dialogue* (Carnegie Council on Ethics and International Affairs), vol. 9, June 1997, 9–11.

41. Steven Mufson, "China's 'Greenspan' Ends Perilous Economic Slide: By Curbing Inflation, Zhu Brings Social Calm," *Washington Post*, 21 August 1997, 1(A), 22(A).

42. Hu Angang, "Xunqiu xinde ruanzhaolu" ("Seeking a New Soft Landing"), *Liaowang (Outlook)*, no. 31 (1997): 12–13.

6

Nuclear Nonproliferation

Weixing Hu

China has moved up the learning curve on nuclear nonproliferation since it joined the Nuclear Nonproliferation Treaty (NPT) in 1992. Beijing's consciousness of nuclear proliferation risks has increased steadily in recent years, and its longtime mistrust and suspicion of the non-proliferation regime was replaced by a more cooperative policy toward international nonproliferation norms and rules. The policy change is not a short-term maneuver but stems from a major shift in Beijing's perception of the international NPT regime as well as its approaches to arms control and international security.

China's evolving policy toward the nonproliferation regime is a good example of how a modernizing country changes its foreign policy behavior to integrate into the existing international order. Beijing's policy shift can be explained by its reoriented foreign strategy as well as structural changes in world politics. Economic reforms and fast economic growth have redefined China's domestic politics and foreign policy agendas. Economic modernization makes China more interdependent with the outside world, creating constraints on its foreign conduct as well as incentives to adapt to the prevailing norms and rules of the international system. In enmeshing itself into the international system, China's domestic agendas and foreign policy goals become more interactive. The new pattern of domestic politics–foreign policy interaction has reshaped Beijing's attitude toward the NPT regime. In order to bring fast economic development to bear on foreign relations, Beijing has consciously changed its policy on nuclear nonproliferation and become more re-

sponsive to structural and normative changes in international nonproliferation regimes.

The degree of China's adjustment to the international nonproliferation regime is also closely related to its interface with major Western powers (especially the United States) over nuclear proliferation issues. As a
major inducer and enforcer for the NPT regime, Washington uses targeted
sanctions and other policy tools to solidify China's adherence to and compliance with nonproliferation rules and export controls. Although Washington's sanctions may not always work, they have had an important impact
on Beijing's perception and its cost-benefit calculation in terms of the NPT
regime.

The nonproliferation regime is a set of international norms, principles, rules, and legal obligations enshrined in the NPT and facilitated by
the International Atomic Energy Agency (IAEA) and the Nuclear Suppliers Group (NSG). The regime prohibits spreading nuclear materials, technology, and equipment that may lead to the processing and producing of
nuclear weapons. From the late 1950s to the 1970s, China was a radical
challenger to the superpower nuclear monopoly and the Western-dominated nonproliferation regime. Beijing rejected the 1963 Limited Test Ban
Treaty and the NPT on the grounds they were discriminatory and helped
maintain the superpower monopoly in nuclear affairs. From the mid-
1980s, when Beijing readjusted its foreign policy toward to a more pragmatic course, the longtime mistrust and suspicion of the nonproliferation
regime began to melt away. The Chinese consciousness of nuclear proliferation risks further mounted when China formally acceded to the NPT in
1992 after holding out for twenty years. Although declared nonproliferation policy does not warrant changes in nuclear export behavior, Beijing
began to learn and play by the international rules of nuclear export controls in recent years. In September 1997 China promulgated a new regulation on nuclear exports, a major step that brings its nuclear export controls close to the internationally accepted standard.[1] This chapter attempts
to explain why China has changed its policy on nuclear proliferation in recent years. It will focus on the domestic dynamism and external factors that
have caused China to learn the norms and rules of nuclear nonproliferation. The chapter also shows how learning can be used as an intervening
factor to explain Beijing's behavioral changes in nuclear export controls
and nonproliferation.

CHINA'S NUCLEAR LEARNING CURVE

Learning is a useful but ill-defined concept in explaining foreign policy
changes, and there has been a proliferating literature on learning and foreign policy changes in recent years.[2] For international relations scholars,

learning involves a major shift in world outlook and conception of international politics that may lead to new thinking on foreign policy goals and approaches to international problems. Learning occurs when policymakers use new information and knowledge to reconceptualize foreign policy goals and strategies to achieve these goals.

International relations scholars also distinguish learning from *policy adaptation*. The former refers to policy change caused by a shift in the central paradigm held by policymakers, whereas the latter indicates a policy change due to tactical adjustment to changes in international relations.[3] In the case of China's policy toward nuclear nonproliferation, it can be better explained in terms of learning rather than in terms of policy adaptation.[4]

The Chinese policy on nuclear nonproliferation evolved with the changes in its perception of nuclear weapons, its relations with superpowers, and its socialization with the nonproliferation institutions. Since Deng Xiaoping's pragmatic foreign policy during the late 1970s, Beijing's position on nuclear weapons and nonproliferation has become more realistic and conciliatory to the existing international regime. The defiant posture against the Western-dominated international norms and regimes on nuclear issues gradually disappeared. The self-righteous attitude was replaced by vigorous efforts to build an image of a responsive major power committed to playing a constructive role in promoting peace and stability in the world. On March 15, 1984, Premier Zhao Ziyang made a long overdue policy statement about the new thinking on nuclear nonproliferation at the National People's Congress. Zhao declared: "China is critical of the discriminatory treaty on the nonproliferation of nuclear weapons and has declined to accede to it. But we by no means favor nuclear proliferation, nor do we engage in such proliferation by helping other countries to develop nuclear weapons."[5] This was a major shift in China's declared nuclear policy. The Chinese government, for the first time, had publicly committed that it would not engage in nuclear proliferation (i.e., helping other states to develop nuclear weapons) or encourage other states to obtain nuclear weapons.

Beijing began to move up on the nuclear learning curve when its perception of nuclear weapons changed and its engagement in IAEA transformed its conception of nuclear nonproliferation. Based on an overall reassessment of the world strategic environment, Chinese leaders have realized that the growing danger of horizontal nuclear proliferation will erode China's security environment. Many Chinese policy analysts have privately argued that a greater number of nuclear states means a greater probability of nuclear war, that the pursuit of egalitarianism in international relations is at the expense of world stability and national security. Thus, preventing nuclear war and proliferation has become a universal norm for every country. Some even argued that the NPT is not discriminatory because both nuclear and nonnuclear weapons states share the same nonproliferation responsibility either by not transferring or not acquiring nuclear weapons.[6]

When considering Chinese nonproliferation policy, the regional security environment is another major factor. China may have assisted the Pakistani nuclear weapons program for reasons that include enhancing its leverage in dealing with Washington's arms sales to Taiwan, balancing an Indian nuclear arsenal, and supporting a long-standing ally. On balance, however, Chinese leaders have realized that nuclear proliferation to neighboring countries will degrade China's nuclear deterrent and complicate the security environment in Asia. Beijing does not want to see a nuclearized Taiwan, which would make reunification more complicated. That is why China insists on the continuation of IAEA safeguards on Taiwan's nuclear facilities. Moreover, it is not in China's interest to see Japan being provoked to acquire nuclear weapons by a North Korean bomb. In fact, North Korea's acquisition of nuclear weapons would be a policy disaster for Beijing. It would fuel Pyongyang's military adventurism, which might drag Beijing into a war it does not want.[7] Thus, it is in China's national interest to help stop or slow the nuclear arms race and proliferation.

China had held out from the NPT largely because of what Beijing argued was the "discriminatory" nature of the treaty. Beijing and Paris had shared a common stand, and each supported the other in holding out from the NPT. But the end of the Cold War transformed Beijing's attitude toward the nonproliferation regime as well as its overall outlook toward world politics. Consequently the psychological resistance to the NPT lessened, paving the way for Beijing to adjust its nuclear policy to be consistent with prevailing nonproliferation norms and principles. China's accession to the NPT in 1991 signified that China had finally embraced the nonproliferation regime after a long period of criticism. Technically, Beijing switched its policy on the NPT in 1991 due to a sudden policy shift by Paris. After the Tiananmen Incident in 1989, Beijing suffered a short period of isolation in its relations with major Western powers. A tattered international image and diplomatic isolation made Chinese leaders feel vulnerable to international pressure on international political and security issues. Angered by the bloody crackdown in Tiananmen, French Pres. François Mitterrand's socialist government broke away from the informal consultation with Beijing on arms control issues and suddenly announced France would accede to the NPT in 1991. This drastic move left China as the only holdout nuclear weapons state. This was the direct spur for Beijing's decision to join the NPT in 1991.

Although the jolting effect of the French move shouldn't be underestimated, China's learning on nuclear nonproliferation was nevertheless a highly complex process. It included what Charles Hermann calls "program changes" (i.e., changes in means by which the goal is addressed) as well as "problem/goal changes" (i.e., changes in the initial problem that policy addresses). It also took place in the process of "international orientation changes."[8] The policy change can be explained by system-level and national-level variables. International structural changes created new problems for China's national security policy and helped redefine the goal of Chinese nuclear policy. But the system-level variables alone are not sufficient to explain the policy change. We must explore China's domestic policy environment to determine the internal dynamics behind the foreign behavioral shift.

THE DOMESTIC SOURCES OF CHINA'S NUCLEAR LEARNING

To understand the substantial change in China's nonproliferation policy since the mid-1980s, we must look into the domestic context in which economic reforms restructured the policymaking process and reoriented Chinese foreign policy. Economic reforms make the boundary between internal agendas and foreign affairs increasingly blurry. The Chinese leadership must consider the domestic effects of foreign policy and the international repercussions of domestic policies. The change on nonproliferation policy does not result from a "change of mind" by one or a group of highest-ranking leaders of the Chinese Communist Party (CCP). Rather, it was driven by the need for international economic cooperation and the domestic bureaucracy advocacy. There are forces within the bureaucracy that feel compelled to adapt China's nonproliferation policy to the prevailing international standards. The entire government may not be seized with the need for change, but some bureaucratic sectors within the government have learned the international regime and advocated for policy redirection.

Economic reforms in China have created a strong domestic need for nuclear cooperation with Western countries. It is China's nuclear industry that became a driving force for a more cooperative stance with the nonproliferation regime. China's nuclear industry employs more than 300,000 workers, with full-spectrum capabilities in uranium mining, processing, metallurgy, fuel fabricating, enrichment, plutonium production, reprocessing, and weapons design. Before the 1980s, the nuclear industry was basically a military nuclear bomb program. Beijing spent tremendous money and built a substantial infrastructure for its bomb project. There were more than a dozen research and plutonium production reactors and a large community of nuclear scientists and engineers working on nuclear weapons. Yet China's civilian nuclear technology was quite underdeveloped, and not a single nuclear power plant had been built for thirty years by the time the Qinshan nuclear power project started in 1983.[9]

In the 1980s, when the military budget and state funding for the defense industry was sharply reduced, nuclear factories had an extremely hard time adjusting to the reduction of military orders, consequent shutdowns, and financial deficits. Conversion of the defense industries became the only way to cope with unemployment and factory closures. In March 1981, Zhang Aiping, then vice premier and the director of the Commission of Science, Technology, and Industry for National Defense (COSTIND), argued that the military nuclear program should integrate into the civilian nuclear industry and produce more civilian goods while keeping up military production. This later became the slogan "Integrate the military and the civilian; guarantee the military and convert to the civilian" (*Junmin Jiehe, Baojun Zhuanmin*).[10] The Ministry of Second Machine Building, in charge of nuclear weapons industry, was changed to the Ministry of Nuclear Industry (MNI) in 1982. Facing an enormous domestic demand for electricity, the new ministry was geared up to become the "second ministry of energy" and shift more resources to civilian nuclear power production under the new policy of *Baojun Zhuanmin* (which means that in terms of importance the largely defense-related nuclear industry must give military production the priority; but, given reducing military production orders, resource allocation must be skewed toward civilian production).[11] The priority of China's nuclear industry began to transform from weapons production to nuclear energy production. In order to push forward the defense industry conversion, the Central Military Commission decided in 1986 to release its control over former defense industry ministries (nuclear, aviation, ordnance, and space) to the State Council. The reorganization meant that the ministries no longer directly report to COSTIND, which administers them on behalf of the Central Military Commission. COSTIND's power was thus reduced to controlling the production and R&D of some high-technology weapons and providing policy guidance for defense industry.[12]

To build a civilian nuclear power industry, China needs advanced Western nuclear technology. And it is only through international cooperation that Beijing can get advanced civilian nuclear technology for its nuclear power programs. MNI was pushing hard within the government to join IAEA from the late 1970s, but the Ministry of Foreign Affairs (MFA) was indifferent and slow to establish a working relationship with IAEA due to a lack of staff with the technical expertise to understand the rules and regulations of IAEA's safeguards system. Upon assessing the benefit and cost with IAEA, MNI argued that China could benefit from joining IAEA and acquire civilian nuclear technology through IAEA's safeguards system as well as technical assistance for programs on the peaceful use of nuclear energy.[13] China's economic modernization depends on advanced technology transfers, foreign investment, and a stable political environment. Without foreign technology transfers, the Chinese industry would be increasingly marginalized in global competition. But most advanced technologies (such as telecommunications, computers, nuclear reactors, satellites, and precision machine tools) are subject to Western export controls. The only way for China to obtain Western technology is to develop international cooperation with Western powers. As a central condition, commitment to nonproliferation would unlock the door to technological bounty.

There was a shift of power in policymaking during the mid-1980s from MFA to MNI. The latter, which had been responsible for administering national nuclear affairs, now became the main voice to speak on nuclear affairs in the international arena. Jiang Xingxiong, then minister of nuclear industry and now president of the China National Nuclear Corporation (CNNC,[14] the succeeding administrative agency in charge of national nuclear affairs), was appointed to the IAEA executive board in 1984, and he became the spokesman for the Chinese policy on nuclear nonproliferation. In each year's IAEA plenary meeting, the Chinese delegation is no longer led by an MFA official but instead by the president of CNNC, who delivers the policy speech on behalf of the Chinese government in Vienna. CNNC has not only technical expertise in international nuclear affairs but also political support from the leadership to have more input in China's nuclear policymaking. This makes CNNC the major agent for policy change in export controls and international nuclear cooperation. The role of MFA is more reflected in policy coordinating among different ministries.

In the defense conversion, the nuclear industry followed a strategy called "walk on two legs." On the one hand, it relies on indigenous efforts to produce more civilian products, and, on the other, it turns more to the world market for international cooperation and customers. With the significant reduction of military orders, most state-supported defense enterprises were virtually in bankruptcy. The state could not pump a large amount of money into their rescue; they must fight for their survival and come back to their feet. The Chinese nuclear industry has shown a great enthusiasm to export what it produces in the international market so as to earn foreign currency to import advanced Western nuclear technology. This brings about a new issue as to how China adjusts its export behaviors to the internationally accepted rules and standards.

LEARNING INTERNATIONAL RULES

As a nuclear weapons state, China's nuclear resources, engineering, and manufacturing capabilities set it apart from other emerging nuclear suppliers.[15] Beijing's nuclear exports have ranged from natural uranium, low- and medium-enriched uranium, fabricated fuel, and heavy water to a research reactor and a 300MW nuclear power plant. Although China has embraced the norms and principles of nonproliferation, China's nuclear exports raise the question whether Beijing would play by the same rules as other nuclear suppliers.

The proliferation allegations against China include exports of nuclear weapons–related technology to Pakistan and suspicious dealings with Iran. Among them, Beijing's alleged international involvement in Pakistan's nuclear program caused the most negative publicity, especially surrounding the nuclear explosions by India and Pakistan in summer 1998. China reportedly assisted in the operation of the Kahuta gas centrifuge enrichment plant and in designing Pakistan's PARR-2 research reactor. The PARR-2 uses highly enriched uranium (HEU) as fuel, and its capacity was increased from 5MW to 10MW in 1991. The latest episode involved charges that China had transferred 5,000 magnet rings potentially usable in gas centrifuges to enrich uranium to weapons-grade level.[16]

Although Beijing has repeatedly denied these charges, insisting instead that all its nuclear exports are peaceful nuclear cooperation, it is still suspected of helping in other countries' nuclear weapons programs. To Western observers, the suspicion is based on the conviction that China's nuclear exports are a type of economic behavior for hard currency and that it provides Beijing foreign policy leverage in regions where it wants to increase its influence. It is fair to say that there is still a gap between China's general nonproliferation posture and its export practice. But we must distinguish between intentional assisting and being insensitive to the established international rules of nuclear exports. In my view, China's nuclear exports, for the most part, fall into the latter category. Beijing may be sympathetic with Pakistan's effort to develop a nuclear weapons program, but the exact nature of the Chinese assistance remains unclear. Much of the evidence about Chinese aid to the Pakistani bomb program is very sketchy. Some of the highly questionable allegations originated from India but were widely cited in the Western media.[17] On all accounts, Beijing has recently stopped assistance.

There is no doubt that China's nuclear export behavior cannot be held up to Western standards and that Beijing is still in the learning process. In China's case, learning took time, sometimes with twists and turns, even "finger burning." From the late 1970s to the mid-1980s most of China's nuclear exports did not require recipient countries to accept IAEA safeguards. This is one of the major reasons that China's nuclear exports caused international concerns. Chinese officials did not have much knowledge about IAEA safeguards before 1984. It was not until joining IAEA that China's knowledge about the established safeguard rules began to grow. The existing nonproliferation regime was created by Western powers, based on Western values and standards. Beijing has long perceived itself as a victim of the regime. The socialization with the nonproliferation regime requires conscious efforts to adjust behavior to international standards. Because of China's distinct strategic and tactical culture in dealing with the international society, the process of learning and socialization with international nuclear regimes is slow and unique. The controversial export activities from the late 1970s to the mid-1980s later became a finger-burning lesson for Beijing, which taught China that irresponsible exports hurt China's image.

As Beijing began to learn about the sensitivity of nuclear exports, it quickly moved up the learning curve of nuclear nonproliferation. Nuclear experts in CNNC, rather than career diplomats in MFA, played the role of agents for change.[18] They introduced internationally shared nonproliferation concepts (such as safeguards, export controls, and inspection) into the policymaking process. In this regard, they became part of the international epistemic community in nuclear nonproliferation that promotes common standards in nuclear dealings.[19] In the 1980s, China signed nuclear cooperation agreements with major Western nuclear suppliers. This helped China to learn nonproliferation regimes. In its nuclear exchanges with the Western countries, China acquired more technical knowledge about nuclear safeguards. In 1984 China received from the U.S. Department of Energy roughly 1,200 documents about nuclear safeguards regulations.[20] Better knowledge about safeguards led to the reconsideration of the previous nuclear export policy. Domestic export control arrangements then began to be discussed, and rules on nuclear exports were initiated. The State Council and CNNC started a hands-on policy on all nuclear export activities.

In adjusting export behavior to international rules and standards, the then MNI announced three new principles concerning nuclear exports: (1) The recipient state should ensure that nuclear imports from China will be used for peaceful purposes only; (2) the imports should be placed under the safeguards of IAEA; and (3) they should not be transferred to any third country without China's consent. On November 14, 1985, a foreign ministry spokesman confirmed that China would require all recipient countries to accept IAEA safeguards, and China is willing to accept IAEA safeguards on some designated nuclear facilities.[21]

China's nuclear cooperation agreements with other countries after 1984 all include a guarantee that nuclear export and import would be used solely for peaceful purposes, and if the recipient country is a non–nuclear weapons state, the export would fall under IAEA safeguards. These agreements also contain a guarantee against retransfer of material or equipment by either party without the prior consent of the other party. In addition, most of the agreements also require that adequate physical security would be maintained on all imported nuclear material and equipment while

within the territory of either party. In the agreements with Japan and Western European countries, China accepts IAEA safeguards on imports of
civilian nuclear technology and equipment. In negotiating the Sino-U.S.
nuclear cooperation agreement, the United States did not request IAEA
safeguards on China's imports from America because China is already a
nuclear weapons state.

On September 20, 1988, the IAEA board of governors approved an
agreement for the application of safeguards in China. In this agreement,
Beijing committed to "accept IAEA safeguards on all source or special fissionable material in peaceful nuclear facilities to be designated by China
within its territory with a view to enabling the Agency to verify that such
material is not withdrawn."[22] From 1987, China began to require recipient
countries to accept IAEA safeguards as a condition for nuclear export. On
September 18, 1987, Chile and IAEA signed an agreement for applying
safeguards on its import of 20 percent enriched uranium (in the form of
UF6) from the People's Republic of China (PRC).[23] On February 20, 1990,
Pakistan and IAEA reached an agreement on applying safeguards on a
miniature neutron source reactor from the PRC.[24] From 1991 to 1993,
IAEA signed similar agreements with Algeria, Syria, and Pakistan concerning the application of safeguards on their imports of a research reactor, a
miniature neutron source reactor, and a nuclear power plant, respectively,
from China.[25]

In a report to the National People's Congress about the government's
decision to join the NPT in October 1991, Deputy Foreign Minister Liu
Huaqiu stated that China would follow a more stringent nonproliferation
policy after acceding to the NPT. He also stated that China wants to see the
international nonproliferation regime pursue a more balanced policy on
nonproliferation, arms control, and peaceful use of nuclear energy.[26]
China's accession to the NPT in March 1992 marked an explicit legal commitment not to provide special fissionable material or equipment especially designed or prepared for the processing or production of nuclear
weapons to any non–nuclear weapons states. As a party to Protocol II of the
Treaty of Tlatelolco, China has already committed not to aid the parties of
the Latin American nuclear-free-zone treaty in violating their joint commitment and not to use or threaten to use nuclear weapons against the region.
In 1987 China signed a comparable protocol under the Treaty of Raro-
tonga, establishing a South Pacific nuclear weapons–free zone.

All nuclear weapons states have a strong self-interest in curtailing the
spread of nuclear weapons, especially on their peripheries. Yet they also
have economic or commercial interests in expanding their own nuclear exports. The challenge for China, as well as for other nuclear suppliers, is
how to balance commercial interests with nonproliferation commitments.
Compared to other nuclear suppliers, China's biggest concern is how to es-

tablish an effective domestic control over exports of nuclear materials, technology, and equipment, which is something very weak in the system. Without effective export controls, all obligations to nonproliferation norms and principles would be meaningless.

ESTABLISHING NUCLEAR EXPORT CONTROLS

An effective export control system requires foreign trade regulations, administrative competence, policy coordination, and enforcement capability, all of which are relatively weak in China by Western standards. Unlike Western nuclear suppliers, China for a long time had no atomic energy statute in place or specific regulations about nuclear export controls. Among Western nuclear suppliers, France, Germany, Belgium, the Netherlands, Switzerland, and the United States all have complex and apparently rigorous special statutory schemes for controlling nuclear-related exports; Britain and Italy rely on their existing general export control laws to regulate nuclear exports.[27] Among the emerging nuclear suppliers, South Korea, India, and Pakistan also have specific nuclear energy statutes that regulate all nuclear trade and activities.[28] The countries without nuclear control statutes (for instance, Britain and Italy) tend to add a nuclear trigger list to their general export control lists. In China, however, no such trigger list was specified, and the general export control laws have been kept vague as to restrictions on nuclear-related products. For a long time, China's nuclear export controls were built basically on administrative management and regulation, not on formal statutes that empower a stringent export control scheme. With the foreign trade system reforms and the weakening of the central government's control capability in the evolving market-oriented economic system, informal administrative control measures are more difficult to carry out.

Beijing has made a few big steps in recent years on establishing effective national export controls on nuclear materials, equipment, and technology, which may lead to processing and production of nuclear weapons. On September 10, 1997, China's State Council promulgated a comprehensive nuclear export control regulation "Rules of Control on PRC Nuclear Exports" (*Zhong Hua Renmin Gongheguo He Chukou Guanzhi Tiaoli*).[29] A "Control List of Nuclear Exports" (*He Chukou Guanzhi Qingdan*),[30] similar to that of the Zangger Committee (a group of nuclear suppliers seeking to exercise control over the exports of nuclear-related technologies), was attached to the regulation. In June 1998 the State Council promulgated a regulation on the control of nuclear-related dual-use items, another step to bring China's nuclear export practice to the international standard. Beijing's new regulation is a major step toward the rule of law for nuclear export controls and brings China's export control system closer to the internationally accepted standards. Economic reforms and fast growing international trade are redefining China's domestic politics and foreign policy agendas. Growing international interdependence creates constraints on Beijing's foreign conduct as well as incentives for Beijing to adjust behavior to prevailing international norms and rules.

China's first specific nuclear export control law was enacted in September 1997. This law, the Nuclear Export Controls Regulation *(He Chukou Guanzhi Tiaoli)*, along with the Nuclear Export Control List *(He Chukou Guanzhi Qingdan)*, is the first comprehensive nuclear export control statute that resembles the nonproliferation legislation in most Western countries. This is a very important achievement in China's nuclear learning, and it took almost fifteen years for China to get to this point after it joined IAEA.

Looking back at China's export control system, the first national export control regulation was the Provisional Rules of Foreign Trade Administration *(Duiwai Maoyi Guanli Zhanxing Tiaoli)*, enacted in December 1950.[31] This law established a system requiring all importers and exporters to have licenses issued by central or provincial foreign trade authorities. But when all private foreign trade companies were nationalized in 1956, all import-export activities fell under the control of state-owned specialized trading corporations, and the licensing system, for all practical purposes, ceased to exist. The economic reforms since 1978 have revitalized China's economy and opened up a long closed economic system. The reforms loosened up tight control on foreign trade as well. In 1980, an export licensing system was reestablished by the Temporary Provisions of Export Licensing System (*Guanyu Chukouxuke Zhidu de Zhanxing Banfa*).[32] The new regulations set out license application procedures, requirements, and responsible institutions. From 1985 to 1988, approximately seven other decrees were issued to articulate detailed rules about licenses application, review procedures, and the jurisdictions of responsible institutions.[33]

Starting from January 1, 1993, another general export control regulation, the Temporary Rules on the Management of Export Goods (*Chukou Shangpin Guanli Zhanxing Banfa*), was enacted.[34] The new regulation reflected important changes laid out in the State Council's 1988 decision on reforms in the foreign trade system. The number of export control goods is reduced by about 50 percent from the previous list. All controlled goods are now placed under four categories: (1) thirty-eight products vital to the national economy will remain under state production and control; (2) fifty-four commodities listed under "voluntary export quota control" will need permits to be shipped to China's key trading partners; (3) passive quota control goods (mainly textile products), their export subject to the quota agreement between China and recipient countries; and (4) twenty-two goods (including some sensitive technological products and scarce domestic goods) that are subject to general export control and require export licenses. Heavy water, rare-earth metals, and dual-use chemical products (ten unspecified items) are on the general control list. But no nuclear material or equipment (except the nuclear-related product, heavy water) is listed.[35]

In theory, the Ministry of Foreign Trade and Economic Cooperation (MFTEC) has jurisdiction over all exports. But in practice nuclear products (such as enriched uranium, research, and power reactors) and other products from the former defense industry ministries have never been placed under its control. The six state-owned ministerial-level corporations for the defense industry are responsible for producing and exporting them. According to the PRC Regulations Regarding the Control of Nuclear Materials (*Zhonghua Renmin Gongheguo Hecailiao Guanli Tiaoli*, issued by the State Council on June 15, 1987), the MNI/CNNC, the National Bureau of Nuclear Safety (NBNS), and CONSTIND are responsible for controlling all nuclear materials in China. A license is required for possessing, utilizing, producing, storing, shipping, or disposing all nuclear or nuclear-related materials in China. MNI is the government organ responsible for administering the control of all nuclear materials; NBNS is charged with supervising the implementation of this regulation and safeguard measures. An application for a nuclear license must be filed with the MNI, which has the power to approve it upon consulting with NBNS and COSTIND, responsible for making specific regulations over the nuclear materials that have been transferred to the military. That explains why nuclear exports have never fallen under the control of MFTEC.

China has a long tradition of not using published laws as a means for export controls. Without clearly defined legal procedures, China's export controls relied more on informal administrative action and coordination. Within the Chinese administrative structure, exports of nuclear materials and equipment must be approved by the directly responsible ministry (*Zhuguan Bumen*). Since CNNC has jurisdiction and administrative power over all nuclear products, it is in a key position to decide on all nuclear exports. It has become more cooperative in recent years with the international nonproliferation organizations in conducting responsible nuclear exports. CNNC approves nuclear exports from its subsidiaries by a form of ratification document (*Pi Wen*) instead of an export license. If other concerned ministries (*Youguan Bumen*) within the government need to be consulted, a joint ratification document (*Lianhe Pi Wen*) is required. The ratification document should mean the same thing as an export license to the Customs Service officials at ports.

The interministerial process often creates more problems than it can solve. Problems appear because of blurred scopes of jurisdiction over nuclear-related matters. For instance, the Qinshan nuclear power plant project involved CNNC (providing reactor and nuclear fuel), the Ministry of

Hydraulic Power and Electricity (the conventional island), and the Commission of Machinery Building Industry (accessories). The conflict of organizational interests among them caused a turf war over future administrative jurisdiction over the plant. The pull-and-haul among the ministries delayed the project decision until the State Council had to arbitrate in 1983 that the project and future jurisdiction should belong to CNNC (MNI at that time).

The 1997 Regulation on Nuclear Export Controls[36] was a major step in bringing Chinese nuclear export controls up to international standards. The regulation provides principles, application and review procedures, and the scope of China's nuclear export controls. This is the first time that Beijing has sought to match its export control system (i.e., its licensing and control lists) to international common practice. The scope of control, established by the attached Nuclear Export Control List, is exactly the same as the first part of IAES's INFCIRC/254. This is because China is now a full member of the Zangger Committee but not the NSG. Compared with previous executive decrees, this regulation is more definitive in depicting the power and responsibility of various government agencies in nuclear export control management. Although MFTEC is the agency issuing export licenses, the China Atomic Energy Authority (CAEA, a state agency in charge of nuclear affairs)[37] is put in the center of the reviewing process for all nuclear export applications. All nuclear exports must be carried out by the state's designated companies, and no individuals are authorized to conduct nuclear or nuclear-related exports. In reviewing nuclear export applications, CAEA, after consulting with COSTIND, MFTEC, and MFA, has discretion to approve or reject.

In terms of safeguards against proliferation, the regulation is more straightforward in comparison with previous executive decrees. It stipulates that China must receive written assurance from the recipient government that the recipient party: (1) will not use the Chinese supplied nuclear materials, equipment, and technology for nonpeaceful explosive purposes; (2) will provide physical protection for the materials and equipment; (3) will put them under IAEA safeguards; and (4) will not transfer to a third party without prior written approval from China. These principles were reaffirmed in the white paper on "China's National Defense," released in July 1998. However, the regulation stops short of requiring full-scope safeguards (FSS) for Chinese supplied nuclear materials and equipment.

This regulation lacks the complexity evident in export control legislation in Western countries. Although simplicity does not mean low compliance, the current Chinese regulation leaves at least three questions unanswered, which might cause concerns in future practice. First, who is really in charge? CAEA, the nominal state authority, is put in the center of the review process, but the authority is really another face of CNNC. It will be difficult for the two agencies to avoid conflict of interests in deciding which exports should be carried out and which exports should not. Second, although China requires written assurance from recipient parties against proliferation, how could China verify the actual end-user and its usage of Chinese supplied nuclear materials and equipment? Assurance from recipients could just be a nominal certificate. Third, because of the lack of the FSS requirement, is inspection power largely discounted?

THE U.S. FACTOR

Proliferation of weapons of mass destruction (WMD) has been one of major issues in Sino-U.S. bilateral relations. Washington, through constructive engagement, has played the role of inducer and enforcer in bringing China's export controls up to Western standards. Nuclear proliferation became an acute issue during the late 1970s, when China began to move toward a market-oriented economic system. Economic reform puts the central government in Beijing in a situation whereby it wants to empower free enterprises on the one hand but needs to regulate their commercial behaviors on the other. This situation created chaos in export controls.

In recent years Washington has consistently voiced concerns to China at various levels of contact (including at the top leadership level) about China's nuclear export behavior. The 1985 Sino-U.S. Peaceful Nuclear Cooperation Agreement was put on hold until Beijing's nuclear exports became more in line with U.S.-accepted standards. There have been sanctions and threats of sanctions against China because of its nuclear dealings with Pakistan and Iran. Now the bilateral dialogues on nonproliferation of WMD have been regularized, and the Chinese leadership has come to understand that proliferation of WMD could be a critical impediment to a stable Sino-U.S. relationship.

As China moves up on the learning curve of nonproliferation, its policy for controlling sensitive technology (including dual-use technology) also changes accordingly. One of the incidents that made Beijing adjust its export policy on sensitive dual-use technology was the ring magnets transfer to Pakistan in 1996. Ring magnets, in the Chinese view, are not nuclear weapons–related technology or materials and should not fall within export controls. But for Western countries, ring magnets are key dual-use items that can be used to produce nuclear weapons materials. The Chinese government's opinions on exporting these items did not change until Washington pressured Beijing and threatened to sanction the Chinese companies involved. After a few rounds of bilateral dialogues over the issue, Beijing gained a better understanding of the nature of the transfer. As a face-saving maneuver, Beijing later openly acknowledged that it was not aware of such a transfer by a Chinese company and would preclude future transfers of such sensitive materials to unsafeguarded facilities.[38] This gave the Clinton administration an excuse to drop the proposed sanctions against the Chinese companies involved.

The post-Tiananmen Sino-U.S. relationship was strained largely over four issues: human rights, Taiwan, trade deficit, and nonproliferation. The nonproliferation problem is an important national security interest for the U.S. foreign policy agenda after the Cold War. As both sides are stuck in a stalemate over the human rights, trade, and Taiwan issues, nonproliferation cooperation becomes the likely breakthrough that could move the relationship forward. For Beijing, the cooperation with Washington on nonproliferation would, first, stabilize the troubled Sino-U.S. relationship after Tiananmen and, second, pave the way for Western technology transfers to China. For Washington, progress in the nonproliferation area demonstrates that the Clinton administration's engagement policy is working; it also opens up the huge Chinese nuclear market to American companies. It is estimated that China will build more than several dozen nuclear power plants in the next forty years, about 50 percent of the total Asian market. Westinghouse estimates that if the ban on nuclear export to China is lifted, it will bring about US$50–60 billion in business for the U.S. nuclear industry.[39]

During Pres. Jiang Zemin's visit to the United States in October 1997, the agreement on nuclear nonproliferation was one of a few concrete results coming out of the summit. In the China-U.S. joint statement issued after the summit, the two countries agreed "to cooperate in implementing the [nonproliferation] convention within a multilateral framework." The Chinese side reiterates that it will place controls on exports of nuclear and dual-use materials and related technology and will take further measures to strengthen dual-use export controls.[40] It is speculated that President Jiang gave a private pledge to President Clinton that China will stop selling nuclear technology and antiship cruise missiles to Iran. In return, President Clinton will certify to Congress that China is no longer helping any other nation develop nuclear weapons. That will activate the 1985 Peaceful Nuclear Cooperation Agreement between the two countries and allow American companies to sell nuclear power reactors to China. The potential deals could have a value of US$15 billion through 2010.[41]

President Clinton's return visit to China in June 1998 saw new progress in Sino-U.S. cooperation on nuclear nonproliferation. The Indian nuclear tests and the worsening arms race in South Asia brought the two sides closer on the issue of controlling nuclear exports to the region. Presidents Clinton and Jiang issued a joint statement strongly condemning the Indian and Pakistani tests and resolving to take necessary measures to curb nuclear weaponization in the region. They also pledged to support the Strengthened Safeguards System administered by IAEA and to take measures to implement more stringent nuclear export controls, especially on nuclear-related exports to South Asia. As a reward for China's cooperation, the United States signed an agreement on peaceful use of nuclear technologies with China, which prepares for the future selling of American commercial nuclear reactors to China.

As Beijing is tightening up domestic export controls, it is still reluctant to join the NSG, a cartel of mainly Western nuclear suppliers. From China's point of view, IAEA is the institutional arm of the global nonproliferation regime, and its nonproliferation control schemes are different from those of multilateral supplier organizations like NSG. China joined the Zangger Committee (the nuclear exporters committee)[42] and adopted the committee's trigger list in October 1997. That trigger list includes export items that require IAEA safeguards under Article III(2) of the 1974 NPT. However, the Zangger list is less comprehensive and stringent than the NSG's control list, which was established after India's "peaceful nuclear explosion" to satisfy the concerns of major nuclear suppliers. China's argument to adopt the Zangger list, rather than the NSG list, is that the former is directly associated with the NPT, whereas the latter is an informal multilateral agreement and thus is not legally binding.

Beijing's concern over NSG is that it blocks technology transfers to developing countries and that China itself is a victim of the West's technology prohibition. And whereas China has maintained a good relationship with IAEA, it wants to keep its distance from NSG. For Beijing, NSG has moved too fast and too far in undertaking stringent export control standards in recent years. The NSG control scheme would impose unreasonable restrictions on international nuclear cooperation, and the developing countries' programs of peaceful use of nuclear energy would be hurt indiscriminately.[43] Beijing argues that nonproliferation export control should strike a balance between preventing proliferation and facilitating peaceful nuclear cooperation and that the international society should reform the existing discriminatory export control systems and multilateral control arrangement.[44]

CONCLUSION

Economic reforms have increasingly integrated China into the existing international system. In the integration process, learning norms and rules of the international system becomes extremely important as Beijing adjusts foreign behavior sufficiently to established international regimes. In order to bring its fast economic development to bear on foreign relations, Beijing is changing its old-fashioned diplomacy and becoming more responsive to structural and normative changes in international relations. The evolution of China's nonproliferation policy has demonstrated that Beijing has gradually adjusted to the established nonproliferation regimes.

For neorealists, states can learn in international politics, though learning is not an independent variable explaining foreign policy changes. States can assimilate the norms and rules of the international system through socialization with international institutions and other states.[45] States are rational actors. They respond to changes in world politics and adapt their behaviors to the established rules and norms in international politics. The structure of the international system rewards good learners and punishes those that fail to learn. Because each state positions itself differently in the international system, the international structure determines or at least constrains the outcomes of each state's learning of international regimes. China's learning of nonproliferation regimes is influenced by its position in the international system and how well it has socialized with international nonproliferation institutions.

The interaction between domestic and foreign policies creates the stimulus for China to learn and play by the international rules in nuclear nonproliferation. The change in nuclear export controls is not only closely related to the extent to which China's domestic reforms have changed its foreign policy agendas but also reflects a shift in Beijing's perception and approaches to international security and nuclear nonproliferation. The U.S. role in this learning process serves as an external inducer and facilitator that keeps pushing Beijing toward compliance with prevailing NPT norms and regulations. But there are limits to China's nuclear learning. Strengthening political institutions and the rule of law will no doubt fortify central control over nuclear exports. Yet incomplete and incoherent reforms could also fragment authority, thereby undermining China's adherence to the nonproliferation regime. For example, in April 1998 COSTIND was replaced by the State Commission of Science, Technology, and Industry for National Defense (SCOSTIND), which no longer represents the military. Meanwhile, PLA now has its own newly created General Armaments Department, responsible for nonnuclear weapons development and exports. Unclear division of labor and overlapping responsibilities between the two agencies could potentially complicate policymaking and policy implementation in terms of China's nonproliferation behavior. Moreover, Beijing has in the past linked its proliferation behavior to strategic interests: It has been more likely to engage in dubious nuclear exports to regions where it has a strategic interest; it has leveraged its proliferation policy to pressure the United States not to export weapons to Taiwan. Finally, Beijing has to balance its security interests and commercial benefits in deciding its future nuclear exports.

NOTES

1. "Zhong hua renmin gongheguo he chukou guanzhi tiaoli"("Rules of Control on PRC Nuclear Exports"), *Remin Ribao (People's Daily)*, 12 September 1997.

2. The pioneer work of using learning to explain nuclear policy changes was Joseph S. Nye, "Nuclear Learning and U.S.-Soviet Security Regimes," *International Organization* 41, no. 3 (Summer 1987). Other works on learning and foreign policy changes include Ernst Haas, *When Knowledge Is Power* (Berkeley: University of California Press, 1990); George Breslauer and Philip Tetlock, eds., *Learning in U.S. and Soviet Foreign Policy* (Boulder, Colo.: Westview Press, 1991); Emanuel Adler, "The Emergence of Cooperation: National Epistemic Communities and the International Evolution of the Idea of Nuclear Arms Control," *International Organization* 46, no. 1 (Winter 1992); Yuen Foong Khong, *Analogies at War: Korea, Munich, Dien Bien Phu, and the Vietnam Decisions of 1965* (Princeton: Princeton University Press, 1992); Jack S. Levy, "Learning and Foreign Policy: Sweeping a Conceptual Minefield," *International Organization* 48, no. 2 (Spring 1994); and Dan Reiter, "Learning, Realism, and Alliances: The Weight of the Shadow of the Past," *World Politics* 46 (July 1994).

3. The difference between learning and adaption is controversial among international relations scholars. At the center of the disagreement is the degree of changes and whether the changes involve a shift in the central policy paradigm. For more discussion, see Ernst B. Haas, "Collective Learning: Some Theoretical Speculations," in Breslauer and Tetlock, *Learning in U.S. and Soviet Foreign Policy*.

4. For more discussion on the learning effect in China's nuclear policy, see Weixing Hu, "The Medium Nuclear Powers and Nuclear Stability," Ph.D. dissertation, University of Maryland, College Park, 1992, chap. 4, "The MNPs, Nuclear Regimes, and Learning." Also see Alastair Iain Johnston, "Learning Versus Adaptation: Explaining Change in Chinese Arms Control Policy in the 1980s and 1990s," *China Journal*, no. 35 (January 1996). Johnston argues that "Chinese behaviour in arms control is more consistent with the absence of a paradigm shift and with the persistence of a free-riding realpolitik calculus" (p. 46). He reaches this conclusion by testing whether China's arms control policy is more reflective of hard realpolitik or idealpolitik, a highly abstract spectrum constructed in three dimensions: frequency of conflict in human affairs, efficacy of violence, and zero-sum nature of the conflict.

5. Premier Zhao Ziyang's government report to the Second Session of the Sixth National People's Congress, Beijing, 15 March 1984.

6. See, for example, Yu Zhiyong, "Some Issues About Reconsidering the NPT," *Shijie jingji yu zhengzhi (Journal of World Economy and Politics)*, no. 6 (1988).

7. To the Chinese leaders, assisting North Korea to have nuclear weapons is something like helping the North Vietnamese during the Vietnam War. Hanoi turned its back against China after the war. This becomes China's Vietnam Syndrome. Despite speculations about Chinese assistance in the North Korean nuclear program, there is no evidence that Beijing has provided Pyongyang with any sensitive nuclear materials and technology that could be used in its nuclear weapons program. The only known Chinese assistance to the North Korean nuclear devel-

opment was that China helped Pyongyang conduct a uranium mining survey of the entire country in 1964. The survey revealed large deposits of commercial-grade uranium ore. See Joseph S. Bermudez Jr., "North Korea's Nuclear Programme," *Jane's Intelligence Review,* September 1991, 404–411.

8. Charles F. Hermann, "Changing Course: When Governments Choose to Redirect Foreign Policy," *International Studies Quarterly* 34 (1990), 3–21.

9. China now has two operating nuclear power stations (Qinshan and Daya Bay), two more under construction, and four have gone through the feasibility study stage and been approved by the State Council.

10. Zhang Chunting, "A Major Reform in China's Military Industry System," *Liaowang (Outlook),* 24 November 1986, 3–4.

11. Li Peng's speech was partly published in *Jingji ribao (Economics Daily)*, 24 January 1985.

12. Xie Guang et al., *Dangdai zhongguo de guofang keji shiye (Contemporary China's Science and Technology for National Defense)* (Beijing: Dangdai zhongguo chubanche, 1992), 160–161.

13. See Li Jiu et al., *Dangdai zhongguo de hegongye (Contemporary China's Nuclear Industry)* (Beijing: Zhongguo shehui kexue chubanshe, 1987), esp. the section on cooperation with the IAEA, pp. 537–542.

14. The China National Nuclear Corporation, despite no longer being a ministry, still directly reports to the State Council. It has the same ministerial status within the council as other former defense industry ministries. With a staff of seven hundred from the former MNI, the CNNC's missions include: making and implementing national nuclear industrial policies; administrating and managing nuclear production, construction, and research; and providing nuclear products for national defense and national energy programs.

15. The emerging nuclear suppliers are countries that are outside of the international nuclear export control accords, such as the Zangger Committee and the London Nuclear Supplier Group. These countries include Brazil, India, Israel, Pakistan, China, South Korea, and South Africa. See William C. Potter, ed., *International Nuclear Trade and Nonproliferation: The Challenge of the Emerging Suppliers* (Lexington, Mass.: Lexington Books, 1990), 3–13.

16. Reuter and Agence France-Presse international news report, 6 March 1996.

17. The British transmission created some credence about the reports. For instance, M. K. Rasgotra, head bureaucrat of India's Ministry of External Affairs, alleged that China provided test facilities in China for a Pakistani nuclear explosion. It was widely cited in the Western press. But when one probes the meanings and origin of them, very little details are available.

18. The Chinese epistemic community on nuclear nonproliferation consists mainly of experts from the Chinese Academy of Atomic Energy, the Chinese Academy of Engineering Physics, the Institute of Applied Physics and Computational Mathematics, and the Beijing Institute of Systems Engineering under COSTIND. Some of these institutions have programs on science and national security, which become think tanks for nuclear policy making.

19. For discussion on the role of epistemic communities in learning, see, for example, Peter M. Haas, ed., "Knowledge, Power, and International Policy Coordination," special issue of *International Organization,* 46 (Winter 1992); and Judith

Goldstein and Robert O. Keohane, eds., *Ideas and Foreign Policy: Beliefs, Institutions, and Political Change* (Ithaca: Cornell University Press, 1993).

20. See Li Jiu et al., *Dangdai zhongguo de hegongye*, 533.

21. Xinhua News Agency, 14 November 1985.

22. IAEA INFCIRC/369, October 1989.

23. IAEA INFCIRC/350, March 1988.

24. The agreement entered into force on 10 September 1991. See IAEA INFCIRC/393, October 1991.

25. IAEA INFCIRC/401 (April 1992), INFCIRC/408 (July 1992), and INFCIRC/418 (March 1993).

26. Deputy Foreign Minister Liu Huaqiu's report to the twenty-second session of the Standing Committee of the Seventh National People's Congress, *Renmin ribao (People's Daily)*, 26 October 1991.

27. France and Germany have enacted two separate regulatory schemes: one for nuclear fuel and materials and another for nuclear equipment and components. For more discussion about the European nuclear export control, see Joel Davidow, *Comparative Study of European Nuclear Export Regulations* (report prepared for Lawrence Livermore National Laboratory), August 1985.

28. A detailed study about export control laws of the emerging nuclear suppliers was prepared by Burrus M. Carnahan et al., *The Legal Foundation for Export Control in the Emerging Nuclear Suppliers: A Comparative Study* (for Los Alamos National Laboratory), September 1990. For a brief discussion on the issue, see Burrus M. Carnahan, "Export Control and Policy of the Emerging Nuclear Suppliers: A Basis for Cautious Optimism," *Eye On Supply*, no. 5 (Fall 1991), 66–76.

29. For the text of the regulations, see *Remin ribao (People's Daily)*, 12 September 1997.

30. The Regulation and attached control list was published in *Zhonghua renmin gongheguo guowuyuan gongbao (Gazette of the State Council of the People's Republic of China)*, no.29 (29 September 1997).

31. It was issued by the then Central Government Ministry of Trade, and a decree of detailed rules, *Detailed Rules Regarding the Provisional Rules of Foreign Trade Administration (Duiwai maoyi guanli zhanxing tiaoli shishi zizhe)*, was enacted by the same ministry on 28 December 1950.

32. It was issued by the State Commission on Import and Export Management and the Ministry of Foreign Trade on 3 June 1980.

33. For instance, *Duiwai jingji maoyibu guanyu chukou xukezheng fenji guanli youguan wenti de tongzhi (Ministry for Foreign Economic and Trade: Notices on Multi-level Management of Export Licenses)* (18 March 1985); *Duiwai jingji maoyibu guanyu chukou xukezheng qianfa yuanzhe he youguan guiding de tongzhi (Ministry for Foreign Economic and Trade: Notices on the Principles and Regulations Concerning Issuing Export Licenses)* (13 January 1988); *Duiwai jingji maoyibu guanyu tiaozheng jingchukou xukezheng guanli de ruogan guiding (Ministry for Foreign Economic and Trade: Several Regulations on Adjusting the Management of Import and Export Licenses)* (1 June 1988).

34. Issued by the Ministry of Foreign Economic and Trade (it changed to the Ministry of Foreign Trade and Economic Cooperation in March 1993) in December 1992. Its text appears in *Guoji maoyi (Intertrade)*, February 1993.

35. Heavy water appears on the control list because the Chinese define it as a chemical product rather than as a nuclear material. It is produced by the Ministry of Chemical Industry and is exported by the China National Chemical Industry Import and Export Corporation (SINOCHEM), a national trading corporation under MFTEC. China Nuclear Energy Corporation can purchase heavy water from the Ministry of Chemical Industry and is entitled to export it at its discretion. For more discussion, see Weixing Hu, "China's Nuclear Export Controls: Policy and Regulations," *Nonproliferation Review* 1, no. 2 (Winter 1994).

36. Before promulgating the regulation, the State Council issued an executive directory called *Guanyu yange zhixing woguo he chukou zhengce youguan wenti de tongzhi (Notice on Issues Concerning Stringently Implementation of the State's Nuclear Export Policy)* in May 1997. The contents of the notice were later overtaken by the regulation.

37. A new state agency that provides nominal control of all nuclear materials and deals with international nuclear organizations.

38. The public statement was made by Foreign Minister Qian Qichen in a meeting with then U.S. Secretary of State Warren Christopher in the Hague, 19 April 1996. The U.S. side accepted the clarification and assurance provided by China and concluded that given the evidence available in this case there was not a sufficient basis to warrant an economic sanction against China.

39. *Wen Wei Pao,* 1 November 1997; *Tai Kung Pao,* 8 November 1997.

40. See China-U.S. Joint Communiqué on 30 October 1997.

41. *International Herald Tribune,* 20 October 1997.

42. It was established in 1972 outside the IAEA framework, responsible for executing nonproliferation norms, rules, and procedures through its safeguards arrangements with member states.

43. Jiang Xinxiong's address to the IAEA General Conference, 21 September 1992, IAEA GC(XXXVI)/OR.344, 43.

44. Ambassador Sa Zukang's speech at the UN First Committee meeting, 14 October 1997.

45. See Kenneth N. Waltz, *Theory of International Politics* (Reading, Mass.: Addison-Wesley, 1979), 74–79; Levy, "Learning and Foreign Policy."

7

Public Images of the United States

Ming Zhang

In 1986 Chinese dissident Fang Lizhi told college students that "I am here to tell you that the socialist movement, from Marx and Lenin to Stalin and Mao Zedong, has been a failure. I think that complete Westernization is the only way to modernize." Fang's call was echoed by numerous voices across campuses in China. The mid-1980s witnessed a great wave of liberalism among Chinese intellectuals with a revival of debate over socialist alienation, humanism, and the current relevance of Marxist economic theory. In 1988 Chinese writer Su Xiaokang wrote in *River Elegy* that "we need to create a new civilization; this time it cannot pour forth from the Yellow River. Like the silt accumulated on the bed of the Yellow River, the old civilization has left a sediment in the veins of our nation. Only deluge can purge us of its dregs. Such a flood is industrial civilization, and it beckons us."[1]

Ten years later, however, China seems to have reversed its public image of the West, the United States in particular. A group of youth wrote a book called *China Can Say No,* leading a spate of literature critical of foreign countries and their culture.[2] The public suspicion, anger, frustration, and assertiveness toward the United States have come across multiple issues related to society, economics, politics, and foreign policy.

Just why have the pro-U.S. Chinese public in general and intellectuals in particular changed their attitudes to resent the United States? And to what extent? This chapter will discuss these questions and their implications for the future U.S.-China relations. The research sources for this chapter are primarily books and articles published in China, supplemented with this author's personal interviews during the past few years. Starting with a general Chinese image of the United States, this chapter will focus on the Chinese images of the U.S. media, U.S. Taiwan policy, and U.S. politics, which have attracted a great deal of attention from the Chinese public. To a large extent, this chapter elaborates the "radical" public view of the United States that is different, though not entirely separate, from Beijing's official policy. The emphasis on the popular view also means to put Chinese perception in a different perspective from other chapters in this book.

A GENERAL IMAGE OF THE UNITED STATES

The Chinese people's general image of the United States has several components: images of U.S. society, images of the U.S. global role and foreign policy, and images of U.S. strategy toward China. Such a general view is seen in many publications printed during the mid-1990s.

According to opinion polls conducted among Chinese youth and reported in *China Youth Daily* (*Zhonguo Qingnian Bao*) in May 1996, the United States was ranked first among the most disliked foreign countries in 1994 (31.3 percent), and again first in 1995 (57.2 percent). On more specific questions, 90 percent believed that the United States is a country with prosperous material life and strong overall national power; 80 percent believed that the United States is a country that highly emphasizes material value and respects enterprises; more than 50 percent believed that the United States works efficiently but that government officials and police are corrupt; 60 percent believed that U.S. society is full of competition and that careers are not stable; 90 percent believed that the United States contains serious problems with drugs, the rich-poor gap, and abusive sexual behavior; 80 percent believed the United States does not really want to promote democracy but rather hegemony in the world; and 90 percent believed that the U.S. government takes a hegemonist and unfriendly policy toward China. These findings were from *China Youth Daily*'s survey (November-December 1995) in Beijing, Shanghai, Shandong Province, Jiangsu Province, and Anhui Province among factory workers, technical professionals, educators, office staff, and college students under age thirty-five.

The authors of *China Can Say No* criticize individual heroism and the pursuit of "corrupt entertainment" in the United States. They argue that Americans, pressed by serious debt crises, broken families, racial discrimination, violent crimes, free sex, and drugs, are extremely pessimistic, confused, and self-destructive.[3]

Others questioned the goal of U.S. foreign policy by asking whether it is for normal interaction or deliberate provocation. They depict the concept of the U.S. "new world order" with the following arguments: In a new world order, the United States does not like to coexist with other countries; the ultimate U.S. goal is not something like global democracy and universal human rights; in essence, the U.S. national goal is to establish a great USA federal empire unifying the world. These authors expound that in American eyes there is no substitute for their leadership of the world and believe that the thrust of U.S. strategy is national strategic economic interest. As for its China policy, these authors argue, the United States wants to see a China absent strong government and efficient management and falling into eventual division and chaos. As a result, the United States does not have to deal with a strong competitor.[4]

Some authors contend that containment of China has become a long-term U.S. strategy and that countercontainment should therefore become China's long-term strategy. They look upon Russia and France as China's potential strategic partners and caution Asian countries not to become a card in the U.S. hand. They emphasize that people should not appease but rather contain racial discrimination and power politics in U.S. foreign policy.[5]

The perception that the United States was pursuing a containment policy toward China fueled Anti-American sentiments. The public believes that the United States has applied all kinds of means to contain China's growth; the blockage of China's membership in the World Trade Organization (WTO), an attempt to revoke the most-favored-nation trading status, and fabrication about China's human rights problems are all tools that are repeatedly used. Some authors contend that whereas a minority in the U.S. administration utter for a hard-line policy toward China some Americans advocate the mingling of "containment" and "engagement." The authors warn that U.S. containment will be constrained by many factors. For example, it will result in two losers (China *and* the United States) and benefit others. In geopolitics, containment would force China to lean toward Russia, Japan, and other strong powers.[6]

As of late 1997, the support for an improved Sino-U.S. relationship was heard more frequently in China. One scholar wrote that "U.S. leaders are reviewing Sino-U.S. relations from a long-term strategic angle. They are determined not to take a part for the whole, not to let some specific issues dominate Sino-U.S. relations."[7] Even on the eve of the October 1997 U.S.-China summit in Washington, however, some Chinese analysts were still suspicious about U.S. policy. They believed that "a deeper analysis of the U.S. policy of 'comprehensive engagement' with China shows that it remains a neutral one. Under a special political climate, it still will waver between 'containment' and 'engagement'."[8]

THE U.S. MEDIA

Chinese public impression of the U.S. media is largely reflected in the book *Behind the Demonization of China.* The authors have education and work experiences in journalism and literature; they either live or once studied in the United States. They are graduates of Nanjing University, Beijing University, Wuhan University, Nankai University, or the Chinese Academy of Social Sciences, some of China's best universities and institutes. Li Xiguang, coeditor, was a visiting scholar to *The Washington Post* in 1995. Liu Kang, coeditor, is a professor at Penn State University in the United States. They believe that the demonization of China by the U.S. media has both short-term goals and long-term interests:

- *Damage Sino-U.S. relations.* U.S. media vilify China and the Chinese people in order to create the Americans' detestation of China. Whenever the Sino-U.S. relationship is repaired and shows a new momentum of improvement, the U.S. media start to make up reports on human rights, Taiwan, weapon exports, Tibet, and other issues. According to the book, these reports generate pressure on Congress and the U.S. administration and turn new opportunities in Sino-U.S. relations back to deterioration.
- *Scare away foreign investors in China.* U.S. media intend to send a message to foreign business people that China does not behave by international rules and that they should not do business with it. The book states that the long-term goal of the media is to isolate and crash China in the world.
- *Divert international public attention from U.S. hegemonism and expansion.* The book provides an example that U.S. media concoct "fake" reports about China's support of a Pakistani missile factory in August 1996, even though the United States sold stinger missiles to Taiwan to induce the killing between the Chinese in the mainland and Taiwan.
- *Boost Japanese militarism and the U.S.-Japan alliance against China.* U.S. media coordinate with Japan in spreading the theory of a "China nuclear threat," implying that Japan, not China, was a victim of war in history.
- *Stimulate Asian nations to follow the United States to build up an anti-China military alliance.* U.S. media caution the American public and military that China is becoming an offensive maritime power.[9]

Authors of *Behind the Demonization of China* further elaborate the means they believe used by the U.S. media:

- *Use a great deal of fake information to create a windproof "stone screen."* The media collect all kinds of "lies" to cover the reality of Chinese social economic development and improved living standards so that the American public cannot see a real China.

- *Dare to make false numbers, repeat them, pour upon the reader, and mislead the reader to believe them as truth.* The media are eager to make up the numbers of how many Tibetans were killed or how many children were abused in China.
- *Do not conduct field investigations.* The media do not double-check their reports about abuses in Chinese orphanages.
- *Cite or publish sources or comments with strong political inclinations.* The media would "never" cite sources sympathetic to China.
- Other means include *language games* and *emotion stimulations.*[10]

Behind the Demonization of China focuses its attack on *The New York Times, The Washington Post,* and Voice of America. Sometimes the authors cite their own encounters in the United States to support their arguments.

Criticism of U.S. media is a common topic among many Chinese publications during the mid-1990s. Among other events, Chinese authors feel outrage over Connie Chung's CBS report on Chinese spies in the United States and Bob Costas's critical comments on the Chinese team during NBC's coverage of the opening ceremonies for the 1996 Summer Olympic Games in Atlanta. On the evening of May 19, 1994, Chung reported that every day many Chinese citizens legally come to the United States. She illustrated that they all look like ordinary people but that some of them are possibly spies. She concluded that several years later these spies will become active and steal American military and technological secrets. During the opening ceremonies in August 1996, Costas commented that China has problems related to human rights, copyright violations, and the threat to Taiwan. As for the Chinese team, Costas said that China built itself into an athletic power amid suspicions of drug use by athletes. Chinese nationals in the United States and in China launched protests against the two reports and received apologies from CBS and NBC. However, Chinese authors are not entirely satisfied by the "implicit" apologies and remain indignant over American "arrogance."[11]

Chinese media often respond to what they believe to be slanderous reports on China in U.S. media. For instance, *People's Daily* once published a commentary criticizing *The New York Times*'s editorial that compared the collapse of the Berlin Wall to what was going to happen to China and predicted the demise of Chinese communism. *People's Daily* commentary concluded that *The New York Times* is very limited in its knowledge about humanities and history.[12] The English-language *China Daily* once warned that *The New York Times* has waged a verbal war on China by constantly misleading the reader and damaging Sino-U.S. relations and rebuked that *The New York Times* suffered from paranoia.[13]

In early 1997, a new book by two journalists entitled *The Coming Conflict with China*[14] was published in the United States. *China Daily* responded immediately by commenting that this book "defames the People's Republic of China and its major achievements over the past decades with sheer fabrication and distortion of facts."[15] The book attempts to caution against the China threat and argues that military conflicts between the United States and China are inevitable in the future.

The Coming Conflict with China generated another wave of Chinese resentment toward the United States, through the media in particular. On April 2, 1997, *Wenhui Bao* (Shanghai) organized a special panel on this book. The following are the excerpts from Chinese scholars' comments:

> At present, Sino-U.S. economic interdependence has increased, military security dialogue has been restored, mutual visits at the top level tend to be frequent and systemized, and congressional members have started to deepen their understanding of China. Nevertheless, some hardliners in the United States attempt to revitalize the discredited containment policy; *The Coming Conflict with China* represents the new gathering of the hawkish forces.
>
> *The Coming Conflict with China* resorts to the method of McCarthyism in attacking American people who have good relations with China and in estranging China's relations with neighboring countries. The book pathetically labels all people showing friendship to China as a "new China Lobby," who are, as the book poses, three kinds of people: business enterprise people, former government officials with economic interests in China, and scholars who advocate engagement with the top Chinese leadership. This is dangerous. McCarthyism in the 1950s once tortured a large number of American people and resulted in a Sino-U.S. confrontation for more than 20 years.
>
> *The Coming Conflict with China* suggests that the United States dispatch military forces to intervene in a future Taiwan Strait crisis. This move would not be tolerated by China and not in the U.S. interest either.
>
> The book reflects the imbalanced psychology of some Americans toward the rise of China.

Many in China feel that almost the entire coverage of China by U.S. media, including TV programs, newspapers, magazines, and radios, is negative. Chinese authors share the impression that Americans think of themselves as the absolute number one in the world after the collapse of the Soviet Union. They argue that ordinary Americans tend to take things for granted and consider their social model an example for other countries. Chinese authors do not agree that American concepts and values are the absolute standards to measure democracy in other countries. They state that the freedom of news has been gradually replaced by vulgar freedom in the United States: Newspeople have lost their moral judgment and social responsibility; utilitarianism is driving the media.[16]

U.S. TAIWAN POLICY

The Chinese public is particularly concerned with one aspect of Sino-U.S. relations: the Taiwan issue. In May 1995 the United States invited Taiwan's leader, Lee Teng-hui, to visit Cornell University, causing a precipitous deterioration in Beijing-Washington relations. Beijing interpreted the invitation as a violation of Sino-U.S. communiqués and a beginning of a U.S. one China, one Taiwan policy. China responded by launching a series of military exercises around Taiwan, lasting until the general election on the island in March 1996. By then the United States had dispatched two aircraft carrier fleets near the Taiwan Strait, aiming to deter the threat from China. The U.S. action seemed to trigger a nationwide anti-American sentiment in China.

Some authors wrote that the United States simply feels reluctant to give up Taiwan, the unsinkable aircraft carrier in the western Pacific; that it is unwilling to keep from intervening in the Taiwan issue, unable to stand by while the Chinese handle their fate by themselves. Instead, the United States wants to play Taiwan as a piece in a larger game. According to these authors, the United States fears that China, if it is unified, will control the sea-lanes of the South China Sea and the Sea of Japan and will readily dash out of Asia to be another world hegemon. The authors comment that these American assumptions are out of date, unwise, and against fundamental U.S. and Chinese interests.[17]

Chinese authors argue that if people were naive enough to believe that the U.S. decision to sell F-16s to Taiwan in 1992 was an expedient prior to George Bush's reelection, then Bill Clinton's action (sending aircraft carriers toward Taiwan) should help people realize the truth. Considering U.S. historical emphasis on the strategic significance of Taiwan, authors believe that the ultimate interest of the United States is to use Taiwan to drag and divide China, as well as Japan and South Korea, in order to dominate the entire Asia-Pacific situation.[18]

Thus, Chinese authors conclude that American intervention in China's internal affairs constitutes one critical reason why the Taiwan issue remains unsettled. Without the American "black hands," the Taiwan issue would have disappeared long ago, and China would have been unified. They argue that the 1979 Taiwan Relations Act passed in Congress is an open violation of international laws and constitutes meddling in Chinese sovereignty; the Taiwan Relations Act is the expression of American hegemonism. The Chinese public also notice public opinion in the United States. For example, 30 percent of Americans would support dispatching U.S. troops to defend Taiwan, an alarming sign to the Chinese public. Chinese authors caution that the United States talks about one China, but its real policy is two Chinas, or one China and one Taiwan.

They call upon Chinese people to be sober-minded and to oppose American hegemonism.[19]

U.S. POLITICS

In response to a comment that Chinese leaders do not understand American political system and misinterpret U.S. China policy, a Chinese author said that the United States does not understand international relations and often make diplomatic jokes.

The author wrote in a book that Chinese and even the ordinary public have the knowledge of the United States as a state with three divided political powers (the executive administration, Congress, and the Supreme Court) and a two-party system. The president has important diplomatic power, but his decisionmaking is restrained by Congress, the National Security Council, interest groups, religious organizations, think tanks, elites, and constituents. The author explains that China understands the U.S. diplomatic disorder caused by its domestic problems and the ambiguity of U.S. China policy but cannot understand why a big diplomatic power like the United States often uses important foreign affairs as chips in domestic struggles and even ignores international laws and bilateral treaties. The author states that this is not forgivable.[20]

A Chinese correspondent asks why U.S. congressmen keep picking on China: Why should they enjoy intervening in and subverting a China that is pursuing reform and opening up pursuant to acts commensurate with its status? The report states that China is not an enemy of the United States, but if a small number of congressmen insist in having such an enemy, in the long run they will turn China into an enemy. The correspondent quotes a former senior official of the Reagan administration who said that "we do not really want to oppose China; but our urgent task is to pose difficulties for Clinton. In this way, the Democrats will have to leave office at the next general election." According to the report, after the Republicans get into office, they would also implement the current policy to develop relations with China. The report comments that one feature of Western democratic politics is attacking each other and that the anti-China strategy of congressmen is to demonize China first and then harass and jeopardize Clinton's China policy by using most-favored-nation (MFN) status as a diplomatic weapon. The report concludes that all politicians who stand up to reproach China are heroes in the United States; as long as this odd tendency exists, China will always be a victim of U.S. political party struggles.[21]

Chinese scholars also criticize "inconsistency" in U.S. China policy. One author wrote that great differences exist in understanding China and actions taken toward it between the U.S. executive and legislative branches and among various government departments. "Often, the differences arise because of conflicting departmental interests. In the circumstances, it is very difficult for the U.S. administration to work out a well-planned policy toward China. . . . In May 1995, for example, the U.S. Congress, State Department, and the White House were bitterly divided over whether to grant Taiwan's Lee Teng-hui a visa to visit the country. . . . In the end, however, Congress prevailed." There are, of course, this author added, cases in which the executive and the legislative branches cooperated in, for example, illegally investigating a Chinese cargo ship suspected of carrying chemical weapon equipments to Iran.[22]

Overall, some Chinese scholars feel that ideological differences between China and the United States are more "unbridgeable" than those in the economic and security areas. In Chinese eyes, the United States has supported China's political dissidents, encouraged the Dalai Lama on the Tibetan issue, enhanced Taiwan's international status, and led other Western countries to embarrass China in international human rights fora. According to one author, Asians, including Chinese, dislike the American notion of human rights and will say "no" to the United States more vehemently and frequently. He sees that the United States will continue to judge Asian nations by its own cultural values and use human rights as an instrument to enlarge U.S. interests in the region. The author states that "many Chinese truly believe that the Asian path of development or the Asian political model provides an alternative to Western-style capitalism and democracy. This 'Asian consciousness' is accompanied by the rise of Chinese nationalism and the so-called 'neo-authoritarianism' that is gaining popularity among younger Chinese intellectuals disillusioned with Western ideas and attitudes toward China."[23]

WHY NEGATIVE IMAGES: THE CHINESE EXPLANATIONS

Why has the Chinese public changed its image of the United States? For different people, the answer can vary greatly. Since this chapter is about Chinese opinions, this section approaches the question by using Chinese interpretations.

First, a negative image of the United States has ascended as Chinese economic growth has maintained a stable trend and the living standard of the Chinese population has improved visibly during the 1990s. Since 1978 the Chinese economy has registered an average 9 percent annual growth rate; despite the uneven distribution of wealth across the nation, most people's living conditions have seen significant improvement. Chinese national confidence and self-identity have increased with these achievements. At the same time, they have opportunities to travel abroad and compare different lifestyles and cultures. Under this situation, American political and economic pressure appeared to have backfired. As a scholar from Shanghai said to a group of China hands in Washington in 1996, "Whereas Americans have a dream, we Chinese also have a dream." Although Chinese families do not own a single house or a car, he explained, they still want to choose and enjoy their own way of life.

Second, economic growth and opening-up do not necessarily lead to assertiveness or criticisms of other countries. However, as the Chinese public sees it, the United States hardly tolerates the rise of another great power, prejudices a non-Western China of great potential, and contains China economically, politically, and militarily. As discussed earlier, the Chinese public is especially critical of U.S. policy toward Taiwan. As a result, confrontation stimulated China's new image of the United States.

Third, according to some Chinese journalists, the demonization of China by the U.S. media has awakened Chinese intellectuals. "Chinese, the youth in particular, have started to awaken from the blind worship of the United States in the 1980s and from the sham American dream." They write that this time it was the public who starts to criticize the United States. The authors contend that although Chinese intellectuals pursue freedom and democracy and ask for human rights Americans forgot that patriotism of Chinese intellectuals is higher than that of their counterparts in any other country. They emphasize that Chinese intellectuals cannot put up with Americans' bullying and damaging of China over issues such as the WTO, MFN status, intellectual property rights, Tibet, and human rights; American behavior in this regard costs the loss of Chinese intellectuals; American pressure and media bias have resulted in a negative U.S. image among the Chinese public.[24]

AN ANALYSIS OF CHINESE IMAGES

The assumption seems to be confirmed that the Chinese image of the United States has deteriorated compared to what it was during the 1980s. This general statement appears even stronger if readers simply review major events (or conflicts) in U.S.-China relations from 1990 to 1996. Nevertheless, how much has the Chinese perception of the United States really shifted? Does anything remain unchanged? Has anything even improved? How should we interpret the changes in the Chinese public image of the United States.

One method to study images is to apply written literature or oral interviews. But images may also exist in objects that do not always take the form of written or oral languages, for example, lifestyle. The New York, New York club in Shanghai, the Ocean Disco in Qingdao, more than 130 McDonalds, many TGIF restaurants, and TCBY ice cream–yogurt stores across the country have attracted millions of children and adults. CNN is on Chinese TV programs in major cities; *Da Niao* (Big Bird) in *Zhima Jie* (Sesame Street) has been produced into a Chinese version in Shanghai.[25] It is hard to say what this new lifestyle means for the younger generation in China, but it is fair to say that "image" is a complex concept that is always evolving; at present, the Chinese public is attacking the foreign culture it is tasting.

Undoubtedly, it is striking to read *China Can Say No*'s call: "We must prepare for war."[26] But the question also arises as to how appealing this kind of extreme rhetoric is. During an interview with the author of this chapter in 1997, a senior fellow at the Shanghai Institute for International Studies said that the book does not represent Chinese intellectuals; China's international experts have different views about the book. He thought that young people's views often tend to be biased, and he was concerned about the method and contents of the future Sino-U.S. dialogue.

Some physicists in Beijing said that the United States attempts to use the issue of human rights to interfere with China's domestic affairs. It does not really understand the situation in China, and it does not really want to improve China's human rights. At the same time, however, these physicists criticized the Chinese government's response to the American disapproval of China's human rights. In the 1990s Beijing has published human rights white papers exposing human rights problems in the United States. These physicists did not believe that blaming others is a good way to solve China's own human rights problems.

A research director in Shanghai also said that the public in China does not believe in the U.S. human rights campaign. The fact is, he continued, that although it has not released all of the political dissidents China has in fact accepted tacitly some U.S. suggestions. For instance, China has permitted defendants to hire lawyers before prosecution, and prison conditions have been improved.

During a talk with the author of this chapter in summer 1997, a taxi driver in Beijing blamed the United States for China's delayed membership in WTO, China's failure to host the 2000 Olympic Games, the Taiwan issue, and the uncertain MFN status (MFN has a wide influence on the Chinese public, and a taxi driver's business is particularly related to China's foreign exchange activities). Then he acknowledged that the U.S. system remains the best in the world; the two parties can check each other.

Mixed attitudes also appear in previously cited literature. Some authors suggest that China should take a balanced posture in the face of any threat. On territorial issues, for example, the government should express a firm policy but ought not to intensify conflicts. China should develop broad foreign relations, clearly identify its interests, and subject its diplomacy to its entire national strategy. They caution that no country can isolate itself from the rest of the world for development—especially a great power like China, which needs international cooperation. Ideology should not set a standard for China's international relations; different systems do not prevent interstate exchanges. China should follow its own rules, not parochial nationalism.[27]

Some even criticize the argument that Sino-U.S. relations have lost their strategic basis and call it nearsighted. They think that in the security area China is an indispensable partner for the United States to handle regional issues and maintain peace and stability. These authors make the following observations:

- An opened-up, not a closed, China more accords with U.S. interests. China and the United States can realize mutual learning between two great Eastern and Western civilizations and mutual supplementation of natural resources through interdependence and market exchange. If the United States insists on a containment policy and excludes China from WTO and other international organizations, China will be forced to close its opened door, which is China's tragedy and the U.S. tragedy as well.
- A prosperous and not a poor and backward China more accords with U.S. interests. As the United States carries out economic sanctions, China's national economy will stagnate and the United States will lose a potential market. A stable China has to be an economically developed China; only as China develops can the United States have a reliable trading partner.
- A stable, not a disturbed, China more accords with U.S. interests. China's turmoil is among one-fifth of the world's population and will bring unrest to the Asia-Pacific region. U.S. support of Taiwan's independence, intervention in Tibet, and gathering anti-China elements will also violate U.S. strategic interests in the Asia-Pacific region.[28]

As the Chinese public image of the United States has turned negative compared with that in the 1980s, it is true that almost every single individual in China who knows something about Sino-U.S. relations has frowned at the U.S. policy. The Chinese public even prepares for the worst in case of a confrontation with the United States. Yet as just elaborated the public does not agree China should sever relations with the United States or simply turn its back. The old impressions from the 1980s and current firsthand involvement in U.S.-China exchanges (such as tourism or academic visits) perhaps yield somewhat more realistic and balanced views. It is rare in contemporary Chinese history to see the public have such diversified and sophisticated images of another country. This improvement is encouraging.

What the Chinese public says, writes, and thinks of the United States constitute its images of the country. Instead of a lengthy critique of the

Chinese image, this chapter turns to some comments on the highlights of the Chinese conception of the United States.

The radical view of the United States was widespread, especially during 1995–1996. Because it emerged as a response to some explosive events in Sino-U.S. relations, the 1996 Taiwan crisis in particular, the radical view has tended to be extreme and emotional. As an eruptive reaction, it has poured blames on others without self-criticism, stared at the surface of events instead of looking into the details, and dramatized the negative but overlooked the positive. The radical view is neither balanced nor constructive.

China Can Say No is known partially for its criticism of U.S. social problems, such as racial discrimination. Unfortunately, the authors themselves become their own target. For example, according to the book, America-born Chinese (ABC) have Chinese appearances but can only speak English and think in an American way. "In white American eyes, they are still Chinese whereas the Chinese society sees them as 'Americans.' These people above all face the crisis of national identity and cannot find their own social group in the American society. Psychologically they can not reach a sense of conversion. Whites have the white society and Chinese have the Chinese society. What society do they belong to?"[29] The authors lost their moral appeal by thus revealing their own racial bias and ignorance. Their arguments are similarly illogical. In some places of the book, the authors have warned the United States to not support ethnic independence in China, but on other pages they advocate that different ethnic groups should live in their own countries. The authors do not seem to appreciate the existence of multiethnic countries in today's world.

Behind the Demonization of China is written by some well-trained journalists and scholars. The authors have tried not to be extreme in describing the U.S. media. For instance, they introduce several American journalists and writers in a positive manner. Nevertheless, an obvious discrepancy still seems to exist between the book and reality. They spend many pages criticizing *The New York Times,* painting it as an anti-China machine. Yet the newspaper has published several major articles that are pathbreaking and not necessarily anti-China. On November 9, 1996, the newspaper published an article, titled "Taiwan's Overtures to U.S. Backfire," exposing how Taipei bought U.S. favor, as during the early 1996 crisis; this report stirred protests from Taipei. On December 3, 1996, it reported "China's Military Stumbles Even as Its Power Grows," a fresh view amid the China threat arguments and perhaps the first of its kind in years. This article led other newspapers, such as the *Washington Post* and even the *Washington Times,* to reevaluate the so-called Chinese military superpower during the following days. Just like Chinese media are critical of the U.S. domestic influence on Washington's China policy, on April 29, 1997, *The New York Times* wrote that

"Clinton's policy is being attacked with new vigor on Capitol Hill, especially by Republicans who see another weapon to use against a Democratic president."

Behind the Demonization of China apparently missed some quality media coverage in the United States, such as PBS programs and *U.S. News and World Report*. As the voice of containment of China reached a peak in late 1995, *U.S. News and World Report* criticized "America's China syndrome" and urged the United States to engage China and its leader, Jiang Zemin, based on long-term strategic interests.[30]

News in the United States is largely free and independent, though profit-driven. It is perhaps accurate to say that a major part of the reportage about China was negative and aggressive during late 1995 and early 1996. Yet the news agencies have no coordinated opinions. It remains debatable whether the U.S. media have both short-term goals and long-term interests to demonize China. It also sounds questionable that all U.S. media resort to unreliable means for their reports.

A final comment falls on the political or ideological nuance of the Chinese image. Many have described the rising Chinese sentiment as anti-Americanism, nationalism, or radical views.[31] Indeed, the Chinese publications demonstrate a strong mentality, self-confidence, and national pride. The public even defends the current Chinese leadership. However, the Chinese literature as a whole does not promote the communist cause; in the Chinese public's eyes, a prosperous and strong China is separate from communist ideology. It is also interesting to note that the Chinese public does not reject democracy, either as a concept or as China's future choice. It criticizes U.S. social and political problems, perhaps with exaggeration, yet embraces the merits of democracy. The prodemocracy characteristics are understandably not spelled out by the Chinese public at the downturn of Sino-U.S. relations; likewise, Western media are more interested in portraying China as an evil communist state rather than a changing society.

CONCLUSION

China has changed at a high speed since the start of economic reforms in 1978; economic growth has transformed daily life in China. As a result, many Chinese have earned good wealth, which affords satellite TVs and travels across the country or overseas. Although the one-party system remains, the Chinese Communist Party has gradually lost control over public life.

A more independent public in China, like in other countries, will prove a complicated variable in foreign relations. This is particularly true for China, because its foreign policy was tightly handled by the central government in the past. Now it is likely that future Sino-U.S. relations will be influenced not only by the U.S. domestic audience but also by the Chinese public, the intellectuals in particular. In that case, some Chinese public opinions, which are critical of the United States and implicitly against the Beijing regime at the same time, will pose a thorny challenge to the Chinese government. Already, Beijing has distanced itself from the radical ultranationalist views discussed in this chapter.

Therefore, leaderships in the two countries will have to adjust to and learn a new decisionmaking process, because the Chinese public will no longer be a dummy variable. However, the public factor will not necessarily obstruct the development of the bilateral relationship. It can also assist or benefit mutual understanding between the two nations and strengthen bilateral ties. As discussed earlier, Chinese opinion has become more sophisticated, diversified, and autonomous. A mature and balanced public opinion will help sustain a durable Sino-U.S. relationship.

The U.S. media have played a large role in U.S.-China relations; during the mid-1990s, it stimulated rather than smoothed out the turbulence between the two countries. Clearly, the Chinese media have got that message and responded vehemently. Conceivably, "a clash of civilizations"[32] in rhetoric if not on battlegrounds can be kindled by correspondents in both countries. Major news agencies on both sides bear the mission and responsibility to avoid such an unnecessary conflict.

At a higher level of public exchange, it is in the long-term U.S. interest for the U.S. Congress to engage rather than confront China. Its counterpart in China, the National People's Congress, is becoming another important power branch with an increasing public base. Active exchange between the two legislatures will facilitate broader bilateral contact and enhanced mutual political understanding.

In the final analysis, public image is a volatile factor in foreign relations, its change being associated with other social and international events. During the 1990s the Chinese public image of the United States has taken a negative turn compared to that during the 1980s. At the same time, the public image was not completely anti-American and xenophobic but was supplemental with elements of positive view; it demonstrated a more complex pattern of change.

Since presidents Zemin and Clinton exchanged summit visits in October 1997 and June 1998, Sino-American relations have stabilized and improved. Clinton's announcement of the "three nos" policy regarding Taiwan reaffirmed the U.S. commitment of "no Taiwan independence, no two Chinas or one Taiwan, one China, and no Taiwan membership in international organizations for sovereign states." As a result, the Chinese public seems to be less interested in criticizing the United States. Whereas Chinese media coverage of the two summits helped lessen the Chinese negative image of the United States, the Clinton-Lewinsky scandal no doubt tarnished the image of the president and his country. No on can predict how the Chinese public image of the United States will evolve. At this juncture, what is certain is that the Chinese image will not be monolithic but rather complex with diverse views. Earlier simplistic and naive Chinese views of the United States have been replaced by a more complex and diverse image with a recognition that conflict and disagreements will persist while cooperation between the two countries is necessary and possible.

NOTES

The author wishes to thank Thomas J. Christensen, Yong Deng, Xinning Song, and Fei-Ling Wang, among others, for their comments on an early draft of this chapter. The author is, however, entirely responsible for the discussion, analysis, conclusion, and any mistakes in this chapter and does not represent any U.S. institutional policy and opinion.

1. Richard Baum, *Burying Mao: Chinese Politics in the Age of Deng Xiaoping* (Princeton: Princeton University Press, 1994), 189, 225. For a historical review of Chinese intellectual perception of the United States, see Yuan Ming, "Chinese Intellectuals and the United States: The Dilemma of Individualism Versus Patriotism," *Asian Survey* (July 1989): 645–654.

2. Song Qiang et al., eds., *Zhongguo keyi shuo bu (China Can Say No)* (Beijing: Zhonghua gonshang lianhe chubanshe, 1996); Chen Feng, ed., *Zhong mei jiaoliang (Trials of Strength Between China and the United States)* (Beijing: Zhongguo renshi chubanshe, 1996); Wang Jianmin, Liu Guofen, and Lei Yuhong, eds., *Taiwan hechu qu (Where Will Taiwan Head To?)* (Beijing: Huawen chubanshe, 1996); Li Xiguang and Liu Kang, eds., *Yaomuohua zhongguo de beihou (Behind the Demonization of China)* (Beijing: Zhongguo shehui kexue chubanshe, 1996); Peng Qian, Yang Mingjie, and Xu Deren, *Zhongguo weishenmo shuo bu (Why Does China Say No?)* (Beijing: Xinshijie chubanshe, 1996); Cai Xianwei, ed., *Zhongguo da zhanlue (China's Grand Strategy)* (Haikou: Hainan chubanshe, 1996); He Jie, Wang Baoling, and Wang Jianjie, eds., *Wo xiangxin zhongguo (I Believe in China)* (Beijing: Zhongguo chengshi chubanshe, 1997). Although these books might not represent the best scholarship in China and might have been published for commercial purposes, the author of this chapter chooses them for a focused study for the following reasons. First, the anti-U.S. sentiment expressed in these books contrasts the much more positive view during the 1980s and deserves serious attention. Second, the negative image of the United States is not an isolated phenomenon; the books selected here are perhaps representative though not necessarily comprehensive. Third, the negative public image coincides with the deterioration of Sino-U.S. relations during the mid-1990s, which has significant policy implications.

3. Song et al., *China Can Say No*, 128.

4. He et al., *I Believe in China*, 176, 204–206.

5. Song et al., *China Can Say No*, 61–67.

6. Cai, *China's Grand Strategy*, 232–234.

7. Tao Wenzhao, "Hurdles Cannot Stop Momentum of Improvement—Basic Trend of Sino-U.S. Relations," *Wen Wei Po*, 23 October 1997, A-7.

8. He Chong, "China and the United States Are Exploring the Possibility of Establishing a 'Strategic Partnership,'" Foreign Broadcast Information Service-China (FBIS-CHI)–97–297, 27 October 1997.

9. Li and Liu, *Behind the Demonization of China*, 45–52.

10. Ibid., 52–59.

11. Peng et al., *Why Does China Say No?*, 212–217.

12. *Renmin ribao (People's Daily)*, 1 February 1997, 3.

13. *China Daily*, 6 March 1997, 4.

14. Richard Bernstein and Ross Munro, *The Coming Conflict with China* (New York: Alfred A. Knopf, 1997).

15. *China Daily*, 14 March 1997, 4.

16. Peng et al., *Why Does China Say No?*, 204, 207, 209.

17. Ibid., 172.

18. He et al., *I Believe in China*, 211.

19. Wang et al., *Where Will Taiwan Head To*, 285–287.

20. Peng et al., *Why Does China Say No?*, 240.

21. *Wen Wei Po*, 25 June 1997, A1.

22. Ai Li, "In Search of a Working Sino-U.S. Relationship," *Beijing Review*, 22 June 1997, 12.

23. Wang Jisi, "The Role of the United States as a Global and Pacific Power: A View From China," *Pacific Review* 10, no. 1, (1997): 13–14.

24. Li and Liu, *Behind the Demonization of China*, 59–62.

25. Ron Gluckman, "The Americanization of China," *Asiaweek*, 4 July 1997, 40.

26. Song et al., *China Can Say No*, 41.

27. He et al., *I Believe in China*, 199, 214.

28. Peng et al., *Why Does China Say No?*, 247, 256, 272–275.

29. Song et al., *China Can Say No*, 201.

30. Mortimer Zuckerman, "America's China Syndrome," *U.S. News and World Report*, 30 October 1995, 10.

31. Ming Zhang, "The New Thinking of Sino-U.S. Relations—an Interview Note," *Journal of Contemporary China* 6, no. 14 (1997): 117–123; Christopher Hughes, "Globalism and Nationalism: Squaring the Circle in Chinese International Relations Theory," *Millennium: Journal of International Studies* 26, no. 1 (1997): 103–124.

32. Samuel Huntington, "The Clash of Civilizations?" *Foreign Affairs* (Summer 1993): 22–49.

8

Sino-U.S. Relations: The Economic Dimensions

Yasheng Huang

Prior to 1980, China pursued an autarkic development strategy. Trade played a very small and passive role in Chinese economic development; foreign capital was not allowed, and China did not have membership in such organizations as the International Monetary Fund and World Bank. Foreign trade was a highly centralized operation, with import and export rights being restricted to fifteen or so foreign trade organizations under the Ministry of Foreign Trade and Economic Relations. Under that system, there was no relationship between domestic procurement prices and international sale prices or between international procurement prices and domestic sale prices. The Chinese currency renminbi (RMB), was not convertible, and the administrative allocation of foreign exchange favored large state-owned importers for the purpose of dealing with absolute shortages in the economy. All the foreign exchange earnings were turned over to the central government.

Between 1980 and 1997, the Chinese external sector developed by leaps and bounds. The annual trade growth exceeded annual economic growth by a large margin, and thus foreign trade has now accounted for around 40 percent of Chinese gross domestic product when the official exchange rate is used for conversion.[1] In 1995, China's two-way trade stood at $180 billion, compared to $20.6 billion in 1978. In 1998, China was the tenth largest trading power in the world; it was thirty-second in 1978. In terms of share of the international trade, China rose from 0.97 percent in the late 1970s to more than 3 percent during the mid-1990s, indicating both the stride China achieved toward opening its economy to the world and the potential possibilities for continued growth.

Foreign capital—mainly foreign direct investment (FDI)—now plays an integral financing role in Chinese economic development. On the institutional side, the Chinese economy has become more integrated into the world economy via trade and investment liberalization and partial RMB convertibility. In pockets of China, such as the fast-growing Guangdong Province, foreign trade and foreign-invested enterprises (FIEs) are the major drivers of economic growth.

Reforms in the foreign sector coincided with reforms in other sectors of the economy. Foreign sectoral reforms have sought to decentralize decisionmaking power to local government officials and to enterprises, to devise various schemes whereby foreign exchange earnings were jointly shared by the government and enterprises in the export business, and to gradually open up China's domestic markets to foreign products. Other trade liberalization measures include partial lifting of the restrictions on currency convertibility, a gradual depreciation of RMB to narrow the gap between official rate and market rate, abolition of export subsidies in 1991, and recently announced measures to lower tariffs.

Along with this development in foreign trade and investment, China has also entered into increasing economic policy conflicts, mainly with the United States. Issues such as trade deficits, intellectual property rights violations, domestic market protection, technology transfer, accession terms to the World Trade Organization (WTO), dumping, unfair competition, and the like, have increasingly dominated the agenda between China and the United States. The purpose of this chapter is to examine a number of problem areas in the economic relationship between China and the United States. The main argument is that a number of unique features of China—the nature of its political regime, its size, its development strategies, the functions of Hong Kong and the role of FIEs in the bilateral trade—have all contributed to the complexity of economic relations between China and the United States.

SINO-U.S. ECONOMIC RELATIONS

An increasingly important component of the Sino-U.S. relations is economic in nature. According to China's State Statistical Bureau, in 1996 China's export to the United States accounted for 18 percent of China's total export value and 12 percent on the import side.[2] It is widely believed that the Chinese figures underestimate the true size of trade with the United States; the main reason is the role of Hong Kong as an entrepôt. Hong Kong transships a significant portion of goods destined to Hong Kong from the People's Republic of China (PRC) to the United States and to other final destination countries; on the import side Hong Kong serves as an intermediate step for many goods that are eventually destined to the PRC. On the investment side, FDI from the United States in 1996 amounted to US$3.4 billion, about 8 percent of China's total FDI absorption. Again this is probably an underestimate because of the overattribution to FDI coming from Hong Kong due to the difficulties of accounting for the investment decisions made by U.S. subsidiaries or branches in Hong Kong.

The economic importance of the United States to China goes far beyond these numerical measurements. The United States wields enormous decisionmaking power and moral authority at organizations such as the World Trade Organization (WTO), International Monetary Fund (IMF), World Bank, and the like. The key impediment to Chinese accession to WTO is the U.S. stance that China needs to further liberalize in those goods and service markets where American firms possess unrivaled competitive advantages. The demands from the United States for rule of law and intellectual property rights have had a direct impact on China's regulatory system and have, more than anything else, directly modified China's notion of economic sovereignty. In addition, the higher technological content of the investments and goods from the United States implies more adverse consequences for China should the relationship deteriorate on a dollar-for-dollar basis as compared with other alternative markets or sources of investments and suppliers of goods.

China's economic importance to the United States has also increased rapidly in recent years. This was highlighted when China persuaded the United States to intervene in the currency market to stabilize the yen and to restore financial calm in Asia. This is probably a watershed event in that it signals China's economic leadership and power on a global scale. One way to gauge that importance is to analyze the losses to the United States should China lose most-favored-nation (MFN) status. According to the International Business and Economic Research Corporation, the costs to American consumers would amount to $27–29 billion per year should Chinese imports come under the higher non-MFN tariffs. The retaliation from China would then cost the United States 190,000 jobs as well as threaten U.S. investments in China.[3]

From the U.S. perspective, "absorption of China" presents three unique problems. First, China is and remains a communist country in its official ideological adherence. Never has any other communist country loomed so large on the world's economic stage; along with this ideological factor, human rights and prison labor charges resonate with the American public more so than similar problems in other countries. Second, no other country has ever played such an important economic role in the world at such a low per capita income. Japan, for example, accumulated large trade surpluses with the United States at a far higher income base. Japan joined the Organization for Economic Cooperation and Development (OECD) in 1964. Because China is a far poorer country than Japan in 1964, the fear is that the trade conflicts with China will be long-lasting. Third, China's trade surpluses with the United States are being accumulated in an unprecedented manner.

Despite the enormous stake of the economic relationship between the two countries, the United States and China are sometimes engaged in a rather dangerous game of economic bluffs with each other. What seems to be lacking is a consensus between the two countries as to the nature of the problems between them and, by implication, as to an accepted approach to solving these problems. Typically, the sharp conflicts over intellectual property rights and other issues were resolved at the last moment, in ways that are often viewed as preponderantly unfair to one side and as a result of compulsion rather than as a result of reaching a common framework of solutions.

Although economic and business analysts often compare the nature and magnitude of China's trade surpluses with the United States to those with Japan during the 1970s and 1980s, in many ways this is quite misleading. For one thing, the actual mechanisms driving up trade deficits between the United States and China, on the one hand, and between the United States and Japan, on the other, are quite different, as we outline in detail below. The implications arising from these trade conflicts for the overall relationship between the two countries are much graver in large part because of the weaker political foundation of the relationship. Unlike Japan in the 1960s and 1970s, which as a bulwark against communism in Asia was allowed a myriad of exceptions to the international trading norms by the United States, China today is viewed increasingly in menacing terms by a growing chorus of voices in the U.S. media and politics. Books with titles such as *The Coming Conflict with China* are best-sellers in America, and every year the U.S. Congress debates granting universal tariff treatment to China—MFN status, which more than 150 countries receive from the United States. In this context, economic conflicts between China and the United States are both harder to manage and far more prone to escalating into the political arena. The stakes are far higher than the similar trade conflicts between the United States and Japan.

TRADE DEFICITS WITH CHINA

In 1996, according to U.S. trade statistics, the U.S. trade deficit with Japan stood at $48 billion; not far away from this number was the U.S. trade deficit with China, at $40 billion. Given the rate of growth of Chinese exports to the United States, many analysts believe that China will soon over-

take Japan as the largest deficit-generating country. In part because of developments on the trade balances, in U.S. media and policy circles there
have been serious charges that China is increasingly behaving like the
Japan of the 1960s and 1970s in terms of its economic conduct. Articles
heralding China as the next economic nemesis for the United States appeared in U.S. media regularly.[4]

Probably the most succinct way to characterize Japanese economic
conduct is mercantilism. *Mercantilism* has two prominent components. One
refers to a systematic effort to drive up trade surpluses with the rest of the
world; it is based on the view that production, not consumption, is the en-
gine of economic growth. The other component is the idea that there
ought to be close business-government collaboration to achieve trade surpluses and other economic goals.

The comparison with Japan is inaccurate and dangerous.[5] The main
similarity between Japan and China during the compared periods is the
fact that both countries had extremely high savings rates relative to that of
the United States. From national income accounting, we know that when
a country has a very high savings rate, its production would typically ex-
ceed consumption, and thus the surplus portion is being exported. Because the United States has had historically low savings rates, its high consumption tends to make the country absorb goods from the rest of the
world, and thus it typically incurs a trade deficit with the rest of the world,
especially with those countries with high savings rates. It is thus no coinci-
dence that the United States tends to have a very high trade deficit with
East Asian countries, which generally have a far higher savings rate than
the United States.

Although the high savings rate in China, as in Japan, tends to drive a
large trade surplus on the part of the United States, it is hard to see why
this is a result of deliberate policy manipulation. Savings rates are a complex phenomenon, and savings habits can be rooted in cultural and institutional factors that are quite beyond the immediate influences of policymakers. Thus the United States needs to recognize that a fundamental
driver of its trade deficits with China and Japan is its low savings rate and
that this is a structural factor in the trade relationship between the United
States and a number of East Asian countries, China included.

That said, there are still many differences between China and Japan in
terms of the reasons behind the large trade deficits, and thus there are very
different policy implications. The first basic difference is that the size of
the U.S. trade deficit with China is subject to dispute, a dispute rooted in
honest differences in accounting conventions and in genuine difficulties
of measuring the role of Hong Kong in Sino-U.S. trade relations. In addition, unlike Japan, China has alternated between global trade deficits and
global trade surpluses, even though its trade balance with the United

States has been running at a chronic surplus. The second difference is that Chinese trade patterns, unlike Japan's during the 1960s and 1970s, are largely driven by market forces and conform with China's comparative advantages rather well. The third difference is the significantly larger role of FDI in the Chinese economy, which has contributed to significant trade expansions in China as well as to the difficulties of assigning economic significance to the trade imbalances between the two countries. Let me examine these three differences in more detail below.

The Size and Nature of China's Trade Surpluses

Standard international trade accounting applies rules of "origin of production" to exports and "final destination" to imports to trade among countries. Under the *rule of origin of production,* a product should not undergo "a significant transformation" en route to its final destination after it leaves its producing country. The dispute between China and the United States has to do with the degree of transformation of Chinese products in Hong Kong after the goods have left China. This issue has not disappeared after China formally incorporated Hong Kong in 1997, as Hong Kong will remain a separate customs territory and a separate member of WTO.

The U.S. trade statistics do not appropriately take into account the fact that the Chinese products have been "transformed" in Hong Kong and thus attribute the full dollar value to China. Chinese trade authorities have attempted to correct this bias since 1993, but they in all likelihood do not cover all the products en route to the United States via Hong Kong. This uncertainty over the degree of export markups has led to extremely different estimates of the size of trade deficits between the two countries. According to the U.S. Department of Commerce, as of 1995 the U.S. trade deficit with China was around $35 billion, but Chinese trade figures show that it was only $8.6 billion. This huge statistical discrepancy has contributed to the animosity seen in the economic relations between the two countries.

There have been a number of attempts to correct these estimates. By one estimate, if U.S. trade data were to be adjusted for export markups, then the trade deficits with China would be lowered by 35 percent on average.[6] Other estimates put the export markups around 21–26 percent of the Chinese export value to the United States, that is, about 21–26 percent of the Chinese export value ought to be attributed to export from Hong Kong, not from China.

Another important issue has to do with the duration of China's trade surpluses. A mercantilist policy regime aims at persistent trade surpluses, and Japan indeed enjoyed a consistent trade surplus until 1993 throughout its economic takeoff era. In contrast, China's global trade surpluses have been cyclical in nature, even when it has enjoyed consistent trade surpluses with the United States. China's recent successes in export expansion can be legitimately attributed to market forces rather than to systematic, government-organized programs to promote exports. It should be acknowledged that China has made limited progress in recent years in moving away from this model. In 1994, authorities abolished the dual exchange rate and merged the market rate and the official rate at the market rate. This amounted to an effective devaluation of the Chinese currency of roughly 50 percent. The action has given a huge boost to China's export performance. China's merchandise trade balance has enjoyed a surplus every year since 1993, rising to US\$19.5 billion in 1996 from a deficit of US\$12 billion in 1993. The sizable trade account surplus is sufficient to offset relatively small nontrade account deficits to yield an overall current account surplus for every year since 1990, except for 1993. Because China has become an attractive site for foreign investments in the last few years, surpluses on current and capital accounts have led to a huge buildup of foreign exchange reserves, to the tune of US\$139 billion by 1998.[7]

Trade Strategy

Trade mercantilism not only strives to achieve a favorable trade balance but also seeks to create "dynamic comparative advantages." Japan during the 1960s and 1970s fit with this pattern very well. The Japanese market was closed to the manufactured imports in order to promote Japanese manufacturing capabilities in these products. The market was closed not necessarily via official policy actions but via a complex network of affiliated firms or *Keiretsu*, which supplied each other on a long-term basis. Government aided this process of import substitution by administrative guidance, tough product standards, testing, and certification procedures to discourage imports. The success of this strategy was the rapid escalation of the technological content of Japanese exports. By 1993, 75 percent of Japanese exports to the United States consisted of machinery equipment, goods that directly competed with U.S. producers.

By contrast, China mainly exports along its comparative advantages, and China's export patterns have indeed become more consistent with its comparative advantages over the years. In 1985, such labor-intensive manufactures as textiles, apparel, footwear, and toys and sporting goods accounted for 29.6 percent of the Chinese total exports; by 1990, the share grew to 40.2 percent.[8] The top three U.S. imports from China in 1995 were (1) baby carriages, toys, games, and sporting goods, (2) footwear, and (3) women's clothing. These are precisely the kind of goods in which the United States has comparative disadvantage, and if the United States does not import these goods from China, it would have to import them from other countries.

Although there are exceptions (addressed later in this chapter), there is no question that Chinese export patterns fit well with its comparative advantages, and as such both export growth and composition are largely driven by market forces rather than by systematic efforts on the part of the government to manipulate trade patterns. Nicholas Lardy has shown that there is an inverse correlation between export performance during 1985–1990 and capital intensity in production, suggesting that more and more resources are concentrated in labor-intensive products in the export sector.[9]

A further indication of the market dynamism is that Chinese township and village enterprises (TVEs)——market-driven, nonstate firms—account for some 30 percent of Chinese export volume. Another indication of market forces is the extent of policy decentralization. There are now some 5,000 or more foreign trade corporations, compared to 15 in 1978. Because of the autonomy and the financial incentives granted to Chinese enterprises, China's trade pattern today is largely dictated by the principle of comparative advantage rather than by the decisions of Chinese planners.

FDI

China has been the largest recipient of FDI among developing countries.[10] In 1997 the Chinese government reported a foreign capital inflow of $64.4 billion and an FDI inflow of $45.3 billion. In 1998, despite the widespread financial turmoil in East Asia and Southeast Asia, FDI inflows into China continued at a strong pace, defying the growing pessimism about China in the Western business community. For the first nine months in 1998, the FDI inflows stood at $31.4 billion, unchanged from the year before.[11] China is now the second largest FDI absorber after the United States. Between 1988 and 1992, a period of rapid worldwide FDI growth, China attracted US$25.45 billion, followed by Singapore, a perennial leader in attracting FDI in Asia, at US$21.7 billion. The FDI growth trend also shows China's leading position in absorbing FDI. The annual average of FDI inflow during 1987–1989 period was 17.63 times that during 1980–1982; Korea is next at 8.99.

A more straightforward way is to compare shares of FDI inflows in gross domestic capital formation as a measure of the contribution of FDI to total investment. On balance, China is more reliant on FDI as a source of investment financing, and it accounts for a larger share of gross national product (GNP), except for two countries, Malaysia and Singapore. China's initial reliance on FDI as a source of capital financing was quite low; its FDI share was only 0.4 percent during 1980–1982, but its share climbed faster than all the other economies. Whereas China's FDI share of gross domestic capital formation increased more than fivefold between the early and the mid-1980s, the Korean and Taiwanese shares increased threefold, and the Indonesian share increased about 30 percent. Singapore has experienced small changes. By 1992, FDI accounted for 4.9 percent of domestic capital formation. Along with the rise of FDI, FIEs have become an increasingly important source of investment financing. In 1981, FIEs in China accounted only for 3.78 percent of China's fixed-asset investment; by 1995, the share has risen to 11.47 percent.[12]

Another measure to show the increasing importance of FDI in the Chinese economy is the share of wholly foreign-owned FIEs of total FDI inflow. By this measure, foreign control has increased appreciably. In 1985, wholly foreign-owned FIEs accounted for 0.77 percent of total FDI inflow; in 1995, the share rose to 36.9 percent (all on an approval basis).[13] A more difficult task is to determine the Chinese share of equity in the other two forms of FIEs, equity joint ventures and cooperative joint ventures. Although the equity share roughly corresponds to shares of operational control in equity joint ventures, in cooperative joint ventures the profit-sharing ratio and operational control are determined by negotiations rather than by equity contributions. There is also a problem with the data. Detailed Chinese/foreign breakdowns of equity shares are not available. The following calculations rely on Chinese/foreign breakdowns of the registered capital of FIEs. In 1993, the foreign share of the registered capital was 47.3 percent in the equity joint ventures, 74.4 percent in the cooperative joint ventures. The wholly foreign-owned FIEs have a 100 percent foreign equity share; thus its increase suggests that foreign control is bound to increase as the FDI regulatory framework becomes more liberal. There is also evidence that foreign control is either close to or has already reached the majority position in FIEs as measured by registered capital. The overall importance of FIEs, however, is still dwarfed by the much less efficient state sector. FIEs in 1997 accounted for 13 percent of the industrial output value, as compared with 26 percent by state-owned enterprises (SOEs); in terms of employment, FIEs employed 3 percent and SOEs employed 55 percent of the nonagricultural labor force.[14]

The significant and growing financing and economic roles of FIEs in the Chinese economy set China apart from Japan and Korea, which absorbed little FDI during their comparable stages of development. This has implications for U.S. economic policies toward East Asia. First, U.S. export to some extent is not a full measure of U.S. companies' penetration of the Chinese market. U.S. companies export directly to China but also produce inside China and sell the locally produced goods there. The benefits from these sales are not reflected in the trade data but are reflected in the corporate earnings of U.S. corporations. Data here are scarce, but there is evidence that U.S. and foreign corporations are capturing a sizeable share of the Chinese market, as indicated in Table 8.1.

TABLE 8.1   Estimates for the Share of Foreign-Invested Enterprises of the Total Domestic Sales and of the Number of Firms (percent)

	Shares of Domestic Sales	Shares of Firms
Industries		
Baby Food	20	
Cosmetics	30	18.8
Glassware	30	3/5[a]
Firms		
Xerox	42	
Motorola	70	

NOTE: The data refer to the early 1990s.
[a]Three out of five leading firms are FIEs.
SOURCES: Chinese Academy of Social Sciences (1994, p. 28), and State Planning Commission (1994).

Second, U.S. trade policy is based on the assumption that political and economic boundaries coincide perfectly. This assumption is increasingly indefensible in light of shifts in industrial locations and of the associated changes in the direction of trade. In Asia, this assumption should be challenged to its core.[15] Kiyoshi Kojima first put forward the hypothesis that some FDI activities are trade-oriented and others are antitrade-oriented.[16] Trade-oriented FDI activities are in areas where home economies are losing comparative advantage and the host economies are gaining comparative advantage. Antitrade-oriented FDI activities are in areas where the host economies have a comparative disadvantage. Although this view has been challenged, especially the claim about antitrade-oriented FDI,[17] the claim about trade-oriented FDI activities does seem to accord with the character of much of the FDI inflow into China.

Hong Kong is an extreme but highly illustrative example of trade-oriented FDI activities and of the impact of this kind of FDI on trade flows. By the early 1990s, four-fifths of Hong Kong manufacturing firms had relocated to China. Such investments have reoriented Hong Kong–China trade patterns: Most of the trade activities are directly related to the subcontracting investment activities undertaken by Hong Kong firms in China. In 1993, 74 percent of Hong Kong's domestic export to China was related to outward processing; of the import from China, it was 74 percent in 1993.[18] In effect, Hong Kong operates as a trading corporation that contracts out production units in China—through the provision of production designs and materials—and purchases and distributes the finished goods worldwide.

The concentration of manufacturing locations in China has caused major changes in the direction of trade with the United States and has vastly complicated the management of trade deficits with the region. Briefly stated, labor-intensive goods that previously came from Korea, Taiwan, Hong Kong, and a number of Southeast Asian countries are now increasingly coming from China. This has produced a widening trade deficit between China and the United States and a dwindling trade deficit with the other two members of Greater China (Hong Kong and Taiwan). Table 8.2 shows that the U.S. trade deficit with China has risen concomitantly with a sharp decline in its deficit with Taiwan and Hong Kong, at least until 1994. This rise in the trade deficit has complicated an already fragile political relationship between China and the United States, for rather unnecessary reasons, because the U.S. deficit with Greater China rose by a far smaller margin: While the U.S. deficit with China rose about sixfold between 1987 and 1992, its deficit with Greater China has risen by 9.6 percent. It is also difficult to argue that the rise in the deficit has been a result of China's import restrictions; the table also shows that China's imports from the United States have grown at a double-digit rate every year, except for 1987 and 1990. A far more plausible reason for the rising deficit with China is the trade reorientations that are associated with shifts in industrial locations in East Asia.

Given this production-trade link, an aggressive bilateral trade stance can lead to a number of undesirable outcomes. Reduced U.S. demand for goods from China can slow down the rapid capital integration between once politically hostile regions, such as Taiwan and Korea, on the one hand, and China on the other. It may also impede the process of import liberalization in China by creating a foreign exchange shortage and a regionwide slowdown of economic growth. These outcomes may not be con-

TABLE 8.2   U.S. Trade Deficit (millions of dollars) and U.S. Import Growth (percent)

Year	U.S. Deficit with:			Annual Growth of U.S. Imports
	China	Taiwan	Hong Kong	
1987	2,796	17,209	5,871	2.42
1988	3,490	12,585	4,550	37.26
1989	6,235	12,987	3,431	18.58
1990	10,431	11,175	2,805	−16.22
1991	12,691	9,841	1,141	21.56
1992	18,309	9,346	716	11.14
1993	22,806	9,404	703	20.08
1994	29,505	9,597	1,745	30.72

SOURCE: Huang, 1998.

sistent with U.S. long-term economic and political interests in the region. A subtle but important implication of the production-trade link is the possibility that U.S. investment and trade interests may be in conflict with each other. Since the 1992 Memorandum of Understanding, the United States has been pressuring China to further liberalize market access to U.S. goods and to phase out internal trade regulations and "onerous" import restrictions, such as import quotas, strict sanitary standards, and the like. However, domestically oriented investments depend on a high tariff structure to be profitable, as illustrated in the case of automobiles, and foreign investors typically request protection when they undertake protection-induced investments.[19] Thus, overly aggressive market-opening measures as demanded by the U.S. trade representative may in fact undermine the interests of U.S. multinational corporations (MNCs) with subsidiaries already established in China. This conflict between U.S. trade and investment interests will come into sharper focus if China agrees to "fast-track" accession terms to the WTO.

WTO: The Nature of the Dispute

The most important international trade agreement China is considering joining is WTO, formerly the General Agreement on Tariffs and Trade (GATT). However, it is extremely difficult to predict how soon China will be able to join WTO. Chinese accession depends on the pace of economic reforms and the extent to which the Chinese economy conforms to market principles. China has been quite aggressive in terms of pursuing trade reforms in the past few years, including abolition of export subsidies, and taking steps toward currency convertibility, and the recently announced economic reform program will go a long way toward making China eligible for WTO membership.

However, the U.S. stance on this matter is critical. China's export success and the rapid growth of per capita income have attracted attention to China's closed domestic markets, especially in those areas in which the government wishes to promote domestic firms, such as automobiles and electronics. China's bid for accession has not been successful in large part because China and the United States cannot agree on a common schedule of market-opening measures. The gist of the dispute revolves around the issue of whether to treat China as a developing or developed economy. WTO provisions confer more extended tariff protection upon developing nations than for developed nations. The U.S. position is that China should be treated as a developed economy and that therefore its pace of import liberalization should be accelerated significantly.

In addition, there are issues related to China's eligibility to join the WTO. The United States argues that the continued subsidization to SOEs, government price controls, and heavy reliance on administrative methods to regulate foreign trade (import controls, sectoral restrictions on scope of activities of the trading corporations, lack of transparency of trade regulations, high levels of the Chinese tariffs, and the problematic role of the SOEs in the economy) will present eligibility problems for China.

For its part, China obviously wishes to join WTO on the most favorable terms possible. There are thorny policy and political problems for the Chinese government, however. In 1993, Chinese economists estimated that WTO/GATT membership might bring about the bankruptcies of 40 percent of Chinese SOEs and result in the unemployment of 24 million urban workers. At the recently concluded national labor union conference, government leaders ensured that workers' rights would not be further eroded. The sectors most heavily hit would be automobiles, electronics, and telecommunications—the sectors that the government has repeatedly declared to be the pillars of the Chinese economy.[20] Because of these problems, it is likely that the Chinese government will continue to insist on developing country status as a means of strengthening domestic firms first in order to weather greater international competition later.

China's analysis of the U.S. stance is often darkly conspiratorial, charging that the true motive is to contain Chinese economic growth. This view is factually incorrect and is fanning dangerous economic nationalism in China. It ought to be acknowledged explicitly that China is quite far from fully qualifying for WTO membership and that the size of China's economy and population justifies treating it as a special case. For example, compared with other East Asian economies, China has relied more heavily on tariffs and quotas to control imports and is far more inward-looking, as evidenced in Table 8.3. As a consequence, China needs to make deeper policy adjustments in order to increase its eligibility for WTO.

China has pledged to reduce its average tariff level from the current 23 percent to 15 percent in 2000. However, even 15 percent is far higher than tariffs in many countries. The average tariff rate for Malaysia, for example, is 9 percent; it is 14.3 percent for Brazil. For OECD countries, the level is about 3–4 percent. Quota restrictions on trade are extensive despite recent reforms. In 1994 China lifted quota requirements on one thousand import items, but the quota restrictions still operate on those industries that China intends to develop, such as automobiles. The inadequacy of Chinese trade reforms is one of the major obstacles to China's accession to WTO.

China's automotive industry illustrates this point.[21] China has granted steep protection to the automotive sector. In Korea, the import liberalization in the automotive sector started during the mid-1980s, roughly thirteen years after the initial period of heavy and chemical industrialization (HCI) drive in 1972; by the late 1980s the legal tariff rates were quite low.[22] Roughly, China's protection level today is about the same level as in Korea during the 1970s, and the import liberalization in 1994 was very limited. As

TABLE 8.3   Indicators of Inward and Outward Development Strategies

	Tariffs	Quota Coverage	Black Market Premium
China	0.254	0.291	n/a
Taiwan	0.073	0.375	0.05
Korea	0.137	0.100	0.09
Indonesia	0.137	0.101	0.04
Malaysia	0.087	0.045	0.00
Thailand	0.294	0.055	−0.01

NOTE: Tariffs refer to average tariffs on imports of intermediate and capital goods between 1985 and 1988. Quota coverage refers to quotas on imports of intermediate and capital goods between 1985 and 1988. The black market exchange rate premium is averaged over the 1980s.
SOURCE: Sachs and Warner (1995).

a result of such high protection, the ratio of after-tax profits to book-value assets in the automotive sector in 1995 was three times that of the manufacturing sector as a whole. This is remarkable considering that the automotive sector is among the most heavily taxed sectors and that considerable capacity expansion during the 1990s has already reduced the profit rate in this sector. The comparison of the policy developments in the two countries is shown in Table 8.4.

A major policy challenge is how to deepen China's integration to the world economy on China's own terms and in ways that maximize economic benefits while minimizing any disruptions. The gains from integration into the world economy eventually should outweigh the costs associated with this process, but there are substantial short-run costs, often born disproportionately by previously privileged government ministries and agencies. Considering the political obstacles, it is thus rather remarkable that the Chinese government has been able to take measures in order to increase its WTO eligibility. The RMB has become convertible on current account operations, although not for capital account operations. The government has also reduced tariffs several times during the 1990s. In 1991, the average tariff level was 39.9 percent, and it came down to 36.4 percent in 1993; another round of reduction in 1996 reduced it to 23 percent. The government plans to reduce the average tariffs to 15 percent in two years.

Given the existing gap for WTO qualifications and given that China is making some progress in this area, there have been a number of proposals by Europeans and Japanese for an intermediate solution. The essence of the compromise is for China to commit to a firm market-opening stance and a reasonable schedule as a condition for its accession. This compromise solution takes into account both the progress China has made and its

TABLE 8.4 Protection and Import Liberalization on Finished Vehicles in Korea and China

	Tariff Levels	Administrative Restrictions
Korea		
1. High protection in the 1970s and early 1980s	Effective protection rate on transport equipment: 327% in 1978 and 124% in 1982	Effective ban on vehicle imports since 1966
2. Liberalization since 1986	Legal tariff rate: 30% in 1988 and 10% in 1993	Phased-in liberalization, first in special-purpose vehicles (1986), commercial vehicles (1987), then passenger cars (1988)
China		
1. High protection in the 1970s and 1980s to mid-1990s	Legal tariff rates ranged from 200% to 240%	Extensive and highly discretionary quota restrictions
2. Limited liberalization since 1994	Legal tariff rates ranged from 110% to 150%	Reduced quota coverage and reduced discretion; published the negative list.

SOURCES: Tariff figures for Korea and China are found in World Bank (1987) and Ministry of Machinery Industry (1994).

rather low base from which it has to make its progress. This would seem to be a sensible approach, and if applied effectively it may very well spur China toward a faster track of opening and reforms.

Bilateral Agreements

Apart from the WTO issue, there are a number of bilateral issues between the United States and China concerning economic relations. Some of these issues have been successfully resolved; others are being resolved through a working framework that will most likely reduce problems in these areas.

As discussed earlier, the Chinese and U.S. governments signed a Memorandum of Understanding on the market access issue in 1992. The memorandum requires the Chinese to phase out internal trade regulations and "onerous" import restrictions, such as import quotas, strict sanitary standards, and the like. The implementation, according to experts in this area, has been problematic and slow on China's part. The Chinese austerity program for the period 1993–1996 reimposed trade controls that had been relaxed, especially in the area of automobiles. In addition, the U.S. trade representative has also been trying to pry open China's vast potential market for services to U.S. firms.

An intellectual property rights agreement with the United States was signed in 1992. This MOU requires improvements in the following areas: (1) extension of copyright protection for the first time to foreign owners of software, books, films, recordings, and the like; (2) removal of the prohibition against the patenting of pharmaceuticals and chemicals; and (3) protection against various forms of unfair competition, including misuse of trade secrets. Computer programs are protected for fifty years as a type of literary work.[23]

Experts in this area agree that China has moved quite far in implementing this agreement. For example, Deng Xiaoping himself put personal emphasis on the importance of protecting intellectual property rights, and China has since joined a number of international conventions on copyrights. This agreement and its satisfactory implementation have been greatly welcomed by high-tech U.S. businesses, and U.S. exports to China in high-tech areas can be expected to increase as a result.

There has also been a long-standing agreement with the United States covering textiles. The agreement was extended for two years from 1992, when it last expired. The agreement imposes textile and apparel quotas on Chinese textile exports to the United States. In the future, issues relating to the Chinese evasion of quotas and use of convict labor in textile production are likely to become problems in the U.S.-China trade relationship. The negotiation to sign another five-year agreement has been proceeded slowly. The United States is currently negotiating with China to crack down on illegal shipments of Chinese textiles to the United States, and China is resisting taking strong measures because the illegal shipments constitute one of the major sources of foreign exchange revenues to the Chinese.

The issue that has overshadowed all other aspects of U.S.-China economic and political relations is the dispute over MFN status. MFN status enables Chinese products to be imported into the United States under the normal tariff treatments that the United States grants to most nations. Removal of MFN can have serious consequences for seven of China's top ten commodities exports to the United States; it has moderate consequences for the other three. Altogether, removal of MFN status can cost up to 40 percent of Chinese exports to the United States.

Thus there are reasons to remain cautiously optimistic about the prospect that MFN status will not be disrupted in the future. First, there have been steady and incremental improvements in Sino-U.S. political relations recently. Jiang's visit to the United States in October 1997 was quite successful, and Pres. Bill Clinton visited China in June 1998, further putting the relationship on the right track. The two countries have also made progress in the human rights dialogue, as evidenced by the U.S. decision to drop the sponsorship of a human rights resolution in the United Nations in 1998.

Second, the U.S. business sector has been very active in lobbying against doing anything to harm MFN, because the stakes are too high. In the last two years, the economic relationship between China and the United States has undergone a qualitative change. China is no longer just a source of cheap shoes and clothes; it is a major purchaser of U.S. goods. Third, China has expressed its willingness to make some human rights concessions. For example, it has released Wei Jingsheng, China's most famous dissident, and it has agreed in principle to inspections by the International Red Cross of its prisons. These are positive developments in Sino-U.S. relations that will help preserve MFN status.

FUTURE PROSPECTS

Ultimately, any alleviation of trade tensions between the United States and China will depend on Chinese progress on two fronts. One is the degree to which the Chinese economy conforms to market principles; the other is some political opening in China. The ascendancy of Zhu Rongji as the new prime minister signals a new era of economic reforms in China. The ultimate benefit of renewed efforts at economic reforms is that reforms will alleviate the ideological character of the Chinese regime. The following sections summarize more recent reforms on the external and domestic fronts.

External Sector Reforms

External sectoral reforms themselves do not necessarily reduce the size of U.S. trade deficits with China, but they would mean a more transparent and open trade regime. Accordingly, trade surpluses with the United States could be more fully attributed to economic factors like savings rate differentials and Chinese comparative advantage rather than to policy manipulation.

A major policy challenge is to deepen China's integration into the world economy on China's own terms and in ways that maximize economic benefits while minimizing any disruptions. During the 1980s, the policy approach was an East Asian–style export promotion in combination with a heavy dose of import substitution. The dual exchange rate regime served this purpose. Under that regime, exporters received RMB earnings at the higher, market-determined rate, whereas importers converted their demand for dollars at the lower, officially determined rate. This arrangement enabled authorities not to penalize exports under an overvalued exchange rate while favoring important SOEs that needed to import key intermediate inputs for domestic assembly operations. In 1994, authorities abolished the dual exchange rate and merged the market rate and the official rate at the market rate, which has fueled a new round of export growth.

China's economic growth has also been fueled by a large inflow of FDI in recent years. (Portfolio foreign investments have been carefully limited by authorities.) Foreign direct investment flow totaled US$41.7 billion in 1996, an increase of 11 percent over 1995. China now is the second largest FDI absorber after the United States. The large FDI inflow has allowed authorities to become more selective in accepting FDI during the last few years. Authorities now favor investments that bring China high-tech capabilities as opposed to those that simply seek low-cost production sites. Also, authorities believe that some of the very generous tax benefits offered to foreign firms to invest in China have created unfair competition between foreign and domestic firms. Beginning in 1995, the government has attempted to scale back a number of policy benefits instituted during the 1980s and early 1990s to attract FDI. For example, company income taxes on the part of FIEs have been equalized with domestic firms, which traditionally have been taxed at a higher rate. Some of the import tariff rebates and value-added tax (VAT) exemptions or rebates for exports of FIEs have either been scrapped or scaled back significantly.[24] These kinds of reforms would move China closer to WTO eligibility as well as create a better environment for U.S. MNCs to invest in China.

Domestic Reforms

Domestic reforms are likely to improve U.S.-China economic relations in three ways. First, the central issue of Zhu Rongji's reform program is to tackle problems in the SOE sector; if this effort is successful, then the initial fear of WTO membership on the Chinese side will be alleviated to some extent. Second, many of the institutional reforms during the 1990s were designed to strengthen the economic power of the central government. A stronger central government will likely be able to press for many of the reforms that the United States is now demanding, for example, in the areas of intellectual property rights and market liberalization. Third, domestic reforms such as privatization and corporatization of SOEs may reduce the ideological character of the Chinese regime, which will improve China's image abroad.

Reforming SOEs has always been a thorny political problem more than a purely economic issue. SOEs are the backbone of socialism, and so an explicit privatization policy may cause legitimacy problems for the regime. There are more practical concerns as well. SOEs perform vital social functions for workers, providing them with housing and health care. Thus, liquidating financially inefficient SOEs without a social welfare system in place can cause political and social instability. For these reasons, the preferred approach during the 1980s was to grant more decisionmaking rights to SOE managers, in the hope that SOEs would become profit-maximizing, and to allow the growth of nonstate firms so that over time China could "grow out of the plan."

During the 1990s, however, this gradualist approach became increasingly untenable due to the massive deterioration in the SOEs' financial performance. SOEs accounted for 41 percent of industrial output value in 1996, compared to 76 percent in 1980. In 1996, 50 percent of SOEs incurred net losses, up from 33 percent in 1994. By the government's own admission, at least 30 percent of all SOEs are effectively bankrupt. This poor performance is in sharp contrast to the vibrant nonstate sector in the Chinese economy. According to one study, the nonstate sector, comprising collective, foreign-funded, and private firms, has accounted for 80 percent of the growth and 90 percent of new job creation during the reform era.[25]

A telling indicator of the efficiency problems related to SOEs is that they often produce goods regardless of market demands. China's gross domestic product (GDP) grew at 9.7 percent in 1996, and studies have suggested that 1–2 percentage points of this growth consist of unsold and poor-quality inventories in the state sector. Excess employment is another problem. Surveys have suggested that about one-third of the 100 million SOE workers can be cut with zero effect on output.

Beginning in 1994, the Chinese government adopted a three-pronged approach toward SOEs, summarized in a slogan: "Grasping the big ones and letting go of the small ones." The first prong is to preserve government control of about one thousand of the largest SOEs but to reform and strengthen them by corporatizing their governance structure, using a conglomeration policy that takes advantage of economies of scale. Here the model is explicitly the *Chaebol* organization in South Korea.[26] The second prong is to permit outright privatization of small SOEs controlled by county governments in China.[27] The third prong is to allow bankruptcies and mergers of truly nonperforming SOEs. In September 1997, at the Fifteenth Party Congress, the Chinese leadership formally affirmed this policy; impetus for and the pace of reforms will accordingly be accelerated.

The institutional reforms are mainly in the financial sector. Problems in China's financial sector are directly related to the inefficiency of SOEs. Despite their poor performance, SOEs absorb roughly 70–90 percent of the loans granted by state banks, even though they account for a rapidly dwindling share of output value. It has been estimated that 20–30 percent of outstanding loans are nonperforming, and the insolvency of Chinese financial institutions has become a major policy concern in the wake of the financial crises in Southeast Asia and Korea.

The inefficient credit demand is being addressed by the aforementioned SOE reforms; however, the Chinese government has also taken measures to address the supply-side issues. One of the reasons for the accumulation of large nonperforming lending is the tendency on the part of state-owned banks to allocate credit on political grounds rather than on economic grounds. These can be related to social welfare considerations, such as maintaining a politically desirable level of employment, but sometimes they can also include personal favors and corruption.

Authorities decided to address this banking problem by separating the political and policy functions from commercial functions. Three policy banks, the State Development Bank, the Agricultural Development Bank, and the Export-Import Bank, were set up in 1994 for the purpose of policy lending so that other banks, mainly the four main state banks—the Industrial and Commercial Bank, Agricultural Bank, Bank of China, and People's Construction Bank—can specialize in commercial lending activities. Over time, the commercial banks are to transfer their policy lending portfolio to the policy banks; before that happens, however, the net worth of these banks is negative, and there are indications that a complete separation between policy lending and commercial lending is proving extremely difficult in reality.[28]

An important institutional reform during this period was to strengthen monetary management functions of the People's Bank of China (PBC), China's central bank. In this area, authorities also believed that the 1980s reforms went too far in decentralizing decisionmaking power to the provinces. In 1995, China passed the Central Bank Law, which forbids overdrafts to government agencies and recentralizes monetary control at the head office of PBC. Also, leaders have discussed the Federal Reserve model, in which regional branches supervise the monetary operations of several states. Currently, regional branches of PBC overlap precisely with local governments, which gives local governments formal and informal power over PBC branches.

The institutional reforms have also strengthened the central government's taxation power. During the 1980s and 1990s, the central revenue collection in proportion to GDP declined continuously, from 9.6 percent in 1986 to 6 percent in 1992. The central leadership viewed this development with alarm, as the fiscal contraction at the center would erode the government's ability to control inflation and effect income transfers across regions. In 1994, the central government set up the National Tax Service, in charge of directly collecting most taxes for the central government; the central government then allocates revenues among provinces according to the established sharing arrangements. The local governments collect their taxes via the Local Tax Service. This is close to tax federalism, and it made central tax revenue independent of local tax efforts. This measure effectively reversed fiscal contraction at the center. The central share of consolidated government revenue rose dramatically, from 22 percent in 1993 to 55.7 percent in 1994; in 1996, it reached 49.5 percent.[29]

The 1994 reform also created a simpler and a more uniform tax structure. The tax reform reduced the number of taxes from thirty-two to eighteen by abolishing a number of tax categories and merging others. The value-added tax is significantly broadened when the product and business taxes are merged with the VAT. This has the effect of unifying previously different rates under different taxes into a single rate. Another important change is a more uniform treatment of domestic firms. Previously, different enterprise income tax rates were applied according to the ownership types of the enterprises, and enterprises often bargained with tax authorities so that effective tax rates differed among different enterprise types and across different enterprises. There is now a single income tax (33 percent) applied to all domestic firms.[30]

CONCLUSION

Sino-U.S. relations are in a fragile state. Chinese officials and observers of America often make the argument that the Chinese and U.S. economies fundamentally complement each other and that there should not be conflict between them. These kinds of pronouncements betray an extremely naive view of the U.S. political and policymaking process. Although the United States is ideologically committed to free trade, it is widely recognized that free trade imposes short-run and often undiversifiable costs on certain groups of the U.S. labor force. It is often the case that U.S. labor wields significant political power in a number of regions, especially the Midwest.

The Chinese government, for its part, sometimes views America through a distinctly Marxian, materialist lens. According to this view, U.S. foreign policy is essentially an instrument to advance U.S. economic and commercial interests. Nothing is farther from truth. The United States probably has sacrificed more of its economic interests in its foreign policy than most other major powers. For this reason, human rights and weapons proliferation are important obstacles to a good relationship between the United States and China, and if not satisfactorily resolved they will have an adverse impact on the economic component of Sino-U.S. relations.

As this chapter shows, on specific trade disputes the Chinese may very well have a legitimate argument, but the problem is that in order to appreciate the Chinese argument it is necessary to have a vast stock of knowledge about many fairly technical and complex issues. It is doubtful that U.S. congressmen and the American public are sufficiently willing or able to appreciate the nuances involved in these issues. Furthermore, it is quite plausible that in the not-too-distant future U.S. investments in China will touch off some political firestorms as charges arise that U.S. companies are exporting jobs to China. If the Chinese trade balance persists in surpluses with the United States, then there will be a double-whammy political fallout, and the sense that China is playing unfairly in both trade and investment will only be strengthened. There are more, not fewer, troubles ahead.

NOTES

1. The figure, 40 percent, is a definite overestimate of trade/GDP share in part because Chinese GDP is undervalued when using the official exchange rate for conversion. The purchasing power parity calculation produces various estimates, but a more reasonable one would put trade/GDP share around 10 percent, similar to the trade/GDP in the United States.

2. State Statistical Bureau, *Zhongguo tongji nianjian 1997 (China Statistical Yearbook 1997)* (Beijing: Zhongguo tongji chubanshe, 1997).

3. For a detailed analysis, see International Business and Economic Research Corporation, *The Costs to the United States Economy That Would Result from Removal of China's Most Favored Nation Status* (Washington, D.C.: International Business and Economic Corporation, 1996).

4. Greg Mastel, "Beijing at Bay," *Foreign Policy,* no. 104 (1996): 27–34; Greg Mastel and Andrew Szamosszegi, "America's New Trade Nemesis," *International Economy,* no. 10 (1996): 10–27.

5. For a good account of the history of U.S. trade with Japan, see Fred Bergsten, *Reconcilable Differences* (Washington, D.C.: Institute for International Economics, 1992).

6. See K. C. Fung, "Trade and Investment Relations Among Hong Kong, China, and Taiwan." Unpublished manuscript, Santa Cruz, University of California, 1995.

7. "Emerging Market Indicators," *Economist* (1997), 108.

8. Nicholas R. Lardy, *China in the World Economy* (Washington, D.C.: Institute for International Economics, 1994), 29.

9. See Nicholas R. Lardy, *Foreign Trade and Economic Reform in China, 1978–1990* (New York : Cambridge University Press, 1992).

10. Elsewhere, I have addressed issues related to China's FDI in greater detail. See Yasheng Huang, *FDI in China: An Asian Perspective* (Singapore: Institute of Southeast Asian Studies, 1998).

11. Craig S. Smith, "Chinese Economy Picks Up on State Spending," *Wall Street Journal,* 19 October 1998, C19.

12. Calculated from State Statistical Bureau, *Zhongguo tongji nianjian 1988 (China Statistical Yearbook 1988)* (Beijing: Zhongguo tongji chubanshe, 1988). State Statistical Bureau, *Zhongguo tongji nianjian 1996 (China Statistical Yearbook 1996)* (Beijing: Zhongguo tongji chubanshe, 1996).

13. The figures are calculated from *China Statistical Yearbook 1991* and *China Statistical Yearbook 1996.*

14. Yasheng Huang, *FDI in China: An Asian Perspective* (Singapore: Institute of Southeast Asian Studies, 1998), 28–29.

15. The best example is the emergence of so-called Greater China, an area encompassing southern China, Taiwan, and Hong Kong where economic integration

has increasingly penetrated political divisions. See R. K. Jones et al., "Economic Integration between Hong Kong, Taiwan, and the Coastal Provinces of China," *OECD Economic Studies*, no. 20 (1993): 115–144.

16. See K. Kojima, "A Macro-economic Approach to Foreign Direct Investment," *Hitotsubashi Journal of Economics*, no. 14 (1973).

17. See J. H. Dunning, "The Determinants of International Production," *Oxford Economic Papers*, no. 25 (1973): 289–336.

18. See Fung, "Trade and Investment Relations."

19. The Indonesian oil boom of the mid-1970s, which increased the attractiveness of the Indonesian domestic market and induced import-substituting FDI, coincided with an intensification of its infant industry phase. See I. J. Azis, "Indonesia," in *The Political Economy of Policy Reform*, J. Williamson, ed. (Washington, D.C.: Institute for International Economics, 1994), 406–407.

20. Liang Dongping. "Yatai jinghehui li de gongjian zhan" ("Maneuvers Within APEC"), *Zhongguo shibao zhoukan (China Times Weekly)*, no. 101 (1993): 36–37.

21. I have analyzed China's auto industry in greater detail. See Yasheng Huang, *Between Two Coordination Failures: The Automotive Industrial Policy in China with a Comparison to Korea* (Ann Arbor: Michigan Business School, 1997).

22. Effective protection rate is the sum of the legal rate and the amount of subsidies; this makes the analysis somewhat incomparable for the 1970s. But the low tariff rates during the late 1980s do indicate a meaningful reduction of import protection, as this reduction also coincided with withdrawals of governmental subsidies to the automotive sector.

23. See Yangmin Wang, "The Politics of U.S.-China Economic Relations: MFN, Constructive Engagement, and the Trade Issue Proper," *Asian Survey* 33, no. 5 (1993): 441–462.

24. Both measures have produced an outcry among foreign companies. Although the tax equalization is meant to level the playing field, foreigners believe that domestic firms have many other advantages, including enjoying lower land rentals and paying lower prices for many essentials. Lower tax burdens are viewed as offsetting these disadvantages on the part of the FIEs. The scrapping of the tariff exemptions is expected to increase the business costs for the FIEs. The U.S.-China Business Council estimates that the business cost will rise by 28 percent. See "How and Why to Survive Chinese Tax Torture," *Economist* (1995): 63–64.

25. World Bank, "China's Growth Path to Twenty-First Century: Recommendations from the World Bank," *Transition* 8, no. 5 (1997): 5–7; Harry Broadman, "A Roadmap for Reform," *Transition* 8, no. 5 (1997): 2–3.

26. See "China and the Chaebol," *Economist* (1997): 97–98.

27. Because of the ideological sensitivity of the issue, the Chinese government does not use the term *privatization* explicitly. Instead, euphemisms such as "ownership change" and "nonpublic ownership" are used to refer to what functionally is a privatization process.

28. See World Bank, *The Chinese Economy: Fighting Inflation, Deepening Reforms* (Washington, D.C.: World Bank, 1996), for a detailed discussion.

29. The tax figures are from *China Statistical Yearbook 1997.*

30. World Bank, *China: Macroeconomic Stability in a Decentralized Economy* (Washington, D.C.: World Bank, 1995), 61–63.

9

China and Its Asian Neighbors: Implications for Sino-U.S. Relations

Bin Yu

Only a few years into the overly celebrated post–Cold War era,[1] the People's Republic of China (PRC) and the United States of America seem to have maneuvered themselves into a new division between the maritime, developed capitalist democracies (with Japan) and the continental, poorer, more centralized states (with Russia).[2] This new "cold peace," ironically, comes with the emergence of the PRC's genuine regional policy during the reform decades, which is the first in its history and perhaps the most consistent and most mutually beneficial for China and other countries. To a large extent, this "regionalization" of the PRC's foreign policy parallels a consistent scaling-down of Beijing's foreign policy from revolutionary to pragmatic, from focusing on political-military matters to those of a "trading state," from global geopolitical maneuvering to matters and policy areas closer to home. Such a paradoxical situation in East Asia—the scaledown of PRC foreign policy and the hardening of U.S.-led alliances—provides China and the United States with challenges and opportunity to shape relations for the coming twenty-first century.

This chapter starts with an analysis of the "lack" of a regional policy during Mao's time. This is followed by an examination of the evolution of China's "regional policy" during the reform decades, accelerated in particular since the 1989 Tiananmen Incident. The final section discusses the implications of China's regional posture to its relations with the United States.

BEHIND CHINA'S "LACK" OF A REGIONAL POLICY

Until recently, China has been viewed as "a regional power without a regional policy," or an Asian power without an Asian policy.[3] At least three factors contributed to this absence of a meaningful regional policy toward Asia: China's traditional cultural and "aloof" domination of its neighbors; the Cold War setting; and the lack of domestic stability since the mid-nineteenth century.

There is no question that China's traditional view fosters a Sino-centric mentality. China's domination of its neighbors was nonetheless based upon the intangible cultural influence, which was significantly different from physical conquest, in the form either of religious wars (such as the Crusades of the Middle Ages) or of colonialism and imperialism of modern times. According to this system, the peripheral countries should acknowledge China's cultural supremacy.[4] Beyond that, there was little direct jurisdiction of these countries by the central kingdom. Ever since the First Qin Dynasty (221–207 B.C.), China proper remained relatively stable and seldom extended beyond the Great Wall in the north and the natural barriers in southern and southwestern China.[5] Indeed, the Great Wall served a dual purpose of keeping the "barbarians" out and the Chinese in. The sense of China's cultural superiority was reinforced by the fact that on several occasions in history China was conquered by foreign powers (the Yuan and Qing Dynasties). Instead of imposing their own cultures onto China, these non-Chinese powers were assimilated into the mainstream of Confucianism, something seldom seen in history. The centripetal power of the traditional Chinese culture reached such a point that successive dynasties in China indeed lacked any meaningful interests in things beyond China proper. The Qing Dynasty (1644–1911), which was the last imperial system in China, even banned overseas sailing for commercial activities. This was one of the main reasons for China's failure to develop a modern capitalist economy and to interact with its neighbors in an equal and mutually beneficial way.

These cultural traits of China's traditional foreign relations may explain a consistent pattern of Beijing's contemporary foreign behavior of relative remoteness toward others and its deep-rooted desire to avoid commitments even to clients and benefactors. Partly because of this, Beijing had never contemplated the creation of a Asian Cominform—an organized grouping of Asian communist parties under its own leadership.[6] In return, China also strongly resents and resists the perceived interference in its internal affairs by its superpower counterpart, either as friend or foe. To a significant extent, contemporary Chinese diplomacy is still deeply rooted in the Confucian morality of "do not do to others what you do not like to be done to you," an ubiquitous statement by Chinese foreign policy makers. Perhaps for the same reason, the PRC under normal circumstances has not been particularly interested in exporting its model of domestic development, even to its closest friends. In the majority of cases, China's past support to Third World insurgencies was for geopolitical, rather than ideological, reasons.[7]

Conventional wisdom about China's "self-denial" approach to Asia overlooks a powerful Cold War international setting that dominated most of the second half of the twentieth century. In the Asia-Pacific, China was the primary target for the U.S.-dominated regional security system. Beijing's inexperienced leaders had few alternatives but to react to such a hostile and encompassing international system for the survival of the new state. In a bipolar world order of the Cold War, overreaction, rather than "appeasement," was the rule of the game for both sides of the Bamboo Curtain. There was a tendency to see everything in terms of two camps. Conflicts were globalized, militarized, zero-sum, in geopolitical terms within the bipolar context. The enemy was not a mere state but a movement, an ideology. There were, therefore, no "peripheries" for these confrontations. Thus, China's conflicts with almost all of its neighbors were regarded by both China and its superpower adversaries as part of the grand strategies of the other side. It so happened that both the Korean War and Vietnam War were waged close to China. Both were regarded by the West as a key to containing China, the most dangerous communist regime, though neither was initiated by China. Within this context, China defined its regional foreign and security policies according to relations with superpowers.

From a purely realist point of view, the absence of China's regional policy during the Cold War was also a function of China's lack of a "sphere of influence" in its periphery. This was considerably different from the Brezhnev doctrine derived from the Soviet domination of Eastern Europe, the East-Asia Coprosperity Rim of Japan during World War II, and the nineteenth-century Monroe doctrine based on U.S. domination of Central America and Latin America. In other words, a clearly defined regional policy tends to associate historically, if not exclusively, with the notion of a sphere of influence and the power-projecting capability of the major powers.

In the final analysis, a coherent and persistent regional policy requires a stable home front. For a century China nonetheless experienced a national decay in the hands of the corrupted Manchus, divided warlords, an inept nationalist regime, repeated foreign defeats, and destructive civil wars. Even under normal circumstances, given the fact that China is a huge country in terms of territory and population, internal problems always gripped Chinese leaders, be they traditional gentries and aspiring intellectuals or radical revolutionaries and conservative generals. Successive regimes thus were unable to have a coherent domestic policy, let alone pursue a clearly defined and integrated regional policy; they merely reacted to regional contingencies on an individual basis and in a half-hearted way. *Ruoguo wu waijiao*—meaning "weak countries have no diplomacy to speak of"—is perhaps an accurate description of China's failure to form a meaningful regional policy during modern times. Although the communists had the best record since the mid-nineteenth century in terms of safeguarding China's territorial integrity and security by engaging perceived hostile forces outside the country, most of their nearly half-century of control of the mainland was nonetheless replete with large-scale political campaigns, elite factionalization, and societal dissolution. For almost thirty years, Mao's romantic but tragic ventures towed the country in a roller-coaster style. It was not until after his death in 1976 that China started to stabilize. For better or worse, Deng's reforms are perhaps the longest period of internal stability that China has enjoyed at any time during the past 150 years.

THE EMERGENCE OF THE PRC'S REGIONAL POLICY

Since the early 1980s, for the first time in China's modern history, a coherent, integrated, and persistent regional policy started to evolve. It was either narrowly defined as *Zhoubian Guanxi* (relations with peripheral states) or *Mulin Youhao* (good neighborly policy). The goal was to create a regional environment of peace and stability conducive to China's modernization.

Beijing's first step toward constructing a genuine regional policy actually started from its policies toward the superpowers during the 1980s. By the early 1980s China's perception of the world was no longer a sharply divided, black-and-white picture. What used to be claimed true either by the two superpowers or by Mao's version of a juxtaposing world did not seem convincing for Deng and other reformers. Rather, the world according to the post-Mao reformers was complex and full of gray areas. Although defining China's relations with other countries purely in terms of the latter's relations with either superpower (*yisu huaxian, yimei huaxian,* meaning "drawing the lines between China and other countries" in terms of their relations with the superpowers) alleviated some of China's pressing security concerns, such rigidity nevertheless antagonized some while it held hostage China's relations with others. A pragmatic policy was therefore both desirable and feasible. China's 1982 Independent Foreign Policy (*Duli Zizu Waijao*) was a natural outcome of this rethinking of relations with superpowers.

Once relations with the superpowers were defined in China's strategic calculus, foreign policy makers in Beijing were ready to move down the priority list of their agenda. As a result, a coherent and more nuanced policy toward China's "peripheral countries" (*Zhobian Guojia*) gradually emerged.

The 1980s did not see radical changes in terms of China's relations with neighbors. Beijing even continued to appear unyielding to its preconditions in normalizing relations with Moscow.[8] But perhaps the most important change in Beijing's dealings with Moscow, between 1982 and the Gorbachev-Deng summit in 1989, was a pragmatic and more flexible approach. During most of the twelve official talks between deputy foreign ministers during six years (1982–1988), the Soviet side refused China's "preconditions" on the grounds of interfering in the internal affairs of the third party. It was not until April 1986 that Gorbachev, the new general secretary of the Communist Party of the Soviet Union (CPSU), indicated some flexibility by agreeing to discuss the regional issues according to China's "three obstacles" agenda. But the Chinese side did not break away from the talks because of the uncompromising position of the Soviets. Nor did Beijing allow this lack of progress in political relations with Moscow to affect other issue areas. On the contrary, Chinese leaders seized every opportunity to meet top Soviet leaders. The first half of the 1980s provided some unusual opportunities for China, including all the "funeral diplomacies." Meanwhile, bilateral exchanges flourished in many other areas, including culture, sports, science and technology, and trade. These developments in relations with Moscow, thought to fall in the category of "big-power politics," nevertheless constituted a crucial step toward defusing the once highly charged and tense relationship in Asia.

While improving relations with Moscow in a piece-meal fashion throughout the 1980s, Beijing also worked independently with many pro-Soviet countries on its periphery. For example, China in 1982 started a joint border inspection with Mongolia as the first step toward normalizing bilateral relations and stabilizing the border situation. A border agreement between the two countries signed in November 1988 was the first of its kind between China and its neighboring states.[9] Until recently, relations with India had gradually and substantially improved and was culminated in December 1988 with Rajiv Gandhi's visit to China, the first visit by an Indian prime minister in thirty-four years. The two countries, which went to war over the border issue in 1962, had held a total of eight talks at the deputy foreign minister level between 1981 and 1987 and stabilized the status quo along the 2,000-kilometer border. In 1988, the two sides agreed to set up a joint working group to oversee the border issue.[10]

Policies toward the Korean Peninsula were paramount and hypersensitive for China. The area was the center for geopolitical contention between the four major powers (Japan, China, Russia, and the United

States), and exclusive control of the peninsula by any large power would deprive others an indispensable security buffer. In modern history, there were several occasions when domination of the peninsula by a foreign power served as a prelude to massive aggression toward China, including the 1894–1895 Sino-Japanese War and Japanese occupation of China during World War II. The fear of a hostile United States occupying Korea was seen as a grave threat to the security of the newly established PRC and therefore played a large role in Mao's fateful 1950 decision to engage the U.S. military in Korea. Although it fought the war to a stalemate, Beijing paid a tremendous price for that three-year "limited war," including sowing the seeds of its discontent in relations with Moscow. China's policy toward the Korean Peninsula has therefore been to keep the delicate equilibrium and stability at any cost; this was true even during Mao's time.[11] With the reorientation of China's domestic policy toward economic modernization, the Korean Peninsula was a key linkage in Beijing's effort to construct a peaceful external environment conducive to China's economic development during the 1980s.

It is within this context that Beijing carefully conducts its relations with both Koreas. In the PRC's diplomatic history, relations with allies prove to be most difficult. There are at least two known cases that Beijing's closest allies (Russia and Vietnam) turned to archenemies within a relatively short period. Managing a "friendly" relationship with North Korea is therefore paramount for Beijing. This was particularly true when China and North Korea developed a growing gap in their domestic politics during the 1980s, when the former underwent a significant "de-Maonization" while the latter reverted increasingly to a suffocating cult of personality. The gap between their foreign policies became apparent with Beijing's omnidirectional diplomacy and North Korea's de facto diplomatic isolation. Yet knowing that there was perhaps little China could do to influence North Korea's domestic setting, Beijing leaders tried to maintain the existing relationship with North Korea. For this reason, top Chinese leaders visited North Korea frequently, and they were reciprocated by North Korean leaders;[12] there were also many informal, top-level consultations. Beijing's public support for North Korea, however, was not unconditional. For example, China chose not to condemn North Korea publicly during the 1983 Rangoon explosion and the 1987 bombing of a South Korean airliner, which drew strong international outcry and destabilized the sensitive peninsula. However, China did not defend the North's behavior. Throughout the 1980s, China made it clear, publicly and privately, that it supported only "peaceful" and "reasonable" means for Korean reunification.[13] Meanwhile, China also worked for long-term goals so that North Korea would eventually find its own way to normal relations with the outside world. For these purposes, North Korean leaders were carefully provided with opportunities to get acquainted with China's reform and other domestic changes. China even brokered a series of U.S.–North Korean diplomatic meetings at the councilor level in Beijing during the late 1980s. The sudden death of North Korean leader Kim Il Sung in 1994 disrupted high-level contacts between the two communist states. The question immediately arose as to how his son and successor, Kim Jong Il, would handle the high-level diplomacy, which had been based on the personal ties between Kim the senior and Chinese leaders.[14]

Meanwhile, South Korea also attracted Beijing's attention, particularly with its economic dynamism and intermedium-level technologies, which were suitable for China's low-level development. In order not to offend North Korea by a diplomatic breakthrough with South Korea, Beijing proceeded carefully with its unofficial and commercial relations with South Korea during the 1980s. It deliberately did not develop formal diplomatic relations with Seoul ahead of the Soviet Union.[15] Specifically, Beijing's approach to Seoul was defined as "separating politics from business." The initial contacts between Beijing and Seoul were actually "defection" diplomacy.[16] Beijing used these opportunities as an excuse for opening contacts. This was followed by a series of sports teams exchanged between the two countries, including China's participation in Seoul of the Tenth Asian Games (1986) and Summer Olympics (1988).

As for economic relations, China's trade with Seoul is the most dynamic. In 1988, indirect trade ties with Seoul, which started in 1983, was replaced by a direct trade agreement. The two sides reached a total trade of almost $2 billion in 1990, four times greater than China's trade with North Korea that year. Since 1992, bilateral trade has grown by 50 percent per year, to more than $20 billion in 1996. China is now the third largest trading partner for South Korea, second only to the United States and Japan. Also, South Korea is the fourth largest trading partner for China after Hong Kong, Japan, and the United States. In the past few years, China has also become one of the largest recipient countries for foreign direct investment (FDI) from South Korea, absorbing a quarter of Seoul's overseas FDI.[17] By the end of the 1980s and early 1990s, China actually enjoyed fair to good relations with both North and South Korea by maintaining "traditional friendship" with the former and exploring opportunities with the latter. This was done without "dumping" relations with North Korea or establishing full diplomatic relations with South Korea.

Taken together, Beijing's "periphery policy" of the 1980s was quite impressive. Although relations with its friends remained stable, relations with its former enemies or unfriendly neighbors were either substantially improved or on the verge of being resolved. To be exact, there were no radical changes and breakthroughs in almost all cases. The PRC nonetheless could claim by the end of the decade the best relationship with its neighbors in its diplomatic history thus far.[18] This peaceful and positive "peripheral environment" also paralleled the relatively stable and positive relations with Washington and Moscow, which would soon be challenged and undermined by a series of developments sometimes beyond the control of Beijing leaders.

1989: CRISIS AND OPPORTUNITIES

The 1989 Beijing crackdown led to a diplomatic isolation of China almost overnight. Ironically, pressures from those influential Western nations also served as catalyst for China to develop a more active periphery policy. In a review of China's post-Tiananmen foreign relations, Chinese Foreign Minister Qian Qichen made Beijing's periphery policy the top priority in China's overall foreign relations. The goal was to maintain a stable and peaceful periphery around China amid a sea of change in other parts of the world, which included the Gulf War, the civil war in former Yugoslavia, and the collapse of Soviet communism.[19] In a matter of a few years, China restored or established diplomatic relations with several influential regional powers, such as Indonesia (August 8, 1990), Singapore (October 3, 1990), Brunei (September 30, 1991), and South Korea (August 24, 1992); significantly elevated relations with India and the Philippines; normalized relations with Russia (May 1989), Mongolia (1989), and Vietnam (November 1991); secured a good start with several newly founded Central Asian states (Kazakhstan, Tajikistan, Kyrgystan, Uzbekistan, and Turkmenistan, all in 1992); and started participating in regional organizations such as the Association of Southeast Asian Nations (ASEAN; 1991). Chinese and Asian leaders and officials frequented each others' capitals at a rate seldom seen. The outcome of Beijing's diplomatic fence-mending with neighboring countries, particularly through ASEAN, was somewhat expected, given that Beijing had long supported ASEAN's effort to oppose Vietnamese expansionism, that China had unilaterally dropped its support for communist insurgencies in many Southeast Asian countries, and its cautious, hands-off policy toward overseas Chinese, who constitute the heart of the entrepreneurial class in virtually every ASEAN state. China's post-Tiananmen diplomatic isolation nevertheless accelerated the effort toward that end.

In relations with the two Koreas, China continues to play an independent but responsible role for the stability of the peninsula[20] by encouraging intra-Korean reconciliation, by endorsing regional nuclear nonproliferation, by disapproving terrorism, by supporting the dual membership of the two Koreas in the United Nations, by working for a peaceful ending of North Korea's nuclear crisis, and by participating in a quadripartite talk for a peace treaty in Korea. In several crisis or near-crisis situations, China has acted with prudent and effective measures.[21] Meanwhile, China has also sent a large quantity of food to famine-plagued North Korea, a timely relief for its old ally.[22] These policies toward the Korean Peninsula parallel and even converge on those adopted by other major powers and therefore are conducive to an improved diplomatic status for Beijing since the 1989 crackdown. Through private consultations China kept the North Koreans informed about its diplomacy that impinged on North Korean interests. The Beijing-Seoul breakthrough was therefore a moderate and somewhat expected aftershock for Pyongyang following Gorbachev's 1990 about-face decision to normalize diplomatic relations with South Korea. There was no question of North Korea's displeasure for China's 1992 normalization of relations with South Korea.[23] However, by pursuing a delayed and measured pace in its crossrecognition of the two Koreas, Beijing was able to save face for the North Koreans and therefore preserve its traditional friendship with the old ally. Beijing's policy toward the Korean Peninsula during the early 1990s served several purposes. Good relations with South Korea proved to be valuable in China's continuous engagement with other major powers, particularly Japan and the United States.

The implementation of China's peripheral policy after 1983 has led to a growing trade and investment relationship with Asian countries. This came largely thanks to China's economic reform and opening-up to the rest of the world.[24] There is no question that China competes with many of its neighbors for markets, resources, and capital in their modernization. The vast Chinese market and its diverse needs, however, also provide numerous opportunities for many of its neighboring states to trade with and invest in China. As China's economy grows stronger, it also starts to export capital, particularly to Central Asian states, Russian Siberia, and some Southeast Asian countries. Even if China itself is increasingly affected by the ongoing currency crisis in Asia, Beijing has kept its promise not to devalue its national currency (RMB), thereby alleviating pressures from other Asian countries, a posture that even Japan is either unable or unwilling to take. Meanwhile, it has provided several billions of U.S. dollars (either through the International Monetary Fund or bilateral agreements) to stabilize Asian economies, such as Thailand and Indonesia, some of the hardest hit.[25]

Needless to say, China's increasing economic relations with its neighbors is designed to serve China's own interests. Such a move to interact economically with almost every country around China has also led to some predictable results. One is general and relative stability in Asia, where many noncommunist countries, though wary of China, do not have to choose between antagonistic relations with either China or other major powers. Many of them have benefited directly or indirectly from the growing economy of China.

Another indirect outcome of China's growing economic activity with neighbors concerns China's relations with former and reforming centralized economies. Each time leaders of those countries came to visit China, they toured the special economic zones (SEZs).[26] The scope and speed of China's opening-up impressed many of them. Gorbachev certainly tried to reform the huge Soviet centralized planning system, but the abortive 1991 coup ended that effort. In 1993, Russian Pres. Boris Yeltsin dropped the Western prescription of "shock therapy" in favor of China's phased and gradual economic reform. Among socialist countries around China, Vietnam is perhaps the most successful in adopting economic reforms similar to China's.[27] Even North Korea is beginning to experiment with SEZs. China's economic opening-up is by no means intended to get the Communist Party out of power. Nor does China intend to force others to follow in its footsteps. The outcome of this gradual linkage with the world trading system is nevertheless impressive: There has been a remarkable absence of ideological polemic between communist states around China, and each (probably except North Korea) is working to gain a more tangible result for its own people while transforming out of rigid economic and social structures.

China's peaceful and mutually beneficial interactions with smaller neighbors also parallel growing and relatively stable working relations with major regional powers, such as Russia and Japan. Despite differences between their respective domestic systems, particularly after the 1989 Beijing crackdown and the 1991 Moscow coup, Beijing and Moscow have developed a more mature bilateral relationship that has resulted in relative stability amid fluid internal and external environments; high-level exchanges with top officials frequenting each other's capital on a regular basis; the busiest border trade along the once longest fortified border in peacetime; and a transition from being on the brink of a Russian nuclear strike against China to the mutual pledge of no-first-use of nuclear weapons against one another, even if Russia in 1997 dropped its no-first-use policy toward other countries.[28] As a result of these developments, Sino-Russian relations are the most stable and perhaps most equal than at any time during the past two centuries.[29]

In the 1990s, it has been a more challenging task for China's foreign policy makers to manage relations with Japan, an economic giant with increasing political influence and military capability. Part of the reason is the gap between Beijing and Tokyo regarding the interpretation of Japan's wartime past. Although China may forgive—but not forget—what Japan did to China during World War II, Japan continues to evade, even whitewash historical legacies.[30] Nevertheless, a cursory look at the twentieth century indicates that the current Sino-Japanese relationship is perhaps the most beneficial and least harmful to both countries.[31] Although this cannot be taken for granted, for both China and Japan aspire to play a bigger regional role during the coming millennium, Beijing and Tokyo have been able to manage some thorny issues, including the dispute over the Diaoyu Islands.

The same pragmatic approach to disputes over historical and contemporary issues can be found in China's relations with the more distant powers, especially regarding issues close to home, such as Hong Kong and Taiwan. Though a communist country, China negotiated with the British a peaceful ending of the colonial rule of Hong Kong, which contrasts sharply with the military takeover of the Portuguese enclave of Goa by India, a democracy. The turnover of Hong Kong on July 1, 1997, was followed by relatively uneventful Chinese rule with a generally optimistic view toward the future being held by Hong Kong people and other major powers.[32] Sino-French relations, too, turned the corner in 1997[33] after a steep downturn during the early 1990s, when Paris decided to sell Taiwan sixty Mirage–2000V fighters.

To be sure, China's relations with other powers and its neighbors are not problem-free. Yet many problems have either been resolved or are being managed. It is therefore fair to state that China's relations with neighboring states have never been better.[34]

MANAGING RELATIONS WITH THE SOLE SUPERPOWER

If the current trend inside and around China continues, it is reasonable to predict that in the medium term China's economy will be more powerful, its economic structure more decentralized,[35] and its politics more liberalized.[36] China will become a more formidable power in East Asia, and its impact and influence will be felt increasingly by its neighbors. Meanwhile, a rising and liberalizing China positively engages neighbors and other major powers, with the exception of the United States.

That exception, however, could be fatal not only to China's regional policy but also to its historic rise to wealth and power. No regional policy in China can be complete without a stable and working relationship with Washington. The issue at stake is simple: The United States is forwardly deployed in the Asia-Pacific. This means that anything "internal" (such as Hong Kong or Taiwan, according to China) or on China's periphery can be viewed by Washington as part of its global concern. Such a geopolitical fact of life is compounded by the physical location of China and its complex relationships with neighbors, many of whom have had territorial disputes with China dating back to ancient times and who are always wary of China's economic might, military potential, and political influence. The sheer size of China's population, territory, and armed forces (no matter how outdated) remains a major concern for neighboring states, regardless of the nature of China's domestic system. It is also true that China pursues an independent foreign policy, maintains the largest ground force in the world, and possesses its own independent nuclear force, which is being modernized at a steady pace. Under these circumstances, even well-intended policies or purely defensive actions by China will be cause for concern by others. These circumstances always provide Washington with opportunities and excuses to project its influence around China.

During the 1990s, Sino-U.S. relations have been in a roller-coaster state at best or drifting toward long-term confrontation at worst. It is ironic that such a trend in Sino-U.S. relations occurs even as Beijing adopts a low-profile, regionalized, economic-oriented, conservative foreign policy[37] and as its relations with the sole superpower are being broadened and deepened. Nonetheless, in almost all areas—be they human rights, trade, security, or arms sales—there seems to be numerous conflicts of interest between China and the United States, between a rising regional power and the lone global superpower. As the twentieth century comes to its end, the strategic drifting of bilateral relations seems to head toward strategic confrontation.

A host of factors and developments, sometimes beyond the control of China and the United States, have contributed to their deteriorating relationship. The impact of the systemic changes starting from the late 1980s, namely, the end of the superpower confrontation and eventually of the bilateral system itself, decommissioned the strategic partnership between Beijing and Washington. The 1989 Beijing crackdown forever changed the image of China in the West. The mere existence of a major communist power in China in a democratizing world, no matter how many changes the country has gone through, makes Beijing the natural target of Western media.[38] These systemic changes, among others, constitute the general environment for a deteriorating, more confrontational relationship between Beijing and Washington during the 1990s, when both sides are bogged down with differences, in contrast to the previous two decades, when they fostered similarities.

At the regional level, three separate but related developments have pushed the two countries down a more difficult path. The first are two parallel trends in Taiwan, where the democratization and Taiwanization of local politics give rise to the effort to gain nominal independence from the Chinese mainland. Despite the surge in economic, cultural, and individual exchanges across the Taiwan Strait during the 1990s, the island is drifting away from the mainland. Meanwhile, the "strategic ambiguity" of the United States with regard to the Taiwan issue indirectly and perhaps directly encourages Taiwan to go independent. By 1995, when Pres. Lee Teng-hui was allowed to visit the United States, Washington's "one China" policy, based on three communiqués with Beijing since the early 1970s, was seen as tilting significantly toward Taiwan or as the beginning of a de facto "two China" policy. The stage was therefore set for a fast decline of the already troubled and fragile bilateral relations between Beijing and Washington. The 1996 Taiwan Strait crisis was the result of all these actions and counteractions. Not only did it bring the two countries close to a tense standoff not seen since the height of the Vietnam War;[39] it also played a major role in reaffirming the shaky U.S.-Japan security treaty, which was damaged by the 1995 Okinawa rape case.

There is no question that U.S. China policy since the Taiwan Strait crisis has been more realistic and more consistent than before. However, the People's Liberation Army's (PLA) show of force also undermines China's efforts during the past twenty years to foster a peaceful relationship with neighbors. Perhaps more than anything else, the crisis highlights the improved power projection capability of the PLA to areas close to home and China's willingness to use that power if necessary. Here, too, is an irony. Since the mid-1980s, China's defense strategy, like its foreign policy, has regionalized considerably. The concepts of total war and people's war were replaced by a focus on localized contingencies. This change of strategic thinking has led to a long-term downsizing, depoliticization, professionalization, and modernization of the Chinese military.[40] Largely because of the crisis, China's regional foreign and defense policies during the past few years have been greeted by neighbors with more suspicion and apprehension, even with countermeasures by other powers. The PLA's show of force in 1995–1996, therefore, brought these deep-seated fears to the surface and fed them into the much publicized "China threat" argument. Partially because of this, the United States has become more determined to stay forwardly deployed in Asia and around China. Thus, a diplomatic and military line of engagement has been drawn around China's periphery and coast. In the eyes of many Chinese policy elites, such a line can be easily switched from engagement to containment, depending on circumstances.[41] Domestic developments and mutual perceptions in the United States and China, however, do not seem conducive to a less confrontational relationship.

The "China Issue" for America

These developments, among others, have presented Washington with unusual and sometimes difficult choices.[42] China is not a Western democracy, and there is little chance of its being Westernized in the foreseeable future. Unlike the former Soviet Union, China has no intention to universalize a Bolshevik-style ideology, and China is a multiethnic nation that seems able to hold together despite ethnonationalism elsewhere in the post–Cold War world.[43] Its foreign policy has been scaled down from global to regional, combining with some of the largest unilateral peacetime reductions of its armed forces during the reform. Perhaps more than at any time during the past 150 years, China wants to work with the United States and the existing international system. The United States, for its part, has benefited enormously from a largely contented, modernizing, and stable China during the past two decades. Unless something extraordinary happens to launch a Cold War–type crusade against such a rising power, which is technically possible, aggression toward China would be a hard sell to U.S. allies, let alone the rest of the world.

Yet the current strategic disparity between the sole superpower and much weaker regional powers like China perhaps cannot last forever. If China's historical ascendance cannot be contained or reversed now, it will be more difficult to do so in the medium and long terms. There is no question that containing or confronting China would be costly. The United States, according to some, may have to do something for its own domestic cohesion.[44] Perhaps the biggest, though mostly unspoken, concern among some in the United States is a psychological and emotional discomfort that the historical rise of China has not been, and will not be, directly administered by the United States, an experience markedly different from the U.S.-led resurrections of Germany and Japan following the devastation of World War II.

These difficult questions and concerns regarding China and U.S.-China relations were very much cut to the core of the so-called great China policy debate of 1997, which politicized U.S. China policy in a way not seen since the McCarthy era of the 1950s. Once again, China was described as "fascist," an "evil empire," and a "militarized state." According to one China observer, the debate was led by the so-called new anti-China groups ranging from the liberal weekly magazine *The New Republic* to the conservative *Weekly Standard*. Their influence has been well beyond that of Washington's foreign policy elite. Not only was China portrayed as the new evil empire, after Ronald Reagan's definition of the former Soviet Union; China specialists were also criticized in a way "eerily reminiscent of that dark [McCarthy] period in American political history." Some of those who used to associate with U.S. China policymaking and analysis were said to link to a vast, conspiracy-type business network with connections to top Chinese officials and corporations at the expense of America's national interests.[45] Even millions of Chinese Americans were accused of being disloyal to the United States because they were "domestic partners" of Chinese communism.[46] Much of this rhetoric is far from truth and is instead based upon imagination, stereotypes, misperceptions, and even racial motivations. It is interesting that these statements resemble strongly those of the Red Guard tabloids during China's Cultural Revolution (1966–1976). Before the accused can be clarified, the damage is done. Such a biased preoccupation with the China issue may go well into the next century. This debate, however, is by no means an isolated and sudden eruption. Ever since the 1989 Beijing crackdown, there has been a growing polemic among the political and intellectual elite in the West regarding the goals, motivations, processes, and outcomes of the PRC's domestic politics and foreign behavior. For example, only in a few years since the late 1980s, U.S. perceptions of China have gone from the China collapse school to one of the China threat. To be sure, these views do not necessarily represent the entirety of the scholarly and political opinions outside China. They are nonetheless the most visible ones these days and have been a potent force behind the roller-coaster ride of Sino-U.S. relations during the 1990s.

The China issue, therefore, has been largely domesticized, particularly during election years. When the media bashes the new evil empire, the politicians echo the rhetoric, though they would quickly forget or reverse what they say.[47] Very often, as observed by Stapleton Roy, U.S. ambassador to Beijing (1991–1995), much of the characterization of China in the U.S. domestic debate does not sound like the China in which he lived for four years.[48] Meanwhile, anything negative about China can be blown out of proportion by the media.[49] Before anything can be clarified, Sino-U.S. relations would quickly drop to a new low ebb. Usually, it takes a much longer time for the two sides to recover from these jolts. Largely because of this, U.S.-China relations have been held "hostage" to the wild swing of public opinions between indifference and have overcharged emotions regarding China. From the Tiananmen Incident to late 1997, there had been no summit meeting to deal with this deeply troubled bilateral relationship, perhaps the most important for the post–Cold War world. Top U.S. officials would try to avoid meeting and dealing with PRC leaders for fear of domestic repercussions.[50] The Clinton administration started as if there was no China policy,[51] then made many flip-flops on the issues of human rights, most-favored-nation status, the visit of Taiwan's president, and so on. Some of these abrupt changes may have even surprised some senior foreign policy makers within the administration as much as their Chinese counterparts. As a result, the credibility and effectiveness of U.S. China policy were called into question.[52]

Beijing's Growing Displeasure

Although Washington essentially put its China policy on autopilot, a negative perception of the United States in China was also brewing together with a rising tide of nationalism across all sectors of Chinese society. Unlike Chinese nationalism of the past, coming when the country was weak and divided, contemporary Chinese nationalism is rising along with the growing Chinese power. For many in China, it seems to be a historical injustice that their country has always been kept out of the international order for much of the twentieth century despite its contribution to the winning side in both World War I and World War II as well as the Cold War.[53]

For China, managing relations with the sole superpower is a difficult job. There is no question that the downturn of the bilateral relationship came with the 1989 crackdown. As a result, the *image* of China in the eyes of the U.S. public has forever changed. The *substance* of China's reform, however, has not been tarnished. If anything, China further opens itself to the outside world to the point of no return. Deng's successors came up with a major reform plan only a few months after his death in early 1997 that would introduce market measures to state-owned enterprises, the core of the socialist command economy. When political commentators across the United States cheered President Clinton's witty remarks to visiting Chinese Pres. Jiang Zemin in October 1997—that China was "on the wrong side of history"[54]—most ignored that China has been traveling significantly away from its shadowy past toward the right side. Nonetheless, in the busy, high-tech world, image—not necessarily substance—may be more important for public consumption.

Although other Western powers and Japan lifted their sanctions a few years after the Tiananmen crackdown, Washington's attitude remained largely uncompromising, and soon its "list" to "punish" Beijing grew quickly into many areas, including human rights, trade, weapons sales, nuclear testing, prison product exports, Hong Kong, Tibet, Taiwan, China's membership in the World Trade Organization (WTO), Beijing's bid for hosting the 2000 Olympics (1993), the search of a Chinese ship *Yinhe* (1993),[55] religious freedom, the fashionable China collapse and China threat arguments, the new and redefined U.S.-Japan Security Treaty (1997), and the ongoing issue related to alleged Chinese illegal campaign contributions during the 1996 elections. It seems that no matter what China does, Washington would not be satisfied.

For the Americans, including some genuinely objective and honest scholars, there is hardly a U.S. grand strategy, let alone a conspiracy, behind all these activities against China.[56] Yet for Beijing, the never-ending accusations from the United States—official or opinioned, organized or disorganized—are by no means isolated, if not carefully orchestrated, efforts of the sole superpower to contain China. As a result of these developments, many Chinese, including liberal-minded members of the political and intellectual elites, perceive the motivations and policies of the United States with deep ambivalence, even strong resentment.[57] They complain that the West largely ignored the worst human rights abuses in China under Mao in exchange for China's strategic partnership against the Soviet threat. Yet after the West "won" the Cold War, it discarded China just when its human rights record was the best in PRC history. All of these pressures from the West have coincided with China's rapid transformation from a highly politicized Leninist state to a more open, albeit still authoritarian, society with considerable and increasing individual freedom, especially in the fast growing private spheres. Some Chinese go so far as to believe that the West is deliberately trying to slow down or even reverse China's modernization drive.

Crisis and Damage Control

As a result of these changes, the feeling of novelty of the 1970s and the partnership of the 1980s in Sino-American relations has been replaced by skepticism and even animosity in the 1990s. Although the overall structure of the bilateral relationship remains and has even expanded to new areas from time to time, mutual trust is being steadily eroded to the point where relatively minor issues can be easily blown out of proportion. Compromise and mutual accommodation are still attainable, but only after hard bargaining and with considerable use of punitive measures, instead of positive rewards, by both sides. Differences instead of common interests between the two countries are highlighted; this represents a marked departure from the mutually accommodating atmosphere at the beginning of the Sino-U.S. rapprochement of the 1970s.

These negative perceptions, policies, and counteractions by both sides culminated in 1996, when the two militaries zeroed in at the Taiwan Strait. The momentum for a showdown, however, had been gathering for years. For many Chinese, the West's unspoken hostility toward China is most apparent in the Taiwan issue. Although Taiwan's independent trend is largely being driven by its domestic dynamics, many in China believe that outside powers are behind Taiwan's drifting toward independence. They point to evidence that the United States and other Western countries have sold Taiwan advanced weaponry in large quantities, upgraded their relations with the island, and showed more willingness to admit Taiwan into various international forums. The 1995 White House decision to allow Taiwan's president to visit the United States as a private citizen was seen as a major betrayal by the United States.[58] Now many in the United States would agree, with the hindsight of history, that Clinton's flip-flop on the visa issue directly led China to fire missiles off Taiwan.[59]

Crises, nonetheless, always offer some lessons and opportunities. Although it jolted the status quo, the 1996 Taiwan Strait crisis also tested the limits on both sides. Both realized the need to stabilize their relations and to readjust the way they engaged one another (perhaps by looking beyond Taiwan if necessary or ignoring the occasional destabilizing rhetoric and behavior of Taiwan). Crises, however, may not always be as generous in offering sobering effects as conventional wisdom suggests. A less noticed yet perhaps more important outcome of the 1996 Taiwan Strait crisis was the closing of the brief window of opportunity in the post–Cold War era for major powers in East Asia to construct a more stable regional framework for the twenty-first century. Instead, the old alliance (U.S.-Japan) is being reinforced while Sino-Russia relations have been solidified. To be sure, China, the United States, and other major powers have cooperated on some occasions to ease tensions in East Asia, particularly on the Korean

Peninsula. And all alliance partners are somewhat evasive about the goals, scale, and degree of their new arrangements.[60] Although it is still premature to conclude that the new geostrategic faultlines in East Asia are finalized, the ambiguity in major-power realignment, intended or unintended, can be misperceived and even lead to dangerous outcomes.

The October 1997 Sino-U.S. summit yielded some symbolic results, such as: the so-called strategic partnership; the hotline agreement between the two capitals; the subsequent signing of an agreement to avoid naval accidents; and U.S. promise to join China's nuclear power projects. The Chinese side released a leading dissident, Wei Jingsheng. Both sides worked hard and carefully in order to build stronger momentum for Clinton's visit to China in 1998. The result of this summitry, however, turned out to be mixed, despite many of its surprises, such as the last-minute decision to televise some of Clinton's activities and speeches in China. Although Clinton reaffirmed some basics in U.S.-China relations,[61] the U.S. Congress quickly passed a series of pro-Taiwan bills to balance or undermine his executive authority, which is also steadily being eroded by his personal scandals. Much of his elaborate trip to China was quickly forgotten.

Beneath these more publicized and seemingly more cooperative gestures during the two summit meetings, however, Washington and Beijing have been working to strengthen their respective strategic postures in East Asia. Diplomatically, the United States and China continue to improve relations with many of China's neighboring countries, including Vietnam, India, Mongolia, Kazakhstan, the ASEAN states, and even North Korea. Militarily, the United States continues to strengthen its forward deployment with 100,000 U.S. troops in the Asia-Pacific within a newly defined and broadened security treaty with Japan. The joint decision during Clinton's 1988 trip to China not to target each other with nuclear weapons is more symbolic than substantive in that hundreds of U.S. intercontinental ballistic missiles can be quickly reprogrammed to target China. These measures by the two sides resemble more those between Moscow and Washington during the Cold War than they do relations between two "strategic partners" for the twenty-first century. Even if some PLA analysts show some considerable respect toward their U.S. counterpart as a consistently "moderate" and "pragmatic" force for "stable" and "healthy" U.S.-China relations,[62] the renewed military contacts serve more as opportunities to size up each other rather than serving mutual trust.

THE U.S.-JAPAN SECURITY TREATY: BACK TO THE FUTURE

Officially signed in September 1997, the new, expanded version of the U.S.-Japan Security Treaty[63] quietly but unambiguously closed the post–

Cold War era in East Asia as large powers maneuver into gradually hardened alliances. Many in China view the newly secured alliance with grave concerns, for several reasons.

First, the new version of the U.S.-Japan Security Treaty is seen by China's policy analysts as covering a much broader geographical area, including the Taiwan Strait, the South China Sea, even the entire Asia-Pacific region. This is a major departure from its predecessor, which would be activated only if Japan was attacked. Perhaps most disturbing for Chinese defense planners is the implicit but unambiguous indication that China has replaced the former Soviet Union as the major target. From the Chinese perspective, the timing of the new revision of the U.S.-Japan Security Treaty, starting one month after the March 1996 Taiwan Strait crisis, suggests that the China issue in general and the Taiwan issue in particular have been the main concerns for Tokyo and Washington.[64] Finally, the U.S.-Japan Security Treaty is seen as a significant threat to China's national unification with Taiwan.[65] Already, the United States has reintroduced the 7th Fleet into the Taiwan Strait (since 1995), with many of its large surface ships coming from bases in Japan. Japanese politicians bluntly told Beijing leaders that Japan would not sit idly by if Beijing uses force against Taiwan, a Japanese colony for some fifty years (1895–1945).[66]

To be sure, the potential of the U.S.-Japan Security Treaty is yet to be fully tapped by both Tokyo and Washington, as the wording of the revised treaty is deliberately vague. Nonetheless, the vagueness of the U.S.-Japan Security Treaty also means flexibility for any contingency that may arise. Moreover, the revived alliance treaty is seen to elevate Japan's role to one of equality from the past junior partnership. More active Japanese foreign and defense policies are likely to follow. In early 1998, less than six months after the new version of the security treaty became official, Japan joined Britain in the United Nations to initiate a bill for automatic military strikes against Iraq, which marks a clear departure from its postwar, low-profile, peace-oriented policy. The North Korean test of a medium-range missile across Japan on August 31, 1998, raised once again the specter of U.S. support for a Japanese missile defense program, that could also involve Taiwan. For Beijing, if Japan in 1951 boarded the ship of Pax Americana by signing the Japan-U.S. Security Alliance Treaty in order to have a "free ride," then Tokyo is now ready to steer, if necessary, the ship of alliance into the twenty-first century.

THE FUTURE: SOME NOT-SO-MODEST PROPOSALS

The pragmatic regional policy of China has gradually taken shape during the past twenty years. China's long-term effort to cultivate good relations with its neighbors, however, has been basically bilateral in nature and at the "microist" level. A more peaceful and stable regional environment is yet to be fully constructed. If anything, the forward U.S. deployment and web of alliances in the Asia-Pacific dictate that Sino-U.S. engagement, be it peaceful or confrontational, will be in East Asia and around China's periphery. This geopolitical posture, perhaps, will not significantly change by the next century, even with the rosiest of projections for China's economic growth. Meanwhile, some of the difficult problems between the two countries—Taiwan, human rights, trade, weapon sales, the South China Sea, and so on—will remain; they may get worse and even erupt from time to time.

Although these problems will continue to be at the top of the agenda for Beijing and Washington well into the next century, political elites in both countries may find it necessary and beneficial to transcend them by inquiring into some long-term issues and questions in order to construct a conceptual perimeter in which the two countries will engage each other during the coming century.

For both countries, the twenty-first century will undoubtedly test, for the first time in modern history, whether the rise of a major power can be peaceful and relatively low-cost, for both China and the rest of the world. That prospect, however, is far from clear, and many uncertainties lie ahead. For China, its historic rise after centuries of decay and decline will undoubtedly exert a multitude of impacts on the world, particularly its neighbors. Chinese foreign policy elites would have to learn how to relate a richer, more powerful China to the rest of the world, even if they have accumulated a great amount of expertise in managing external relations when the country was weak, poor, and sometimes deeply divided. For the United States, its twentieth-century accomplishments in pacifying fascist Germany and militarist Japan and containing communist Russia will perhaps provide little guidance in dealing with a country like China. Can the United States—which fought its way onto the world stage during the twentieth century—be able to tolerate, absorb, and manage the rise of a major, non-Western power without a last-ditch fight?

This question may sound hypothetical today. Political and intellectual elites of both countries, however, will have to face it early in the next century. The challenging task for both countries is that issues regarding rising and status quo powers cannot be simulated in an abstract, controlled environment, for they have engaged, and will continue to engage, each other in a complex situation in East Asia, where the rises and falls of great powers (China, Japan, Russia, and the United States) during the past two hundred years seem to have been parts of an enduring geopolitical game. The fact is that East Asia now faces the rise of not one but two regional powers: China and Japan. Despite an essentially peaceful intercourse between the two Asian powers during the second half of the twentieth century, a historical reconciliation of the Franco-German type is yet to be achieved. Although such a state of affairs provides the United States with opportunities to insert its influence, there are limits in playing one against another. The Japan question will become particularly and increasingly acute early next century as Japanese elites move to make the country a "normal" power, ridding Japan of the internal and external constraints to exercise its sovereign rights, such as armaments and the use of military force. Yet for all three parties, as well as the rest of the Asia-Pacific, the current "abnormal" situation, in which Japan does not have "real" foreign and defense policies, of the past fifty years happens to be the most peaceful and prosperous era in the region.[67] Will a "normal" Japan continue to behave the same way? The future prospect may be even less encouraging for Beijing given the fact that an increasing number of Japanese aspiring to correct Japan's incomplete power status do not exactly understand or accept how and why this anomaly was imposed upon their country in the first place.

If that is the trend in Japan, political elites in China may have to realize that U.S. hegemony, for all its perceived "misbehavior" toward China, including a high-handed China policy since the late 1980s, also parallels, even provides, a historical opportunity for the modernization of China, something that other hegemonic powers, be they European colonialists or Japanese militarists, could never do. Then if a forwardly deployed American presence would continue in the foreseeable future, a logical conclusion for Beijing is to accept the U.S. presence around China's periphery, work with the United States on regional issues, and maximize its interest within the U.S.-dominated world trading system. Although the United States has power, China should have patience.

In the final analysis, a stable and peaceful periphery has to start from home. Short of a massive nuclear exchange, which is highly unlikely, the biggest potential threat to the survival of China's existing system would come from within, not from the outside. Specifically, the most challenging task for China is whether sociopolitical stability, currently the longest stretch in 150 years, can be sustained. That prospect appears more difficult in the future as the Asian economies continue to destabilize. The type of near double-digit economic growth that China has experienced during the past twenty years will be unlikely to continue, as the country had officially entered a "buyers-market" economy by early 1998. A near saturated home market also means less opportunity for millions of Chinese entering the already oversupplied job market. Meanwhile, continuous sociopolitical liberalization will lead to increasing societal input into foreign policy–making. As a result, the public sentiments and opinion will have more sway over the policymaking elite, which has so far been relatively free of societal constraints. Finally, a set of stable and legitimate value systems for the cohesion of the Chinese nation needs to be convincingly articulated, developed, and institutionalized by Chinese political and intellectual elites. Otherwise, in the wake of Mao's romantic, bankrupt communism, and with the influx of Western liberalism and commercialism, China's modernization can be difficult and even dangerous.

It is against this backdrop that China engages the United States into the next century in East Asia, a region vital for China's security and survival and for America's sense of leadership and pride.

NOTES

1. According to Frances Fukuyama, the end of the Cold War means the end of "history," in which Western liberalism triumphed over fascism and communism. The "posthistory" era would be relatively uneventful and even boring. Fukuyama, *The End of History and the Last Man* (New York: The Free Press, 1991).

2. In early April 1996, Tokyo and Washington reaffirmed the shaky security alliance and opened the door for a much bigger Japanese military role in the future alliance and regional affairs. Later in the month, Beijing and Moscow elevated their "constructive partnership" into a "strategic" one.

3. Steven I. Levine, "China in Asia: The PRC as a Regional Power," in *China's Foreign Relations in the 1980s*, Harry Harding, ed. (New Haven: Yale University Press, 1984), 107–114; Michael H. Hunt, "Chinese Foreign Relations in Historical Perspective," in Harding, *China's Foreign Relations*, 1–42; Samuel S. Kim, *China In and Out of the Changing World Order* (Princeton: Princeton University Press, 1991), 84.

4. See Lucian W. Pye, *China: An Introduction*, 4th ed. (New York: HarperCollins Publishers, 1991), 120.

5. Several dynasties did reach parts of central Asia and today's Siberia. There was, nevertheless, little effective and durable administration of these areas due to their harsh natural conditions.

6. Harold C. Hinton, "China as an Asian Power," in *Chinese Foreign Policy: Theory and Practice*, Thomas W. Robinson and David Shambaugh, eds. (Oxford: Oxford University Press, 1995), 348–374.

7. For an excellent discussion of China's foreign behavior, see Harry Harding, "China's Co-operative Behavior," in Robinson and Shambaugh, *Chinese Foreign Policy*, 375–400.

8. This refers to Beijing's demand for the removal of the three major "obstacles" in normalizing relations with Moscow. They are: (1) Soviet withdrawal from Afghanistan; (2) stopping assistance to Vietnam's occupation of Cambodia; and (3) reduction of Soviet troops along Sino-Soviet border and from Mongolia.

9. Tian Zengpei, ed., *Gaige kaifang yilai de zhongguo waijiao (China's Foreign Policy During the Reform and Open Door Period)* (Beijing: World Knowledge Publisher, 1993), 27–28.

10. Ibid., 101–110.

11. In his 1975 visit to China, North Korean leader Kim Il Sung clearly hinted that he was ready to use force to unify the country, similar to what the North Vietnamese just did. Mao apparently persuaded him not to do so. The militant rhetoric dropped in Kim's farewell speech, and he instead stressed "peaceful" efforts to

unify the country toward the end of his visit to China. See *Peking Review,* 25 April and 2 May 1975.

12. See Tian Zengpei, *China's Foreign Policy,* 20–21.

13. See *Renmin ribao* (*People's Daily,* henceforth *RMRB*), 12 July 1996.

14. The lack of high-level contacts between China and North Korea, however, is largely due to the three-year mourning period following's Kim Il Sung's death in 1994, a common practice by Confucianist scholars.

15. Beijing eventually established full diplomatic relations with Seoul in August 1992, two years after Moscow did the same in September 1990. But Beijing's cautious move after the "Soviet betrayal" gave Beijing two years of additional time to solidify its political ties with Pyongyang, at least formally.

16. In 1982 and 1983, two Chinese air force pilots defected to South Korea; in May 1983, a Chinese civilian aircraft was hijacked to Seoul; in March 1985, a PLAN torpedo boat also defected. Although Seoul refused Beijing's requests for the return of pilot and plane in the first two cases, Seoul's position softened in 1983, with the return of the airliner and all the crew members and the torpedo boat in 1985. See Lu Ning, *The Dynamics of Foreign-Policy Decisionmaking in China* (Boulder, Colo.: Westview Press, 1997), 124–126.

17. Tian Zengpei, *China's Foreign Policy,* 24–26; *RMRB,* 11 and 14 December 1996.

18. With a few exceptions, for example, relations with Vietnam and Afghanistan. China's relations with the two countries had to wait for the breakthrough in the Beijing-Moscow negotiations on normalization of relations.

19. *RMRB,* 16 December 1991.

20. Publicly, China during the 1990s opposes any disturbance to the status quo coming from either side of the 38th Parallel.

21. This includes the recent issue of Taiwan's proposed shipping of nuclear waste to North Korea and the defection of a top North Korean leader to South Korea in Beijing in 1997. Mr. Hwang Jang Yop, the top theoretician of North Korean's ideology of *juche,* defected to South Korea while he was in Beijing for a "shopping trip." Hwang was one of the eleven secretaries of the ruling Workers Party and roughly the twenty-fifth–ranking leader in the North's hierarchy. *The New York Times,* 13 February 1997.

22. China has provided North Korea with 120,000 tons and 70,000 tons of grain in 1996 and 1997. *Beijing Review,* 12–18 May 1997, 12.

23. In reaction to Beijing's diplomatic breakthrough with Seoul, North Korea opened direct trade relations with Taiwan in 1992 and in June 1996 sent a deputy minister to Taipei for more economic assistance. *Shijie Ribao (World Journal),* 21 and 23 June 1996.

24. In the ten years between 1979 and 1988, there were four waves of China's opening-up along coastal regions: the 1979 decision to set up four special economic zones; the 1984 decision to open up fourteen coastal cities; the 1985 decision to open up the Yangtze River and Pearl River deltas in the Xiamen region across the Taiwan Strait; and the 1988 decision to open up an additional 140 cities and counties along coastal regions of China, including the Liaodong and Shandong Peninsulas and the Hainan Island (it became a province in April 1988). By this point, 292 counties and cities with a population of 200 million along the vast

coastal areas of China were opened up for direct foreign trade and investment. This trend was accelerated in the 1990s, including the 1991 decision to open twenty-one new high-tech parks throughout the country, and 1992 decision to grant twenty inland cities and provinces liberal trade and investment polices similar to those coastal regions. By the end of 1992, there were five hundred trading ports throughout China. See RMRB, 15 May 1996; Chen Shu et al., "Zhongguo jingji dui-wai kaifang shisi nian, 1979–1992" ("The Fourteen Years of China's Economic Opening-Up, 1979–1992"), *Nankai jingji yanjiu (Nankai Economic Studies)*, no. 2 (1993): 55–66.

25. Chinese Pres. Jiang Zemin was quoted as saying that China was willing to contribute some $4–$6 billion to the IMF's effort to stabilize the currency crisis in Asia. *Shijie Ribao,* 17 December 1997.

26. This includes Gorbachev of the former Soviet Union, Yeltsin of Russia, Kim Il Sung of North Korea, Castro of Cuba, and Vietnamese and Central Asia countries' leaders.

27. Partially because of that, Vietnam has recently become one of the largest rice exporters in the world, second only to Thailand and the United States. Its urban and trade reforms also make the country one of the hottest investment havens in the region.

28. *Shijie Ribao,* 26 December 1997, A-4.

29. Russia's historical expansion to Asia was temporarily checked by the 1689 Treaty of Nerchinsk with the Qing Dynasty, after a number of military clashes between the two countries. By the late eighteenth century, however, Russian expansion into areas on China's periphery regained momentum, and clashes became increasingly frequent. This culminated in the signing of the Sino-Russian Treaty of Peking in November 1860, when the entire northern frontier of China was open to Russia's political and commercial influence. See A. Doak Barnet, *China and the Major Powers in East Asia* (Washington, D.C.: Brookings Institution, 1977), 21–22; Joseph Fletcher, "Sino-Russian Relations, 1800–1862," in John Fairbank, ed., *The Cambridge History of China, Volume 10: Late Ch'ing, 1800–1911,* pt. 1 (Cambridge: Cambridge University Press, 1992), 347. This time frame indicates a more conflictual relationship because of Russia's constant expansion during much of the nineteenth and twentieth centuries.

30. Japan is the only country in Asia that China has ever gone to full-scale war with and was defeated by repeatedly in the past one hundred years. Of the fourteen wars Japan waged between its 1868 Meiji Restoration and its defeat in World War II, ten targeted China. See Xi Laiwang, *Ershiyi shiji zhongguo zhanlue da cehua: waijiao molue (China's Grand Strategy into the Twenty-First Century: Strategic Calculus of China's Diplomacy)* (Beijing: Hongqi chubanshe, 1996), 133.

31. If the first half of the twentieth century was a period of Japanese military aggression against China, bilateral relations were also a victim of the rigid Cold War international system and China's domestic instability between the 1950s and 1970s.

32. A recent poll shows that the confidence level is high for 93 percent of the British companies that have invested some £70 billion and employed 300,000 local people. *Shijie Ribao,* 1 and 8 September 1997.

33. French President Jacques Chirac visited Beijing in May 1997.

34. China declared this as early as 1992. See He Fang (deputy director, Center for International Studies, State Council), speech delivered at the 1992 NPC meeting, *RMRB*, 3 April 1992.

35. Unlike the rise of Japan, which benefited largely from the Korean War and Vietnam War, or the "Little Dragons," whose "neoindustrial Confucianist" state guided the modernizing society, the reform decades in China have seen a progressive weakening and erosion of the extractive and distributive ability of the central government. Deng's decision to go to a family farming system in 1978 essentially turn the vast countryside in China back to a system similar to the Confucianist empire, where the emperor is far away. For the East Asian model, see Ezra Vogel, *The Four Little Dragons: The Spread of Industrialization in East Asia* (Cambridge: Harvard University Press, 1990), 92–103.

36. China is known for its economic, not political reforms. Yet to say there is no political change in China is simply untrue. If anything, China has pursued a different sequence to free the people from Maoist totalitarian rule. In contrast to the sweeping, radical, "illiberal," and sometimes violent democratization in some parts of the world in recent years, Deng Xiaoping allowed for a gradualist and bottom-up approach to achieve democratic self-governing for the vast Chinese rural areas. Since the early 1980s, an increasing number of Chinese rural areas across China have, through direct elections, adopted some "self-governing" mechanisms, including villagers' committees and villagers' representative assemblies. In 1982, the system of self-governing was formally written into the PRC Constitution. This system is a radical departure from the village governing system of "the People's Commune" under Mao, where a few cadres and CCP members made all important decisions. By 1985, 948,628 villagers' committees existed in China. This grassroots democratization was even accelerated after the 1989 Beijing crackdown. By 1996, more than 85 percent of rural officials were directly elected through competitive elections. According to the Ministry of Civil Affairs, which supervises the procedure, eighteen provinces went through elections for the third term of their villagers' committees. By 2000, all villages in China should have adopted this self-governing system through substantial, effective elections. Fareed Zakaria, "The Rise of Illiberal Democracies," *Foreign Affairs* (November/December, 1997); Jiang Wandi, "Grassroots Democracy Taking Root," *Beijing Review*, 11–17 March 1996, 11–14; Yan Jiaqi, "June 4th Led to Major Changes in China," *Shijie Ribao*, 22 May and 23 December 1996.

37. See Robert S. Ross, "Beijing as a Conservative Power," *Foreign Affairs* 76, no. 2 (March/April 1997): 33–44; Andrew J. Nathan and Robert S. Ross, *The Great Wall and the Empty Fortress: China's Search for Security* (New York: W. W. Norton, 1997).

38. Before 1989, Western media focused on the changes that had taken place in China from Mao's legacies. Today, they focus on China's continuities of communism. Either is adequate. Both are misleading.

40. In some twenty years (1975–1996), China cut more than half of the PLA forces from its peak of 6 million in the mid-1970s. At present, another cut of a half-million is pending.

41. Interviews with Chinese foreign and defense policy scholars, 1996 and 1998.

42. See *The New York Times*, editorial, 2 July 1995.

43. Non-Han minorities are a fraction of the total population.

44. According to Samuel P. Huntington, even if China's current system collapsed or was destroyed, China would remain China. Historically and theoretically, "the United States, perhaps more than most countries, may need an opposing other to maintain its unity." Otherwise, the United States would collapse like the former Soviet empire. See Huntington, "The Erosion of American National Interests," *Foreign Affairs* (September/October 1997), 32.

45. For a description of this debate, see David Shambaugh, "The United States and China: Cooperation or Confrontation," *Current History* (September 1997): 241–245.

46. These people include many prominent former government officials, such as Kissinger, Eagleburger, Haig, Shultz, Cheney, Scowcroft, Vance, Muskie, Woodcock, Christopher, etc. See John B. Judis, "Chinatown," *New Republic* (10 March 1997): 17–20; Peter Beinart, "Domestic Partners," *New Republic* (10 March 1997): 12–14.

47. An earlier episode was on May 19, 1994, when CBS anchor Connie Chung suggested that many, if not all, Chinese Americans may work for China's intelligence. Presidential candidate Bill Clinton attacked the "butchers of Beijing" and insisted on human rights linking with MFN. He then delinked human rights from MFN halfway into his first term.

48. Quoted from Richard Solomon, in a speech to the Asian Studies Center Symposium, "The United States and China into the Twenty-First Century," sponsored by the Heritage Foundation, in *Heritage Lectures,* no. 551 (Washington D.C.: Heritage Foundation, 1996): 17.

49. To be fair, the media do the same thing to domestic affairs, that is, to selectively report some, particularly negative, facts, in order to attract audiences. Nonetheless, though audiences can reasonably quickly detect the "bias" of some reporting on domestic affairs due to their familiarity with the subjects, their opinions on foreign affairs tend to be swayed by fewer and fewer quality media outlets on foreign news. For the dwindling of media reporting on foreign news, see Garrick Utley, "The Shrinking of Foreign News," *Foreign Affairs* (March/April 1997).

Partly because of this, the U.S. general public is among the least informed about international news among industrialized democracies. For some recent studies, see Stephen Bennett et al., "Citizens' Knowledge of Foreign Affairs," *Press/Politics,* 1(2) (1996): 10–29.

50. It is widely believed that Vice President Gore's trip to Beijing in March 1997 will cost him his year 2000 presidential bid.

51. Conversation in late 1992 with Harry Harding, then a senior fellow at the Brookings Institution, who recalled some evening calls from White House staffers who asked his opinion about what should be the administration's China policy.

52. Robert Zoellick, speaking to the conference "Sino-American Relations at the Summit," *Heritage Lectures,* no. 601 (Washington, D.C.: Heritage Foundation, 15 October 1997): 12.

53. The strong sense of betrayal by the West was behind the "May 4th" Movement in 1919, when many Chinese intellectuals switched from pro-Western democracy to Bolshevism after European democracies decided to turn Shandong Province over from Germany to Japan, instead of returning it to China, an ally of

the Western democracies during World War I. Just two years after this, the Chinese Communist Party was founded. The CCP led and was carried by a powerful nationalist tide in China despite all the odds imposed against it by both internal and external forces. This genuine nationalist force, however, was considered more a satellite of Russian communism than of an indigenous Chinese origin during the early years of the Cold War. Amid the Cold War, China, a communist power, became a de facto ally of the West. During the post–Cold War era, China finds itself again being treated by some in the West, particularly the United States, as a communist but not a normal and major power; this situation is similar to that at the beginning of the Cold War.

54. Remarks made during the White House official reception, October 1997.

55. The U.S. government insisted, based on a CIA report, that the Chinese cargo ship *Yinhe* was carrying chemical weapons materials to Iran. The ship was later searched by a joint team of Americans, Saudis, and Chinese, and no weapons-related chemicals were found. There was no apology from the United States for the incident. On a separate occasion, a State Department spokesman suggested that the Chinese crew dumped the material into the open sea. This, however, was unlikely because the ship was closely followed and monitored by the United States Navy.

56. See Ezra F. Vogel, ed., *Living with China: U.S. Relations in the Twenty-First Century* (New York: W.W. Norton, 1997), 29; Richard Solomon, speech at "The Asian Studies Center Symposium: Taiwan–Hong Kong–PRC–United States: The New Quadrille," in *Heritage Lectures*, no. 600 (Washington, D.C.: Heritage Foundation, 31 July 1997): 7; Zoellick, *Heritage Lectures*, 14.

The "no conspiracy" argument, however, is misleading at best. It ignores the *effect* of those "unintended" actions by major powers or superpowers toward smaller and weaker counterparts. Indeed, it may not require any conspiracy by a superpower like the United States to inflict considerable damage on a weaker country. A domestic analogy is racial relations in the United States, where the white majority tends to insist on the "no-conspiracy" argument regarding the issues of church burning and racial discrimination in numerous areas, whereas considerable "uninstitutionalized" discriminatory effects are being felt by minorities.

57. President Clinton encountered some very critical comments and questions with regard to U.S. China policy following his televised speech at Beijing University in 1998. Most of the U.S. media, however, interpreted these questions and comments as staged.

58. This decision was made only after a few weeks when Secretary of State Warren Christopher informed his Chinese counterpart that the United States would not issue a visa for President Lee. According to a recent—though belated—acknowledgment in an editorial in *The New York Times*, the result of Taiwan's successful lobbying activities among U.S. lawmakers and academia meant they then demanded the White House issue the visa for Lee. The White House was therefore driven by all these forces to a decision that brought the two countries closest to a real showdown in twenty-five years. *The New York Times*, editorial, "The Taiwan Factor," 14 April 1997. But between 1995 and 1996, almost all major U.S. media urged to get tough with the Chinese by putting more pressure on Beijing, including inviting Mr. Lee to the United States.

59. Remarks by William Perry, former Secretary of Defense (1992–1996), during the question-and-answer session following his dinner speech made for the conference "America's Alliances with Japan and Korea in a Changing Northeast Asia," August 22, 1997, Stanford University Faculty Club. Also see Zoellick, *Heritage Lectures.*

60. Although the United States and Japan remain ambiguous about the scope of the newly defined treaty, particularly over the issue of Taiwan and China, China and Russia tend to quickly dismiss any implication of their strategic partnership for the third party.

61. On 30 June 1998, Clinton made a "three-nos" statement regarding the Taiwan issue, namely, no support for Taiwan's independence, no support for "two Chinas" or "one Taiwan, one China," and no membership for Taiwan in international organizations that require statehood. See *Far Eastern Economic Review,* 16 July 1998, p. 16.

62. Liu Jinsong, "Zhongmei junshi guanxi de lishi yanbian: wenti he qianjing" ("Historical Evolution of Sino-U.S. Military Relations: Problems and Prospect"), *Zhanglue yu guanli (Strategy and Management)*, no. 5 (1997): 105–113.

63. See Japan-U.S. "Joint Declaration on Security Alliance for the Twenty-first Century," issued on 17 April 1996 after a summit meeting in Tokyo between Prime Minister Ryutaro Hashimoto and Pres. Bill Clinton; Associated Press, 24 September 1997.

64. In fact, efforts to revise the U.S.-Japan Security Treaty started in response to the North Korean nuclear weapons program before the 1995–1996 Taiwan crisis. But most of China's policy analysts perceive the Taiwan crisis as the impetus for the U.S.-Japan treaty revision. For Chinese views, see China Society of Strategy and Management, ed., "Guoji xingshi fenxi baogao" ("1997–1998 Study Reports on International Situation"), *Zhanglue yu guanli (Strategy and Management)*, no. 1 (1998), 58–59; Ren Donglai, "Xingchengzhong de mei ri zhouxin jiqi dui dongya de yingxiang"("The Evolving U.S.-Japan Axis and Its Influence in East Asia"), *Zhanlue yu Guanli (Strategy and Management)*, no. 5 (1996): 51–53.

65. The Information Office of the PRC State Council, "Zhongguo de guofang" ("China's National Defense"), *RMRB,* 28 July 1998, 2–4, 5.

66. *Shijie Ribao,* 4 May 1996.

67. This is in sharp contrast to Japan in the first half of the century, which fought all three major powers—China, Russia, the United States—before it was pacified by the combined forces of all three, including atomic weapons.

10

Taiwan: From Peaceful Offense to Coercive Strategy

Suisheng Zhao

The Taiwan issue is one of the most sensitive aspects of Sino-American relations. To understand China's views on Sino-American relations, we have to understand Beijing's views on the issue of Taiwan. Taiwan was cut off from the mainland China in 1949 when the Kuomintang or Nationalist Party (KMT) was defeated by the Chinese Communist Party (CCP) in a civil war. Relations across the Taiwan Strait were characterized by one crisis after another during the 1950s and 1960s. However, since the late 1970s, Beijing has adopted a "peaceful offense," and economic and culture exchanges have developed rapidly in recent years. However, after more than a decade of a "peaceful reunification offense," Beijing suddenly launched one wave after another of military exercises, including missile tests aimed at Taiwan, prior to Taiwan's first direct presidential election in March 1996. The military exercises were part of a coercive strategy aimed at stopping the perceived momentum of Taiwan independence and Taiwanese collaboration with foreign forces through the use of force in an exemplary and demonstrative manner. This chapter focuses on the shift in Beijing's perceptions of Taiwan's internal politics and international status in an attempt to explain the shift in Beijing's policy from peaceful offense to coercive strategy. I argue that peaceful offense and coercive diplomacy are two sides of the same coin: Coercive logic is embedded in peaceful offense. For Beijing, Taiwan is a vital issue of unsolved sovereignty and the most important consideration in its diplomatic policy. Beijing's adoption of coercive strategy is a result of accumulated frustration, anxiety, and anger over the perceived Taiwanese independence movement driven by Taiwan's democratization, Lee Teng-hui's personal support, and foreign intervention. There is an inherent dynamic that could drive cross-strait relations into a vicious cycle of peace and coercion if Beijing and Taipei cannot negotiate to stabilize the relationship across the Taiwan Strait.

FROM PEACEFUL OFFENSE TO COERCIVE DIPLOMACY

Beijing's peaceful reunification offense was launched on January 1, 1979, when the Standing Committee of the National People's Congress, during its fifth session, published a "Message" to the Taiwan people, hoping that "Taiwan returns to the embrace of the motherland at an early date so that we can work together for the great cause of national development." The new policy was fully elaborated on September 30, 1981, by Ye Jianying, the vice chair of the NPC Standing Committee, in his nine-point proposal for peaceful reunification. Ye suggested talks between the CCP and the KMT and specifically proposed *santong* (three links, i.e., commercial, postal, and travel) and *siliu* (four exchanges, i.e., academic, cultural, economic, and sports) as the first steps to "gradually eliminate antagonism between the two sides and increase mutual understanding."[1] Later, Deng Xiaoping posed a formula of "one country, two systems" as a viable way for reunification. Beijing's peaceful offense reached a new stage when Jiang Zemin, general-secretary of the CCP and the president of the People's Republic of China (PRC), made an eight-point proposal on January 30, 1995, suggesting that the two sides across the Taiwan Strait start negotiations "on officially ending the state of hostility between the two sides and accomplishing peaceful reunification step by step." He suggested that, as the first step, an agreement should be reached on officially ending the state of hostility in accordance with the "one China" principle.

There are three major policy components embodied in the peaceful offense. The first is promotion of economic and cultural exchanges and peaceful negotiations to end the military confrontation across the Taiwan Strait. The second is the one China principle. Under the premise of one China, socialism in the mainland and capitalism in Taiwan will coexist. Taiwan will enjoy a high degree of autonomy, which includes administrative power, legislative power, independent judiciary power, a power to keep its own troops, and certain powers of foreign affairs, such as signing commercial and cultural agreements with foreign countries, although "only the PRC represents China in the international arena."[2] The third is reservation of the use of force as a last resort. Beijing has reiterated, in a nonambiguous way, that to safeguard the one China principle it will not give up the use of force should the situation require it.

Beijing's leaders turned to a peaceful reunification offense during the late 1970s partly because they perceived the opportunities created by the change in Beijing's international status. In 1971 Beijing took Taipei's seat in the UN General Assembly and Security Council. In 1979, the United States switched its diplomatic recognition from Taipei to Beijing. These changes isolated Taiwan in the international arena and also altered Beijing's perception of international relations, from the inevitability of world war to "peace and development" as the main world trend. Beijing felt that the island, which accounts for only 0.003 percent of Chinese territory and less than one-fiftieth of its population, was not, and would not be in the foreseeable future, a major threat to the mainland. As a result, Beijing became more confident in its ability to resolve the Taiwan issue on its own terms and wanted to create a friendly environment for early reunification.

Beijing's peaceful offense brought about some desirable changes in cross-strait relations. The most significant change is the rapid increase in economic interactions. Despite a feeble start in 1979, total trade value across the strait exceeded $20 billion in 1995, a significant portion of the total trade of both sides. Taiwan ranked second (after Japan) as mainland China's major supplier and was its seventh largest export market. In the meantime, the mainland attracted a large amount of Taiwan's investment. According to Taiwan's official statistics, between 1991 and 1995 the Taipei government approved 11,254 investment applications to the mainland with a total value of $56.45 billion; Beijing's statistics shows 31,780 Taiwan investment applications with a total value of $114.27 billion. According to Beijing's official figures, Taiwan invested $31.62 billion on the mainland. This ranked Taiwan the second largest investor in China next only to Hong Kong–Macao ($49.6 billion). The mainland has become the most important outlet for Taiwan's overseas investment, accounting for about 50 percent of the island's total investment abroad during the first quarter of 1995, far exceeding its second country of investment, the United States (21.42 percent).

Because of these desirable changes, Beijing's sudden military exercises in the Taiwan Strait shocked many people outside China. Starting July 21–25, 1995, the People's Liberation Army (PLA) launched a series of surface-to-surface ballistic missile tests in the East China Sea, just 150 kilometers off the tip of northern Taiwan. During August 12–25, 1995, Beijing held a second series of military exercises, including three days of guided-missile, cannon, and other military tests in the sea 136 kilometers north of Taiwan. In November, PLA marines and tanks made a beachhead landing exercise from amphibious landing craft, backed by jet fighters and naval vessels. In March 1996, before Taiwan's direct presidential election, Beijing conducted a new wave of military exercises. On March 8, the PLA launched missiles in two areas: one was nineteen nautical miles from

Keelung, Taiwan's second busiest seaport, the other twenty-eight nautical miles from the harbor of Kaochung, the third largest container port in the world. During March 18–25, joint ground, naval, and air military exercises were conducted in the Taiwan Strait. *The New York Times* stunned the world with a report that China had completed plans for a "limited" attack on Taiwan after Taiwan's presidential election in March 1996. Charles Freeman, the former U.S. assistant secretary of defense who had traveled in China earlier, was quoted as warning of a "missile strike per day." The article even referred to what might be interpreted as an oblique Chinese threat to use nuclear missiles against U.S. cities if Washington intervened. This news seemed to be confirmed by the statement of Beijing's Xinhua (New China News) Agency: "To strive to end the disunity of the country and nation by peaceful means in no way means allowing the process of peaceful reunification to be delayed indefinitely. If some people were to dare separate Taiwan from Chinese territory, the Chinese people would defend the country's sovereignty and territorial integrity *with blood and lives*" (emphasis added).[3] Beijing particularly warned the U.S. not to intervene in the crisis:

> We should like to advise the U.S. government not to miscalculate, not to underestimate the will of the Chinese government to safeguard its national sovereignty and dignity, and not to underestimate the ability of Chinese government to face whatever challenges. China today is no longer the old China that was weak, could be bullied, and allowed itself to be trampled upon, but is a dragon that stands firm in the East.[4]

Beijing further declared that "if the US anti-China forces, along with Lee Teng-hui and his like, are perverse and collude with each other in pursuing two Chinas, or one China, one Taiwan, China has the *methods, strength, and confidence* to smash their plot" (emphasis added).[5] Despite Beijing's warning, the Clinton administration sent two aircraft carriers, *Independence* and *Nimitz*, toward the direction of the Taiwan Strait. This action led many people to believe that relations across the Taiwan Strait were in a major crisis and that war was about to break out any moment.

However, war did not break out. Beijing declared its successful conclusion of military exercises following Lee Teng-hui's reelection as Taiwan's president. Beijing's missile firings should be viewed as a form of "coercive diplomacy." According to the definition by Alexander George, the general intent of *coercive diplomacy*

> is to back a demand on an adversary with a threat of punishment for noncompliance that will be credible and potent enough to persuade him that it is in his interest to comply with the demand. . . . Coercive diplomacy is essentially a diplomatic strategy, one that relies on the threat of force

rather than the use of force to achieve the objective. If force must be used
to strengthen diplomatic efforts at persuasion, it is employed in an exemplary manner . . . to demonstrate resolution and willingness to escalate to
high levels of military action if necessary.[6]

As a coercive strategy, Beijing was not starting a war but sending a loud
message by harsh words and missiles launched in the Taiwan Strait. The
military exercises were part of Beijing's crisis bargaining strategy. Beijing
used military exercises as an instrument in diplomatic bargaining, that is,
as a tool for the political purpose of pressuring Taipei to halt perceived independent tendencies and warning the United States to stop what it perceived as intervention in Chinese internal affairs. In international relations, "Policy makers view crisis bargaining as a test of a state's power and
resolve, so that unsuccessful outcomes are seen as resulting from a failure
to demonstrate sufficient resolve."[7] The theory behind such a coercive
strategy is that "effective . . . bargaining [is] dependent on exploiting the
other side's fear of war through the use of credible threats and punishments, that is, on demonstrating a willingness to accept the risk of war to
achieve state objectives."[8]

To exploit Taiwan's fear of war and to make coercive strategy credible,
Beijing purposely created an atmosphere of secrecy in which the PLA was
preparing military maneuvers before and after the announcement of missile tests. In the meantime, news media were mobilized to launch an attack
on proindependence forces and assert Beijing's resolve to halt Taiwan's
slipping away from the motherland. Conducting field research in Beijing
during summer 1995, I found Beijing's political circle was permeated with
an atmosphere of "ten thousand years are too long; seize the day, seize the
hour" and the feeling of urgency to teach Taiwan a lesson. One most popular saying was *changtong buru duantong* (long pain is worse than short pain;
meaning that it would be better to resolve the issue of Taiwan earlier rather
than later).[9]

In spite of the rhetoric and military maneuver, Beijing's plan was not to
invade Taiwan but to use the threat of force to change the behavior of the
leaders in Taipei and Washington. This was revealed by Liu Huaqiu, then
director of the foreign affairs office of Beijing's State Council, who visited
Washington one day before the third wave of missile tests. On March 8, Liu
held a meeting with Anthony Lake, the White House national security ad-
viser. Although the content of their meeting was kept confidential, news
leaked that Liu gave the U.S. government explicit assurance that the PLA
would not attack Taiwan and urged the United States to stay out of the
cross-strait quarrel.[10]

Beijing's adoption of coercive strategy, to a great extent, reflected Beijing's perceptions of the undesirable change in Taiwan's internal and ex-

ternal situations. Beijing became disappointed, frustrated, and angered by
the development of the Taiwan independence movement and foreign intervention in the Taiwan issue. The following sections will analyze the
major factors that affected Beijing's perceptual shift and that led to the coercive strategy.

BETWEEN EXPECTATION AND FRUSTRATION

One important component of Beijing's peaceful offense was the policy of
promoting cross-strait exchanges, which in turn was subordinated to a lofty
political objective: national reunification. Although Beijing's leaders consider Taiwan a renegade province of China, they view the growing network
of economic exchange as a means of diminishing the risk that Taiwan
would drift toward permanent separation. Beijing held high expectation
for economic interaction as a way to develop political relations and push
for political negotiations. Beijing's leaders were quite open about their political objectives. At a National Work Conference on Taiwan in 1991,
China's Pres. Yang Shangkun said, "We should promote political integration through the economy, compel the Taiwan authorities to talk with us by
manipulating the Taiwan people's opinion and lead exchanges between
the two sides in a direction favorable to reunification with the motherland."[11] His successor, Jiang Zemin, reiterated this point of view, saying that
"enhancing cross-Strait economic exchanges and cooperation . . . will be
useful in boosting the development of cross-Strait relations and national
reunification."[12] Specifically, Beijing's policy was *yi shang cu zheng, yi min cu
guan* (to peddle politics through business, to influence government
through the people). For political purposes, Beijing gave preferential
treatment to Taiwanese investment and tolerated a huge trade deficit with
Taiwan: around $14.8 billion in 1995, which far exceeded Taiwan's trade
surplus with the United States. Beijing intends to use Taiwanese business-
men to bring the island closer to the motherland by setting up its own political constituency on the island for the "three links" advocated by Beijing,
whereby a large number of entrepreneurs will have a vested interest to
please or at least not offend the Beijing government. In this case, as a Taiwanese scholar has indicated, "Taiwan's political leadership would have to
worry about a gradual emergence of interest-based, rather than ethnicity-
based, 'China Lobby' inside Taiwan."[13]

However, Beijing's expectation turned to frustration because the Taiwan government was quite effective in resisting pressure from the private
sector to lift the ban on direct trade and direct air and sea links with the
mainland. Taiwan's Mainland Affairs Council frequently commissioned private polling agencies to conduct telephone surveys on this issue; most of
these surveys produced the intended outcomes, that is, the majority op-

posed an unconditional removal of the existing bans. Taiwan's official policy toward cross-strait exchanges is *qukuan laiyan* (leniency for going, strictness for coming), which is in line with Taipei's political position of *shanbu* (three no's, i.e., no contact, no negotiation, no compromise) as a response to Beijing's proposals for three links and four exchanges. From 1988 to 1994, about 50,000 mainlanders were given permission to visit Taiwan, although there were around 7 million visits by Taiwan residents to the mainland during the same period. Two semiofficial institutions, the Strait Exchange Foundation (SEF) on the Taiwan side and the Association for Relations Across the Taiwan Strait (ARATS) on the mainland side, began consultation in 1992. Wang Daohan and Koo Chen-fu, chairs of the two institutions, met in Singapore for the first time in 1993. However, these contacts were strictly confined to nonofficial and nonpolitical levels. They conduct only *shiwu xing xieshang* (practical consultation) rather than *zhengzhi tanpan* (political negotiation). Political relations between the two governments remain officially nonexistent. The Qiandaohu (Thousand Islands Lake) Incident in 1994 highlighted the political mistrust. On March 31, 1994, twenty-four Taiwan tourists and some mainland tourists were robbed and burned to death by three armed criminals during a boat tour on the Thousand Islands Lake in China's Zhejiang Province. Although the Chinese government took this incident seriously and punished the criminals within one month, as in the past it did not provide information to news media until the case was solved. Taiwanese news media tried to gather firsthand information on the tragic spots and reported to the public as soon as possible. The rejection of Taiwanese correspondents' immediate investigation and interviews caused suspicion as to Chinese military involvement and an official cover-up, thereby triggering an angry reaction from Taiwan. This tragic incident was highly politicized in Taiwan's media. Lee Teng-hui consequently called the PRC a "bandits regime" and the CCP a "party consisting of evil forces" and said that "Chinese people should have gotten rid of this government long ago." The Chinese leaders and military were unhappy about these attacks after the allegation of Chinese military involvement turned out to be false. This incident deepened the estrangement between the two sides, although nonofficial exchanges continued to grow.

Beijing felt very frustrated by the indirect, one-way, nonofficial, and nonpolitical nature of the contacts. In a new effort to break the political deadlock, Jiang made the eight-point proposal for high-level negotiations in 1995. According to my interview in China, Jiang's statement was the result of a longtime reevaluation of the Taiwan situation by mainland leaders and offered different points of emphasis from Deng's original formula of "one country, two systems." For example, taking into account the fact that Taiwan has established a pluralistic political system and that the KMT alone can no longer represent Taiwan, Jiang's proposal did not mention the negotiation between the KMT and the CCP but instead proposed a "talk with the Taiwan authorities"; Deng's original formula proposed negotiations only between the two parties. Furthermore, Jiang added that "representatives from the various political parties and mass organizations on both sides of the Taiwan Strait can be invited to participate in such talks." Jiang for the first time called for an equal negotiation. By using the word *equal*, Jiang avoided the sensitive issue of central/local government, which was Beijing's long-term emphasis. So far as the content of negotiations is concerned, Jiang stressed that "on the premise that there is only one China, we are prepared to talk with the Taiwan authorities about any issues including all matters of concern to the Taiwan authorities." It goes without saying that "all matters" include the issue of international space, the political status of Taiwan after reunification, and even the designation, flag, and form of a unified China.

Beijing expected a positive response from Taipei. Beijing's Xinhua commentary said that the eight-point proposal "opened up a new chapter in the development of relations between the two sides of the Strait. President Jiang's suggestions, along with the first preparatory consultation between the ARATS and the SEF for the Wang-Koo meeting in late May of 1995, created a favorable atmosphere for cross-straits relations."[14] With the "favorable atmosphere," Beijing expected to move the cross-strait relationship from the phase of discussing practical issues to the phase of political contact and negotiation. In an interview with China's official media, one senior fellow at Beijing's Peace and Development Research Center revealed that "putting an end to the hostility across the strait was an intermediate stage in the transition toward political negotiation and peaceful reunification."[15] Beijing was preparing for a breakthrough in cross-strait exchanges following Jiang's proposal. A special meeting of major responsible cadres held by the Ministry of Public Security in February 1995 predicted that from then on cross-strait exchanges would see a major increase. The meeting called upon "exit and entry administrative personnel [to] make early preparations for direct exchanges conducted by people on the two sides of the Taiwan Strait."[16]

Beijing was disappointed when SEF Chair Koo Chen-fu said that the topics planned for discussion at the second Ku-Wang meeting would not include preparatory negotiations for the ending of bilateral hostilities. "This *xieshang* [consultation] is different from *tanpan* [negotiations]."[17] Lee Teng-hui's six-point response in April further disappointed Beijing, because it was regarded as declining Jiang's proposal. Beijing criticized Lee for requiring the mainland to acknowledge "the reality of divided rule between Taiwan and the mainland." In Beijing's view, "this is actually asking the mainland to recognize two Chinas first and then discuss the issue of the reunification." Beijing also noted that in his six-point proposal Lee did not mention a word about the "one China" prerequisite and instead demanded that Beijing first give up the resort to force against Taiwan as a prerequisite for talks between the two sides. In Beijing's view, this "reversed the order of cross-strait negotiations and the ending of the state of hostility between the two sides" and "can only encourage Taiwan independence." Beijing believed that Lee's demand on Beijing to commit itself to nonuse of force is a "political hoax" and stated that "Beijing will not fall into this political trap." Beijing was particularly upset when Lee stated that the two sides should jointly maintain the prosperity of and promote democracy in Hong Kong (HK) and Macao and saw this statement as an attempt to share the benefits of Beijing's recovery of HK and Macao. Beijing indicated that in the course of negotiations over the resumption of China's sovereignty over HK, which were arduous, Taiwan never offered any moral or substantial help to Beijing. In 1983, Taiwan's foreign ministry issued a statement opposing Beijing and Britain holding talks and refusing to recognize agreements reached in the talks. Thus, Taiwan "did not express even a little consideration for the national cause in the recovery of the country's territory and sovereignty."[18]

In spite of all these disappointments, Beijing refrained from launching large-scale criticism of Lee's six-point response, because, leaving aside its disputed contents, Lee's response objectively created a precedent for dialogues between the leaders of Taipei and Beijing. Therefore, Beijing continued its reconciliatory policy and did not stop preparing for the second round of Wang-Koo talks. As the two-day meeting to prepare for the second Wang-Koo talks concluded on May 28, the two sides reached a preliminary consensus on regularizing and institutionalizing the Wang-Koo talks and decided that the second round would be held in Beijing on July 20, the third in Taipei the next year.

PERCEPTIONS ON TAIWAN'S DEMOCRATIZATION AND INDEPENDENT MOVEMENT

Although Beijing was looking forward to beginning negotiations with Taipei, its frustration and anxiety only grew as it observed undesirable changes that had negative effects on the reunification cause, including: (1) the change in Taiwan's internal politics, particularly the rapidly developed democratization and independent movement; (2) the change in the personal attitude of Lee Teng-hui, Taiwan's president and chair of KMT, toward off reunification; and (3) the change in Taiwan's international status as a result of its "pragmatic diplomacy."

Following nearly four decades of authoritarian rule by the KMT, democratic forces began to gain ground in Taiwan during the mid-1970s. Political space for electoral competition gradually opened up, the degree of political contest intensified, and the scope of political discourse in the public domain widened. Beginning in the mid-1980s, various authoritarian legal constructs—notably, the thirty-eight-year-old decree of martial law and the prohibition of new political parties and new newspapers—were dismantled, and rules for democratic politics were gradually established. Entry barriers to organized political competition were removed, and a number of opposition parties appeared. Notably, the Democratic Progressive Party (DPP) was established on September 28, 1986, and openly called for Taiwan independence.

Beijing watched the political democratization on the island with some grave misgivings. It was particularly worried about the implication of democratization for Taiwan's future. Beijing viewed the rapid rise of the DPP with strong disapproval and was concerned with the development of Taiwan independence activities. Beijing also became disturbed when Taiwan authorities determined that Taiwan independence speeches and deeds were within the limits of free speech. Xinhua commentary noted that on the pretext of democracy Taiwan independence activists were allowed to return to Taiwan from abroad to conduct open activities in the island. On the pretext of free association, Taiwan independence organizations competed freely in the political system, thus "providing Taiwan independence with a political space and a potential opportunity for holding office." Beijing particularly pointed out hints of Taiwan independence in the following activities: pushing for amending the constitution; election of a new national assembly; and direct election of the president in Taiwan, Penghu, Jinmen, and Mazhu.[19]

Beijing's concern over the Taiwan independence movement was aggravated by its view that the KMT's power to control the island was on the decline and the KMT itself began leaning toward independence. Beijing reported in 1994 that "in recent elections, despite the KMT's overwhelming victory, the proindependence-DPP seized the mayorship of Taipei City, while the New Party seized several seats in the provincial assembly and city councils. This shows that the era when the KMT had absolute control over the island's political resources has passed."[20] Beijing was particularly upset to find that since the beginning of the 1990s "the Taiwan authorities' attitude toward Taiwan independence has changed from making one concession after another to providing assistance and support in a disguised form."[21]

It seemed to confirm Beijing's concern when support for independence increased steadily in Taiwan's polls. For example, surveys carried out by Gallup Inc. (Taiwan) and the Public Opinion Survey Foundation (Taipei) during the early 1990s indicated that despite the progress made in cross-strait economic integration in recent years, support for independence, opposition to Beijing's "one country, two systems" policy, and resistance to reunification rhetoric were all increasing. In surveys conducted between 1989 and May 1994, the percentage of respondents who "strongly agreed" or "agreed" that Taiwan should be independent rose from 8.2 percent (December 1989), to 12 percent (December 1990), 12.7 percent (June 1991), 15.1 percent (October 1992), 23.7 percent (May 1993), and 27 percent (April 1994). In May 1994, after the Thousand Islands Lake Incident, support for independence increased again to 27.3 percent.[22]

At the Asia-Pacific Economic Cooperation (APEC) Seattle Summit in November 1993, Taiwan's minister of economic affairs caused quite a stir with his references to "two sovereign nations across the Taiwan strait." Beijing's leaders were further convinced that the Taiwan independence movement was gathering momentum. Prior to the military exercise in mid-1995, Beijing had found a perplexing political centrifugal tendency and even identified a three-step plan for Taiwan independence promoted by the Taiwan authorities, namely,

> Implementation of constitutional reform, announcing that the ruling power of the KMT would be confined to Taiwan, Penghu, Jinmen, and Mazhu; making arrangements for the direct election of the president so as to create a political environment characterized by the initiatives in being the people's hands; and unfolding flexible diplomacy to strive for the international community's recognition of Taiwan as an independent political entity.[23]

PERCEPTIONS ON LEE TENG-HUI: A PERSONAL FACTOR

Beijing's anxiety also came from its perceived change in Lee Teng-hui's personal attitude toward reunification with the mainland. Beijing's policymakers gradually realized that, after consolidating his power, Lee freed himself from the need to compromise with domestic political forces that had in the past restricted his ability directly to confront Beijing's reunification policy. As the mainstream political leader, Lee became more and more proindependent. Taiwan might break away from the mainland even if the DPP is not in power. Beijing's adoption of coercive strategy in 1995 was, to a great extent, due to the change in its appraisal of Lee Teng-hui.

In the early years after Lee took office, he adopted a vague political stance. Beijing's leaders could not tell whether Lee belonged to the reunification faction or the independent faction, because Lee attempted to win support from both factions. During the late 1980s, Beijing had some hope for Lee, believing that only a handful of people, led by the DPP, demanded independence and that Lee was in any event better than the DPP. Because Lee was not involved in China's civil war and should have no personal animosity toward the CCP, he might carry less of a historical burden. For this reason, he could play a role and make contributions to solving the Taiwan issue.

However, Beijing became increasingly frustrated by Lee's two-pronged approach in handling the island's politics. On the one hand, he tried to placate the traditional forces within his party by presiding over the formulation of the "Guidelines for National Reunification" and announced the three stages of communication and cooperation with the mainland. On the other hand, he tried to win the support of the DPP and the centrifugal force by painstakingly pushing talks on reunification into the next century "in an attempt to put them off so as to seek change, orienting toward the international community, expanding pragmatic diplomacy, and tolerating Taiwan independence activities."[24] Lee persisted in three prerequisites with regard to cross-strait relations: the mainland makes a commitment to refrain from the use of force, recognizes Taiwan's status as a political entity on equal footing, and allows Taiwan space in international activities. Through reorganization on several occasions, Lee succeeded in elbowing out senior KMT officials, notably Premier Hao Bochun, who adhered to the reunification of China and appointed figures with independence tendencies.

Beijing was compelled to reassess Lee and eventually came to conclude that "Lee and the Taiwan independent elements are actually in the same boat."[25] In an interview, one senior fellow at the China Institute for International Strategic Studies said Lee's true nature was reunification in form but independence in reality. He pointed out the main manifestation of Lee's double-dealing tactics: "When in public, on official occasion, or out of some political need, he made comments advocating reunification, but he was not talking sincerely. Unlike those undisguised statements by advocates of Taiwan independence calling for changing the national flag and name and setting up a Republic of Taiwan, Lee's approach to spreading his separatist views was gradual and quiet."[26]

An article published by *Liaowang* (*Outlook Weekly*) in Beijing in June 1995 summarized three major shifts from the one China stand that the Taiwan authorities had made after Lee came to power:

> 1) From early 1988 when Lee came to power to March 1991 when the Taiwan authorities publicized the Guidelines for National Unification, after some attempts at "one country, two governments" and "one country, two regions," the Taiwan authorities basically took the attitude and adopted the principles of "two equal political entities" in its regulating and coping with the relations between the two sides of the Taiwan Straits. 2) Since 1992 the Taiwan authorities have wavered greatly on the issue of one China, and have begun slipping gradually toward a two China stance by putting forward the theory of "splitting country and rule by separate

regimes," and starting its "elastic diplomacy." 3) Since early 1993 the Taiwan authorities have come out into the open with their stand of two Chinas. Following his tour of the Middle East, Lee went to the U.S. so as to create two Chinas distinguishably in the world.[27]

Beijing became particularly angered by two events it saw as having clearly expressed Lee's independence quest. One was Lee's interview with Japanese writer Ryotaro Shiba in March 1994; the other was Lee's visit to the United States in May 1995. In his meeting with Shiba, Lee talked about "the sorrow of being a Taiwanese" and told him that "the KMT is an alien regime," "the ROC is a sovereign state," and "the CCP has never set foot on Taiwan, nor has it ever levied taxies in Taiwan. How can it insist on Taiwan's being part of the mainland?" Lee proposed a slogan: *jingying da Taiwan, jianli xing zhongyuan* (operating a large Taiwan, setting up a new China) and compared himself to Moses, saying that he would lead his followers to escape from Egypt, cross the Red Sea, and build another country in another place. Beijing believed that the analogy undoubtedly was Lee's self-analysis of his political direction and that Lee's Taiwan independence mentality was now told in an undisguised confession: "Letting others leak information as a trial balloon and waiting until the right moment to announce his own position is a trick Lee frequently employs."[28]

Beijing particularly resented Lee's talking to a Japanese writer, because Beijing had become increasingly suspicious about Japan's intentions in the Taiwan issue. After the normalization of relations between China and Japan in 1972, Taiwan disappeared from Japanese media coverage for more than twenty years. Under the principle of one China, most news organizations eliminated their Taiwan branches and concentrated on reporting only mainland news. The only newspaper that still had special correspondents in Taipei was *Sankei Shimbun,* which was generally accepted as a right-wing paper. *Taiwan* almost became a forbidden word in Japan. However, this situation was changing. The most noticeable change was that the media had lifted the ban on Taiwan news. In May 1993, *Asahi Shimbun* published on the front page nineteen items introducing tanka written by Taiwanese. Tanka is a traditional style of Japanese poetry composed with thirty-one syllables. In the fifty years after the war, elder Taiwanese who received Japanese education have continued to write poems in Japanese. *Asahi* is the leading left-wing newspaper in Japan and the hired press of the intellectual circles. In the past, it would have considered the heritage of the greater East Asian Coprosperity Sphere as shameful and disgraceful and would have refused to publicize it. The above-mentioned tanka were later published by the Chiying Publishing House under the title *Taiwan Wanye Collection* and evoked great repercussions. Shortly after, in July 1993, the *Asahi Weekly* magazine began to serialize *Taiwan Kiko,* by historical author Shiba Sentaro. This series emphasized the history of Taiwan, including the period of Japanese occupation and the period between recovery and the end of martial law. Later in May 1994, *Asahi Weekly* published a conversation between Shiba and Lee Teng-hui. This caused great repercussions in Beijing. If the *Taiwan Wanye* collection and *Taiwan Kiko* gave Japanese makeup lessons in history, this latter conversation allowed the Japanese to understand the current status of Taiwan.

Shortly after this, the incident at the Asian Games in Hiroshima occurred. Lee wanted to go to Japan, and Beijing at once threatened to boycott the games. Lee did not make the trip in the end. But Lee's name appeared in conspicuous places for several weeks in all major Japanese newspapers. Through this incident, Taiwan successfully claimed space and attention in Japanese newspapers. At the same time, Japan did not show appreciation for the intolerant attitude of mainland China. The biggest winner of the Hiroshima incident was Lee. The lifting of the Taiwan taboo in Japan found expression mainly in the media and public opinion. Meanwhile, the Japanese government appeared to be getting closer to Taiwan below the surface. When the Asian Games incident occurred, some Japanese officials commented in private that it was impossible for Japan to ignore forever this economically strong country of 20 million people. Hsu Lite, deputy president of the Taiwan Executive Yuan, later led a group to Japan, reportedly a substitute plan initiated by the Japanese. In addition, in the past Taiwan reporters stationed at Tokyo were not allowed inside the foreign affairs building. Since 1993, this restriction had been loosened. Japan was forming the image of a new Taiwan, which includes two factors, as indicated by an author in Hong Kong: "One is the Taiwanese Taiwan. The Japanese began to think that the Taiwan issue is actually not a conflict between two Chinas, but a conflict between China and Taiwan. The second is democratic Taiwan. In a modern society, democracy has such positive connotations as being safe, free, open, and civilized."[29]

After his meeting with Ryotaro Shiba, Lee repeatedly clarified that he had no pro–Taiwan independence sentiment. Yet Beijing saw a host of activities that violated the one China principle. In the two years following, Taiwan conducted four military maneuvers, with the mainland as their target; Lee attended three of them and made speeches "sowing discontent among Taiwanese compatriots regarding the mainland." In the meantime, Lee pursued vacation diplomacy and private visits to the Middle East, Southeast Asia, and South America, striving to expand the international living space and participate in international organizations. Beijing contended that "all these were aimed at creating the conditions for realizing his dream of Taiwan independence."[30]

Lee's U.S. visit in 1995 was another major event that infuriated Beijing. This visit was seen as the prelude to the "Exodus," directed and performed by Lee, whose position was to demand that Beijing acknowledge Taiwan as an independent political entity by moving China's "family affairs" into the international arena. During his U.S. visit, Lee played the role of Taiwan's president and propagated the existence of the Republic of China (ROC) in Taiwan. Beijing was convinced that Lee's trip aimed at taking advantage of "the mind-set of some people in the U.S. who do not want to see a unified, powerful China, but are in a hurry to play the Taiwan card."[31] A special article in *Renmin ribao* reported, "Lee no longer covered himself up, and has unmasked his false pursuit of reunification. . . . Through a series of performances, Lee has revealed his true capacity as the cardinal founder of Taiwan independence." Beijing noticed that in his speech at Cornell, Lee mentioned "the ROC in Taiwan" on seventeen occasions, chanted the slogan of "challenging the impossible," and stressed that Taiwan is a country with "independent sovereignty."[32] In Beijing's view, Lee totally stripped away the mask he had kept in place for years and exposed his true aim: pursuing two Chinas; Lee had made up his mind to go further down the road toward splitting China. "He thinks that he has already saved up certain political capital; that he has already used the power in his hands to get rid of those who hold different views; and that he has the backup of some foreign forces, including the U.S.; thus he can do things in a big way."[33]

In summer 1995, Beijing concluded that Lee would brazenly campaign for Taiwan independence after being elected president in March 1996 and that the mainland must make preparations for this possibility.[34] On June 16, Beijing's Taiwan Affairs Office and ARATS jointly declared that the second Koo-Wang meeting would be indefinitely postponed. The official-controlled media in Beijing lashed out at certain forces in Taiwan for having taken "a series of actions that poisoned the atmosphere of the talks and impaired cross-straits ties."[35] While preparing for the missile tests and military exercises, Beijing organized a large-scale campaign of media articles attacking Lee Teng-hui. By mid-August 1995, more than four hundred articles were written.[36] Taking the lead was the first series of four articles jointly signed by commentators from *People's Daily* and Xinhua, the official mouthpieces of the CCP and the State Council respectively. One Xinhua commentary revealed the impact of Lee's meeting with Shiba and his U.S. visit upon Beijing's policymakers in their decision to adopt a coercive strategy:

> In his talks with Ryotaro Shiba, a Japanese, Lee had already revealed his true Taiwan independence colors, but Beijing exercised great restraint out of consideration for peaceful reunification. However, Beijing could no longer show tolerance toward Lee's visit to the US to create two Chinas. Hence, with Lee going further step by step in his move to create two Chinas, Beijing made stronger and stronger responses.[37]

To a great extent, Beijing attributed its new policy of coercion to Lee's provocative personal actions. One Xinhua commentary said, "Because of Lee's attempt to increase his importance with foreign support, his willingness to be a play thing for foreigners, and his continuous sliding on the path leading to Taiwan independence, the present situation in cross-strait relations, which nobody wanted to see, has come about."[38]

PERCEPTIONS ON THE FOREIGN ROLE

Another perceived change in the cross-strait relations that eventually prompted Beijing's new assertiveness was collaboration between Taiwan authorities and pro–Taiwan independence forces in foreign countries, especially in the United States, to perpetuate Taiwan's political separation from China.

After its exclusion from the UN, Taipei's international status deteriorated rapidly. The visit of Pres. Richard Nixon to Beijing in 1972 caused Taipei a great deal of diplomatic derecognition. As Taipei became more and more isolated from world affairs, it adopted a more flexible approach to advance *shizhi guanxi* (substantive relations) with countries that had cut off official ties with Taipei by keeping semiofficial or unofficial relations. Although this helped its failing diplomatic luck to a certain degree, Taipei still could not prevent its presence in world affairs from decreasing. In the early 1990s, Taipei began a new approach, known as *tanxing waijiao* (elastic diplomacy) or *wushi waijia* (pragmatic diplomacy), which distinguished itself from substantive diplomacy by abandoning its one China policy and its insistence on being the only legitimate Chinese government in the international arena. In 1990, when Saudi Arabia established diplomatic relations with Beijing, Taiwan for the first time decided not to terminate official links. Rather it was Riyadh, under pressure from Beijing, that broke with Taipei. In January 1993, Taipei's first foreign affairs report called for an expansion of international links without regard for reactions from mainland China. In July 1994, a white paper on cross-strait relations stated that Taipei would "no longer compete with Beijing for the right to represent China in the international arena."[39] Pragmatic diplomacy utilized Taiwan's greatest assets: economic power and foreign exchange reserves. Thanks to its economic and financial aid, Taiwan could achieve full diplomatic relations with Grenada, Liberia, Belize, the Bahamas, Lesotho, Guinea-Bissau, Bolivia, Nicaragua, and others.

The Taiwan government originally tried to maintain a balance between pragmatic diplomacy and mainland policy so as to benefit from both of the two fronts. However, after the end of the Cold War, Taipei attempted to "exploit the U.S. post–Cold War readjustment of its relations with China to make a breakthrough therein. Whenever a step forward is achieved in cross-strait relations, two steps will have been taken in the international aspect of the relations."[40] One article in *China Daily* said that "Lee Teng-hui is attempting to sacrifice development of two-sided relations by expanding his pragmatic diplomacy." The article questioned Taipei: "Which is more important for Taiwan: International space or cross-strait relations?"[41] Beijing was particularly concerned with Taiwan playing the U.S. card, because U.S. intentions for Taiwan had been a great puzzle to Beijing's policymakers ever since the normalization of diplomatic relations between the two countries. In Beijing's eyes, the U.S. government was double-dealing: It had pledged unequivocally in the three joint communiqués that the Beijing government is the "sole legitimate government of China," that "Taiwan is part of China," and that within these limits the United States would "maintain cultural, commercial, and other unofficial ties" with Taiwan. However, following the establishment of diplomatic relations with China, the U.S. Congress passed the Taiwan Relations Act (TRA), a law that reinstated recognition of Taiwan's position as a quasisovereign state; it directly contravenes the communiqué on the establishment of diplomatic relations between Beijing and Washington. TRA granted Taipei representatives in the United States access to U.S. courts, diplomatic privileges, and other prerequisites reserved to sovereign states. As necessary for Taiwan's defense, TRA endorsed U.S. arms sales to the island and specified that the president and Congress would decide the nature and quantity of such sale based exclusively on their judgment of the requirement for Taiwan's security.

One reason for the two-pronged U.S. China policy is the existence of the pro-Taiwan China lobby, which emerged during the 1930s and 1940s, when the KMT's T. V. Soong (prime minister and finance minister), Chiang Kai-shek, and his wife (Soong's sister), Soong May-ling, cultivated their high-level U.S. contacts assiduously to garner U.S. help in bolstering their staggering economy and unsuccessful war effort. After the United States severed diplomatic ties with Taiwan, the China lobby continued to work to bring numerous U.S. journalists, scholars, politicians, and other officials to Taiwan in all-expenses-paid trips to initiate and strengthen a wide range of linkages. President Clinton, while governor of Arkansas, was invited to Taiwan four times, through his connection with the China lobby. Taiwan has become a major donor to some of America's best-known centers for public policy and also provided funds to prominent universities supporting Asian studies. The Chiang Ching-kuo Foundation for International Exchange was founded in fall 1989 with an endowment of $100 million; it dispenses about $7 million every year, most of it to U.S. universities, conferences, and researchers. The China lobby's efforts paid off particularly well during the 1990s. For a long time, Taiwan's authoritarian system had little appeal to the U.S. public and proved a constant source of embarrassment to Washington. Taiwan's democratization helped to remove the political sore spot and facilitated a favorable reorientation of Washington's Taiwan policy. The Bush administration approved the sale of F-16 jet fighters to Taiwan in 1992. The Clinton administration sent Federico Peña, U.S. secretary of transportation, to visit Taiwan, and for the first time the secretary entered Taiwan's presidential offices and foreign ministry buildings to hold official meetings with President Lee and Foreign Minister Chian in December 1994. The Clinton administration also modestly upgraded the status of Taiwan's diplomatic representation in the United States after completing its Taiwan policy report in September 1994. Eventually, conceding to congressional pressures, Clinton gave a green light to Lee to visit the United States in May 1995.

When they were told that the U.S. government decided to issue an entry visa to Lee Teng-hui, Beijing's leaders were caught by surprise and were at loss as to what to do. This decision broke U.S. promises and openly changed the policy that forbids Taiwan leaders from visiting the United States, which had been successively upheld by past administrations over nearly seventeen years. Beijing's leaders received relevant forecasts only two days before the U.S. State Department officially announced Lee's visit. On May 16, the foreign ministry submitted a report to the CCP, stating that although anti-China U.S. congressmen were stepping up their efforts to operate with Lee in campaigning for one China, one Taiwan, the foundation of Sino-U.S. relations made it impossible for the U.S. government to make a substantial change at present. Less than one week later, however, the U.S. government made the decision to grant Lee an entry visa. Jiang and Qian were very embarrassed. Their policies toward the United States and Taiwan were under heavy criticism. Jiang's position suddenly changed from being the core to being the focus of pressure from all aids. In late May, a position paper submitted to the Central Military Commission (CMC) and the State Council by military leaders supported and pressed for firm, substantial measures against U.S. challenges as well as necessary measures against the Taiwan authorities and Lee. Chi Haotian, China's defense minister, at a reception marking the sixty-eighth anniversary of PLA's founding, revealed this position by vowing that "the PLA will not give up the option of using force when necessary. If certain foreign forces should meddle with China's reunification and promote an independent Taiwan, or if the Taiwan authorities are bent on splitting the motherland, we will not sit idle and let it go unchecked."[42] My China field trip during summer 1995 found Beijing's political cycle buzzing with the report that Jiang felt beleaguered during those days and finally resolved to make a self-criticism within the leadership. An extraordinarily enlarged Politburo meeting was called to examine China's policies toward Taiwan and the United States, acknowledging that it was wrong for China not to have made substantial responses to, and taken appropriate measures against, repeated premeditated attempts by the United States over the past few years to violate the three Sino-U.S. communiqués, thus landing China in a passive position.

Although the Clinton administration repeatedly clarified that Lee's visit was "personal" and "private," a Chinese foreign ministry spokesman insisted that "because of his special stature, Lee's visit to the U.S. in whatever capacity and under whatever pretext is of an official nature."[43] Beijing indicated that even Lee himself made no effort to hide that fact; he declared in a rally in Taiwan that "the most important thing about my visit to the U.S. is to illustrate the existence of the ROC," and "we must let the whole world recognize the existence of the ROC." In Beijing's eyes, "this blatantly shows the political purpose of this so-called personal visit. By permitting him to visit the U.S., Washington is brazenly supporting his attempt to create two Chinas or one China one Taiwan."[44]

Beijing regarded Lee's U.S. trip as a long-planned plot and was worried about the momentum that Taiwan's pragmatic diplomacy gathered thanks to U.S. support. Beijing noted that "Taiwan is currently a member of 795 nongovernmental international organizations, 83 of which were joined by Taiwan in recent years." In Beijing's view, "this shows that the international space for Taiwan's economic and cultural development is very broad."[45] Thus, Beijing was very suspicious of Taiwan's continued efforts to expand its international living space. After becoming president, Lee visited Singapore in March 1989, followed by the Philippines, Indonesia, Thailand, South Africa, and Central America in 1994. In early April 1995, Lee took a private trip to the United Arab Emirates and Jordan in the Middle East. Annoyed by Taiwan's *jingqian waijiao* (money diplomacy), the official PRC news agency, Xinhua, accused that in order to enable Lee to visit the United States the Taiwan authorities lobbied the U.S. Congress at large expense. The Institute for Comprehensive Research of Taiwan, set up by a trusted Lee follower, signed a three-year, $5.7 million lobbying contract with the Cassidy Public Relations Company in the United States. From 1988–1991, the Institute of International Relations spent $1.18 million on lobbying in the United States. In 1994, to support its frequent lobbying activities and to promote public relations, Taiwan's Ministry of Foreign Affairs earmarked as much as NT$340 million from its classified budget for "special expenses," spending most of the money on U.S. politicians. Xinhua quoted a U.S. attorney general's report to Congress that the fifty-one companies serving as Taiwan's lobbying agencies registered with the U.S. Justice Department received total rewards of more than $5.103 million. Of these fifty-one companies, eleven were hired by Taiwan's International Trade Bureau of the Ministry of Economic Affairs, and twelve were hired by Taiwan's semiofficial Foreign Trade Association. During 1988–1991, these two Taiwanese institutions spent $3.825 million and $4.195 million, respectively, on lobbying activities.[46]

Beijing became particularly alerted when Taiwan's Vice Foreign Minister Fang Jinyan (Fang Chin-yen) said that Taiwan was willing to use $1 billion to buy membership in the UN. Beijing strongly opposed Taiwan's efforts to enter the UN and held that neither the German nor Korean model is applicable in solving the problem of China's reunification. In Beijing's view, the division of Germany and Korea was a result of World War II and was confirmed by international agreements, whereas Taiwan's separation from the mainland resulted from civil war and thus remains a part of China's domestic affairs. The dual entry of the two Koreas and two Germanies into the UN was regarded as conducive to relaxing tensions. In the case of China, the PRC eventually replaced the ROC in 1949 even though the Taiwan regime continued to occupy the China seat in the UN; but the PRC ousted the ROC in the UN as regulated by UN Resolution 2758 in 1971. Given the influential Taiwan independence movement and Taiwan's geographical separation from the mainland by the Taiwan Strait, Taiwan would definitely move toward independence if accepted into the UN and recognized by the international community.

Beijing was very sensitive to the involvement of foreign forces, especially Americans, in the Taiwan issue because it believed that the United States may use the Taiwan card to contain China. After the end of the Cold War the structural support of the strategic relationship between Beijing and Washington was removed, and their relations became disoriented. As an American scholar indicated in 1991, "For the first time, with the disintegration of the Soviet Union and the absence of a new credible enemy, the U.S. must deal with China for its own sake and decide where the Chinese fit in the American concept of a new world order."[47] Quickly, the differences and conflicts that the two countries had sought to downplay over ideology, human rights, trade, arms sales, Taiwan, and so on began to surface. The sudden recognition of China's rise as the next superpower competing with the United States in the post–Cold War world further complicated the relationship. Because of the success of economic reforms since the late 1970s, China's record of economic growth has been astonishing to the world. Deng Xiaoping hoped to quadruple the economy from its 1978 level by the year 2000. This goal was achieved at the end of 1995. China's economic output in turn is to be doubled by 2010. Within a generation or so, current optimists predict, a country once dismissed as the "sick man" of Asia could have the largest economy in the world. Western media began to talk about China as the "coming power," "an economic center of gravity in Asia," "a military mover and shaker," and "a peer of any of the Western powers that once nibbled at China's fringes and brought emperors low." China suddenly became the world's center in post–Cold War security calculations. The oldest problem in diplomacy was raised: how the international community is to manage the ambitions of a rising power. The expression of a new containment was applied increasingly to China. One Chinese scholar indicated that "for Beijing, recognition of China's rise came just as unexpected as it did for other countries."[48] Policymakers in Beijing felt that the concept was concocted by Western politicians to sell the so-called China threat theory. Beijing became furious when Winston Lord, Clinton's assistant secretary for East Asian affairs, said after Lee's visit: "The U.S. hoped to improve its relations with China, but the two countries would likely be hostile to each other for a long time to come." For Beijing, this implied that the United States may possibly contain a rising China in the same way it did with regard to communist expansion during the Cold War. One article in *Renmin ribao* said,

> In the eyes of some Americans, China's very existence is a great threat to the system of the West, whereas China's rapid economic growth is even a more serious challenge to the U.S. They worry that China's development will alter the global pattern, and that unfavorable changes in the balance of power will take place. Hence, in seeking countermeasurements from the obsolete cold war policy files, some people have gone so far as to take containment—a typical cold war concept—as an option in shaping U.S. policy toward China.[49]

Beijing suspected that U.S. policy was an attempt to sabotage China's peaceful reunification and to let China twist in a state of long-term split. The Taiwan card served this purpose. Li Jiaquan, deputy director of the Institute of Taiwan Studies in the Chinese Academy of Social Sciences, presented this view by stating that the vigorous growth of economic, trade, and cultural exchanges across the Taiwan Strait worried certain people in the United States who were hostile toward China. They feared that if both sides of the Taiwan Strait improved their relations steadily they would eventually talk about the issue of peaceful reunification. In their mind, China was a potential enemy and that a reunified and powerful China was not in their interests. "These people believe that only by maintaining a state of division and conflict across the Taiwan Strait can Taiwan be used to contain China."[50]

Beijing's suspicions seemed confirmed when news came that the U.S. aircraft carrier *Nimitz* passed the Taiwan Strait on December 19, 1995. A Chinese foreign ministry spokesman said that although the Taiwan Strait is an international waterway where foreign warships have a right of "harmless" or "innocent" passage, China was nonetheless "highly concerned" that a U.S. aircraft carrier passed through the sensitive strait "in view of tension there."[51] This event was seen as a manifestation of a new U.S. Cold War mentality and a demonstration of U.S. power against China. Beijing worried about an international domino effect, that Japan and other nations might follow the U.S. lead in supporting the Taiwan independence movement. Nationalism and anti-American sentiment ran high. Beijing felt a new sense of urgency and, following its first two waves of missile tests in July and August 1995, decided to conduct the third wave of military exercises closer to Taiwan in March 1996.

CONCLUSION: THE OBJECTIVE OF THE COERCIVE STRATEGY

This analysis has shown that Beijing's adoption of coercive strategy was not a result of differences in ideology and social and political systems between the two sides or because Beijing planned to press Taipei for immediate reunification. Rather, it was a result of accumulated frustration, anxiety, and anger over the perceived momentum for Taiwan independence, momentum spurred by Taiwan's democratization, Lee Teng-hui's personal support, and foreign intervention. For Beijing, Taiwan is a vital issue of unsolved sovereignty and the most important consideration in its diplomatic policy. In Beijing's view, the missile tests provided a most forceful reminder to Taiwan: that Beijing would not tolerate Lee Teng-hui's efforts to win international recognition for his government—which Beijing sees as a covert bid for independence—beyond a certain point. Lee Teng-hui tested those limits beginning in the early 1990s, and Beijing used coercive strategy to make its limits clear. The objective of coercive strategy was to send a loud message to Taipei and Washington: If Taiwan independence emerges and if foreign countries interfere in what Beijing considers China's internal affairs, then Beijing would settle it by military means. As stated by Xinhua in announcing the coercive policy, "The missile tests [were] aimed at foreign forces' interference in China's reunification and at the schemes for Taiwan independence."[52]

Coercive diplomacy is a crisis bargaining strategy supplementary to peaceful reunification policy. Beijing saw the undesired change in cross-strait relations as resulting from a failure to demonstrate sufficient resolve to support its peaceful reunification policy. China's historical experience has convinced Beijing's leaders that the established international order is a rough-and-tumble place where possession of substantial force and demonstrated willingness to use it are prerequisites for securing its interests. Adopting a "bullying" strategy of bargaining, Beijing exploited the fear of war in Taiwan and the United States and used the threat of war for a desired behavioral change. This strategy relied heavily on severe threats and punishments until and unless Beijing's terms for peaceful reunification were accepted. It was a rational decision—from Beijing's viewpoint—in order to achieve its objectives. As long as Beijing perceives a desirable outcome resulting from coercive strategy, it would have no reason to discontinue peaceful reunification policy. Beijing has long made clear that the mainland would never recover Taiwan by the use of force except under "three kinds of conditions" emerging on Taiwan (i.e., independence, invasion by foreign forces, and disturbance).

After Taiwan's presidential election, Beijing suspended military actions and declared a victory for coercive strategy, just as Taipei and Washington each claimed success for their strategies in dealing with the crisis. Beijing declared a victory because it saw the impact of the military exercises on U.S. policy. The United States is alarmed at the near upset of the diplomatic balance in the Taiwan Strait and has weighed in emphatically with Taiwan about the necessity not to unilaterally upset things again. Sentiment in the U.S. Congress has shifted from Newt Gingrich's "why don't we just recognize Taiwan" to an awareness that this issue needs to be handled carefully. One big lesson for Clinton was that he needed to take steps to make sure this kind of crisis didn't happen again. To do so, he has repeatedly reassured the PRC about U.S. policy toward Taiwan as a key element in his revitalized engagement policy. The upshot is that U.S. support for Taiwan was reduced, not increased, as a result of the crisis. Since late 1996 U.S. attitudes toward the PRC and Taiwan shifted away from Taiwan and toward some sort of modus vivendi with Beijing. Although China policy remained controversial, it was clear that most critics of engagement had no stomach for fighting the PRC over Taiwan's self-determination, and they made this view known to Taiwan in various ways. One analyst wrote after Jiang Zemin's visit to Washington in October 1997, "the Taiwan straits flared up to near-crisis proportions in 1996 with missile firings and aircraft carrier movements. Some future explosion could be worse and could spark a global crisis if opportunists thought we could be stretched too thin to deter actions we otherwise could not tolerate."[53] Another important lesson the United States drew from the crisis is that movement toward separatism in Taiwan is dangerous and should not be encouraged. Thus, there has been a long series of Clinton administration statements against Taiwan independence, eventually culminating in a reaffirmation of the U.S. "three no's" policy during Clinton's visit to China in summer 1998: no Taiwan independence, no two Chinas or one Taiwan, one China, and no Taiwan membership in international organizations for sovereign states.

To the Taiwanese people, Beijing also demonstrated the devastating consequences of independence. Beijing noted that investors, intimidated by the military exercises, sold shares in panic and rushed to buy gold, customary in times of instability, and that the Taiwanese stock market index plunged to its lowest level. Taiwan's central bank had to dip into its $89 billion reserve to bolster the local currency. The tensions also hampered Taiwan's economic growth. According to Taiwan's official report, Taiwan's economic growth in the fourth quarter of 1995 plummeted to a five-year low of 4.86 percent, well off the forecast of 6.34 percent for the quarter.[54] Given the demonstrated consequences, Beijing's policymakers believed that the Taiwanese people and their leaders would have to rethink the independence movement. Although Lee Teng-hui won a landslide victory with 54 percent of the vote, Xinhua pointed out that the antiindependence candidates won more votes than the proindependence group (24.88 percent versus 21.13 percent), implying that the mainland's military exercises had a direct effect on the independence movement, which 41 percent supported in a 1993 poll. Xinhua underscored this effect in announcing the conclusion of the military exercises: "Beijing's opposition to separatism and 'Taiwan independence' has . . . dealt a heavy blow to the 'Taiwan independence' and separatist forces . . . The facts show that the broad masses of the people in Taiwan demand stability and development of the relations across the Taiwan Strait and were casting aside 'Taiwan independence.'"[55] This is not simply a "face-saving" statement. Beijing's perception comes from its conviction that due to the vulnerability of Taiwan's export-oriented economy even a low-intensity conflict would do it tremendous damage. Although only a minority in Taiwan favored reunification with the mainland in the near future, there are strong forces that wish accommodation with the mainland because most Taiwanese people are too vulnerable to stand up to a prolonged period of psychological terror and economic privation and therefore have come to terms with reality. Based on this conviction, Beijing believes that "stability, relaxation, and improving cross-strait relations are the mainstream of Taiwan's popular will."[56]

After the military exercises, both sides across the Taiwan Strait made some conciliatory gestures. Taipei stopped pushing for Lee to visit Atlanta to attend the centennial Olympic Games after his reelection as president. Taiwan also canceled military exercises planned for April 7–10, 1996. An editorial published by *South China Morning Post* stated that "Taiwan has wisely listened to the voice of reason and postponed live fire military exercises."[57] In his May 20 speech, Lee Teng-hui made an important concession by backing off from his stand of meeting Beijing's leaders only in an international setting and said that he was willing and had the support of Taiwan's 21.3 million people to embark on a journey of peace to Beijing and meet with leaders there. Although Beijing's response was to wait and see not only Lee's "words" but also his "deeds," it reaffirmed that Jiang Zemin's eight-point proposition remains the guiding principle of Beijing's policy toward Taiwan.[58]

As a result of conciliatory gestures by both sides, Taiwan's SEF and the mainland's ARATS resumed their meeting in Beijing in October 1998, thus opening up possibilities for political negotiations in the future. These events show the complementary role of coercive strategy to peaceful reunification policy. Beijing's peaceful offense will not be interrupted as long as it is confident that Taiwan's independence movement is under control. My interviewees in Beijing confirm that Chinese leaders have not planned to press Taiwan for immediate reunification. Deng Xiaoping initially defined national reunification as one of the three major tasks to be accomplished during the 1980s.[59] When the 1980s passed, Deng said he could wait another one hundred years. His premise was that Taiwan would not declare independence. Beijing's calculation is that "the time is advantageous for mainland China," as indicated by Liu Ji, vice president of the Chinese Academy of Social Sciences and a close personal aide to Jiang Zemin. According to Liu, China will keep on "the trend of development that has already lasted for two decades. . . . When the economy of mainland China comes close to, equal to, or surpasses the level of Taiwan, there will be no need for negotiation—the issue will be settled naturally."[60] But before that day arrives, Beijing wants to make sure that Taiwan will not declare independence and that the reunification issue is a matter beyond dispute. As long as Taiwan does not formally seek recognition as a separate country, Beijing will let it be a country in everything but name, symbol, and formal diplomatic practice.

In this case, whether or not Beijing will use coercive strategy again will depend on Beijing's perception of changes in the future relationship across the Taiwan Strait. Beijing might perceive three possible scenarios. The first is that both sides will work together to normalize and improve bilateral relations and push them in a benign direction. Thus, cross-strait relations would undergo a gradual reconciliation. After serious preparation, both sides might even enter into political negotiation and jointly attempt to end hostilities under the one China principle. The second is that Taipei will continue moving toward independence. Thus, tensions will increase and escalate into new crises. The third scenario is that Taipei will try to reduce cross-strait tensions and agree to hold peaceful negotiations yet continue to work for more international recognition and independence. The first scenario would be the ideal development, whereby Beijing continues its peaceful offense without resorting to force. The second scenario will further provoke Beijing's coercive measures. The third scenario may drive the cross-strait relationship into a vicious cycle of peace and coercion. The bottom line for Beijing is that "the day when Taiwan declares independence will be the day war begins."[61] By adopting the coercive strategy in 1996, Beijing drew a line, making clear it wants any Taiwanese leader to think many times before crossing it again.

NOTES

An earlier version of this paper was presented at the International Conference on Preventive Diplomacy for Peace and Security in the Western Pacific, jointly sponsored by the 21st Century Foundation and the Pacific Forum CSIS in Taipei, 29–31 August 1996. I wish to thank my colleague at Colby, Kenneth Rodman, for stimulating conversations during the months of the Taiwan Strait crisis. Comments and criticisms from Hung-mao Tien, An-chia Wu, and other conference participants are appreciated. Qimao Chen and Andrew Nathan read through an early version of the manuscript and made valuable comments. A new version of the paper was presented at a workshop in the Sam Nunn School of International Affairs, Georgia Institute of Technology, on 7 February 1998. I would like to thank the constructive comments from the workshop participants, particularly Yong Deng, Fei-Ling Wang, and Thomas J. Christensen. Of course, the author is solely responsible for the view and accuracy of fact in the paper.

1. *Beijing Review* 24, no. 40, 5 October 1981, 11.

2. *White Paper,* "The Taiwan Questions and Reunification of China," *China Daily,* 1 September 1993, 4–5.

3. Xinhua News Agency, 27 July 1995.

4. Editorial, "Do Not Underestimate China's Will to Safeguard Its Sovereignty," *Ta Kung Pao,* 3 June 1995, A2.

5. Kang Yanwen, "Anti-China Forces in the United States Should Not Imagine That They Can Play the Taiwan Card," *Ta Kung Pao,* 18 June 1995, A2.

6. Alexander George, "Introduction: The Limits of Coercive Diplomacy," in *The Limits of Coercive Diplomacy,* Alexander L. George and William E. Simons, eds. (Boulder, Colo.: Westview Press, 1994), 2.

7. Russell Leng, "When Will They Ever Learn? Coercive Bargaining in Recurrent Crises," *Journal of Conflict Resolution,* no. 27 (September 1983), 415.

8. Russell Leng, *Interstate Crisis Behavior, 1816–1980: Realism Versus Reciprocity* (Cambridge: Cambridge University Press, 1993), 191.

9. One senior Chinese official told me that "China will stand firm even risking its economic benefits and world image. It will not 'kowtow' to Washington." Personal interview notes, Shanghai and Beijing, 18 July–2 August 1995.

10. One well-connected Chinese friend told me that the Clinton administration would not take the risk of going to war with China by sending two carriers to the Taiwan Strait if it was not assured that Beijing did not intend to invade Taiwan. From this perspective, this friend complained that the Clinton administration betrayed Beijing because the Chinese government, by giving its assurance of no-war intention, was to prevent the United States from overreacting to Beijing's military exercises. However, Washington took advantage of the information that Liu Huaqiu passed to Lake and bolstered its naval forces near Taiwan.

11. "Chinese Communist Party Central Committee Document no. 3 (1991): Central Committee Notice Concerning How to Further Promote Taiwan Work," *Zhongguo shibao,* 14 April 1991, 7.

12. "Economic Work Toward Taiwan as the Foundation for Political Reunification," *Zhongguo shibao,* 16 April 1994, 1.

13. Yun-han Chu, "The Politics of Taiwan's Mainland Policy," paper presented at the conference "Political Development in Hong Kong and Taiwan," Hong Kong, 8–9 February 1996.

14. "Lee Ruins Cross-Straits Talks," *China Daily,* 2 August 1995, p. 4.

15. Xinhua News Agency, 31 March 1995.

16. "Security Organs Urged to Protect Compatriots," *Xinhua,* 21 February 1995.

17. Ibid.

18. Zhang Min, "Lee Teng-hui Has Nothing New to Offer in His Six-Point Program," *Xinhua,* 10 April 1995.

19. Xinhua Commentary, 16 June 1995.

20. Li Hsiao-chu, "Taiwan Elections Impact on Future Political Situation on Island and Cross-Strait Relations," *Zhongguo tongxun she,* 4 December 1994, in Foreign Broadcast Infomation Service (hereafter cited as FBIS) CHI-94–235, 7 December 1994, 68.

21. Fan Liqing, "How Can We Treat Lightly the Pro-Taiwan Independence Sentiment that Runs Rampant on the Island?" *Xinhua,* 8 June 1995.

22. "The Trend Toward Taiwan Independent Is Stable," *Zhongguo shibao,* 3 June 1994, 4.

23. He Chong, "Lee Teng-hui Unmasks His False Pursuit of Reunification," *Renmin ribao* (overseas ed.), 21 June 1995, 5.

24. Xin Qi, "An Irresponsible and Adventurous Move—On Lee Teng-Hui's Private Visit," *Xinhua,* 8 June 1995.

25. Qu Xiangqian, "Lee Teng-hui Has Torn Off His Own Mask," *Renmin ribao* (overseas ed.), 19 June 1995, 5.

26. Duanmu Laidi and Liu Shizhong, "New Revelations of the True Nature of Reunification in Form but Independence in Reality," *Xinhua,* 11 June 1995.

27. *Xinhua,* 12 June 1995.

28. *Xinhua,* 11 June 1995.

29. Xin Jing, "Sayonara Taiwan Taboo, Japanese Society Rediscovers Taiwan," *Jiushi niendai (The Nineties),* 1 March 1995, 62–64, in FBIS-CHI-95–111, 9 June 1995, 99.

30. He Chong, "Is Lee Teng-hui Moses or a Chessman?" *Xinhua,* 7 June 1995.

31. Ren Huiwen, "Beijing Reassesses the U.S. and Lee Teng-hui," *Hsin Pao,* 16 Jule 1995, 23.

32. He Chong, "Lee Teng-hui Unmasks His False Pursuit of Reunification," *Renmin ribao* (overseas ed.), 21 June 1995, 5.

33. Qu Xiangqian, "Lee Teng-hui Has Torn Off His Own Mask," *Renmin ribao* (overseas ed.), 19 June 1995, 5.

34. As one U.S. analyst observed during the crisis, "I am convinced, based on talks with mainland officials, that Beijing three months ago believed that Mr. Lee would openly challenge the 'one China' principle—if only by declaring independence then, by pushing for and accepting an official 'state visit' to the United States or committing some other act that would be interpreted by Beijing as a de facto statement of independence." Ralph A. Cossa, "China's Missile Exercises Are Likely to Backfire," *International Herald Tribune* (Singapore), 9–10 March 1996.

35. "Lee Ruins Cross-Straits Talks," *China Daily,* 2 August 1995, 4.

36. *China News Analysis* (HK), 15 September 1995, 1.

37. *Xinhua,* 27 June 1995.

38. "Beijing Media Urge to Keep Taiwan by Force," *Xinhua,* 19 July 1995.

39. Kay Moller, "A New Role for the ROC on Taiwan in the Post–Cold War Era," *Issues and Studies* 31, no. 2 (February 1995), 84–85.

40. *Xinhua,* 8 June 1995.

41. "Lee Ruins Cross-Straits Talks," *China Daily,* 2 August 1995, 4.

42. *China Daily,* 1 August 1995, 1.

43. *Xinhua,* 29 July 1995.

44. Li Jiaquan, "Lee's U.S. Visit Defies Agreement," *Beijing Review,* 26 June–2 July 1995, 19–20.

45. Beijing Central Radio, "Commentary Urges Taiwan to Value Relations," 14 July 1995, *FBIS-CHI-139,* 20 July 1995, 52.

46. Fan Liqing, "Lee Teng-hui Buys Admission Ticket to Enter the U.S. Without Regarding to the Cost," *Xinhua,* 7 June 1995.

47. Nancy B. Tucher, "China and America: 1949–1991," *Foreign Affairs* 70, no. 5 (Winter 1991/1992), 75.

48. Jia Qingguo, "Reflections on the Recent Tension in the Taiwan Strait," *China Journal,* no. 36 (July 1996), 97.

49. Liu Liandi, "What Evil Intentions has the U.S. Harbored in Playing the Taiwan Card?" *Renmin ribao* (overseas ed.), 21 June 1995, 6.

50. Li Jiaquan, "Lee's U.S. Visit Defies Agreement."

51. *Xinhua,* 30 January 1996.

52. "Beijing Media Urge to Keep Taiwan by Force," *Xinhua,* 19 July 1995.

53. Ben Stavis, "Untying the Taiwan Knot," *Foreign Policy Research Institute Bulletin* 6, no. 2 (February 1998) (electronic ed.).

54. Deborah Shen, "Straits Tensions Hinder Local Economic Growth," *Free China Journal,* 1 March 1996, 3.

55. *Renmin ribao,* 24 March 1996, 1.

56. *Wen Wei Po,* 29 March 1996, A2, in FBIS-CHI-96–068, 8 April 1996, 45.

57. *South China Morning Post,* 3 April 1996, in FBIS-CHI-96–065, 3 April 1996, 86.

58. For Beijing's response to Lee's 20 May speech, see *Renmin ribao,* 24 June 1996, 1.

59. Deng Xiaoping, "The Present Situation and the Tasks Before Us," in *Selected Works of Deng Xiaoping, 1975–1982* (Beijing: Foreign Language Press, 1983), 224–258.

60. Liu Ji, "Making the Right Choice in Twenty-First Century Sino-American Relations," *Journal of Contemporary China* 7, no. 17 (1998), 99.

61. Ibid.

11

Pride, Pressure, and Politics: The Roots of China's Worldview

Thomas J. Christensen

M ost parents will likely recognize the *Sesame Street* skit in which characters point out a series of letters or objects and invite in song, "One of these things is not like the other / One of these things is not the same." If the chapter contributors for this book were gathered together for such a skit, I would doubtlessly stick out in the lineup. Despite the fact that I am not Chinese by ethnicity or nationality, the differences between me and my Chinese colleagues might not be as great as they seem. I have spent a good part of the last six years studying the questions raised in this book: How do contemporary Chinese elites and citizens perceive Beijing's interactions with the outside world, and how might those perceptions influence China's foreign relations in the post–Cold War era?

As one would expect in a concluding chapter, below I will tie together some of the themes presented. But I will try to go one step further, comparing the outlook of the authors here with my own views and with the views of their compatriots, with whom I have interacted in Beijing during the past six years. While attending the conference that preceded publication of this book, it occurred to me that the extraordinary scholars who contributed chapters to this volume are worthy of study themselves. For the serious Western student of China's foreign relations, they are rather awe-inspiring. They are, perhaps, the most qualified observers of Chinese foreign policy attitudes in the world. They enjoy enough insider status to not only understand but empathize with the Chinese attitudes they study. This is something even the most qualified foreigners have difficulty doing.

But the authors here have also spent enough time outside of the mainland to gain some of the objectivity of Western China analysts, a trait many of the contributors' compatriots in universities and think tanks in China have difficulty attaining. Moreover, if China continues to open up to the outside world and the fear of foreign influence in government circles decreases, these cosmopolitan scholars' views of China and its place in the world should become increasingly influential in the thinking of Chinese decisionmakers. For all of these reasons, I am most grateful to the scholars here for including me in this project.

CHINA'S FRUSTRATED REALISM AS A FORCE FOR STASIS AND CHANGE

In both form and content the contributions here confirm the increasingly popular thesis that contemporary Chinese perceptions of the international world accord with "realism" or "realpolitik": Elites in the Chinese Communist Party (CCP) view nation-states as the most important actors in the world; they consider international political challenges in terms of power and national interest rather than as an ideological struggle; they look with a good deal of suspicion on international institutions and the global norms those institutions sometimes advocate.[1] The contributions here show that Chinese realism is deeply rooted and stubborn and that the Hobbesian view of international politics that underpins realism is particularly acute in China because of the century of humiliation (now really a century and a half), in which a previously ascendant Chinese empire had been bullied and aggravated by the world's great powers. Ironically, however, the chapters also suggest that China's realpolitik quest to restore its place among internationally recognized great powers might actually be the most important force pushing China into international institutions and agreements that could, in the long run, transform Chinese thinking about international politics.

The chapters by Fei-Ling Wang and Yong Deng clearly illustrate that Chinese elites view international politics largely as a competition for power and prestige. In fact, the latter's chapter drives this point home in a new and rather compelling way. Yong Deng not only demonstrates that there are relatively few Chinese government intellectuals actually considering the world from fundamentally nonrealist perspectives (e.g., globalization, multilateralism, or common interests/interdependence); he shows that the ones who have made such an intellectual journey have battled against the resistance of others as well as the resistance of their own minds. Their struggle for intellectual identity may be an allegory representing the struggle for international identity that the Chinese nation will experience during the next century. In Yong Deng's portrayal, when creative thinkers such as Li Shenzhi or Wang Yizhou venture away from a vision of world politics centered on supreme state sovereignty and stark international anarchy, they seem a bit lost and find themselves, in the end, being pulled back by the strong gravitational force of the realist/victim view of China's foreign relations. In this view, international norms and institutions are just the tools of great powers bent on keeping China in its current undesirable place in the international distribution of wealth and power. So, as Yong Deng reports, new thinkers like Wang Yizhou sometimes are forced to surrender to realist conclusions such as this: "Rationally speaking, the international society is still in the state of anarchy governed by power politics."

Yong Deng is right to focus on scholars such as Wang and Li, because they are, in a sense, hard test cases. Finding strong strands of cynicism and frustration in their writings underscores the pervasiveness and stubbornness of the garden-variety realism that drives the thinking of mainstream foreign policy analysts in China today. The fact that their new thinking is still marginal in government circles also sheds light, by contrast, on the current mainstream Chinese mindset. In reading Yong Deng's chapter, one is reminded of how, in Jonathan Spence's classic *The Gate of Heavenly Peace*, the frustrations and struggles of Western-influenced "new thinkers" in China since 1895 placed in a clearer light the deep-seated nature of the dominant Chinese political thought of their times.[2] But, as Yong Deng also argues, the mere existence of new writings that emphasize globalization and liberal perspectives on international relations in China can still be seen as a breakthrough and a harbinger of increased intellectual diversity.

There are several reasons for the pervasive emphasis on power and competition in Chinese foreign policy analysis. One important one is underscored in the contributions here. In the Maoist era, free discourse on international affairs was forbidden, and there was a top-down orthodoxy that was highly ideological and openly contemptuous of realpolitik (*qiangquan zhengzhi*), a term representing something so evil as to border on great power hegemony (*baquan*), the great bogeyman of all postcolonial ideologues. During the reform period, as communist ideology was soundly rejected in the minds of Chinese elites (if not always in their public statements), the CCP and its academies have turned to the outside world for new theoretical perspectives on international relations. Absorption of new ideas from the outside world takes time, however. At the most mundane level, complex, often jargon-filled texts need to be translated into Chinese. At the political level, acceptable new trends in thinking must first be approved by elites who are understandably nervous about the professional risks of intellectual adventurism. The result is that only a select group of books gets translated over time. As Yong Deng shows, the books selected and taught often have been realist in their bent.

There are several reasons for the popularity of realist works in China. First, the works of authors such as Hans Morgenthau, Kenneth Waltz, and Robert Gilpin are the standard-bearers of their respective generations of international relations scholars in the West. Moreover, they propose theories that take no clear ideological position and, more often, even reject ideology as a basis for foreign policy making. Although they suggest a strong opposition to any ideology in foreign policy making—and that would certainly include communist ideology—they at least cannot be construed as being pointedly anticommunist.[3] Therefore, nervous Chinese scholars may find these works to be the safest diversion from traditional CCP orthodoxy.

A second, perhaps more important reason that realism finds such fertile soil in China is China's historical disappointment with and bitterness toward the world's great powers. Rightly or wrongly, Beijing elites and Chinese citizens alike view China as always on the receiving end of great power machinations. As a result, they find it difficult to believe that anything but the struggle for dominance drives the foreign policies of the world's most powerful actors.

Worse yet, as was discussed by several scholars at the conference that preceded publication of this book, Chinese citizens view some of the biggest disappointments in Chinese diplomatic history as resulting from the West's high-profile efforts to redefine international politics along some normative, principled line that diverges from power politics. In fact, many trace the birth of modern Chinese nationalism to May 4, 1919, when a group of Chinese took to the streets to protest China's unequal treatment at Versailles. Treating China as an exception to their new norms of national equality and respect for sovereignty, the great powers at Versailles granted Japan territorial booty in China for Japan's support of the Allies during World War I. The somewhat utopian Western rethinking of international politics during the 1930s, particularly that of the United States, meant that when Japan raped and pillaged China for years the United States did little but protest diplomatically. By merely refusing to recognize Japanese acquisitions in Manchuria and northern China and leveling universal arms embargoes against all combatants, the United States arguably hurt the weaker Chinese forces much more than their Japanese enemies. After World War II, Beijing would be excluded from the United Nations until 1971. As authors point out in this volume, since George Bush's call for a new world order, Chinese elites and many Chinese citizens believe that the United States has used global norms as a cover to interfere in Chinese domestic affairs (e.g., human rights criticisms), frustrate China's efforts to improve its international standing and image (e.g., opposition to the Beijing Olympics), and, according to the most conspiratorial version of the theory, to destabilize the Chinese polity as part of a long-term containment strategy (e.g., alleged encouragement of Taiwanese and Tibetan independence and support for political dissidents in China).[4]

As I have argued elsewhere, the details of China's century of humiliation matter a great deal in understanding China's current foreign policy problems.[5] First, China does not simply take the realist view that all great powers are equally dangerous. Ship for ship, plane for plane, and soldier for soldier, Chinese elites and the Chinese public view Japanese power as more threatening than any other nation's power. This fear derives from the brutal legacy of the Japanese occupation of China during the 1930s and 1940s. It also derives from the scarring defeats at the hands of Japan during the war of 1894–1895, after which Japan was awarded territorial concessions, including Taiwan. Because this was the first time in modern history that China had been defeated and carved up by an Asian power, as opposed to a Western power, this event was particularly poignant in the long record of China's humiliation. Given China's traditional dominance in the region, that initial loss to Japan during the late nineteenth century made a deep impression.

The widespread and deeply held mistrust of Japan helps explain why China has reacted so negatively to the prospect of any change in the traditionally American-dominated security alliance with Japan. As Yu Bin points out, the fear of a militarily resurgent Japan is a major factor in China's regional security strategy. As my own research suggests, whether it appears that the United States might abandon Japan because of U.S.-Japan disputes or whether the United States might seek to strengthen the bilateral alliance by expanding its scope and urging Japan to play new military roles, Chinese analysts worry greatly. Whether Japan is abandoned or encouraged by the United States, Chinese security analysts believe that Japan will be more likely to build up independent military power that would, almost by necessity, pose a grave security threat to China. Though the fear of strong powers in the neighborhood is fully in accord with realism, scenarios in which some of the roles of the much stronger United States are adopted by a weaker Japan should not trigger alarm bells according to realist logic. Only the particular dislike and distrust of Japan can explain why a Japanese aircraft carrier seems much scarier to Chinese analysts than an equally powerful American one.[6]

Another place where the details of China's history of humiliation comes into play is in its relations with outside powers over the Taiwan question. Taiwan combines all of the worst lessons of the century of humiliation for China. There is a strong sense that Taiwan's separation from the mainland is the last unrecovered part of the Chinese national body, which began being carved up during the Opium War. Worse yet, Taiwan was separated from the mainland in 1895 by the Japanese. Moreover, Taiwan was promised to China by the great powers at the Cairo Conference in 1943 as a reward for China's considerable contribution to the defeat of Japanese fascism. From Beijing's perspective, America's willingness to protect Taiwan from the mainland since 1950 is just another example of how power, not principle, operates in international politics. Finally, with the death of communism as a legitimizing force for the CCP, nationalism is an increasingly important force for political stability in China, and toughness on Taiwan is perhaps the most important measure of any leader's nationalist credentials. As Fei-Ling Wang points out in his chapter, a tough policy toward Taiwan independence gains consensus perhaps more easily than any other policy position in present-day China. On the other side of the same coin, if Taiwan were allowed to gain de jure independent legal status, leaders would run the risk of being labeled modern-day Li Hongzhangs, Li being the man who is rather unfairly blamed for the 1895 Treaty of Shimonoseki ceding Taiwan to Japan. Moreover, there is a fear that softness in the face of Taipei's provocation would send a green light to separatists throughout the Chinese empire, especially in regions with large minority populations, such as Tibet and Xinjiang. Finally, as Fei-Ling Wang points out, the fear of Yugoslavization in Beijing is only exacerbated by the declining financial and political authority of the central government over the regions during the 1990s.[7]

Given China's outstanding sovereignty disputes, including Taiwan, the Spratlys, and the Diaoyudao Islands (Senkaku), its desire to become a great power, and its mistrust of multilateral institutions and norms, it is not surprising that Chinese officials and thinkers have not been at the forefront in the new push to create regional multilateral institutions designed to build confidence and cooperation in the security arena, to foster global consensus on environmental, human rights, and proliferation problems, and to allow international mediation in bilateral sovereignty disputes. The chapters by Jianwei Wang and Fei-Ling Wang show how the strong realist streaks in the thinking of Chinese security elites led initially to dismissal of the need for formal regional security arrangements and a fear of an enlarged and more influential Association of Southeast Asian Nations (ASEAN). In the early days of the ASEAN Regional Forum (ARF), Chinese analysts expressed much more than just skepticism. They wanted to know what power and interests were behind the veil of multilateral norms. The answer was usually twofold: The United States was encouraging processes of regional multilateralism so as to prevent China from becoming a regional and global rival to American hegemony; and ASEAN, particularly with the inclusion of Vietnam, could easily become an anti-Chinese containment alliance.[8]

As Jianwei Wang writes, because of the prevalence of realist thinking, multilateralism is generally viewed as a tool of great power competition rather than as something fundamentally new in international politics. He writes:

Based on its own experience, China believes that in any institutionalized multilateral regime, sooner or later there would be a competition for leadership. China, still considering itself relatively weak among the major powers in the region, does not want to be involved in such a struggle too early as it could be in an unfavorable position.... China suspects that proposals for a collective security regime in the Asia-Pacific may have the implication of containing China as a rising power.

China has participated in ARF since its first meeting in 1994. China's initial agreement to do so probably was based on two calculations: Beijing feared being left out of any international organization regardless of its mission, because Chinese leaders still have a complex about being treated like a second-class citizen; Chinese leaders also may have hoped that by participating they could undercut any concrete action by the organization that might hurt China's interests. So, at the July 1994 ARF conference and in earlier multilateral meetings with Southeast Asian representatives, China effectively blocked any meaningful discussion of territorial disputes involving Chinese claims.[9] It has also worked in the past to block the creation of formal multilateral reassurance regimes in East Asia, like the Organization for Security and Cooperation in Europe (OSCE), that might lead to condemnation of China's development and/or deployment of force projection capabilities.[10]

But realism and cynicism may also be a force for change in Chinese views of the outside world and in Chinese foreign policy strategies. As recent works by Paul Evans and Iain Johnston have shown, in China there is a small but growing community of true believers in the benefits of arms control, confidence-building measures, and multilateralism more generally. These new thinkers are represented in certain government think tanks and in specific offices within the Ministry of Foreign Affairs.[11] Somewhat like their Soviet counterparts from the early 1980s, these experts are cosmopolitan and have been greatly influenced by interactions with foreigners in both government-to-government and track-II dialogues.[12] This phenomenon may help explain China's seemingly less suspicious and somewhat more proactive posture in ARF and with ASEAN countries over time. Since the first ARF meeting in July 1994, China seems increasingly willing to discuss issues related to the Spratlys, and in 1997 Beijing even hosted a conference on confidence-building measures, cosponsored by Manila. As Johnston and Evans argue, these developments, though nascent, should not be dismissed as mere rhetoric and showmanship. China is indeed capable of participating in meaningful multilateral agreements, as is demonstrated by the recent agreements on border demarcation and confidence-building measures pounded out with Russia and the former Soviet republics in Turkish Central Asia.[13] But Jianwei Wang warns that China's recent overtures to ARF, though meaningful, do not mean that China wants ARF to develop into a formal "arbitrator of regional conflict." Instead, it is more likely that China is increasingly reassured that ASEAN is not dominated by Washington and that China, by participating and limiting the scope of ARF, can be assured that Chinese interests will not be compromised.[14]

The rise of a small group of true believers in multilateralism as a new way of conducting international relations within the Chinese government is a significant event. However, if we want to explain the recent warming toward multilateralism in the statements and actions of the CCP, the beliefs of these new thinkers cannot provide a sufficient explanation. They are simply too small in number and treated with too much suspicion by many of my interlocutors, particularly those in more traditionally conservative sections of the government, such as the People's Liberation Army.[15] As my interviews in 1996 and 1998 suggest, understanding the changes in the perceived security threats facing China may go a long way toward explaining the new spoken interest in multilateralism in Beijing. It seems that a combination of reduced fear of ASEAN collusion against China, however justified, and an increasing fear of developments in U.S. bilateral diplomacy in the Asia Pacific, particularly with Japan and Australia, has convinced many formerly skeptical analysts that multilateralism may be the best alternative for China given the risks posed by business as usual. Yong Deng suggests this in his chapter when he questions the full sincerity of calls for multilateral security dialogue when they follow immediately after complaints about U.S. bilateral diplomacy. Since China both fears and has little influence over various aspects of U.S. bilateral diplomacy, such as the strengthening of the U.S.-Japan alliance, accepting a bigger role for multilateral dialogue, if not the creation of formal multilateral security institutions, may be the least unpleasant method to reduce the threat posed by U.S. bilateralism.[16]

In the case of growing acceptance of multilateralism, both new ideas and external pressure familiar to realists matter a great deal. Many in China are quick to point out that foreign pressure only leads to more conservative and belligerent reactions in China, but this may only sometimes be true. As with China's growing interest in multilateral dialogue as a response to foreign pressure, Yu Bin's work on China's regional strategy suggests that China has tried to play a more active and constructive role in the region since the 1980s, at least partially as a response to the sanctions and stigmatization leveled against China by the West following Tiananmen. Whether intended or not, this outcome of great power pressure may be seen as a positive one, even if, at the same time, Western complaints about China's domestic repression also carried real costs in spurring popular nationalism and a "rally around the flag" effect.

In other areas, material sanctions or security threats may be unnecessary for changing China's behavior. Purely normative pressures can help alter China's definition of what it means to be a prestigious great power and thereby influence core Chinese security policies. As Hu Weixing argues in his chapter, it was the fear of being left alone outside the great power club following Tiananmen and the French accession to the Nuclear Nonproliferation Treaty (NPT) that compelled China to sign on to the Treaty in 1992. This occurred, according to Hu, despite China's long-running suspicion of multilateral counterproliferation treaties and organizations, such as the International Atomic Energy Agency (IAEA). As Johnston and Evans point out, it is very difficult to understand China's 1996 accession to the Comprehensive Test Ban Treaty (CTBT) without understanding that international normative pressures on China actually can have important constraining effects on Chinese behavior in the security realm.[17] In his chapter, Jianwei Wang similarly claims that China's fear of appearing obstructionist in the UN prevents it from actively opposing resolutions with which Beijing disagrees in principle. Arguing along the same lines, he points out that China participates in other multilateral organizations at least partially because China does not want to appear obstreperous by remaining outside them.

The most important normative pressure that can be applied to China is defining for Beijing what it would take for China to be considered by the other great powers as a respected member of the great power club. Having adopted a more standard realist logic at the time of China's accession to the CTBT, this author, for one, was surprised that China did not continue with its traditional delaying tactic of demanding unachievable compromises from the United States, such as a no-first-use pledge, as preconditions for Chinese participation.[18] A realist might counter that a range of factors may have mitigated the costs of accession for the Chinese: China may have learned quite a bit from the tests it conducted just before it acceded to the treaty; it may have learned much from espionage in the West and in Russia; and it may have faith that in the near future it will be able to simulate nuclear explosions with computers. Still, even if adhering to the CTBT does not stop Chinese nuclear modernization in its tracks—and it almost certainly has not—nobody seems to dispute the fact that the CTBT carries real opportunity costs for China's nuclear modernization. This, then, suggests that external pressure, both economic and normative, brought China on board the CTBT even though it runs against China's security interests as normally measured by realists. If, as part of its goal to become a normal great power, China buckled to the opprobrium of other great powers on the test ban issue and sacrificed real military strength in the process, the role of norms and changing definitions of what it means to be a great power are clear. Along these lines, we may see increased participation in multilateral organizations and in confidence-building regimes if China becomes convinced that participation is not only the "norm" for a modern great power but also actually a prerequisite for being considered a great power by others, a goal that has driven the most important Chinese foreign policy behavior since the late Qing Dynasty.

If multilateralism is not just a strategy to pursue national interests but can be an entirely different way of considering international politics, as some Western theorists suggest, then China has a long way to go before it accepts true multilateralism.[19] Since multilateralism has become more tolerable to many in China largely because of realist frustrations relating to U.S. bilateral diplomacy, many of those who now claim to be more open-minded about the benefits of multilateral fora have not undergone any fundamental shift in worldviews. But perhaps this is how shifts in worldviews take place: in stages and with unintended outcomes. Today's pragmatic shift could become tomorrow's ideational change for an increasing number of Chinese elites.

DOMESTIC POLITICS, PUBLIC OPINION, AND THE FUTURE OF CHINESE POLITICS

Many of the authors in this volume have addressed one of the most important questions facing foreign leaders as they engage an increasingly open China: What will Chinese politics look like in the twenty-first century and what effect will foreign countries have in determining that outcome? The contributions should be quite sobering to optimistic Western analysts who foresee a more democratic and, therefore, more peaceful China on the horizon. The chapters will be particularly jarring to those Westerners who believe that only foreign pressure can help speed the process of CCP demise, democratization, and moderation in Chinese foreign relations. The evidence and analysis presented here offer a few rebuttals to those positions: (1) The Chinese public, especially the intellectual elite, has grown more conservative, nationalistic, and supportive (however grudgingly) of the CCP regime during the 1990s; (2) foreign pressure fuels nationalism, not liberalism in China and actually makes public opinion and elite politics more conservative than they would otherwise be; and (3) Chinese democracy, if it were to come relatively soon, would actually make Chinese foreign policy more unpredictable and, perhaps, belligerent in the short-to-medium term.

At the most basic level these lessons jibe well with my own experiences in China during the 1980s and 1990s. Chinese government and university intellectuals seem much more conservative than they were during the heady months before the Tiananmen massacre or during the years immediately following the 1989 crackdown. As Ming Wan points out, this trend is present in the entire society, not just in the intellectual elite. Western observers of China often fail to recognize that just because "the voice of Chinese society is not heard does not necessarily mean that society shares the views of dissidents."

Some of the arguments made by intellectuals in China for respecting the political status quo are made along reactive, nationalist lines: China needs to stand up to outside pressure, and for all of its faults the CCP provides the stability and authority to fend off foreign incursions better than any imaginable alternative regime. Others emphasize the long-term goal of true liberal democratization but take a Huntingtonian position about why there must be political stability and economic development in the next decades so that the societal and institutional groundwork can be laid for eventual peaceful and comprehensive democratization (*quanmian minzhuhua*).[20] This latter position is consistent with Ming Wan's seemingly contradictory finding that on the one hand average citizens would prefer more civil liberties and a free press in the abstract, but that on the other hand those same citizens so cherish economic and political stability that they generally do not view confrontation with authorities as a justifiable means to pursue their abstract desires. Ming Wan notes that there is a similarly conservative intellectual trend among his fellow Chinese scholars abroad. Like many in China, they too support "gradual developmentalism" for the People's Republic of China (PRC).[21]

It seems to this outside observer that a good deal of the new conservatism, though very real, is rooted at least as much in a newly intensified nationalism in China as it is in intellectual theories about gradual socioeconomic change. As Fei-Ling Wang suggests, this new nationalistic trend, particularly among Chinese youth, is partially a backlash against Western pressure on human rights and other criticisms of China's political system. As both Ming Zhang's and Fei-Ling Wang's chapters strongly suggest, many in China have drawn the conclusion that a foreign attack on the CCP is, in effect, an attack on the Chinese nation. That conclusion has been fostered by the CCP, which finds itself without an ideological message in the wake of its systematic and intentional destruction of everything communist except its Leninist, one-party dictatorship. As Fei-Ling Wang points out, because the CCP has been successful in equating its regime stability with national security, many average Chinese now have the impression that Chinese national security is extremely vulnerable, even though from an objective perspective the Chinese nation has not been so safe since before the Opium Wars. Ming Zhang's and Yu Bin's findings about attitudes in China regarding conspiracies against China perpetrated by the United States and Japan fully accord with Fei-Ling Wang's portrayal of a widespread exaggeration of the security threats faced by the Chinese nation.

Popular Chinese nationalism appears to this observer to be more complex and much stronger than just a reaction to specific foreign pressures followed by a "rally around the regime" effect. It seems to have a great deal to do with an identity crisis in the post-Mao PRC and a desperate search for some political message that can both unify the Chinese nation and provide a nonideological basis for criticizing a leadership that is often viewed as corrupt, inefficient, and self-serving. The implicit criticism of the current leadership that runs through much of the nationalist rhetoric one hears in China is almost certainly what makes the central government in Beijing so ambivalent about popular nationalist sentiments. Sometimes the Chinese state drums up nationalism over issues like Taiwan in order to bolster its legitimacy at home and demonstrate resolve abroad. Yet at other times the government cracks down on nationalist protests against foreign nations before they grow into wider movements. So, in 1996, the CCP dissuaded academics in Beijing from protesting against Japanese rightist activities in the disputed Diaoyudao (Senkaku) Islands. As one retired Chinese military officer told me, the fear was that "on the first day, the protestors would demonstrate against Japan; the next day they would protest against the government for being too soft on Japan; and on the third day they might even call for an overthrow of the CCP." He pointed to how anti-Japanese protests in 1919 and during the 1930s quickly became forces for domestic political opposition.[22]

If one accepts the argument of Jack Snyder and Edward Mansfield that poorly institutionalized new democracies are actually more belligerent than stable authoritarian states, one might view CCP restraint of democratic forces as a force for peace in the region.[23] As Fei-Ling Wang points out, the would-be nationalist protestors advocated a much tougher policy toward Japan during the 1996 minicrisis over Diaoyudao/Senkaku than did the authoritarians in Beijing's Zhongnanhai compound. At the conference, several scholars agreed that fast-paced democratization would make Chinese foreign policy more unstable and aggressive, not less so.

Despite making many important and valid points in discussing the issues of foreign pressure and the growing nationalism in China, the authors here may be missing something critical to understanding Chinese domestic political trends and foreign influence on those trends. Though the average Chinese citizen might sincerely cite foreign pressure on China as the root cause of the new nationalist tendencies, this is not necessarily the only or even most important cause of this phenomenon. The nationalist trends are almost certainly as rooted in the national identity crisis cited above, and the domestic political problems that flow from that crisis, as they are in the particular actions of foreign powers toward China. By understanding this, we may better assess when foreign pressure might be counterproductive and when it actually may be helpful in reducing the chance of hypernationalism and aggressive foreign policies in China in the post–Cold War world.

A good example for such a distinction is provided by an analysis of the 1995–1996 minicrisis between the United States and China over Taiwan. The common wisdom in China and in several chapters in this book is that America's support for Taiwan and coercive diplomacy toward China only fostered the growing nationalism and conservatism in Chinese politics. Given America's stated goals of a more moderate, less nationalistic China, one might draw the conclusion from such an analysis that U.S. China policy from May 1995 through March 1996 was an unmitigated disaster. But if one views currents of virulent nationalism in China as a domestic force largely independent of the policies of foreign leaders, and one breaks down the crisis into distinct chapters, one may draw very different conclusions about the failures and successes of U.S. policy.

Suisheng Zhao argues convincingly that the U.S. State Department's granting of a visa to Pres. Lee Teng-hui to visit Cornell University not only sparked widespread nationalism in China and increased support for the CCP regime generally but also, within the regime itself, discredited voices for moderation in international politics and reconciliation in cross-strait relations, most notably Foreign Minister Qian Qichen. After all, as Zhao points out, in January 1995 Beijing offered its most conciliatory posture to date toward Taiwan in Jiang Zemin's eight-point proposal. Certainly advocates of moderation toward Taiwan and the United States looked bad when the Clinton administration reversed its pledge to the contrary and granted the visa to President Lee. China's reaction to this about-face in U.S. policy is well known: phased military exercises beginning in July 1995 culminating in extensive missile firings and live-fire surface exercises in March 1996 prior to Taiwan's first presidential election. China toughened its stance toward Taiwan either because the voices of moderation in China changed their attitudes about the Taiwan problem and Sino-American relations, because their voices were muted by the less moderate, more belligerent elements of the CCP elite, including the military, or, most probably, because of some combination of these two factors.

In March 1996, the United States reacted to the last, most provocative round of missile exercises by sending not one but two aircraft carrier battle groups to the area around Taiwan as a general warning against Chinese belligerence. Citing the very angry response to this U.S. policy by even generally liberal groups such as college students, young professors, and beneficiaries of international trade and investment, many in China saw this U.S. policy as one that only increased Chinese nationalism and violent opposition to Taiwan's efforts to increase its international profile.[24] Several of the contributors to this book seem to agree with this analysis. But if one takes virulent nationalism in China seriously as a largely domestically driven force, related as much to the death of communism as it is rooted in foreign pressure on China, one might draw a very different conclusion. Although it is indisputable that the dispatch of U.S. carriers led to an angry reaction in China, one must ask what the result of U.S. passivity would have been in the face of a clearly provocative and hard-line Chinese policy. In such an instance would not the harder-line thinking inside and outside the CCP have been fully vindicated and would not popular Chinese national pride and confidence have increased to dangerous levels at the same time? If China had been rewarded for allowing policy to be driven by the risk-accepting, devil-may-care attitudes described by Suisheng Zhao in his chapter (under the heading *changtong buru duantong*, "long-term pain is worse than short-term pain"), then could not Chinese nationalism have inflated to very dangerous proportions? If one sees both moderate and hyperna-tionalist streaks coexisting in the Chinese government and in Chinese soci-ety, then one can understand that hypernationalism can be caused not only by the failure of moderate policies like those pushed by Jiang Zemin and Qian Qichen in early 1995 but also by the success of hawkish policies like those being promoted in March 1996. So, even if one views the grant-ing of a visa to Lee Teng-hui in spring 1995 as a policy of little foresight, one might still view the tough American posture in March 1996 as quite wise. Moreover, one can have the same reason for both determinations: the desire to increase the power of the voices of moderation and decrease the volume of hypernationalism in postcommunist China.[25]

CONCLUSION

The contributions to this book demonstrate that Chinese perceptions of the great powers differ wildly from those countries' own self-perceptions. Few in Japan would portray Japan as a military threat to the region; few in America would consider the U.S. media as systematically unfair to China, as Ming Zhang argues; nor would many Americans view the growing U.S.-China trade deficit as largely a mirage created by inaccurate U.S. account-ing practices, as Yasheng Huang argues. The contributions here do much more than just report the publicly stated views of common citizens and elites in China. By agreeing with those viewpoints in certain cases, the au-thors here suggest the veracity and sincerity of their compatriots' ex-pressed opinions. As Ming Wan argues, Chinese scholars entrenched in American universities are largely protected from political reprisals for their views and are exposed to a much freer marketplace of ideas. So, when they draw conclusions similar to those of their compatriots at home, it suggests that the statements and writings of those compatriots in China are more likely to be heartfelt and deep-seated and less likely to be merely reflec-tions of a short-lived, superficial, and fabricated party line.

China's perspectives on international relations should provide practi-cal lessons and cautionary warnings for foreigners as they seek to engage

China in the economic, military, and political spheres. The lessons of the chapters here warn outside powers against the folly of trying to transform Chinese domestic politics quickly by means of direct, external pressure. Although agreeing in principle with that lesson, I personally think the reader should also consider that this lesson can, in key instances, be overlearned. The common view in China is that the new trend of Chinese nationalism is fundamentally a reaction to outside pressure. A corollary is that pressure on China never plays a constructive role in shaping China's foreign policy attitudes. But if one considers these positions, however heartfelt, as only partially correct, and if one also considers internal sources for growing Chinese nationalism, one may be more selective in deciding when it is and is not appropriate to accommodate China. Although pressure may often backfire and harden China's attitudes toward a range of international initiatives, pressure and even normative stigmatization aimed at China may sometimes also produce desirable outcomes. The benefits and opportunity costs of any given strategy toward China, including the risk of encouraging hypernationalism, can only be determined by an analysis of the domestic political situation and intellectual atmosphere in China at the time and whether or not the domestic trends are moving in a positive or a negative direction.

There are two ways for foreigners to foster hypernationalism in China, not just one. The first, wisely cautioned against by the contributors to this volume, is to cultivate hypernationalism by putting undue pressure on moderate Chinese leaders with reasonable international agendas. The second way to foster hypernationalism, not emphasized here, is to accommodate and reward belligerent and uncooperative policy initiatives with passivity or even concessions. If foreign observers view Chinese nationalism as a complex entity created as much at home as abroad, then they may be more able to avoid stumbling into either trap.

NOTES

1. Thomas J. Christensen, "Chinese Realpolitik," *Foreign Affairs* 75, no. 5 (September/October 1996), pp. 37–52; and "Realism with Chinese Characteristics: Beijing's Perceptions of Japan, the United States, and the Future of East Asia Security," a research report submitted to the Asia Security Project at Harvard University's Olin Institute for Strategic Studies, November 28, 1996. For related works, see Alastair Iain Johnston, *Cultural Realism: Strategic Culture and Grand Strategy in Chinese History* (Princeton: Princeton University Press, 1995); see also his "Cultural Realism and Strategy in Mao's China," in Peter Katzenstein, ed., *The Culture of National Security* (New York: Columbia University, 1996).

2. Jonathan Spence, *The Gate of Heavenly Peace* (New York: Viking, 1981).

3. In fact, both Morgenthau and Waltz criticized the thinking of the emotional anticommunists in the West fairly early in the Vietnam War. See Hans Morgenthau,

Politics Among Nations: The Struggle for Power and Peace, 4th ed. (New York: Alfred A. Knopf, 1967), p. 12; and Kenneth Waltz, "The Politics of Peace," *International Studies Quarterly* 11, no. 3 (September 1967): 199–211.

4. These conclusions are fully in accord with the author's interview research in Beijing during 1993–1998.

5. Christensen, "Chinese Realpolitik," and "Realism with Chinese Characteristics."

6. See ibid.

7. For an excellent discussion of Beijing's decreasing extractive capacity and its implications, see Wang Shaoguang, "Falling State Extractive Capacity in China and its Results," *21 shiji (Twenty-First Century)* (Hong Kong), no. 21 (February 1994): 5–14.

8. Author's interview research, 1994. One military officer considered counting the expanded ASEAN (with Vietnam) as a future fifth great power in the East Asia region, along with China, Japan, the United States, and Russia. For other discussions of Chinese concerns about regional multilateralism, see Gerald Segal, "East Asia and the 'Constrainment' of China," *International Security* 20, no. 4 (Spring 1996): 107–135; and Christensen, "Chinese Realpolitik." One theme that came up repeatedly in discussions in 1994 was that the United States was pushing for a new "Asia Pacific Community" (*Xin taipingyang gongtongti*) as a way of expanding the Asia-Pacific Economic Cooperation forum (APEC) into the security arena. The origin of the idea seemed as concerning to many analysts as the idea itself. Given the zero-sum logic of realist thinking, the belief seems to have been that if such a forum is in the U.S. interest, it must not be in China's. One published 1994 analysis of U.S. foreign policy refers to such efforts cynically as "so-called multilateralism." See Jin Junhui, "Kelindun zhengfu de waijiao zhengce sixiang chuxi" ("A Basic Analysis of the Foreign Policy Thinking of the Clinton Administration"), *Guoji wenti yanjiu (International Studies)*, no. 2 (1994): 1–5.

9. See Allen S. Whiting, "ASEAN Eyes China," *Asian Survey* 37, no. 4 (April 1997): 299–322. Also see Jianwei Wang's contribution in this volume (Chapter 4, "Managing Conflict: Chinese Perspectives on Multilateral Diplomacy and Collective Security").

10. As Jianwei Wang argues in his contribution here, China has been more open to multilateralism in the economic realm than it has in the security realm.

11. Alastair Iain Johnston, "Learning Versus Adaptation: Explaining Change in Chinese Arms Control Policy in the 1980s and 1990s," *China Journal*, no. 35 (January 1996): 27–62; see also his "International Relations Theory and Chinese Foreign Policy: The Role of 'Fuzzy' Variables," unpublished manuscript, 1994; Alastair Iain Johnston and Paul Evans, "China's Engagement of Multilateral Institutions," in Johnston and Robert S. Ross, eds., *Engaging China: The Management of an Emerging Power* (London: Routledge, forthcoming). This community is identified in Jianwei Wang's contribution here (Chapter 4). Such a trend is also consistent with the minority, nonrealist schools of thought that Yong Deng identifies in the Chinese government think tanks and academy.

12. Matthew Evangelista, "The Paradox of State Strength: Transnational Relations, Domestic Structures, and Security Policy in Russia and the Soviet Union," *International Organization* 49, no 1 (Winter 1995): 1–38; and Robert G. Herman,

"Identity, Norms, and National Security: The Soviet Foreign Policy Revolution and the End of the Cold War," in Katzenstein, *The Culture of National Security*.

13. Johnston and Evans, "China's Engagement."

14. Agreeing with Wang Jianwei's viewpoint on China's gradual and still limited acceptance of multilateralism is Wu Xinbo, "Integration on the Basis of Strength: China's Impact on East Asian Security," working paper of the Asia/Pacific Research Center, February 1998.

15. As Chinese interlocutors reported to me in 1996, the foreign ministry (*Waijiaobu*) is so reviled in other sections of the government that it is now often referred to as the *Maiguobu* (translated as Ministry of Compradors or, perhaps, Ministry of Traitors).

16. Author interviews, 1996 and 1998. Also see Zhou Jihua, "Rimei anbao tizhi de qianghua yu dongya de anquan" ("The Strengthening of the U.S.-Japan Security Arrangement and the Security of East Asia"), *Riben xuekan (Japan Studies)*, no. 4 (1996): 31–42. For an excellent analysis of ASEAN concerns and hopes about China, see Whiting, "ASEAN Eyes China." After the "strengthening" or "upgrading" of the U.S.-Japan alliance in the 17 April 1996 Clinton-Hashimoto communiqué and increased attention to Australia and South Korea in U.S. global strategy, many analysts seem to be reconsidering the value of multilateralism, both in ARF and in Northeast Asia. Without any solicitation, several interlocutors in 1996 raised multilateral dialogue as a constructive alternative to the trends in U.S. bilateral diplomacy. It was notable that the issue was raised by the analysts themselves, not by me, and that it was raised by both civilian and military analysts. They would often raise multilateral alternatives to current arrangements after complaining about the 17 April communiqué and statements by U.S. officials and academics that the U.S.-Japan relationship is the keystone of East Asian security.

17. Johnston and Evans, "China's Engagement."

18. For discussion of previous Chinese amendments to CTBT proposals, including no-first-use clauses and peaceful nuclear explosions, see Banning N. Garrett and Bonnie S. Glaser, "Chinese Perspectives on Nuclear Arms Control," *International Security* 20, no. 3 (Winter 1995/1996): 43–78.

19. For the argument that multilateralism can be understood as a shift in the meaning of international politics, and as more than just a new tactic for each country to pursue unilateral goals, see John Gerard Ruggie, "Introduction," and James Caporaso, "International Relations Theory and Multilateralism: The Search for Foundations," in Ruggie, ed., *Multilateralism Matters: The Theory and Praxis of An Institutional Form* (New York: Columbia University Press, 1993), chaps. 1–2.

20. Samuel P. Huntington, *Political Order in Changing Societies* (New Haven: Yale University Press, 1968).

21. For an interesting take on these issues, see Edward Friedman, "Democratization: Generalizing the East Asian Experience," in Friedman, ed., *The Politics of Democratization* (Boulder, Colo.: Westview Press, 1994).

22. Author interview, 1996.

23. Edward D. Mansfield and Jack Snyder, "Democratization and the Danger of War," *International Security* 20, no. 1 (Summer 1995): 5–38.

24. Author's interviews in Beijing, 1996 and 1998.

25. Making a similar argument for a mixed policy of toughness and conciliation toward Eastern Europe at the end of the Cold War depending on the political winds at the time is Jack Snyder, "Averting Anarchy in the New Europe," *International Security* 14, no. 1: 5–41.

Selected Bibliography

CHINESE-LANGUAGE SOURCES

Cai Xianwei. *Zhongguo da zhanlue: Lingdao shijie de lantu* (*China's Grand Strategy: A Blueprint for Leading the World*). Haikou: Hainan Press, 1996.

Chen Hanwen. *Zai guoji wutai shang: Xifang guoji guanxi xue jianjie* (*On the International Stage: A Brief Introduction to Western IR Theory*). Chengdu: Sichuan renmin chubanshe, 1985.

Chen Shu et al. "Zhongguo jingji duiwai kaifang shisi nian, 1979–1992" ("The Fourteen Years of China's Economic Opening Up, 1979–1992"). *Nankai jingji yanjiu* (*Nankia Economic Studies*), no. 2 (1993): 55–66.

Chen Feng, ed. *Zhong mei jiaoliang* (*Trials of Strength Between China and the United States*). Beijing: Zhongguo renshi chubanshe, 1996.

China Society of Strategy and Management, ed. "Guoji xingshi fenxi baogao" ("1997–1998 Study Reports on International Situation"). *Strategy and Management*, no. 1 (1998).

Chinese Academy of Social Sciences. "Liyong jingwai zhijie touzi yu kaifang guonei shichang" ("Utilizing Foreign Direct Investments and Opening Domestic Markets"). *Jingji yanjiu cankao* (*References on Economic Research*), no. 173 (1994): 22–33.

Deng Xiaoping. *Deng Xiaoping wenxuan* (*Selected Works of Deng Xiaoping*), vol. 3. Beijing: Renmin chubanshe, 1993.

———. *Deng Xiaoping wenxuan, 1975–1982* (*Selected Works of Deng Xiaoping*), vol. 2. Beijing: Renmin chubanshe, 1986.

Feng Tejun and Song Xinning, eds. *Guoji zhengzhi gailun* (*Introduction to International Politics*). Beijing: Zhongguo renmin daxue chubanshe, 1992.

Gao Jingdian, ed. *Guoji zhanlue xue gailun* (*Introduction to the Study of International Strategy*). Beijing: Guofang daxue chubanshe, 1995.

———. *Deng Xiaoping guoji zhanlue shixiang yanjiu* (*A Study on Deng Xiaoping's Thoughts on International Strategy*). Beijing: Guofang daxue chubanshe, 1992.

Gao, Hongjun. "Zhongguo gongmin quanli yishi de yanjin" ("The Awakening of Consciousness of Rights among Chinese Citizens"). In *Zouxiang quanli de shidai zhongguo gongmin quanli fazhan yanjiu* (*Towards an Era of Rights: Research on De-*

velopment of Civil Rights in China), ed. Xia Yong. Beijing: Zhongguo zhengfa daxue chubanshe, 1995.

Han Lianlong et al., eds. *Dangdai zhongguo waijiao* (*Contemporary China's Diplomacy*). Beijing: Zhongguo shehui kexue chubanshe, 1987.

He Xin. *Zhonghua fuxing yu shijie weilai* (*China's Revival and the World's Future*, vols. 1–2). Sichuan: Sichuan renmin chubanshe, 1996.

Hu Angang. "Xunqiu xinde ruanzhaolu" ("Seeking a New Soft Landing"). *Liaowang* (*Outlook*), no. 31 (1997): 12–13.

———. *Zhongguo xiayibu* (*The Next Step of China*). Chengdu: Sichuan renmin chubanshe, 1996.

Hu Wei. "Lun lengzhanhou guoji chongtu: dui 'wenming fanshi' de piping" ("Conflicts in the Post–Cold War World: A Critique of the 'Civilization Paradigm'"). *Fudan xuebao: shehui kexue ban* (*Fudan Journal: Social Sciences Edition*), no. 3 (1995): 254–262.

Information Office of the PRC State Council, "Zhongguo de guofang" ("China's National Defense"). *Renmin ribao,* 28 July 1998, 2, 4, 5.

Jin Junhui. "Kelindun zhengfu de waijiao zhengce sixiang chuxi" ("A Basic Analysis of the Foreign Policy Thinking of the Clinton Administration"). *Guoji wenti yanjiu* (*International Studies*), no. 2 (1994): 1–5.

Jin Yinzhong and Ni Shixiong. *Guoji guanxi lilun bijiao yanjiu* (*A Comparative Study of International Relations Theory*). Beijing: Zhongguo shehui kexue chubanshe, 1992.

Li Jiu et al. *Dangdai zhongguo de hegongye* (*Contemporary China's Nuclear Industry*). Beijing: Zhongguo shehui kexue chubanshe, 1987.

Li Shengzhi. "Quanqiuhua yu zhongguo wenhua" ("Globalization and Chinese Culture"). *Meiguo yanjiu* (*American Studies*), no. 1 (1995): 126–138.

———. "Quanqiuhua: ershiyi shiji de daqushi" ("Globalization: Grand Trend in the Twenty-First Century"). *Keji daobao* (*Science and Technology Herald*), 3 June 1993, 5.

Li Xiguang and Liu Kang, eds. *Yaomuohua zhongguo de beihou* (*Behind the Demonization of China*). Beijing: Zhongguo shehui kexue chubanshe, 1996.

Liang Dongping. "Yatai jinghehui li de gongjian zhan" ("Maneuvers within APEC"). *Zhongguo shibao zhoukan* (*China Times Weekly*), no. 101 (1993): 36–37.

Liang Shoude. "Guoji zhengzhi xue zai zhongguo" ("The Study of International Politics in China"). *Guoji zhengzhi yanjiu* (*Studies of International Politics*), no. 1 (1997): 1–9.

———. "Lun guoji zhengzhi xue de zhongguo tese" ("On the Theory of International Politics with Chinese Characteristics"). *Guoji zhengzhi yanjiu* (*Studies on International Politics*), no. 1 (1994): 15–21.

Liang Shoude, ed. *Guoji zhengzhi xinglun* (*New Introduction to International Politics*). Beijing: Beijing daxue chubanshe, 1996.

Liang Shoude and Hong Yinxian. *Guoji zhengzhi xue gailun* (*Introduction to International Politics*). Beijing: Zhongyang bianyi chubanshe, 1994.

Liu Jiang. "Zhongmei guanxi de xianzhuan he fazhan qushi" ("The State and Prospects of Sino-American Relations). *Shijia xinshi yanjou* (*Studies of the World Situations*), no. 26 (1997).

————. "Shixi zhongmei jianshixin zhanlue huoban guanxi" ("Preliminary Analysis of the Sino-American Strategic Partnership"). *Shijie xinshi yanjou (Studies of the World Situations)*, no. 47 (1997).

Liu Jinsong. "Zhongmei junshi guanxi de lishi yanbian: wenti he qianjing" ("Historical Evolution of Sino-U.S. Military Relations: Problems and Prospect"). *Zhanglue yu guanli (Strategy and Management)*, no. 5 (1997): 105–113.

Liu Zhenhuan. "Ping lianheguo haiyang fa" ("Comment on the UN Law of the Sea"). *Guofang (National Defense)*, no. 15 (15 November 1996): 14–16.

Luo Weilong. "Zhongguoren yao shuo bu" ("The Chinese Want to Say No"). *Taipingyang xuebao (Pacific Journal)*, no. 2 (1995).

Ministry of Machinery Industry. *Qiche gongye fuguan duice yanjiu keti baogaoji (Automotive Industry and GATT Membership)*. Beijing: China Automotive Technology Research Center, 1994.

Ni Shixiong and Jin Yinzhong, eds. *Dangdai meiguo guoji guanxi lilun liupai wenxuan (Selected Readings in Contemporary American International Relations Theory)*. Shanghai: Xuelin chubanshe, 1987.

Niu Jun. "Duoshi zhichiu: Zhongmei guanxi de xianzhuang ji qianjing" ("The Troubling Time: Current Situation and Prospects of Sino-American relations"). *Meiguo yanjiu (American Studies)*, no. 4 (1995).

Peng Guangqian and Yao Youzhi, eds. *Deng Xiaoping zhanlue shixiang lun (On Deng Xiaoping's Thoughts on Strategy)*. Beijing: Jiefangjun kexue chubanshe, 1994.

Peng Qian, Yang Mingjie, and Xu Deren. *Zhongguo weishenmo shuo bu (Why Does China Say No?)* Beijing: Xinshijie chubanshe, 1996.

Ren Donglai, "Xingchengzhong de mei ri zhouxin jiqi dui dongya de yingxiang" ("The Evolving U.S.-Japan Axis and Its Influence in East Asia"). *Zhanlue yu Guanli (Strategy and Management)*, no. 5 (1996): 51–53.

Ren Rongrong: "Dadongmeng de jueqi he zhongguo de duice" ("The Rise of a Greater ASEAN and China's Policy"). *Yatai cankao (Asia-Pacific Reference)*, no. 38 (16 September 1996).

Ren Xiao. "Zhenzhi wenhua de fanxing" ("A Reflection on Political Culture"). *Zhongguo shuping (China Book Reviews)*. (Hong Kong), no. 1 (1994).

Shi Xiuyin. "Zhongguo shehui zhuanxing shiqi de quanli yu quanli" ("Public Power and Rights during the Transformational Period in China"). In *Zouxiang quanli de shidai zhongguo gongmin quanli in China fazhan yanjiu (Towards an Era of Rights: Research on Development of Civil Rights)*, ed. Xia Yong. Beijing: Zhongguo zhengfa daxue chubanshe, 1995.

Shi Yongming. "Yatai anquan huanjing yu diqu duobian zhuyi" ("Security Environment in Asia-Pacific and Regional Multilateralism"). *Guoji wenti yanjiu (International Affairs)*, no. 1 (1996): 41–47.

Song Qiang et al. *Zhongguo keyi shuo bu—Lengzhanhou shidai de zhengzhi yu qinggan jueze (China Can Say No—The Political and Emotional Choice in the Post–Cold War Era)*. Beijing: Zhongguo gonshang lianhe chubanshe, 1996.

Song Qiang et al. *Zhongguo haishi neng shuo bu—Zhongguo keyi shuo bu xupin: Guoji guanxi bianshu yu women de xianshi yingfu (China Still Can Say No—The Sequel to China Can Say No: The Variables in International Relations and Our Realistic Handling)*. Beijing: Zhongguo wenlian chubanshe, 1996.

Song Xinning. "Guojia liyi de lilun renshi" ("A Theoretical Understanding of National Interests"). *Zhongguo shehui kexue jikan* (*Chinese Social Sciences Quarterly, Hong Kong*), no. 20 (Autumn 1997).

————. *Guoji zhengzhi jingji yu zhongguo duiwai guanxi* (*International Political Economy and Chinese Foreign Relations*). Hong Kong: Hong Kong shehui kexue chubanshe, 1997.

State Planning Commission. "Woguo liyong waiguo zhijie touzi wenti de yanjiu baogao" ("Report on the Problems in Utilizing Foreign Direct Investments in China"). *Jingji yanjiu cankao* (*References on Economic Research*), 1994: 2–59.

State Statistical Bureau. *Zhongguo tongji nianjian* (*China Statistical Yearbook*). Beijing: Zhongguo tongji chubanshe, various years.

Tang Tianri. "Anquan hezuo de xin moshi" ("New Model in Security Cooperation"). *Liaowang* (*Outlook*), vol. 31 (1997): 44.

Tang Yongsheng. "Zhonghe anquan yu zhongti zhanlue" ("Comprehensive Security and Grand Strategy"). *Shijie zhishi* (*World Affairs*), no. 20 (16 October 1996): 16–17.

Tang Yongxing. "Zhongmei guanxi jinru yige xinde lishi jieduan" ("Sino-American Relations Have Entered a New Historical Stage"). *Shijia xinshi yanjou* (*Studies of the World Situations*), no. 26 (1997).

Tian Zengpei, ed. *Gaige kaifang yilai de zhongguo waijiao* (*China's Foreign Policy During the Reform and Open Door Period*). Beijing: Shijie zhishi chubanshe, 1993.

Wang Hexing. "Quanqiuhua dui shijie zhengzhi, jingji de shida yingxiang" ("Ten Influences of Globalization on World Politics and Economics"). *International Studies*, no. 1 (1997): 10–15 and 33.

Wang Huning, "Deng Xiaoping tongzi dui guoji zhanlue de sikao" ("Comrade Deng Xiaoping's Thoughts on International Strategy"). *Wenhui bao*, 26 February 1994.

Wang Jianmin, Liu Guofen, and Lei Yuhong, eds. *Taiwan hechu qu?* (*Where Will Taiwan Head To?*). Beijing: Huawen chubanshe, 1996.

Wang Jisi. "Ezhi haishi jiaowang?" ("Containment or Engagement?"). *Guoji wenti yanjiu* (*International Affairs*), no. 1 (1996).

Wang Jisi, ed. *Wenming yu guoji zhengzhi—Zhongguo xuezhe ping hengtingdun de wenming chongtulun* (*Civilizations and International Politics—Chinese Scholars' Responses to Huntington's Theory of Civilizational Clashes*). Shanghai: Shanghai renmin chubanshe, 1995.

Wang Taiping, ed. *Deng Xiaoping waijiao shixiang yanjiu lunwenji* (*A Collection of Research Papers on Deng Xiaoping's Thoughts on Diplomacy*). Beijing: Shijie zhishi chubanshe, 1996.

Wang Yizhou. "Lianheguo haiyangfa gongyue yu zhongguo" ("The UN Law of Sea and China"). *Taipingyang xuebao* (*Pacific Journal*), no. 2 (Summer 1996): 9–17.

————. *Dangdai guoji zhengzhi xilun* (*Analysis of Contemporary International Politics*). Shanghai: Shanghai renmin chubanshe, 1995.

Wei Yang. "Guojia liyi gaoyu yiqie" ("National Interests Take Precedence Over Everything"). *Liaowang Outlook*, no. 19 (1997): 1.

Wen Jieming et al., eds. *Yu zhongshuji tanxin* (*Chatting with the General Secretary*). Beijing: Zhongguo shehui kexue chubanshe, 1997.

Xi Laiwang, *Ershiyi shiji zhongguo zhanlue da cehua* (*China's Grand Strategy into the Twenty-First Century: Strategic Calculus of China's Diplomacy*). Beijing: Hongqi chubanshe, 1996.

Xiao Ding. "Ya ou hezuo yu fazhan wenti yantaohui jiyao" ("Summary of the Symposium on Asian-European Cooperation and Development"). *Xiandai guoji guanxi* (*Contemporary International Relations*), no. 7 (1996): 42–53.

Xie Guang, et al. *Dangdai zhongguo de guofang keji shiye* (*Contemporary China's Science and Technology for National Defense*). Beijing: Dangdai zhongguo chubanche, 1992.

Xu Ming, ed. *Guanjian shike: dangdai zhongguo jidai jiejue de 27 ge wenti* (*Crucial Moment: The 27 Issues That Need to Be Urgently Solved*). Beijing: Jingri zhongguo chubanshe, 1997.

Yan Xuetong. *Zhongguo guojia liyi fengxi* (*An Analysis of China's National Interests*). Tianjin: Tianjin renmin chubanshe, 1996.

———. "Xifangren kan zhongguo de jueqi" ("Westerners View China's Rise"). *Xiandai guoji guanxi* (*Contemporary International Relations*) no. 9 (1996).

Yang Chenxu. "Jianxi dongya anquan wenti" ("An Analysis of East Asian Security Issues"). *Guoji wenti yanjiu* (*International Studies*), no. 3 (1994).

Yang Hongshan. "Wandong nongcun 'jidujiao re' diaoca yu sikao" ("An Investigation of and Reflection on the 'Christianity Craze' in Rural East Anhui"). *Jianghuai luntan* (*Jianghuai Forum*), no. 4 (1994).

Yang Jianyong. "Guanyu woguo zhoubian anquan huanjing de fenxi yu sikao" ("An Analysis of and Reflection on the Neighboring Security Environment of Our Nation"). *Yatai cankao* (*Asia-Pacific Reference*), no. 34 (19 August 1996).

Yu Quanyu. "Ba renquan lilun yinxiang shenru" ("Furthering Human Rights Research"). Preface in the books of the Human Rights Book Series by Liaoning Renmin Chubanshe (Liaoning People's Press) in 1994.

Zhang Jiliang. *Guoji guanxi gailun* (*An Introduction to International Relations*). Beijing: Shijie zhishi chubanshe, 1990.

Zhang Tuosheng, ed. *Huanqiu tongci liangre: Yidai lingxiumen de guoji zhanlue shixiang* (*Same to the Whole Globe: The International Strategic Thoughts of a Generation of Leaders*). Beijing: Zhongyang wenxian chubanshe, 1993.

Zhao Gancheng. "Yatai diqu xinzhixu yu zhongguo de zeren" ("The New Order in Asia-Pacific and the Responsibility of China"). *Guoji wenti luntan* (*Forum on International Issues*), no.2 (1996).

Zhao Xiaochun. "Lun lengzhan hou guojia liyi de xinbianhua" ("On New Changes in National Interests in the Post–Cold War era"). *Guoji guanxi xueyuan xuebao* (*Journal of the Institute of International Relations*), no. 1 (1995): 1–7.

Zhou Jihua, "Rimei anbao tizhi de qianghua yu dongya de anquan" ("The Strengthening of the U.S.-Japan Security Arrangement and the Security of East Asia"), *Riben xuekan* (*Japan Studies*), no. 4 (1996): 31–42.

ENGLISH-LANGUAGE SOURCES

Adler, Emanuel Adler. "The Emergence of Cooperation: National Epistemic Communities and the International Evolution of the Idea of Nuclear Arms Control." *International Organization* 46, no. 1 (Winter 1992).

Aron, Raymond. *Peace and War: A Theory of International Relations* (Translated from the French by Richard Howard and Annette Baker Fox). New York: Praeger, 1967.

Baker, James. "America in Asia: Emerging Architecture for a Pacific Community," *Foreign Affairs* 70, no. 5 (Winter 1991/92).

Barnett, A. Doak. *China and the Major Powers in East Asia.* Washington, D.C.: The Brookings Institution, 1977.

Barnett, Doak, et al. *Developing a Peaceful, Stable, and Cooperative Relationship With China.* New York: National Committee on American Foreign Policy. July 1996.

Baum, Richard. *Burying Mao: Chinese Politics in the Age of Deng Xiaoping.* Princeton: Princeton University Press, 1994.

Bergsten, Fred. *Reconcilable Differences.* Washington, D.C.: Institute for International Economics, 1992.

Bernstein, Richard, and Ross H. Munro. *The Coming Conflict with China.* New York: Knopf, 1997.

Betts, Richard K. "Wealth, Power, and Instability: East Asia and the United States after the Cold War." In *East Asian Security,* ed. Michael Brown, Sean M. Lynn-Jones, and Steven E. Miller. Cambridge: M.I.T. Press, 1996.

Breslauer, George W., and Philip E. Tetlock, eds. *Learning in U.S. and Soviet Foreign Policy.* Boulder, Colo.: Westview Press, 1991.

Broadman, Harry. "A Roadmap for Reform." *Transition* 8, no.5 (1997): 2–3.

Butterfield, Herbert, and Martin Wight, eds. *Diplomatic Investigations.* Cambridge: Harvard University Press, 1966.

Buzan, Barry. "From International System to International Society: Structural Realism and Regime Theory Meet the English School." *International Organization* 47 (1993): 327–352.

Buzan, Barry, Richard Little, and Charles Jones. *The Logic of Anarchy: Neorealism and Structural Realism.* New York: Columbia University Press, 1993.

Calder, Kent E. "Asia's Empty Tank." *Foreign Affairs* 75, no. 2 (March/April 1996): 55–69.

Carr, E. H. *The Twenty Years' Crisis, 1919–1939.* London: Macmillan, 1939.

Cashman, Greg. *What Causes War? An Introduction to Theories of International Conflict.* New York: Lexington Books, 1993.

Chan, Alfred L., and Paul Nesbitt-Larking. "Critical Citizenship and Civil Society in Contemporary China." *Canadian Journal of Political Science* 28, no. 2 (June/July 1995): 293–309.

Chan, Anita, and Robert Senser. "China's Troubled Workers." *Foreign Affairs* 76, no. 2 (March/April 1997): 104–117.

Chen, Jie, Yang Zhong, and Jan William Hillard. "The Level and Sources of Popular Support for China's Current Political Regime." *Communist and Post-Communist Studies* 30, no. 1 (1997): 45–64.

China in Brief: Factors Fueling China's Rapid Economic Development. Beijing: New Star Publishers, 1995.

Chiu, Hungdah. "Chinese Attitudes Toward International Law of Human Rights in the Post-Mao Era." In *Chinese Politics from Mao to Deng,* ed. Victor C. Falkenheim. New York: Paragon House, 1989.

Choucri, Nazli, and Robert C. North. *Nations in Conflict: National Growth and International Violence.* San Francisco: W. H. Freeman, 1975.

Christensen, Thomas. "Chinese Realpolitik." *Foreign Affairs* 75, no. 5 (September/October 1996): 37–52.

Cronin, Andrey K., and Patrick M. Cronin. "The Realistic Engagement of China." *Washington Quarterly* 19, no. 1 (Winter 1996): 141–169.

Deng, Yong. "Managing China's Hegemonic Ascension: Engagement from Southeast Asia." *Journal of Strategic Studies* 21, no. 1 (March 1998): 21–43.

———. "Chinese Relations with Japan: Implications for Asia-Pacific Regionalism." *Pacific Affairs* 70, no. 3 (Fall 1997): 65–80.

———. *Promoting Asia-Pacific Economic Cooperation: Perspectives from East Asia.* New York: St. Martin's, 1997.

Dittmer, Lowell, and Samuel Kim, eds. *China's Quest for National Identity.* Ithaca: Cornell University Press, 1993.

Dougherty, James E., and Robert L. Pfaltzgraff Jr. *Contending Theories of International Relations,* 4th ed. New York: Longman, 1997.

Doyle, Michael. "Liberalism and World Politics." *American Political Science Review* 80, no. 4 (December 1986): 1151–1169.

Evangelista, Matthew. "The Paradox of State Strength: Transnational Relations, Domestic Structures, and Security Policy in Russia and the Soviet Union." *International Organization* 49, no. 1 (Winter 1995): 1–38.

Evans, Paul. "The New Multilaterialism in the Asia-Pacific and the Conditional Engagement of China." In *Weaving the Net: Conditional Engagement with China,* ed. James Shinn. New York: Council on Foreign Relations, 1996.

Farber, Henry S., and Joanne Gowa. "Polities and Peace." *International Security* 20, no. 2 (Fall 1995): 123–146.

Fletcher, Joseph. "Sino-Russian Relations, 1800–1862." In *The Cambridge History of China, Volume 10: Late Ch'ing, 1800–1911,* pt. 1, ed. John Fairbank. Cambridge: Cambridge University Press, 1992.

Friedman, Edward. "The Challenge of a Rising China: Another Germany?" In *Eagle Adrift: American Foreign Policy at the End of the Century,* ed. Robert J. Lieber. New York: Longman, 1997.

Friedman, Edward, ed. *The Politics of Democratization.* Boulder, Colo.: Westview Press, 1994.

Friedman, Edward, Paul Pickowicz, and Mark Selden. *Chinese Village, Socialist State.* New Haven: Yale University Press, 1991.

Fukuyama, Francis. *The End of History and the Last Man.* New York: The Free Press, 1991.

Fung, K. C. "Trade and Investment Relations Among Hong Kong, China, and Taiwan." Unpublished manuscript, Santa Cruz, University of California, 1995.

Gallagher, Michael. "China's Illusionary Threat to the South China Sea." *International Security* 19, no. 1 (Summer 1994): 169–194.

Garrett, Banning N., and Bonnie S. Glaser. "Chinese Perspectives on Nuclear Arms Control." *International Security* 20, no. 3 (Winter 1995/96): 43–78.

Garver, John. "China Pushes Through the South China Sea." *China Quarterly,* no. 132 (December 1992).

George, Alexander. "Introduction: The Limits of Coercive Diplomacy." In *The Limits of Coercive Diplomacy,* ed. Alexander L. George and William E. Simons. Boulder, Colo.: Westview Press, 1994.

Gilpin, Robert. *War and Change in World Politics.* New York: Cambridge University Press, 1981.

Goldman, Merle. "Politically-Engaged Intellectuals in the Deng-Jiang Era: A Changing Relationship with the Party-State." *China Quarterly,* no. 145 (March 1996): 35–52.

Goldman, Merle, Perry Link, and Su Wei. "China's Intellectuals in the Deng Era." In *China's Quest for National Identity,* ed. Lowell Dittmer and Samuel S. Kim. Ithaca: Cornell University Press, 1993.

Goldstein, Avery. "Great Expectations: Interpreting China's Arrival." Working Papers Series of the Christopher H. Browne Center for International Politics, University of Pennsylvania, March 1997.

———. "Trends in the Study of Political Elites and Institutions in the PRC." *China Quarterly,* no. 139 (1994): 714–730.

Golstein, Judith. *Ideas, Interests, and American Trade Policy.* Ithaca: Cornell University, 1993.

Haas, Ernst. *When Knowledge Is Power.* Berkeley: University of California Press, 1990.

Haas, Peter M., ed. "Knowledge, Power, and International Policy Coordination." *International Organization* 49, no. 1 (Winter 1995): 1–38.

Harding, Harry. "International Order and Organization in the Asia-Pacific Region." In *East Asia in Transition: Toward a New Regional Order,* ed. Rober Ross. Armonk, N.Y.: M. E. Sharpe, 1995.

———. *A Fragile Relationship: The United States and China Since 1972.* Washington, D.C.: The Brookings Institution, 1992.

———. *China's Second Revolution.* Washington, D.C.: Brookings Institution, 1987.

Harding, Harry, ed. *China's Foreign Relations in the 1980s.* New Haven: Yale University Press, 1984.

Hermann, Charles F. "Changing Course: When Governments Choose to Redirect Foreign Policy." *International Studies Quarterly* 34 (1990): 3–21.

Hinton, Harold C. "China as an Asian Power." In *Chinese Foreign Policy: Theory and Practice,* ed. Thomas Robinson and David Shambaugh. New York: Oxford University Press, 1993.

Hoffmann, Stanley. "An American Social Science: International Relations." *Daedalus* 106, no. 3 (1979): 41–60.

Huang, Yasheng. *FDI in China: An Asian Perspective.* Singapore: Institute of Southeast Asian Studies, 1998.

———. *Between Two Coordination Failures: The Automotive Industrial Policy in China with a Comparison to Korea.* Ann Arbor: Michigan Business School, 1997.

———. "Why China Will Not Collapse?" *Foreign Policy,* no. 99 (Summer 1995): 54–68.

Hughes, Barry B., Steven Chan, and Charles W. Kegley Jr. "Observations on the Study of International Relations in China." *International Studies Notes* 19, no. 3 (Fall 1994): 17–22.

Human Rights Watch/Asia. "China: Chinese Diplomacy, Western Hypocrisy, and the U.N. Human Rights Commission" 9, no. 3 (C) (March 1997).

Huntington, Samuel P. *Political Order in Changing Societies.* New Haven: Yale University Press, 1968.

Huntington, Samuel. "The Erosion of American National Interests." *Foreign Affairs* (September/October 1997).

———. "The Clash of Civilizations?" *Foreign Affairs* (Summer 1993): 22–49.

International Business and Economic Research Corporation. "The Costs to the United States Economy That Would Result from Removal of China's Most Favored Nation Status." Washington, D.C.: International Business and Economic Corporation, 1996.

Jacobson, Harold K., and Michel Oksenberg. *China's Participation in the IMF, the World Bank, and GATT: Toward a Global Economic Order.* Ann Arbor: University of Michigan Press, 1990.

Jervis, Robert. *Perception and Misperception in International Politics.* Princeton: Princeton University Press, 1976.

Jia Qingguo. "Reflections on the Recent Tension in the Taiwan Strait." *China Journal,* no. 36 (July 1996).

Johnson, Chalmers. "Containing China: U.S. and Japan Drift Toward Disaster." *Japan Quarterly* (October-December 1996): 10–18.

Johnston, Alastair Iain. "Cultural Realism and Strategy in Mao's China." In *The Culture of National Security: Norms and Identity in World Politics,* ed. Peter Katzenstein. New York: Columbia University Press, 1996.

———. "Learning Versus Adaptation: Explaining Change in Chinese Arms Control Policy in the 1980s and 1990s." *China Journal,* no. 35 (January 1996).

———. *Cultural Realism: Strategic Culture and Grand Strategy in Chinese History.* Princeton: Princeton University Press, 1995.

Johnston, Alastair Iain and Robert S. Ross, eds., *Engaging China: The Management of an Emerging Power* (London: Routledge, forthcoming).

Jones, R. K., et al. "Economic Integration Between Hong Kong, Taiwan, and the Coastal Provinces of China." *OECD Economic Studies,* no. 20 (1993): 115–144.

Katzenstein, Peter, ed. *The Culture of National Security.* New York: Columbia University Press, 1996.

Kelliher, Daniel. "Keeping Democracy Safe from the Masses: Intellectuals and Elitism in the Chinese Protest Movement." *Comparative Politics* 25, no. 4 (1993): 379–396.

Kennan, George. "Containment: Then and Now." *Foreign Affairs* 65, no. 4 (1987): 885–890.

Kennedy, Paul. *The Rise and Fall of the Great Powers: Economic Change and Military Conflict from 1500–2000.* New York: Random House, 1987.

Khong, Yuen Foong. *Analogies at War: Korea, Munich, Dien Bien Phu, and the Vietnam Decisions of 1965* (Princeton: Princeton University Press, 1992).

Kim, Samuel S. *China In and Out of the Changing World Order.* Princeton: Princeton University Press, 1991.

———. "Thinking Globally in Post-Mao China." *Journal of Peace Research* 27, no. 2 (1990): 191–209.

———. *China, the United Nations, and World Order.* Princeton: Princeton University Press, 1979.

Kim, Samuel S., ed. *China and the World: Chinese Foreign Relations in the Post–Cold War Era.* Boulder, Colo.: Westview Press, 1994.

King, Gary, Robert O. Keohane, and Sidney Verba. *Designing Social Inquiry: Scientific Inference in Qualitative Research.* Princeton: Princeton University Press, 1994.

Kleinberg, Robert. *China's "Opening" to the Outside World: The Experiment with Capitalism.* Boulder, Colo.: Westview Press, 1990.

Kwak, Tae-Hwan, and Edward A. Olsen, eds. *The Major Powers of Northeast Asia.* Boulder, Colo.: Lynn Rienner Publishers, 1996.

Lapid, Yoseph. "The Third Debate." *International Studies Quarterly* 33, no. 3 (1989): 235–254.

Lardy, Nicholas R. *China in the World Economy.* Washington, D.C.: Institute for International Economics, 1994.

———. *Foreign Trade and Economic Reform in China, 1978–1990.* New York: Cambridge University Press, 1992.

Legro, Jeffery W. "Conceptual Revolutions in Foreign Policy: America after the World Wars." Paper presented at the Annual Meeting of the American Political Science Association, San Franscisco, 28 August–1 September 1996.

Lei, Guang. "Elusive Democracy: Conceptual Change and the Chinese Democracy Movement, 1978–1979 to 1989." *Modern China* 22, no. 4 (October 1996): 417–447.

Leng, Russell. *Interstate Crisis Behavior, 1816–1980: Realism Versus Reciprocity.* Cambridge: Cambridge University Press, 1993.

Levine, Steven I. "China in Asia: The PRC as a Regional Power." In *China's Foreign Relations in the 1980s,* ed. Harry Harding. New Haven: Yale University Press, 1984.

Levy, Jack. "Learning and Foreign Policy: Sweeping a Conceptual Minefield." *International Organization* 48, no. 2 (Spring 1994): 279–312.

Li, Liangjiang. "Popular Demands for Village Elections in Rural China." *Human Rights Dialogue,* Carnegie Council on Ethics and International Affairs, vol. 9 (June 1997): 9–11.

Lieberthal, Kenneth. *Governing China: From Revolution Through Reform.* New York: W. W. Norton, 1995.

Liu, Ji. "Making the Right Choice in Twenty-First Century Sino-American Relations." *Journal of Contemporary China* 7, no. 17 (1998).

Lu, Ning. *The Dynamics of Foreign-Policy Decisionmaking in China.* Boulder, Colo.: Westview Press, 1997.

Mansfield, Edward D., and Jack Snyder. "Democratization and the Danger of War." *International Security* 20, no. 1 (Summer 1995): 5–38.

Mastel, Greg. "Beijing at Bay." *Foreign Policy,* no. 104 (1996): 27–34.

Mastel, Greg, and Andrew Szamosszegi. "America's New Trade Nemesis." *International Economy,* no. 10 (1996): 10–27.

Michael Hunt. *The Making of a Special Relationship: The United States and China to 1914.* New York: Columbia University Press, 1983.

Morgenthau, Hans, and Kenneth Thompson. *Politics Among Nations: The Struggle for Power and Peace,* 6th ed. New York: Knopf, 1985.

Nathan, Andrew J., and Tianjian Shi. "Cultural Requisites for Democracy in China: Findings from a Survey." In *China in Transition,* ed. Tu Wei-ming. Cambridge Harvard University Press, 1994.

Nathan, Andrew, and Robert Ross. *The Great Wall and the Empty Fortress: China's Search for Security.* New York: Norton, 1997.

Nye, Joseph S. Jr. "China's Re-emergence and the Future of the Asia-Pacific." *Survival* 39, no. 4 (Winter 1997–1998): 65–79.

———. "The Case for Deep Engagement." *Foreign Affairs* 74, no. 4 (July/August 1995).

———. "Neorealism and Neoliberalism." *World Politics* 40, no. 2 (January 1988).

———. "Nuclear Learning and U.S.-Soviet Security Regimes." *International Organization,* 41–43 (Summer 1987).

Organski, A. F. K., and Jacek Kugler. *The War Ledger.* Chicago: University of Chicago Press, 1980.

Potter, William C., ed. *International Nuclear Trade and Nonproliferation: The Challenge of the Emerging Suppliers.* Lexington, Mass.: Lexington Books, 1990.

Powell, Robert. "Anarchy in International Relations Theory: The Neorealist-Neoliberal Debate." *International Organization* 48, no. 2 (Spring 1994).

Pye, Lucian W. "China: Not Your Typical Superpower." *Problems of Post-Communism* 43, no. 4 (July–August 1996).

———. *China: An Introduction,* 4th ed. New York: HarperCollins Publishers, 1991.

Rachman, Gedeon. "Containing China." *Washington Quarterly* 19, no. 1 (Winter 1996): 129–139.

Reiter, Dan. "Learning, Realism, and Alliances: The Weight of the Shadow of the Past." *World Politics* 46 (July 1994).

Robinson, Thomas, and David Shambaugh, eds. *Chinese Foreign Policy: Theory and Practice.* New York: Oxford University Press, 1995.

Rosenberg, Justin. "What's the Matter with Realism?" *Review of International Studies* 16, no. 4 (October 1990).

Ross, Robert. "Beijing as a Conservative Power." *Foreign Affairs* 76, no. 2 (March/April 1997): 33–44.

Rown, Henry S. "The Short March: China's Road to Democracy." *National Interest* (Fall 1996): 61–70.

Roy, Denny. "The 'China Threat' Issue: Major Arguments." *Asian Survey* 36, no. 8 (August 1996): 758–771.

———. "Hegemon on the Horizon? China's Threat to East Asian Security." *International Security* 19, no. 1 (Summer 1994): 149–168.

Ruggie, John G. "Multilateralism: The Anatomy of an Institution." *International Organization* 46, no. 3 (Summer 1992): 561–598.

———. "Continuity and Transformation in the World Polity: Toward a Neorealist Synthesis." *World Politics* 35, no. 2 (1983): 261–285.

Ruggie, John G., ed. *Multilateralism Matters: The Theory and Praxis of An Institutional Form.* New York: Columbia University Press, 1993.

Russet, Bruce. *Grasping the Democratic Peace.* Princeton: Princeton University Press, 1993.

Sachs, Jeffrey D., and A. Warner. "Economic Reform and the Process of Global Integration." *Brookings Papers on Economic Activity,* no. 1 (1995): 1–95.

Schlesinger, James, et al. *Toward Strategic Understanding Between America and China.* New York: National Committee on U.S.-China Relations, December 1996.

Segal, Gerald. "East Asia and the 'Constrainment' of China." *International Security* 20, no. 4 (Spring 1996): 107–135.

Seymour, James D. "Human Rights in Chinese Foreign Relations." In *China and the World: Chinese Foreign Relations in the Post–Cold War Era,* ed. Samuel S. Kim. Boulder, Colo.: Westview Press, 1994.

Shambaugh, David. "The United States and China: Cooperation or Confrontation?" *Current History* (September 1997): 241–245.

————. "Containment or Engagement of China? Calculating Beijing's Responses." *International Security* 21, no. 2 (Fall 1996): 180–209.

Shinn, James, ed. *Weaving the Net: Conditional Engagement with China.* New York: Council on Foreign Relations Press, 1996.

Shirk, Susan. "Internationalization and China's Economic Reforms." In *Internationalization and Domestic Politics,* ed. Robert Keohane and Helen Milner. New York: Cambridge University Press, 1996.

————. "Chinese Views on Asia-Pacific Regional Security Cooperation." *Analysis,* The National Bureau of Asian Research 5, no. 5 (1994).

Sikkink, Kathryn. *Ideas and Institutions: Developmentalism in Brazil and Argentina.* Ithaca: Cornell University Press, 1991.

Snyder, Jack. "Averting Anarchy in the New Europe." *International Security* 14, no. 1: 5–41.

Song, Xinning. "The IR Theory-Building in China: Tradition, Function, and Characteristics." Manuscript, Department of International Politics, Chinese Renmin University, 1997.

Spence, Jonathan. *The Gate of Heavenly Peace.* New York: Viking, 1981.

Sutter, Robert G. *Shaping China's Future in World Affairs: The Role of the United States.* Boulder, Colo.: Westview Press, 1996.

Swaine, Michael, and Donald Henry. *China: Domestic Change and Foreign Policy.* Santa Monica, Calif.: Rand Corporation, 1995.

Van Ness, Peter. "The Impasse in U.S. Policy Toward China." *China Journal* no. 38 (July 1997): 139–150.

Vogel, Ezra F., ed. *Living With China: U.S. Relations in the Twenty-First Century.* New York: W. W. Norton, 1997.

Vogel, Ezra. *The Four Little Dragons: The Spread of Industrialization in East Asia.* Cambridge: Harvard University Press, 1990.

Walder, Andrew G., and Gong Xiaoxia. "Workers in the Tiananmen Protest: The Politics of the Beijing Workers' Autonomous Federation." *Australian Journal of Chinese Affairs* 29 (January 1993): 1–29.

Waldron, Arthur. "Deterring China." *Commentary* 100, no. 4 (October 1995).

Waltz, Kenneth. "The Politics of Peace." *International Studies Quarterly* 11, no. 3 (September 1967): 199–211.

Wan, Ming. "Chinese Opinion on Human Rights." *Orbis* 42, no. 3 (Summer 1998): 361–374.

Wang, Jisi. "The Role of the United States as a Global and Pacific Power: A View From Beijing." *Pacific Review* 10, no. 1, (1997).

Wang, Fei-Ling. "To Incorporate China: A New Policy for a New Era." *Washington Quarterly* 21, no. 1 (January 1998): 67–81.

————. *From Family to Market: Labor Allocation in Contemporary China.* Lanham, Md.: Rowman & Littlefield, 1998.

————. "Ignorance, Arrogance, and Radical Nationalism." *Journal of Contemporary China* 6, no. 14 (Spring 1997): 161–165.

————. "Coping with China as a Rising Power." In *Weaving the Net: Conditional Engagement with China,* ed. James Shinn. New York: Council on Foreign Relations, 1996.

Wang, Jianwei, and Zhimin Lin. "Chinese Perceptions in the Post–Cold War Era: Three Images of the United States." *Asian Survey* 32, no. 10 (October, 1992): 902–917.

Wang, Shaoguang. "Estimating China's Defense Expenditure." *China Quarterly,* no. 147 (September 1996): 889–911.

Wang, Yangmin. "The Politics of U.S.-China Economic Relations: MFN, Constructive Engagement, and the Trade Issue Proper." *Asian Survey* 33, no. 5 (1993): 441–462.

Wendt, Alexander. "Collective Identity Formation and the International State." *American Political Science Review* 88, no. 2 (June 1994): 384–396.

————. "Anarchy is What States Make of It: The Social Construction of Power Politics." *International Organization* 46 (1992): 395–421.

Whiting, Allen S., ed. "ASEAN Eyes China: The Security Dimension." *Asian Survey* 37, no. 4 (April 1997): 299–322.

————. "Chinese Nationalism and Foreign Policy After Deng." *China Quarterly,* no. 142 (June 1995): 295–316.

————, ed. Special issue on Chinese Foreign Relations, *The Annals of the American Academy of Political and Social Science,* vol. 519 (January 1992).

World Bank. "China's Growth Path to Twenty-First Century: Recommendations from the World Bank." *Transition* 8, no. 5 (1997): 5–7.

————. *The Chinese Economy: Fighting Inflation, Deepening Reforms.* Washington, D.C.: World Bank, 1996.

————. *China: Macroeconomic Stability in a Decentralized Economy.* Washington, D.C.: World Bank, 1995.

Yee, Albert. "The Causal Effects of Ideas on Policies." *International Organization* 50 (1996): 69–108.

Yu, Bin. "The China Syndrome: Rising Nationalism and Conflict with the West." *Asia Pacific Issues* (Analysis from the East-West Center), no. 27 (May 1996).

————. "The Study of Chinese Foreign Policy: Problems and Prospect." *World Politics* 46 (January 1994): 235–261.

Yuan Ming. "Chinese Intellectuals and the United States: the Dilemma of Individualism Versus Patriotism." *Asian Survey* (July 1989): 645–654.

Zakaria, Fareed. "Speak Softly, Carry a Veiled Threat." *New York Times Magazine,* 18 February 1996, 36–37.

Zhang, Ming. "The New Thinking of Sino-U.S. Relations—an interview note." *Journal of Contemporary China,* no.14 (1997): 117–123.

————. "The Shifting Chinese Public Image of the United States." *Strategic Forum* (National Defense University, Washington, D.C.), no. 89 (November 1996).

Zhao, Suisheng. *Power Competition in East Asia.* New York: St. Martin's, 1998.

————. "Chinese Intellectuals' Quest for National Greatness and Nationalistic Writing in the 1990s." *China Quarterly,* no. 152 (December 1997): 725–745.

Zheng, Yongnian. "Development and Democracy: Are They Compatible in China?" *Political Science Quarterly* 109, no. 2 (Summer 1994): 235–259.

Zhong, Yang, Jie Chen, and John M. Scheb II. "Political Views from Below: A Survey of Beijing Residents." *PS: Political Science and Politics* 30, no. 3 (September 1997): 474–482.

Zhou, Kate Xiao. *How the Farmers Changed China: Power of the People.* Boulder, Colo.: Westview Press, 1996.

Index

township and village enterprises
(TVEs), 166
TVEs. *See* township and village
enterprises

UNDOF. *See* United Nations
Disengagement Observer Force
UNEF II. *See* United Nations
Emergency Force II
UNFICYP. *See* United Nations
Peacekeeping Forces in Cyprus
United Nations, 13; Chapters VI and
VII Operations, 78–80; China and,
24, 74–75; China and Haiti and
Guatemala, 81; peacekeeping
operations, 76
United Nations Disengagement
Observer Force (UNDOF), 75
United Nations Emergency Force II
(UNEF II), 75
United Nations Human Rights
Commission, 102
United Nations Peacekeeping Forces in
Cyprus (UNFICYP), 76
United Nations Transitional Authority
in Cambodia (UNTAC), 77–78, 79
United States, "manifest destiny" of, 30
UNTAC. *See* United Nations
Transitional Authority in Cambodia
U.S. engagement policy, 7–10
U.S. media, 98, 144–46, 196–97
U.S. security treaty with Japan, 9, 57,
144, 195, 198, 200–1, 210n60,
210n64
U.S.-China cooperation on nuclear
technologies, 133–5
U.S.-China summits, 143, 174, 198, 200,
233

VAT. *See* value-added tax

value-added tax (VAT), 176, 179
Vietnam, 8, 33, 76, 200
Vietnam War, 185, 195, 207n35, 244
village elections, 112, 207n36

Waldron, Arthur, 5
Waltz, Kenneth, 57, 242
Wang, Daohan, 217, 218, 225
Wang, Jisi, 56
Wang, Yizhou, 58, 241
weapons of mass destruction (WMD),
133
Wei Jingsheng, 30, 97, 110, 200
White Paper on National Defense, 57,
95n46, n53
white papers on human rights, 99–100
Wight, Martin, 48
WMD. *See* weapons of mass destruction
World Trade Organization (WTO), 2,
11, 14, 34, 54, 143, 150, 152, 160,
161, 170–73
WTO. *See* World Trade Organization

Xiao, Qiang, 105
Xinjiang, 38, 244. *See also* ethnic
separatism
xitong, 102–3

Yan, Xuetong, 51, 56
Yang, Shangkun, 216
Ye, Jianying, 212
Yeltsin, Boris, 192
Yinhe Incident, 198, 209n55
Yugolavization, 26, 244

Zakaria, Fareed, 5
Zangger Committee, 129, 132, 135
Zhong, Yang, 10, 109, 110, 111
Zhou, Kate X., 112
Zhu, Rongji, 22, 113, 176

About the Editors
and Contributors

Thomas J. Christensen (Ph.D., Columbia University) is associate professor of political science and a member of the Security Studies Program at the Massachusetts Institute of Technology. He was previously associate professor of Government at Cornell University. He is the author of *Useful Adversaries: Grand Strategy, Domestic Mobilization, and Sino-American Conflict, 1947–1958* (Princeton: Princeton University Press), and several articles on international relations theory and Chinese foreign policy in journals such as *International Organization, International Security,* and *Foreign Affairs.*

Yong Deng (Ph.D., University of Arizona) is assistant professor in political science and international studies and associate director of the Center for International Studies, Benedictine University. He is the author of *Promoting Asia-Pacific Economic Cooperation: Perspectives from East Asia* (New York: St. Martin's), and has published numerous articles in journals such as *China Quarterly, Pacific Affairs, Asian Survey, Journal of Strategic Studies, Fletcher Forum of World Affairs,* and *East Asia: An International Quarterly.*

John W. Garver (Ph.D., University of Colorado) is professor at the Sam Nunn School of International Affairs, Georgia Institute of Technology. He has written many articles and books the most recent of which are *Face Off: China, the United States, and Taiwan's Democratization* (Seattle: University of Washington Press), and *The Sino-American Alliance: Nationalist China and American Cold War Strategy in Asia* (Armonk: M. E. Sharpe). He is a member of the National Committee on U.S.-China Relations and serves on the editorial boards of *China Quarterly, Journal of American–East Asian Relations,* and *Journal of Contemporary China.*

Weixing Hu (Ph.D., University of Maryland) is associate professor of international relations at the University of Hong Kong. He was previously assistant professor in the Department of Political Science, University of Detroit–Mercy. He coedited *Strategic Views from the Second Tier* (Newark: Transactions) and has published articles in journals such as *Pacific Review, Journal of North East Asian Studies,* and *Journal of Contemporary China.*

Yasheng Huang (Ph.D., Harvard University) is associate professor at Harvard Business School. He was previously assistant professor in the Department of Political Science, University of Michigan at Ann Arbor. His other professional affiliations include Research Fellow, William Davidson Institute, Michigan Business School, and Fellow, Center for Chinese Economic Research at Tsinghua University. He is the author of *Inflation and Investment Controls in China: The Political Economy of Central-Local Relations during the Reform Era* (New York: Cambridge University Press) and *FDI in China: An Asian Perspective* (Singapore: Institute of Southeast Asian Studies). He has published many articles in journals such as *World Politics, Foreign Policy,* and *China Quarterly.*

Ming Wan (Ph.D., Harvard University) is assistant professor in the Department of Public and International Affairs, George Mason University. He held postdoctoral fellowships from the Program on U.S.-Japan Relations, the John M. Olin Institute for Strategic Studies, and the Pacific Basin Research Center of Harvard University. He has published articles in journals such as *International Studies Quarterly, Pacific Affairs,* and *Pacific Review.*

Fei-Ling Wang (Ph.D., University of Pennsylvania) is assistant professor at the Sam Nunn School of International Affairs, Georgia Institute of Technology. He was previously assistant professor at the United States Military Academy (West Point). He is the author of *Institutions and Institutional Change in China: Premodernity and Modernization* (London: Macmillan), *From Family to Market: Labor Allocation in Contemporary China* (Lanham: Rowman & Littlefield), and *Tacit Acceptance and Watchful Eyes: Beijing's Views About the U.S.-ROK Alliance* (Carlisle Barracks: Strategic Studies Institute). His articles have appeared in journals such as *Problems of Post-Communism, Journal of Contemporary China,* and *Washington Quarterly.*

Jianwei Wang (Ph.D., University of Michigan) is assistant professor of political science at the University of Wisconsin, Stevens Point, and senior research fellow of the U.S. Atlantic Council. Previously he was a research fellow in the Program on International Politics and Economic at the East-West Center and at the United Nations Institute for Disarmament Research in Geneva. He is the author of *Managing Arms in Peace Processes: Cambodia* and is a contributor to *Wavering the Net: Conditional Engagement with China* (New York: Council on Foregin Relations). He has published several articles in journals such as *Asian Survey.*

Bin Yu (Ph.D., Stanford University) is associate professor in the Department of Political Science, Wittenberg University, and faculty associate at the Mershon Center, Ohio State University. He was a research fellow at the Center for International Studies, State Council, China (1982–1985), the president of Chinese Scholars of Political Science and International Studies, Inc. (1992–1993), and visiting fellow at East-West Center, Honolulu, Hawaii (1994–1995). He is the author or editor of three books and many articles on East Asian security, mainland China-Taiwan relations, U.S.-China relations, and Chinese foreign policy in journals like *World Politics, Asian Survey, Harvard International Review, Political Science Quarterly, The Historians,* and *Modern China Studies.*

Ming Zhang (Ph.D., Purdue University) is a specialist on Asian security based in Washington, D.C., and was previously a research analyst in the United States–China Business Council, the Library of Congress, and a research fellow at the National Defense University. He is the author of *Major Powers at a Crossroads: Economic Interdependence and an Asia Pacific Security Community* (Boulder: Lynne Rienner) and *A Triad of Another Kind: U.S., China, and Japan* (New York: St. Martin's). His articles have appeared in *Journal of Contemporary China, Defense News Weekly, Strategic Forum, Journal of Communist Studies and Transition Politics,* and *Australian Journal of International Affairs.*

Suisheng Zhao (Ph.D., University of California–San Diego) is associate professor in the Department of Government, Colby College, and the founding editor of *Journal of Contemporary China.* He was a research fellow in the Economic Research Center, State Council of China, and assistant professor in Beijing University. He is the author of *Power by Design: Constitution-Making in Nationalist China* (Honolulu: University of Hawaii Press), *Power Competition in East Asia: From the Old Chinese World Order to Post–Cold War Regional Multipolarity* (New York: St. Martin's), and coeditor of *Decision-Making in Deng's China* (Armonk: M. E. Sharpe). He has published widely on Chinese politics and foreign policy and East Asian international relations in both Chinese and English languages. His English articles have appeared in *China Quarterly, World Affairs, Asian Survey, Journal of Northeast Asian Studies, Asian Affairs, Issues and Studies, Problems of Post-Communism, The Journal of East Asian Affairs, Journal of Contemporary China,* and elsewhere.